TRANSACTIONS

OF THE

AMERICAN PHILOSOPHICAL SOCIETY

HELD AT PHILADELPHIA
FOR PROMOTING USEFUL KNOWLEDGE

NEW SERIES—VOLUME 66, PART 1
1976

THE GERMAN CENTER PARTY
1890–1906

553746

JOHN K. ZEENDER

Department of History, Catholic University of America

THE AMERICAN PHILOSOPHICAL SOCIETY
INDEPENDENCE SQUARE
PHILADELPHIA

May, 1976

TO MY WIFE

It was the party of Ausgleich [compromise] aspiring to a dynamic redress of political forces in a daily restored balance and compromise. For this course it was often denounced by its opponents as an unscrupulous, unprincipled, opportunistic power group unfit for German politics. In a way it was a stranger to the German party system and approached more the typical patterns and politics of Western constitutional parties. Attracting members from different social strata and divergent ideological leanings, it had to resolve basic conflicts within its own ranks and thus became a school of politics par excellence.

Sigmund Neumann, "Germany: Changing Patterns and Lasting Problems," in *Modern Political Parties* (Chicago, 1956), p. 358.

PREFACE

This is a study of the German Center and its relations with the German Imperial government in the period 1890–1906 when this essentially Catholic party held the decisive position in the Reichstag. During that time Germany was undergoing a profound economic change accompanied by tensions between an older society, consisting of landed, artisan, small business, and ecclesiastical elements, and a more recent urban industrial society that was itself split into capital and labor. In domestic affairs and in the ambitious foreign policy it pursued especially in the late 1890's and after, the Imperial government transformed tension into crisis. Between 1890 and 1906 the Reichstag had to deal with a major army bill, three proposals for the building of a modern navy, two highly controversial economic programs, and several measures aimed at the suppression of the Social Democrats or their trade unions.

The Center approved some legislation which has not won the approval of historians, in particular the naval bills, which did serious damage to Germany's dealings with Great Britain, and the great tariff measure of 1902 that imposed high food prices on the German working classes. But it did refuse to permit any tampering with the existing popular suffrage and it chose finally to oppose the campaign against Social Democracy. Instead it convinced the government that it should follow the course of moderate social reform. Often opportunist, sometimes stubborn and morally committed, the Center was instrumental both in reconciling to a degree the positions of the government and its opponents and in maintaining the independence of political forces the Imperial regime would have liked to absorb or destroy.

My analysis of the Center's political conduct is complicated for the Center was a complex party. Bismarck once said:

> There are not two souls in the Center but seven ideological tendencies which portray all the colors of the political rainbow from the most extreme right to the radical left. For my part I admire the skill which the coachman of the Center [Ludwig Windthorst] demonstrates in leading all these contradictory spirits so elegantly.[1]

Windthorst had been disappointed over the failure that he and his senior colleagues had experienced during the early 1870's in their efforts to make the Center into a great moderate conservative party on a broad Christian basis. Yet the lack of an explicit conservative program or manifesto may have been the salvation of the Center since it allowed the party to sustain a loose unity and a fairly large disparate electorate through its concern with the problems of the Catholic church and its membership.

In 1890 most Catholics, residents of rural or provincial regions, approved policies or social systems that might be called conservative. But they had to make choices in their primary allegiances to institutions or to try to balance them. The higher Catholic aristocracy, especially the nobility of north Germany, wanted their party to follow the direction of the hegemonial Prussian monarchy that could provide their sons with administrative careers, and to collaborate with the Prussian Conservatives, with whom they shared common interests in the defense of aristocratic privilege and agrarianism. They were undoubtedly sincere, however, in their belief that such a course would eventually be beneficial to the Catholic Church.

Two other conservative groups, the corporatists and integralists, were largely rooted in Prussia also, though they were both hostile in greater or lesser measure to the spirit of the Prussian monarchy. They shared a common ideal, the absolute independence of the church from the state. The corporatists, whose leaders were usually noblemen and priest intellectuals, also rejected free enterprise and the bureaucratic state for being rationalist in mentality and disruptive of the ordered, traditional ways. They preserved the romantic vision of a decentralized society in which representative bodies of vocational organizations like the guilds and agrarian and commercial chambers would legislate on economic matters. They thought of themselves as social reformers because they sought to preserve the artisan and peasant classes through the establishment of a controlled economy. Their aim was the restoration of a social order in which the nobility would govern under the spiritual direction of the churches. And much as they disliked the Prussian bureaucratic state, they wanted the Center to work in close harmony with the Prussian Conservatives against the prime enemy, the liberal and leftist parties.

The integralists were principled opponents of liberalism and they also recalled the injuries done to their church by the Prussian bureaucracy during the Kulturkampf. Mostly middle-class laymen and priests, they were primarily intent on achieving the specific aims of the Church itself rather than a Christian social order: the liberation of the Church from the controls left over from the Kulturkampf settlement of 1886–1887 and the application of Catholic doctrines to national and state legislation. Though they and their supporters came mostly from limited areas in the west, their press could have extensive influence over their co-religionists when the Center came into conflict with the government over issues of interest to the Church.

It was a severe handicap to the leading Catholic conservatives that they could not fully use the principles

[1] Hans Joachim Schoeps, *Bismarck über Zeitgenossen, Zeitgenossen über Bismarck,* (Frankfurt/Main, 1972), p. 234.

of federalism in their own behalf. Bavarian Centrists, chiefly peasants, artisans, and clergymen, were painfully conscious that the empire was only in theory a federal state, since the Prussian and Imperial governments had the same ruler and first minister. Prussia also dominated the Federal Council of States and its minister of war represented the Imperial army before the Reichstag. Understandably the Catholic electorate of Bavaria, three-fourths of the total voting population in that kingdom, favored opposition to the national government rather than the policy of responsibility and support. For several years Bismarck played with the idea of promoting a conservative Catholic ministry in Bavaria that would balance against the conservative Protestant government in Prussia, but the notion came to nothing.

In the 1880's Bismarck, eager to discredit the popular and oppositional wing of the Center, liked to refer to the democratic elements in the party. I do not believe that we can categorize members of the Center's left wing as either liberals or democrats, terms which were really only applicable to those persons who belonged to parties committed to freedom of thought and popular sovereignty. Some Catholics had been prominent in liberal politics in the 1850's and early 1860's, but the liberals' advocacy of German unification at the expense of Catholic Austria and their resentments against the dogma of papal infallibility soon created nearly insurmountable walls between the liberals of all degrees and most Catholics. Nevertheless, the majority of lawyers, businessmen, editors, and academicians in the Center believed in the superiority of the constitutional order. They assumed that it was better for their church, their class and society as a whole. Their faith in the values of a capitalist system based on individual initiative and competition and their impatience with guild concepts were hardly less intense than that of their liberal counterparts.

German soil was not well suited, however, to liberalism in any form, secular or Catholic. Like so many secular liberals those in the Center became increasingly conservative in their politics by the end of the century. The desire of the Catholic clergy to secure their church's emancipation from the Kulturkampf legislation of Prussia and other states and the resentments of many Catholics against their government and the Prussian-German monarchy in particular made it possible for the liberal Centrists to control their party for most of its history after the Kulturkampf. But the aim of the Center had been to win acceptance from the Prussian-German monarchy, not to change its structure. Hence it moved increasingly further to the right in the 1890's and the early 1900's, though never to the position of reaction. But that change was also due in some measure to the insistence of its real electorate—small shopkeepers, artisans, industrial workers and agrarians—that the party attend to their economic needs. The Center had become by that time a moderate conservative social party on a Catholic foundation.

My work is based primarily on the extensive Ernst Lieber papers which are scattered between the Archiwum Archideicezjalne in Wrocław, Poland (prior to 1945 the Episcopal Archive of the Diocese of Breslau, Germany), the Pfälzische Staatsbibliothek in Speyer, Rhineland-Palatinate and the Lieber home in Camberg, Hesse. I have used the papers of Georg Cardinal Kopp, probably the leading Catholic churchman in Germany in the period under study, and Felix Porsch, a prominent Centrist, which are also in the Archiwum Archideicezjalne. I found valuable material in the papers of Karl Bachem at the Stadt-Köln Historisches Archiv. For my further research in archives and libraries see my bibliographical essay at the end of this study.

The undertaking of the research for this work would not have been possible without the generosity of the Fulbright Commission, the American Philosophical Society, and my own university. I owe special debts to my two friends and colleagues, Thomas R. West and Robert Trisco, who read substantial parts of my manuscript and made invaluable suggestions to me for its improvement, and to Professor Max Braubach, Ellen Giesberts, Dr. Erich Kuphal, now deceased, Ernst Köppen, Dr. Ernst Lieber, Dr. Karl Nolden, and Congressman Clement Zablocki. I profoundly regret that Professor Hajo Holborn is no longer with us so that I could try to thank him for the extensive assistance he gave me in a variety of ways while I was doing my research.

The staffs of these institutions were of considerable help to me: the Stadt-Köln Historisches Archiv, the Pfälzisches Staatsbibliothek, Speyer, the Archiwum Archidiecezjalne in Wrocław, Poland, the university libraries in Cologne and Bonn, the German Documents Section of the National Archives in Washington, and the Mullen Library of my own university.

Above all I owe a special acknowledgment to my wife for her typing of the manuscript and other assistance and to her and our children for their patience and encouragement.

THE GERMAN CENTER PARTY, 1890–1906

JOHN K. ZEENDER

CONTENTS

1. INTRODUCTION

I believe that it is not only possible, but advisable, to form a [Catholic] party between or above the existing parties; sometimes honorably combining with them, sometimes promoting an independent policy by making use of the dissensions of the others.

August Reichensperger, January, 1860.[1]

Windthorst was indeed a statesman who did not calculate with romantic imponderables. . . . He was a realistic politician through and through.

Bismarck, August, 1890.[2]

Throughout its history under the empire the German Center took a special pride in the unity which was the source of its strength and parliamentary influence. The minority status of the large Catholic population, approximately one-third of the whole nation,[3] the strong influence of the Catholic Church over its members and effective party leadership were the decisive elements in the maintenance of a unity which was sometimes threatened by the centrifugal tendencies of certain ideological, regional, and class groups. Its leaders were aware, however, that Catholic support for a confessional party could not be taken for granted. They never forgot that the first Center party of the Prussian

Landtag, initially named the Catholic Fraction, had suffered a complete collapse in the mid 1860's.

Catholic political parties came into existence in many German states between the end of the Napoleonic wars and the early 1850's because their founders believed that Catholicism was a total culture. While there were debates in Catholic circles about the exact content of that culture, the basic motive for the foundation of the Catholic parties was undoubtedly a desire to provide a defense in a new constitutional order for a Catholic way of life.

The armies of revolutionary France and Napoleon had broken the thin shells of the small and medium-sized Catholic states governing societies in which the church was the center of life and the economy virtually static. Austria and Bavaria were the only Catholic states still standing after 1814 and the Austrian monarchy was concerned primarily with its Italian possessions, even though the ruler was the president of the new German Confederation. The Catholic Church was under bureaucratic control everywhere in Germany, including Bavaria. The Catholic educated classes found themselves virtually excluded from the higher levels of the administrative, judicial, and university systems of the regions in which they lived. The Catholic professional man, the merchant and the artisan, stood often in competition with non-Catholics more accustomed to life in a competitive society and better equipped psychologically, financially, and technologically to use the machine and modern financial devices. Catholics by baptism or by continuing practice like Josef Görres, the noted journalist, Gustav Mevissen, the prominent industrialist, both from the Rhineland, Franz von Buss, the Baden social reformer, Franz Waldeck, a distinguished Westphalian liberal, and Ludwig Windthorst, a leading minister of state in Protestant Hanover prior to 1866, were major exceptions to that general rule. It is not surprising that many Catholic leaders liked the old corporative system giving to the clergy, aristocracy, peasantry, and guilds of merchants and craftsmen automatic representation in regional parliamentary bodies, and disliked its replacement by the liberal system providing a central legislature and basing suffrage on districts, population, and property ownership.[4]

Possibly a milder atmosphere for the Church and Catholics existed in Prussia after 1815 than in some

---

[1] Letter to the editor, *The Rambler* 2 (January, 1860) : p. 238.

[2] *Bismarck Gespräche. Von der Entlassung bis zum Tode*, Willy Andreas, ed. (Bremen, 1963), p. 83.

[3] In 1905 Catholics made up twenty-five million or thirty-six per cent of the total German population of sixty million. I have been unable to find precise statistics for the number of Polish Catholics in the empire but they were probably somewhere in the neighborhood of three million five hundred thousand or four million. The Alsatian Catholics numbered one million four hundred thousand in 1905. Though the Poles and Alsatians maintained their own parties, the Polish clergy and population in Silesia supported the Center almost exclusively till the last decade or so before World War I. See *Staatslexikon*, Julius Bachem, ed. (3rd rev. ed., Freiburg, 1911) 1: pp. 1262, 1578; 4: p. 315.

[4] On Catholic social and economic traditions before 1850 see Franz Schnabel, *Deutsche Geschichte im Neunzehnten Jahrhundert* (4 v., 2nd ed., Freiburg, 1951) 4: 195 ff. Also Clemens Bauer, *Deutscher Katholizismus. Entwicklungslinien und Profile* (Frankfurt am Main, 1965), p. 37 ff.

other non-Catholic German states. In Baden, where Catholics made up a slight majority of the population, the traditionally tense relations between them and the Protestant minority were exacerbated by the ability of liberal Protestants, already dominant in the economic and cultural life of the state, to exercise influence on the government and its policies. But Prussia was the largest and most powerful state in Germany, except for Austria, and its Catholic population, German and Polish, made up a strong third of the total population.[5] During and after the Kulturkampf the development of relations between that state and the Catholic Church was to influence similar relations in Baden, Hesse, Württemberg, and other states with smaller Catholic populations.

The German Catholics who lived under Prussian rule after the Napoleonic period had nothing initially in common besides their religion. Mainly peasants, the German and Polish Catholics of Silesia, in southeastern Prussia, had lived under Prussian rule since 1740 and were submissive to the bureaucratic system. They had little or no contact with the Rhineland and Westphalia, Prussia's new acquisitions in the west. Under Protestant economic leadership, the Rhineland was beginning to develop that urban and capitalistic life which was to distinguish it markedly from all other Catholic regions in Prussia and wider Germany. Within that province the Catholic aristocracy and educated middle class had sharply differed over the question of whether the Prussian state should maintain the Napoleonic Code, which provided for free enterprise and equality before the law.[6] The crown was reluctant to do so, but it finally capitulated on that question to the defenders of the French Code. It is difficult to see how the various Catholic provinces and their upper classes could have come together in any manner if it had not been for the difficulties between the state and their church.

It was extremely hard, as tactful people on each side were to discover, to reconcile the state's confidence in its own authority with the Church's exalted view of its own rights and mission. The Prussian bureaucracy was highly trained, dedicated, and honest, but as Bismarck later complained, it was also anti-clerical and anti-Catholic.[7] It was accustomed to the German Protestant tradition in which the monarch was the official head of the Church; its officials, graduates of universities, believed that they represented trained intelligence, and they regarded the Catholic Church as an obstruction to progress and rational administration. Since the state supported the churches and the clergy, they

undoubtedly expected the clergy to be agents of the state.

By the 1830's the Prussian monarchy was faced with a new kind of Catholic bishop. The destruction of the Catholic states and the secularization of church properties had led to a greater emphasis among the clergy on spirituality, religious devotion and closer communion with the laity. Perhaps to their surprise, bishops found that they enjoyed not only authority among Catholics but considerable popularity as well. The most impressive and influential figure in Germany prior to Windthorst's rise to popular leadership was Wilhelm von Ketteler, an ascetic Westphalian aristocrat and bishop of Mainz in Hesse from 1850 to 1877.[8]

Under the circumstances it was probable that a collision would occur at some early point between the Prussian state and the episcopacy. After a prolonged dispute over the procedures to be used in mixed marriage, then common in German states, the government took the uncommon steps of jailing the archbishop of Cologne, Clemens von Droste-Vischering in 1837 and then the archbishop of Posen, Robert Dunin in 1838. The arrests of the two churchmen provoked angry waves of protest from Catholics throughout Germany in which genuine indignation and anti-Prussian prejudice were mixed. The government's assault on the churchmen's dignity had incalculable consequences. It created for the first time a Prussian and wider Catholic public opinion and the psychological basis for a later Catholic political movement.[9] When the revolution of 1848 came, Catholic deputies at the Frankfurt national assembly and at the Prussian constitutional assembly collaborated on the drafting of articles providing for the freedom of the churches. The Frankfurt Assembly proved, of course, to be a failure, but the Prussian legislature survived and the crown handed down a revised constitution in 1850 providing for the liberties of the churches.

The formation of a Prussian Catholic party was probably inevitable with the appearance of a Prussian parliament and enough Catholic deputies to make up a respectable parliamentary group. The founders, August Reichensperger (1808–1895) and Peter Reichensperger (1811–1892), were well known in German Catholic circles; August had sat in the Frankfurt national assembly and Peter in the Prussian constitutional assembly during the revolution of 1848–1849.[10] But they might have had difficulty in creating a viable party if the government had not awakened the doubts of

---

[5] Eugene Anderson, *The Social and Political Conflict in Prussia 1858–1864* (Lincoln, Nebraska, 1954), p. 423.

[6] See Schnabel, *Deutsche Geschichte* **4**: pp. 190–191.

[7] Rudolf Lill, "Die deutschen Katholiken und Bismarcks Reichsgründung, in: *Reichsgründung, Tatsachen, Kontroversen, Interpretationen,* Theodor Schieder and Ernst Deuerlein, eds. (Stuttgart, 1970), p. 359.

[8] But Schnabel notes that Ketteler was the last of the bishops to be a public figure: Schnabel, *Deutsche Geschichte* **4**: p. 215.

[9] On that controversy and its importance in German history: *ibid.,* pp. 131–151. Hajo Holborn, *A History of Modern Germany 1648–1840* (New York, 1963), pp. 505–506.

[10] For detailed biographical sketches of the two brothers consult the *Staatslexikon* (3rd rev. ed.) **4**: pp. 470–491. Schnabel provides the best synthesis of their political ideas: *Deutsche Geschichte* **4**: pp. 199–202.

other Catholic deputies about its commitment to the religious articles of the new constitution. The Ministry of Public Worship and Education had continued to claim the patronage rights to certain church livings which it had taken over from private persons and religious societies. The minister, Karl von Raumer, created more of a furor in 1852 when he imposed restrictions on the missionary preaching of the Jesuits in the Catholic diaspora and forbade seminarians to attend the Jesuit German College in Rome.

The Reichenspergers, who were sons of the general secretary of the Rhineland under the French occupying forces and capable jurists themselves, had a double motive in organizing a Catholic party. They wanted freedom for their church, equality of treatment for it with the Evangelical Church and maintenance of its influence in the state schools. They also hoped to use their party as a lever to force the government to open more of its offices to Catholics and give them social and economic opportunity. It is probable that the various ministries maintained low quota restrictions on the appointment of Catholics throughout the Prussian administrative and judicial system, since their numbers in the central ministries, superior presidencies of the provinces, district presidencies, and country councilorships were considerably lower than the Catholic "cultural lag" might have justified. The Reichenspergers and Hermann von Mallinckrodt, their leading Westphalian colleague, undoubtedly felt they were held back in their governmental careers by the bureaucracy's discrimination against Catholics. The question of parity in public administration was important for educated Catholics because so few of them could gain places in industry, commerce, and banking. The Catholic Church itself could reasonably fear that some of its more talented and ambitious members might look on Catholic orthodoxy as a barrier to a career.[11]

Unlike the later Center parties of the Landtag and and Reichstag, the Catholic Fraction, renamed the Center Fraction in 1859, did not possess mass support. Most members of the Catholic lower classes abstained from voting in parliamentary elections; they were apparently discouraged from doing so by the Prussian three-class system of suffrage which was heavily weighted in favor of the more affluent taxpayers.[12] After its first year of existence the party lost most of its aristocratic members who disapproved of its collaboration with the liberal groups in the Landtag. The

Catholic urban and rural lower middle classes and the industrial workers and the aristocracy would undoubtedly have supported the Catholic party if their church was in any danger from the state. But the ministry had withdrawn the Raumer decrees soon after the formation of the Catholic Fraction, though it continued to make life difficult for the Catholic press.[13]

The fact that their party was heavily dependent on the loyalty of the Catholic urban and rural middle classes was not a matter of initial concern to its leaders. They assumed that the Catholic Fraction, fifty-seven or fifty-eight members strong, would hold the balance between the Conservatives and the several liberal factions for the foreseeable future. During the army bill controversy of the early and mid-1860's, however, most of the party's earlier supporters either voted for liberal candidates or did not cast ballots.[14] The Conservative and Center parties went into a decline while the liberal groups, especially the new Progressive party, achieved impressive parliamentary strength.

The reasons for the dissatisfaction of its earlier electors with the Catholic party's course are evident enough. Why the Reichenspergers failed to respond to their disaffection is less clear. During the 1850's the Catholic Fraction and the liberal groups stood in opposition to the reactionary Manteuffel regime, a course which appealed to the deep anti-Prussian instincts of the Catholic middle classes in the western provinces. The joint efforts of the Reichenspergers and their liberal allies to promote liberty and equality for all minority groups—Catholics, nonconformist Protestants, and Jews—appealed to the confessional interests of middle-class Catholic voters but also to their desire to be progressive. The collaboration between the Catholic Fraction and the liberals had been so close there was discussion in the late 1850's between some of their members over a possible fusion of the Catholic Fraction and one or more of the liberal groups, an action which the Reichenspergers successfully opposed.[15] Many Catholic middle-class electors were at first puzzled, then incensed in the years between 1862 and 1864 when the Center's leadership did not join the new Progressive party in opposition but sought to devise a compromise on the army bill issue which would be favorable to the crown. The Center suffered heavy losses in the elections of 1862 and 1863 and passed out of existence in 1866.

---

[11] Karl Bachem, *Vorgeschichte, Geschichte und Politik der deutschen Zentrumspartei* (9 v., Cologne, 1927–1932) **2**: pp. 131–132. Schnabel, *Deutsche Geschichte* **4**: p. 118.

[12] Throughout Prussia only twenty-seven per cent of the voters in the third category participated in the election of 1863. Eugene Anderson claims that the participation of Catholics from all three classes in the elections of the early 1860's was lower than that of Protestants from the same social groups: *Social and Political Conflict in Prussia 1858–1864*, pp. 413, 424–425.

[13] Bachem, *Zentrumspartei* **2**: pp. 113–121.

[14] Anderson, *Social and Political Conflict in Prussia*, pp. 424–425. *Staatslexikon* (3rd rev. ed.) **4**: p. 478.

[15] Bachem, *Zentrumspartei* **2**: pp. 155–156. The editors of the English Catholic review, *The Rambler*, had apparently attempted to promote the cause of the fusion by publishing an editorial article in which they claimed that there should be no more than two parties in any parliamentary body. August Reichensperger took sharp issue with their position, arguing that Catholic parties had different fundamental aims from those of other parties. See fn. 1 above.

FIG. 1.   Ernst Lieber.

It would be logical to assume that the Reichen-spergers chose such a problematic course because they expected the ministry to end the traditional discrimination against Catholics in the administrative and judicial branches of the civil service in payment for their support. Mallinckrodt had already spent the year 1859–1860 in the Ministry of Interior for the apparent purpose of promoting the careers of Catholics in the government and Peter Reichensperger brought up the question of "parity" when he met with Bismarck in 1863 to discuss the army bill and the Center's efforts to secure its passage in a modified form. Mallinckrodt's and Reichensperger's attempts to change the governmental policy toward Catholics proved to be unsuccessful. Nevertheless, the Center leadership continued to support the government.[16]

The breakdown in the parliamentary balance after 1858 was the actual cause of the shift in the Center's orientation at the end of the decade. The elections of that year marked the beginning of the liberal dominance of the Landtag which was to last for two decades. Their identification with the ideals of national unification, constitutionalism, and free enterprise now worked handsomely to their benefit.[17] Even though Franz Waldeck, the leader of the Progressive party was a

practicing Catholic,[18] the Reichenspergers believed that a strong liberal majority would be less likely to respect the traditional role of the Catholic Church in public life, especially in education, than the monarchy.

The new ruler William I (1858–1888) had sought from the commencement of his reign to win the affections of Catholics because he intended to challenge Austria's sole leadership in Germany. Even though he did not try to break the entrenched opposition of Prussian bureaucracy to the introduction of parity in civil service appointments, William I accorded a freedom to the Catholic Church that it did not possess in the Catholic states of Germany. In the early 1860's the Progressives still upheld the old liberal ideal of a united Germany under a liberalized Prussia's leadership. The Reichenspergers assumed, however, that the Prussian crown would be willing to accept a compromise plan for the reformation of the German Confederation which would provide for a division of authority between Austria, Prussia, and the middle states.[19]

The Center party finally passed out of existence in 1866, the year in which Prussia expelled Austria from Germany and annexed Hanover, Hesse-Kassel, Nassau, and Frankfurt. The shock of those events which left Catholics in a minority position in Germany and made some of them "involuntary Prussians" did not lead to a revival of the Center. It was only when Catholics began to fear for the security of the Church in 1869 and 1870 that they became receptive to proposals for its restoration.

That threat did not come in the first instance from the Prussian state, although Bismarck's later conflict with the Center and the Catholic Church contributed significantly to the popularity of the party among Catholics. The hostility of the liberals, especially those of the new National Liberal party, was due to a mixture of contrivance, conviction, and euphoria. Bismarck had humiliated the Prussian liberals by demonstrating that the Prussian monarchy and its army were alone capable of bringing about the unification of the nation. The National Liberals, made up of nationalists from some of the states annexed by Prussia in 1866 and some of the former Progressives, needed a new unpopular political enemy and found it in the Catholic Church, in particular the Papacy and the religious orders. The Papacy did present a sizable target to German liberals. It had issued in 1864 the Syllabus of Errors which rejected any Catholic compromise with liberal doctrines and institutions, and in 1869 convoked the first Vatican Council for the purpose of securing a proclamation of papal infallibility as a dogma. But the resistance of Bavaria and the southern states to the creation of a national state under Prussian leadership may have done more to provoke the more nationalist

16 Bachem, *Zentrumspartei* 2: p. 163. *Staatslexikon* 4: p. 478.
17 *Ibid.*, pp. 477–478.

18 Bachem, *Zentrumspartei* 2: p. 78.
19 *Staatslexikon* 4: p. 478.

liberals. They assumed that the Catholic Church was the primary source of that opposition; they were also confident that with the support of a new national government and liberal public opinion they could make the Catholic Church into a national church though subject to liberal state governments.[20]

Under the circumstances any events that gave symbolic expression to the growing ideological tensions in Prussia were likely to have a political impact upon nervous Catholics, clerical and lay. In June, 1869, the destruction of a small Berlin convent by a crowd of young artisans produced an effect upon Catholics comparable to the shock that their parents had felt some thirty years earlier when the government arrested Archbishop Droste-Vischering.[21] Later that year the Committee of Petitions of the Landtag, dominated by National Liberals, reported out a bill calling for the expulsion of religious orders from Prussia. Both events, combined with the long anti-papal campaign in the liberal press, created the resonance in some Catholic circles that Peter Reichensperger and some other old Centrists needed. Despite the opposition of a few Catholic parliamentarians, the Reichenspergers were able to convince most of their Catholic colleagues in the Landtag in December, 1870, that they should create a new Center party. Some weeks later they made preparatory steps to form a similar party in the new Reichstag after its election in the following spring.[22]

The new Center parties in the two Berlin parliaments reflected the traditional views of the Reichensperger brothers on party organization. They wanted to form a Catholic constitutional party, like the old Catholic Fraction, that would sit in the middle of the Landtag and Reichstag between the Conservatives and the liberal groups. The question of their church's security was the overriding issue of concern to the Prussian clergy and devout Catholics; the one sentence paragraph of the program of the Prussian Center stated baldly that is special aim was the maintenance and further development of constitutional rights in general and "the freedom and independence of the Church and its institutions in particular."[23] In drafting the program for the Reichstag Center, the Reichenspergers took account of two other elements important to the success of the national party, the South Germans and the lower classes. They stressed that the Center would defend the remaining rights of the states, an obvious gesture to the Bavarians who feared Prussian ambition. Following a reference to the support of constitutional rights, among those of the churches, the program also expressed the Center's concern with the well-being of all national classes.[24]

Ludwig Windthorst, relatively new to Catholic politics, would have preferred a different kind of party. Though his Protestant political associations influenced his thinking, the political situation itself seemed to validate his belief that it would be better for Catholic parliamentarians to combine with Protestant conservatives in the formation of a broad popular conservative party.[25] Windthorst apparently thought that a Catholic party would not be strong enough to control the parliamentary balance and that it could become isolated—as indeed it did after 1871.

Even though Windthorst was a politician of broader vision than the Reichenspergers, his knowledge of the actual political situation in Prussia was partly inferior to theirs. The Catholic and Protestant populations and their clergies were not ready in the year 1870–1871 for an interconfessional party. Nevertheless, the other leaders came to agree with Windthorst that it would be advisable for the Center to try to win Protestant members. Some eight to ten Hanoverian Protestants, bitter against the Prussian Conservatives who had approved Prussia's annexation of their state, eventually moved into the Center as guest members. Two others joined it as well, one of them Bismarck's old patron, Ludwig von Gerlach.[26] By and large the effort was a failure, though the presence of a small Protestant minority in the Center made clear that it was a political rather than a strictly confessional party. The failure was far less serious however than the inability of the party leaders to draw the Conservatives into a coalition with the Center before or during the early Kulturkampf.

At the time of its formation the leaders of the Center failed to anticipate a major Kulturkampf, since they did not expect the Prussian monarchy or the Conservatives to support to any significant degree a legislative campaign against the Catholic Church, in particular the religious orders. But the existence of the party was itself an incitement to that movement. No doubt the mere existence of a Catholic party when the Church was free in Prussia and in a time when confessional passions

---

[20] Heinrich von Sybel, historian and National Liberal, was to say in 1873 that the Prussian bishops would not resist the efforts of Bismarck to impose controls on the Church since they had capitulated to the pope on the question of papal infallibility: see Prince Chlodwig zu Hohenlohe-Schillingsfurst, *Denkwürdigkeiten* (2 v., Stuttgart, 1907) **2**: p. 95.

[21] Ernst Lieber, Windthorst's successor, said publicly in 1895 that the creation of the new Center party might not have taken place if it had not been for the convent incident in Berlin: *Frankfurter Volksblatt*, September 27, 1899.

[22] On the tensions between the nationalist liberals and Catholicism see Bachem, *Zentrumspartei* **3**: p. 90 ff.

[23] Wilhelm Mommsen, *Deutsche Parteiprogramme* (Munich, 1960), p. 218.

[24] *Ibid.,* p. 222.

[25] The role of Windthorst in the foundation of the new Center is obscure; see Bachem, *Zentrumspartei* **3**: pp. 127–128. According to Mallinckrodt's notes Windthorst favored the creation of a "Conservative Peoples' party" in 1870: Otto Pfulf, S.J., *Hermann von Mallinckrodt* (Freiburg, 1892), p. 370. He had tried earlier without success to interest Bavarian Catholic leaders in the establishment of a new Conservative party. George Windell, *The Catholics and German Unity 1866–1871* (Minneapolis, 1954), p. 286.

[26] Bachem, *Zentrumspartei* **3**: pp. 142–147.

FIG. 2. Julius Bachem.

The Kulturkampf was decisive for the early growth and viability of the Center party. Most likely Bismarck's dependence on the strong majority of the liberal bloc would have made it necessary for the Prussian monarchy to seek closer state control over the schools and civil marriage, measures in keeping with the standard legislation of the western world. But the chancellor and the liberal coalition, except for individual members, were eager to create a national Catholic Church under state control. Throughout the empire most of the religious orders were banned and all priests were made subject to possible criminal prosecution for remarks made in the pulpit. Other laws in Prussia stripped the bishops of their disciplinary power over the lower clergy and vested them in a special state court. By 1876 priests were unable to read Mass without governmental permission and most of the Prussian bishops were in prison or in exile; over a thousand parishes were without priests. It was a repetition of the mistake of 1837 all over again but on a far more massive and extensive scale. Later collaboration between the Center and the Prussian-German monarchy was to be hampered by the recollection on the part of many Catholics that they, the sick, and the dead were often denied religious services and that bishops had to sit in jail or flee the country.[28]

The angry or worried Catholic reaction to the Kulturkampf was evident by the second parliamentary election of 1874. Only seven hundred thousand Catholics had voted for the Center deputies running for the Reichstag in 1871 and some middle-class electors had probably continued to support one of the liberal or conservative parties. But in 1874 the Center polled one million four hundred thousand votes and increased its mandates in the Reichstag from fifty-eight to ninety-one. In all later elections its strength was to be always somewhat above that figure.[29] Its actual strength was even greater since there were usually from eight to ten Hanoverian Protestant members the party could regularly count upon along with the Polish and Alsatian parties containing together twenty-seven or twenty-eight members. The danger actually existed that resistance to the Kulturkampf would spawn competing Catholic organizations. Felix von Löe and Karl zu Löwenstein, two ultra-conservative Catholic noblemen, prominent in the executive committee of the annual Catholic Congress, had founded a mass movement in 1872, the Mainz Catholic Association, patterned after

were sharp was an acute annoyance to Bismarck. The insistence of the senior Centrist leaders, the Reichenspergers, Herman von Mallinckrodt and Bishop von Ketteler, that the Reich government and the Reichstag should introduce the liberal articles on the freedom of the churches that the old Prussian constitution contained also upset the chancellor, who was concerned over the sensitivity of the states to any further invasion of their sovereignty and to the feelings of their Protestant citizens. The senior Prussian Centrists, with the possible exception of Mallinckrodt, had come after 1866 to approve of Prussia's claims to hegemony in Germany; but the prominence of Windthorst, the most resourceful of the anti-Prussian German particularists in the period before and after 1866, led Bismarck to regard the new Center as an enemy of his empire. The chancellor was further agitated by the presence in the Center's leadership group of his own former deputy, Karl von Savigny, who had broken with Bismarck in 1866 because he thought the chancellor not protective enough of state rights.[27]

---

[27] Friedrich von Holstein, one of Bismarck's subordinates, later insisted that the chancellor's attitude toward the Center underwent a drastic change when he saw Windthorst and Savigny in its parliamentary representation: *The Holstein Pa-*

pers, Norman Rich and Martin Fisher, eds. (4 v., Cambridge, 1963–1965) 1: p. 59. And see Martin Spahn, *Das Deutsche Zentrum* (Mainz, 1906), p. 54.

[28] The most detailed recent study of the Kulturkampf is by Erich Schmidt-Volkmar, *Der Kulturkampf in Deutschland 1871–1890* (Göttingen, 1962). For a balanced brief treatment consult Holborn, *A History of Germany 1840–1945*, pp. 261–266.

[29] Fritz Specht and Paul Schwabe, eds., *Die Reichstagwählen von 1887 bis 1903* (2nd ed., Berlin, 1906), pp. 310–311.

the model of Daniel O'Connell's earlier Catholic Association in Ireland. Löe, the actual founder and leader, was a capable organizer but a stubborn reactionary.[30] Fortunately for the Center, the Prussian government destroyed the Mainz Catholic Association when the ministry ordered its dissolution in 1876.

It is not surprising that Windthorst became party leader after Mallinckrodt's death in 1874. A brilliant debater, he had shouldered the chore of dueling with Bismarck on the floor of the Landtag and Reichstag, and he did so successfully.[31] But the preference of the South Germans for Windthorst may have been the decisive factor in his ascendancy. He had been prominently if secretly identified with the South Germans in their efforts to block Bismarck's efforts to unite Germany under Prussian leadership after 1866, whereas Peter Reichensperger had publicly supported Prussia.[32]

Windthorst had not quickly become the hero of the Catholic minority. Nature had been unkind to him. He was short, homely, bald, and near-sighted. Speaking to a small parliamentary audience, which was the typical kind in the Landtag or Reichstag he was effective because he could bring his charm, humor, and powerful intellect to bear on his auditors; but he lacked a strong voice and the gift of moving or overpowering rhetoric. Yet in the later Kulturkampf, with the church in disarray and most of the bishops in jail or in exile, he became for most Catholics the symbol of their security and legal opposition to governmental violence.

Windthorst's major contributions to his party, church, and people came not during the Kulturkampf but in the next decade. Catholics would have supported the Center in the 1870's under any other leader. The party itself had no choice but to move along a single track, the line of defense, and to remain unified whatever the differences were within its ranks. That situation was to change after 1878 when the Center was confronted with a future which was both reassuring and disturbing.

In 1878 and 1879 Bismarck made his historic break with liberalism. Unable to impose his will on the left wing of the National Liberal party, which wanted some share in the Prussian government and differed with Bismarck on the trade and the Socialist questions, the chancellor turned upon the National Liberals. After a brief period of indecision the party's right wing decided to submit to the chancellor, while its left elements moved to a new relationship with the Progressives; they were to form the Radical party in 1884. In 1879 the Center had joined the Conservatives in supporting Bismarck's first tariff bill, which represented a break with the earlier economic and financial policies of the liberal coalition. Under the Franckenstein financial clause of the new tariff measure, named after the Center's chairman,[33] all income from the tariff above one hundred thirty million marks was to be turned over to the states. The Center appeared to be moving into a firm coalition with the government and the Conservatives.

It was a bitter awakening for the rest of his senior colleagues when Windthorst and Bismarck did not effect a political reconciliation after their initial partnership on the tariff bill.[34] The Centrist leader chose to keep his party in formal opposition for another decade. The Center was to support the government on important legislation from time to time and elements in the Center would do so on other measures. The most impressive collaboration came in the field of social law, though Bismarck and Windthorst sometimes sharply differed on its details, and Windthorst did not dare to clash directly with the chancellor on the issue of the harsh anti-Socialist law, which violated the constitutional rights of Socialists and workers, so part of the Center always voted with the government to ensure its renewal.[35] The remainder, led by Windthorst, always attacked it.

Throughout the 1880's Windthorst had to contend with vigorous Centrist opposition to his course. The new pope, Leo XIII, shared the disappointment of the Reichenspergers and the leading noblemen of the Reichstag and Landtag Center parties. He was desperate to win the support of the leading statesman in Europe for the Vatican's efforts to regain the papal temporal power in Italy. He deferred, therefore, to Bismarck's insistence that Bishop Georg Kopp, in whom the chancellor had confidence, instead of Windthorst should negotiate the peace settlement between the Prussian Catholic Church and the Prussian state. His eagerness to strengthen his rapport with the chancellor was to be even more evident in 1887 when he attempted unsuccessfully, at Bismarck's request, to determine the Center's decision in the debates on the Septennat, Bismarck's seven-year army bill, an action which threatened the unity and existence of the Center.

The primary cause for the incompatibility between the chancellor and Windthorst was due to a conflict in

---

[30] Bachem, *Zentrumspartei* **3**: pp. 276–277.

[31] August Reichensperger acknowledged Windthorst's indispensability to the Center in this respect: Ludwig von Pastor, *August Reichensperger, 1808–1895* (2 v., Freiburg, 1899), pp. 397–398.

[32] His former colleague, Paul Majunke, implied that the south Germans' preference for Windthorst was decisive in his successful bid for the leadership: "Ludwig Windthorst. Ein Lebensbild," *Frankfurter zeitgemässe Broschüren* (Frankfurt, 1891), p. 186. Eduard Jörg, the leader of the Bavarian Catholic party from the 1860's to the 1880's, later wrote that his party would have gladly accepted Windthorst as minister-president of its state: *Historisch-politische Blätter für das katholische Deutschland* **107** (1891): p. 539.

[33] On Franckenstein see the *Allgemeine Deutsche Biographie* **49** (Berlin, 1912): pp. 226–234. Cited hereafter as the *ADB*.

[34] Johannes Heckel, "Die Beilegung des Kulturkampfes in Preussen," *Zeitschrift der Savigny-Stiftung für Rechtsgeschichte* **50** (1930): p. 226 ff.

[35] In May, 1884, thirty-seven Centrists voted with the government for the renewal of the anti-Socialist law: Werner Pöls, *Sozialistenfrage mit den angeblichen Staatsreichpläne Bismarcks*, Historische Studien, **377** (Lubeck and Hamburg, 1960): pp. 74–75.

their basic political aims. Bismarck, encouraged by the Conservatives, wanted to destroy what was left of independent liberalism. He claimed later in his memoirs that the Progressives had begun in 1877 to collaborate with the Center in the parliament and in elections and that the alliance had been the reason he had been forced to abandon the Kulturkampf.[36] Bismarck lost some of his concern about liberalism by 1888 because the new German Radical party nearly collapsed in the elections of 1887, which was fought over the Septennat, and the liberal Crown Prince Frederick came down with cancer in the same year. Even though Bismarck depended partly on the support of the National Liberals after the Septennat elections he fell out with them too. The National Liberal leader, Rudolf von Bennigsen, was to complain to Windthorst in the late 1880's that it was impossible to do anything with Bismarck.[37]

Unlike his senior colleagues, Windthorst preferred to experience continued tension with Bismarck than to depend on the favor of the chancellor and on the reliability of the Conservatives as allies. He knew from his own experience that the Prussian state respected power and nothing else. The Center, he believed, could move the chancellor to meet its demands in Prussian or German affairs only if it were always capable of confronting him with a defensive majority coalition composed of its own members, the Radicals, the Social Democrats, the Poles, and the Alsatians. The partial collapse of the Radicals in the Septennat elections proved the validity of Windthorst's thesis, for it cost the Center its decisive position in the Reichstag from 1887 to 1890 and left it virtually impotent. Before and during that uncomfortable period Windthorst insisted that local Center leaders throw support to Radical candidates whenever they could afford to do so, and it was partly through that aid that the Radical party survived as a factor in the Reichstag.[38] Windthorst's concern for the survival of the Radicals also reflected his earlier experiences with the Conservatives. A moderate conservative himself when he entered the Reichstag in 1871, he had been apparently disillusioned over the failure of the Prussian Conservatives to join forces with the Center and said openly to the Reichstag that they were not true conservatives. But during the course of the Kulturkampf and after it he also came to the further conclusion that they were far less reliable than the Radicals in a defense of constitutional rights.[39]

The disagreements between Windthorst and his own leading colleagues reflected significant ideological and social dissonances in the Center party as well as differences on matters of tactics. The first Prussian Catholic Center had been predominantly a parliamentary party of middle-class civil servants, professional men and priests. The Reichstag Center contained two large elements, approximately equal in numbers, of noblemen and of middle-class members. A small group of priests, who probably numbered one-seventh of the parliamentary party, made up the rest of its membership.[40] The line of division in the Center did not run directly between the aristocracy and the bourgeois members, since some wealthy noblemen, for ideological or regional reasons, associated themselves with Windthorst[41] while some bourgeois civil servants often voted with the aristocratic wing of the party. But Windthorst revealed his natural affiliations when he said publicly in 1885 that his successors would come from younger Prussian Centrists like Ernst Lieber, a bourgeois intellectual from Hesse-Nassau, Felix Porsch, a lawyer from Silesia and Matthew Wiese, a popular Rhineland industrialist.[42]

In the early 1880's the conservative Centrists thought they could exploit the unpopularity of liberalism among the majority of their co-religionists. The National Liberals and their close allies, the Free Conservatives, had been in the forefront of the Kulturkampf, a fact that remained long fixed in the minds of Catholic voters; it was a Radical, Rudolf Virchow, the noted virologist, who had given that campaign its name. The later 1870's and the 1880's were bad times for the lower middle classes and workers throughout Germany. Conservatives, clerical and lay, readily tracked the troubles of these unfortunates to one source: liberalism. At the Catholic Congress of 1884 a priest speaker warned:

the whole social order threatens to break down because of the poisons of liberalism, first of all the workers, wholesale, then the class of large landowners and finally small business.[43]

The chairman of the Reichstag Center, Georg von Franckenstein, was the formal leader of the aristocratic Centrists but his political ambition was to become the minister-president of his state, Bavaria.[44] Though he was apparently an excellent chairman, he lacked the political and parliamentary skills of Burghard von

[36] Otto von Bismarck, *Gedanken und Erinnerungen* (3 v., Stuttgart, 1898) 2: p. 134.

[37] *Allgemeine Zeitung,* March 16, 1897.

[38] August Bebel, the leader of the Social Democrats, claimed in October, 1886, that the Radicals could collapse in the next elections and then be absolutely dependent on the grace of the Center and his own party: *Briefwechsel mit Friedrich Engels,* Werner Blumenberg, ed. (The Hague, 1965), p. 295.

[39] *Kölnische Volkszeitung,* July 12, 1897.

[40] From my analysis of the names of the Centrist deputies in the Reichstag in the 1880's: *MdR Biographisches Handbuch der deutschen Reichstages,* Max Schwarz, ed. (Hanover, 1965), pp. 251–506. There were fourteen priests in the Reichstag Center after the elections of 1890: *Germania,* March 20, 1890.

[41] One of them, Franz von Ballestrem, owner of estates and mines, was the eighth wealthiest person in Silesia: Henri Moysett, "L'esprit Publique en l'Allemagne," *Le Correspondant* 241 (1910): p. 633.

[42] At the Catholic Congress of that year: *Verhandlungen der 39. General-Versammlung der katholische Deutschlands zu Münster* (Münster 1885), p. 346. Hereafter cited as *VGVkD.*

[43] F. E. Filthout, *Deutsche Katholiken 1848–1958 und Soziale Frage* (Essen, 1960), p. 62.

[44] See fn. 32 above.

Schorlemer-Alst, the chairman of the Prussian Center and the successor to Mallinckrodt as the leading Westphalian in the Center parties of the Reichstag and Landtag. Schorlemer was well equipped by reason of his talents, background, and office to be the natural leader of the Center's conservatives. Self-assured, genial, and dynamic in personality, he was both a ready debater and a colorful public speaker with a booming voice. An old cavalry officer, he had been decorated by William I himself for his services to the Prussian crown during the revolution of 1848 and later served in the three Prussian wars of the period between 1864 and 1871. But despite his attachment to the Prussian state, he had made vigorous attacks on Bismarck and the government throughout the Kulturkampf and therefore remained a popular figure among the middle-class Catholics.[45]

Like the Catholic ultra-conservatives of the corporatist movement, Schorlemer and his friends wanted to fix the attention of their party on social issues rather than on constitutional and political questions. The corporatists, usually aristocrats, priest scholars, and lay integralists looked back through the mist of Romanticism to the medieval corporative order which had survived in wide parts of Central Europe. They rejected capitalist free enterprise, which they thought was destroying the old productive classes of society, the peasantry and the craftsmen. They apparently assumed that the Protestant and Catholic conservatives could prevail upon the Prussian-German monarchy to take the initiative in restoring the powers or the influence of the guilds, the provincial parliamentary estates and the churches, destroying liberalism in the process.[46] But Schorlemer and most of his aristocratic allies were too close to the thinking of Bismarck, Prussian officials, and the then dominant capitalistic wing of the Conservative party to believe that they would be willing to approve changes which could lame the national economy, the monarchy, and the international posture of the state.

Schorlemer had been a pioneer in the work of organizing the peasantry in associations, and his activities stimulated other noblemen and priests in the early 1880's to follow his example. Felix von Löe in the Lower Rhineland, Karl von Huene in Silesia, and Felix von Wambold in Hesse were the leading founders of regional Christian peasants' associations, using the model set up by Schorlemer twenty years earlier. The formal objectives were the spiritual and vocational education of their members, but the immediate aim was the freeing of the peasantry through collaboration from the debt which threatened the whole class. Unlike the more famous Agrarian League founded by Junkers in eastern Prussia in 1892, the Christian peasant movement was made up of autonomous regional associations which were supposed to stay out of politics. It was in the nature of things, however, that Schorlemer, Huene, and other prominent Catholic agrarians involved in the movement profited politically from it.[47]

The Catholic conservatives included other classes in their social vision. Like Ketteler before them, Schorlemer and Chaplain Franz Hitze, a Westphalian priest, were vigorous promoters of the causes of the more traditional working classes, the artisans and craftsmen. Schorlemer was probably the author of the Center's first legislative proposal for social reform, which one of Ketteler's nephews presented to the Reichstag in March, 1877; it provided for the imposition of restraints upon free enterprise and for the revival of the guilds, and it was probably these points that called down upon the proposal the ridicule of the liberal majority.[48] It is doubtful that Schorlemer, unlike the Catholic corporatists with whom Hitze was identified for some years, believed that the government would in fact ever approve the complete restoration of the guilds and their right to determine who could practice a craft. But the bill of 1877 also contained measures for social reform of industrial conditions. Schorlemer and Franz Hitze were articulate spokesmen for the unskilled workers of the mines and factories, as Ketteler had been. The issue associated itself easily with conservative Catholic social policy, for most Catholic workers were employed by non-Catholic employers. Schorlemer achieved a ready reputation with workers as their friend by exposing some of the miserable conditions in which miners had to try to make a living in the pits which were owned either by the state or by non-Catholics in the Ruhr.[49]

The underside of Conservative philosophy was anti-Semitism. Under the influence of the prominent Lutheran court pastor, Adolf Stöcker, the Conservatives adopted anti-Semitism as an aid to their competition with Radicals and Social Democrats; and a decade later in Austria Karl Lueger was to create a strong Catholic party by its use. In Germany, the Christian peasants' associations founded to free the peasantry from dependence on Jewish moneylenders and cattle merchants were strongholds of anti-Semitism. It was also widespread among small retailers and craftsmen who competed with Jewish merchants, owners of warehouses and peddlers in limited markets. Since they were often from lower middle-class families themselves the lower clergy tended to share the prejudices of the *Mittelstand* against the Jews.

---

[45] Bachem, *Zentrumspartei* 5: pp. 20–25; *ADB* 54 (1912): pp. 158–166.

[46] For their thought consult: Ralph Bowen, *German Theories of the Corporative State* (New York, 1947), p. 96 ff.; also Emil Ritter, *Die Katholisch-Soziale Bewegung Deutschlands im Neunzehnten Jahrhundert und der Volksverein* (Cologne, 1954), pp. 56–83.

[47] See Bachem, *Zentrumspartei* 3: p. 422 ff.; Georges Blondel, *Études sur les populations rurales de l'Allemagne et la crise agraire* (Paris, 1912), pp. 233–249.

[48] Ritter, *Volksverein*, pp. 123–124.

[49] *ADB* 54: p. 161.

The spread of anti-Semitism among the Catholic bourgeoisie and better educated clergy owed much, however, to the Kulturkampf. They believed that the Kulturkampf was a conflict between orthodox Christians like themselves and former Christians over the nature of the state; therefore they became annoyed or even angry when prominent liberal deputies of Jewish backgrounds like Eduard Lasker participated in the debates on the confessional school system or in attacks on the Catholic Church.[50] In 1873 and 1875 the Bavarian *Historisch-politische Blätter* stressed the influence of Jewish businessmen on the national economy; in the latter year *Germania,* then edited by two robust anti-Semites, Paul Majunke and Christopher Cremer, published a series of articles in which it charged that the Kulturkampf was the work of Jews who wanted to distract popular attention from the responsibility of Jewish speculators for the economic recession of 1873. Majunke and Cremer had probably initiated *Germania's* campaign for the tactical purpose of embarrassing the liberal parties in the Kulturkampf. It was not surprising therefore, that Schorlemer received extensive backing in the Prussian Center when he asked his colleagues in November, 1880, to support the Conservatives in a parliamentary attack on the Jews.[51]

That the Center did not join in the campaign was due solely to Windthorst. He had earlier brought about the removal of Majunke and Cremer from *Germania.*[52] He threatened to resign his mandate if his party approved Schorlemer's proposal.[53] In his own brief remarks to the Landtag on the Jewish question he reminded his colleagues of that body that the Jews were a minority and needed protection.[54] Windthorst undoubtedly considered the harm that Centrist anti-Semitism could do to the party's relations with the Radicals; but his position was deeply grounded in his rectitude, his humanity and the respect that his defense of German Catholicism strengthened in him for the rights of all minorities.

It is not surprising that anti-Semitism, latent in times of economic stability, would be virulent in some Catholic districts during bad times. This was evident in the Rhineland, the most advanced Catholic province in Germany, during the debates on the Jews of November, 1880, and again in the early 1890's. Peter Reichensperger, who had promoted the cause of Jewish equality in the 1850's, had agreed to act as a mediator between Schorlemer and Windthorst in their disagreement on the Jewish question, but both Reichensperger and Julius Bachem, his young Rhenish colleague, spoke unfavorably about the Jews. While they insisted that no one wanted to take away any constitutional rights from Jews they implied that there was a place for restraints on their economic activities.[55] Unlike Windthorst, they were the leaders of a regional party which thought much about the appeal of anti-Semitism to the retailers and artisans who had to compete with superior commercial enterprise and energy of Jewish merchants and peddlers. In the next decade Julius Bachem was to advocate specific legislation aimed against Jewish merchants.

In opposing anti-Semitism, Windthorst may have been colliding with only a part of the conservative Center faction. But social affiliation and philosophy put him at odds with much of Centrist conservatism. The deputies closest to him were young intellectuals or journalists, enterprising businessmen, an occasional magnate, and a few priest colleagues. One of his closest aides, Ernst Lieber, had seriously considered an academic career; another, Georg von Hertling, had actually chosen one. Windthorst had tried unsuccessfully to entice into the party Lujo Brentano, the noted liberal economist who was Lieber's closest friend and Hertling's cousin.[56] This group of Catholic middle-class intellectuals and journalists was quite small and tightly connected: the Bachem cousins, Julius and Karl, who were apparently doubly related, were also distant cousins of Brentano,[57] and some of the parliamentarians in Windthorst's group or editors close to it had known one another in their university years.

Windthorst himself, to be sure, had a deeply conservative strain. Though he was apparently untouched by Romanticism and the Catholic revival, he was a believing Catholic deeply attached to his church but respecting the religious convictions of Protestants and Jews. In his fundamental political beliefs he was certainly a moderate conservative for he remained personally loyal to the deposed Guelf dynasty of Hanover under which he had held high office.[58] Yet some of his political views and even more his social and economic outlook were not distinguishable from those of the radical liberals. He wanted a society and economy based upon the supremacy of the law; life in a Prussian state with a nearly omnicompetent bureaucracy and an arbitrary chancellor were galling to him. He was especially

[50] Joseph Hess, *Der Kampf um die Schule in Preussen 1872–1906* (Cologne, 1912), p. 28.

[51] Paul Massing, *Rehearsal for Destruction* (New York, 1947), pp. 17–19. Walther Frank, *Hofprediger Adolf Stöcker* (Hamburg, 1935), p. 195 ff.

[52] On Windthorst and Majunke: Bachem, *Zentrumspartei* 5: pp. 192–193.

[53] Pastor, *August Reichensperger* 2: p. 191.

[54] Bachem, *Zentrumspartei* 3: p. 419. Also, R. Lill, "Die deutschen Katholiken und die Juden 1850–1933"; *Kirche und Synagoge,* K. H. Rengstorf und S. v. Kortzfleisch, 2 (1970): pp. 381–384.

[55] Lill does not agree with Bachem's claim that Windthorst was satisfied with Reichensperger's remarks on the issues under debate: *ibid.,* p. 384. Bachem, *Zentrumspartei* 3: p. 419.

[56] Lujo Brentano, *Mein Leben im Kampf um die sociale Entwickelung Deutschlands* (Jena, 1931), pp. 68–69.

[57] Karl Bachem, *Die Bachem Familie von Erpel und Köln* (Cologne, 1937), table II.

[58] His Reichstag colleague, Ludwig Bamberger, said that Windthorst was basically a conservative: Erich Eyck, *Auf Deutschlands Politischen Forum* (Erlenbach-Zurach and Stuttgart, 1965), p. 51.

enthusiastic about the freedom enjoyed by the churches in Great Britain and the United States and the lack of religious controversy in their legislative bodies.[59] Though Windthorst throughout the 1890's refused to risk a direct conflict with Bismarck and his own right wing over the renewal of the anti-Socialist law, he was undoubtedly sincere in warning Bismarck that the chancellor was mistaken in believing he could defeat ideas by force.[60] His distaste for the anti-Socialist law was of one piece with his opposition to the Kulturkampf, anti-Semitism, and exceptional legislation against the minority ethnic groups. It is more difficult to define with any precision what Windthorst's exact views were on social reform, since he kept in mind the susceptibilities of his Radical allies, who were, with minor exceptions, ardent believers in the validity of the principles of *laissez faire*. We cannot determine whether his absence from the Reichstag during the introduction of the Center's social program of 1877 was due to illness, his personal dislike for its proposals or concern for his alliance.[61] But Windthorst, unlike most of his conservative associates, believed that Catholic Germany needed more, not less, industry and commerce.[62] It is probable that his early years in Hanover, a Protestant state with long connections with Great Britain, and his practical intelligence had made him an early convert to capitalism. Though he lived modestly himself and was extraordinarily thoughtful to others, he seemed not to have understood the extent to which the life of many workers was a bitter struggle for existence.[63] In 1877 he sought without success to prevent the election to the Reichstag of Gerhard Stötzel, a Catholic miner and editor. Nevertheless it may have been partly at his encouragement that in 1879 Franz Brandts, a prominent textile manufacturer in the Rhineland, founded "Workers Welfare," an association for Christian employers willing to promote a humane relationship between employers and employees. Though Brandts established a familiar and warm relationship with his own workers, the association did not receive substantial sup-

port from either Catholic or non-Catholic employers.[64] It is clear, in any case, that Windthorst would have preferred solutions to the social problem that did not involve governmental intervention in industry or the formation of trade unions.

As Bismarck recognized, Windthorst's strength in politics lay in his realism and willingness to compromise. He knew the crucial value of the peasant vote to his party and the influence that the Catholic agrarians could exercise over the peasantry on agricultural questions. Though he preferred free trade, he went along with his agrarian colleagues who wanted the Center to support the three tariff bills presented by the government between 1879 and 1886. The last of those measures provided the relatively high rate of five marks per two hundred weight of wheat.[65] And while Windthorst distrusted Catholic corporatists almost as much as he did Socialists, for both rejected free enterprise, he did not oppose the bills initiated by his conservative colleagues and members of the Conservative party which would give the guilds public status; their proposals stipulated that the craft guilds should be able to prescribe certain regulations binding on journeymen and apprentices and to tax masters and journeymen for the support of courts of arbitration in certain crafts.[66] The growth of the Social Democratic movement, the Center's support of agricultural tariffs, and the restlessness of Catholic workers over the party's concentration on issues left over from the Kulturkampf made the need to take legislative action on behalf of factory labor even more pressing than the necessity for protection of artisans. The question Windthorst faced was not whether the Center would promote social measures for industrial labor but what form they should take.

The social legislation which Windthorst accepted did not fit either his convictions or the interest of his relations with the Radicals. He and his young aides, Lieber and Hertling, preferred a program of worker protection calling for a six-day week, safety precautions, sharp restrictions on the working time of women and children, courts of arbitration, and eventual limitation on the working day of male adults. Such provisions reflected the traditional concern of the Catholic Church for the family; they were also in harmony with the liberal thesis that the state had to provide in some measure for the physical security of its citizens. But

[59] *VGVkD zu Münster* (Münster, 1885), p. 349. *Verhandlungen des Reichstages,* October 30, 1889: p. 58. In April, 1879, he queried the papal nuncio whether the Vatican would be willing to approve the separation of church and state in Prussia, adding that a favorable response to the question would facilitate relations with the liberals: "Aus Windthorsts Korrespondenz," *Stimmen aus Maria Laach* **82** (1912): p. 259. The Vatican's response was apparently negative.

[60] Hans Rosenberg, *Grosse Depression und Bismarckzeit* (Berlin, 1967), pp. 200–201, fn. 190.

[61] See Ritter, *Volksverein,* p. 112.

[62] Though he did so in a humorous vein he once told a gathering of young businessmen that he always advised parents to encourage their sons to enter industry or commerce: *VGVkD zu Coblenz* (Coblenz, 1890), pp. 148–149.

[63] Addressing himself specifically to workers in the audience at the Catholic Congress of 1879 he said that he had always been "a hard worker himself": *VGVkD zu Aachen* (Aachen, 1879), p. 63.

[64] Julius Bachem, "Vom Rhein. Eine Ära von Schwierigkeiten nicht zuletzt für Centrum," *HpB* **111** (1893): p. 455.

[65] On the Center and the tariff question in the 1880's see Johannes Croner, *Die Geschichte der agrarischen Bewegung in Deutschland* (Berlin, 1904), p. 21 f; Franz S. Pichler, *Zentrum und Landwirtschaft* (Cologne, 1898), p. 60.

[66] Volksverein für das katholische Deutschlands, *Die Sozialpolitik der deutschen Zentrumspartei* (München-Gladbach, 1903), pp. 70–74. The Center voted in 1885 for one of the major objectives of the master craftsmen, a bill requiring all persons who wanted to practice a trade to give formal proof of competence, but the Federal Council refused to approve the measure.

Bismarck was rigid in his insistence that the Reichstag would have to accept his program of insurance for the sick, the injured, and the aged, which rejected the liberals' premise that the individual should be responsible for his own financial welfare. Franckenstein, the chairman of the Reichstag committee concerned with social legislation, and Schorlemer finally prevailed upon the reluctant Windthorst to accept the chancellor's proposals. The Centrist leader did so but he insisted successfully in the debates on the insurance bills for the injured and the sick in 1884 and 1885 that they contain no provision for a state subsidy and that their administration be decentralized. In 1889, however, when the Center was out of power in the Reichstag, Bismarck secured the passage of an old-age insurance measure which provided a state subsidy. That Franckenstein, the chairman, Peter Reichensperger, and ten other Centrists helped to bring about its victory made Bismarck's success doubly painful to Windthorst and his aides. Relations were never the same again between the members of the Windthorst group and Franckenstein, who was to die at the beginning of the next year.[67]

Windthorst's easy triumphs over his aristocratic rivals were probably due to his resistance to the Kulturkampf and the credit he received for the conclusion of that war upon independent Catholicism, even though he had been excluded from the settlement. Most Prussian Catholics, if not for the same reason, had tended toward opposition to the government in the past and the Kulturkampf had enormously intensified that state of mind, especially among the clergy. No Prussian churchman could hope to secure an important bishopric unless he had been identified with the Windthorst wing of the Center in the 1880's.[68] In the south, above all in Bavaria, the traditional mood was that of opposition to the Prussian government at any price.

The more serious concerns of the Center's leaders were really with the future of the party. The brief history of the first Prussian Center had demonstrated that no Catholic party could hope for a permanent lease on life. With the end of the Kulturkampf and a return to normal relations between the Prussian state and the Catholic Church, divisive economic and social issues would become more prominent in Catholic politics, as indeed they had done to a considerable extent between 1879 and 1887. Windthorst told Bishop Kopp near the end of the Kulturkampf settlement that the Center needed an issue involving struggle and uniting Catholics.[69]

A campaign against the anti-Jesuit law after 1887 might seem ideal for Windthorst's purposes. The law was national in scope and affected the sensibilities of Catholics throughout the empire. It banned all teaching and preaching orders, except for a few like the Benedictines who were decentralized, and it permitted any state government to expel their individual members from its territory overnight. Once the anti-Socialist law had been revoked in 1890, it was to be the only law of exception on the Imperial statute books. But Windthorst apparently believed that Bismarck could or would not move to rescind the whole law. One of the express purposes of the Evangelical League, founded in 1887 by Protestants close to the Free Conservative and National Liberal parties, was to block the return of the Jesuits and other orders to Germany. While Windthorst hoped to secure the early deletion of the expulsion paragraph of the law, neither he nor informed Catholic churchmen thought that the question of the orders' return would be ripe for several years.[70]

Windthorst believed that the school issue in Prussia had promising potential for the Center. After the passage of the School Inspection Act of 1872, the Prussian Ministry of Public Worship and Education had affirmed the sovereign control of the state over school instruction, including the teaching of religion. Government officials appointed the teachers, made up the syllabus and selected the reading materials for religious instruction. Since there was no law which committed the Prussian state to the absolute maintenance of the confessional school system, the Ministry of Public Worship and Education could, if it chose to do so, decree the building of new interconfessional schools.[71] Some of the smaller southwestern states had already based their school systems on the interconfessional principle.

Windthorst had undoubtedly planned from an early date to attempt to secure a revision of the state's school policies, but he later found additional reasons for doing so. The political significance of the school question became evident in 1879 when the lower clergy in nearby Belgium organized a successful national school strike of Catholic children against an anticlerical government. Other prominent German Catholics also grasped the significance of the Belgian school strike. Felix von Löe and Karl zu Löwenstein, the leaders of the defunct

---

[67] On the Center, Bismarck, and social legislation in the 1880's consult Ritter, *Volksverein,* pp. 114–125; Bachem, *Zentrumspartei* 4: ch. 2: Georg von Hertling, *Erinnerungen aus meinen Leben* (2 v., Munich and Kempten, 1920) 2: p. 105 f.

[68] Bishop Kopp had hoped to become archbishop of Cologne. Later Pope Leo XIII had to impose Kopp on the cathedral chapter of Breslau after its canons had refused to elect him: Hermann Hoffman. "Die Breslauer Bischofswählen in preussicher Zeit," *Zeitschrift des Vereins für die Geschichte Schlesiens* 77 (1941): p. 227 ff.

[69] Heckel, "Die Beilegung des Kulturkampfes," p. 226.

[70] On the antagonism of the new League to the Catholic orders see Fritz von der Heydte, *Gute Wehr, Werden, Wirken und Wollen des Evangelischen Bundes* (Berlin, 1936), p. 62 f. Bishop Kopp told Leo XIII in 1889 that Bismarck had good will toward the Catholic Church but was kept from making any new concessions by the Evangelical League's opposition: draft of a report, dated July, 1889, Kopp Papers, File 34, Wrocław.

[71] See Hess, *Der Kampf um die Schule in Preussen 1872–1906,* ch. 1. Hess was a Rhineland Centrist but his study is factual.

Mainz Catholic Association, concluded that they could use the school issue in the German states as a device to build a new national Catholic association. After receiving approval from the pope, they asked the Catholic Congress in August, 1879, to approve such an organization. Windthorst, working unobtrusively, managed to deflate the plan.[72] Nevertheless, the difficulties with Löe and Löwenstein must have strengthened him in his assumption that he would have to take the initiative on the school issue at a suitable time.

The validity of that assumption was proven in 1888, when Windthorst used the school question as the central issue in the Landtag elections. For the first time several of the Prussian bishops along with the archbishop of Cologne, Philipp Krementz, in the van, intervened in an electoral campaign and warned that Catholics should not vote for any candidate who was not ready to defend the rights of the Christian schools.[73] That statement meant that the candidate should be ready to support Windthorst's school bill, which called for the restoration of the churches' role in the approval of teachers of religion, and in the selection of syllabuses and reading materials.[74] As Windthorst had foreseen, the Landtag election of 1888 ended in a significant victory for the Prussian Center and reinforced his own position of party leadership though Bismarck ignored the Center's school proposals. Two years later, after the national elections of 1890, the Reichstag Center recovered its old position in the national parliament, a happy event that was somewhat dimmed by the achievements of the Social Democratic party, which polled more popular votes than the Center itself. But the Center, aided by its electoral alliances, won far more mandates and was easily the largest party in the Reichstag, with one hundred and six seats.

In the last years of his life Windthorst reached the apotheosis of his career in Catholic politics and leadership of the Catholic minority. The annual Catholic congress had become by the mid-1880's an opportunity to see, hear, and fete Windthorst rather than an occasion for the meeting of the leaders and members of Catholic associations. It was an ironic twist in the career of a former leading adviser of the Protestant king of Hanover, but there was a certain consistency in Windthorst's life, for the Center party upheld the constitutional principles that had been even more important to him than the Guelf dynasty.

Nevertheless, the career of the old Centrist leader had a certain incompleteness. Always the realist, he had never been satisfied with opposition—which, he insisted, ended in sterility. Windthorst liked to compare the Prussian state with a speeding locomotive and to say that he intended to jump aboard, work its brakes and, if necessary, lay a hand on the throttle.[75] But his important substantial achievements lay behind him after Bismarck and the Papacy ratified the peace settlement of 1886. The future relationship between his party and the state was still uncertain at his death in 1891, as was the succession to his leadership.

In the mid-eighties Windthorst looked forward to the early coming of a regime in which his allies from the Radical party, Ludwig Bamberger and Eugen Richter, would have influence. There would be no Bismarck and there would be an end to exceptional laws and the threat of state intervention in the economy. The Catholic Church would recover its complete freedom. Young men who shared Windthorst's economic views would attain the leadership of the party. But that was not the direction of events. Bismarck used the Septennat issue to weaken the Radicals in 1887 and Frederick III was already a dying man when he succeeded his father in March, 1888.[76] The new ruler, William II, had earlier come under the influence of advisers who had a strong distrust of the Center and Windthorst. They believed that the Prussian government should extend itself to maintain the restored alliance of the Conservatives and Free Conservatives with the National Liberals, the so-called Cartel group, since the National Liberals were the only one of these three parties with some influence in southern Germany.[77]

Windthorst drew the logical consequences from the new state of affairs in Berlin. His political conduct was to reveal more than ever the hard core of realism in his political personality. With the Center's recovery of its pivotal position in the Reichstag after the elections of February, 1890, he and Bismarck moved toward each other. The negotiations between them are still shrouded in obscurity but reliable conclusions can be drawn about their respective proposals. The government's military experts were confident that the deterioration of Russo-German relations and the apparent rapprochement between the Tsarist empire and France dictated a major expansion and reorganization of the German army. In domestic affairs Bismarck was obsessed with the belief that he had to continue a punitive campaign against the Social Democratic party, its press, and other institutions after the Reichstag refused any further renewal of the old anti-Socialist law in February, 1890. The old Center leader was undoubtedly

---

[72] On the question of a new Catholic school association on a mass basis and the evidence of internal Catholic disagreement over it: *VGVkD zu Aachen* (Aachen 1879), pp. 108–115, 362, 372, 374.

[73] *Kölnische Volkszeitung*, October 10, 1888.

[74] Eduard Hüsgen, *Ludwig Windthorst*, (Cologne, 1907), pp. 307–309.

[75] *Stimmen aus Maria Laach* **82**: p. 148: Quotation from an Ernst Lieber speech, *Kölnische Zeitung*, September 25, 1899.

[76] Windthorst told a confidant of the crown prince in February, 1888, that it would be highly worth while if the future emperor were to rule only for a year: Robert Lucius von Ballhausen, *Bismarck-Erinnerungen* (Stuttgart, 1921), pp. 418–419.

[77] On the anti-Centrist thinking of the new ruler's advisers see J. C. G. Röhl, "The Disintegration of the Kartell and the Politics of Bismarck's Fall from Power," *Historical Journal* **9** (1966): pp. 60–89.

ready to make concessions on the army and socialist questions, politically sensitive though they were certain to be. He had said on several occasions in previous months that international conditions would keep Germany from doing anything to stop the armaments race, so he was undoubtedly ready to support a new army bill.[78]

Though the Center had helped to defeat the anti-Socialist law, Windthorst had earlier indicated his willingness to approve of a measure aimed at the Socialists that would be based on existing law.[79] His own fear of the attractiveness of Socialist ideas to workers and of the resourcefulness of Socialist agitators and organizers was scarcely less than Bismarck's. When he had finally approved of the establishment of Catholic workers' associations several years earlier, he had warned that priests should be at their head to protect their members from bad influences.[80] In return, Windthorst expected the chancellor to compel a reluctant Prussian ministry to meet the Center's desires for a Prussian school bill favorable to the churches and for the revocation of the expulsion article of the anti-Jesuit law.[81] The Center leader undoubtedly envisioned as a further result of his new alliance with the chancellor an exclusion of the National Liberals from the inner coalition of the Conservatives and the Center. But Count Helldorf, the leader of the Conservatives at the time, told William II about the secret negotiations between the chancellor and Windthorst and Bismarck's dismissal from office followed within a few days.[82]

The chancellor's fall from power soon after their meeting was a heavy shock to Windthorst, who knew that his own time was running out.[83] Nevertheless, he continued his efforts to bring his party together with the government. He knew and liked Bismarck's successor, General Leo von Caprivi, with whom he had dealt many times in the mid-1880's when Caprivi, then chief of the Naval Admiralty, had sought to work in harmony with the Center and Radicals on naval expenditures. He knew that the new chancellor, nervous and uncertain in his difficult position, was especially concerned about the success of his first bill to the Reichstag, a minor army proposal which was to prepare the parliament for a major program a year or so later.

The early debates over the little army bill demonstrated, however, how difficult it could be to turn the Center from the easy work of opposition to the burdens of political responsibility. At a time when he enjoyed unparalleled prestige and influence among the Catholic people, Windthorst had to engage in the grueling labor of trying to win his party for the new army proposal. His colleagues had discovered the more ambitious plans of the Prussian Ministry of War and some of them had decided to start the campaign against these projects right away by attacking the minor proposal which was their introductory wedge. Windthorst went through a harrowing experience before he succeeded in bringing most of his party into line behind a slightly modified government bill.

Even though the initial opponents of the measure came from all parts of the Center's popular wing, the most serious problem was the clear conflict of political interest between the Prussian and Bavarian elements in the party. No prominent Prussian member really dared to spoil the possibility of compromise, for either the defeat of the bill or apathetic Centrist support for it might alienate the king-emperor still further and cost the party a favorable Prussian school bill and other concessions to the Church.[84] But the Bavarian members were concerned over the reactions of their own voters to the Center's approval of a military bill. Windthorst in 1889 had already anticipated having serious difficulties in convincing the Bavarian contingent and its associates in the Bavarian party at home that the Center should back the government in necessary army legislation.[85] After the emperor had agreed to a minor reduction in the length of time some recruits would serve, Windthorst was finally successful in getting most of his party to approve the little army bill. Windthorst had prepared the way for passage by presenting four resolutions to the Reichstag which were supposed to impose restraints on the government in its planning of the major army program. Though they were elastic, their existence was to make it possible for the opponents of the later bill to point to them in the debates of 1892 and 1893 on the army.[86]

The government had understood that the Center's leaders would expect and in fact need a *quid pro quo*

---

[78] *Stenographische Berichte der Verhandlungen des Deutschen Reichstages.* October 30, 1889: p. 58. *Germania,* January 23, 1890.

[79] Pöls, *Sozialistenfrage,* p. 84.

[80] *VGVkD zu Münster* (Münster 1885), p. 352.

[81] Ballhausen, *Bismarck-Erinnerungen,* p. 521; Spahn, *Zentrum,* p. 87.

[82] J. C. G. Röhl, *Germany without Bismarck* (Berkeley, 1967), pp. 53–55; and E. Zechlin, *Staatsreichpläne Bismarcks und Wilhelms II, 1890–1894* (Stuttgart, 1929), p. 77.

[83] He said to a young colleague that "Bismarck has gone too early for us." Karl Bachem, Notes dated September 7, 1898. Bachem Papers, Stadt Köln Historisches Archiv, File 63.

[84] Ernst Lieber went along initially with the opponents of the bill in order to preserve his influence with them but later provided the compromise that enabled some of them to vote for the measure: Lieber, Journal, June 16, 1890.

[85] Windthorst and most of his colleagues were upset when the Bavarian government refused in early 1890 to give permission for the holding of the annual Catholic Congress in Munich later that year. Windthorst on that subject: *VGVkD zu Coblenz* (Coblenz, 1890), pp. 75–76. Also Hertling, *Erinnerungen* 2: pp. 75–76, 122–123.

[86] They were old demands of the left-liberals: the government should abandon any plan to introduce universal military service, consider annual budgetary approvals of army expenditures, and think seriously about shortening military service to two years and lessening the period spent by recruits in training: See Heinz Goebel, *Die Militärvorlage, 1892–1893,* (Ph.D. diss., University of Münster, 1935), p. 35.

for their party's support of the army bill and other legislative proposals. William II and his advisers undoubtedly hoped also to strengthen the position of the aristocrats and other conservative elements in the party, who would benefit in any case from the Center's shift to the right. In February, 1890, William II invited Bishop Kopp and Franz Hitze to participate in an international conference on social problems to be held later in Berlin. Later the Caprivi government announced its intention of presenting to the Reichstag a program for the protection of workers which duplicated the proposals made unsuccessfully by the Center in the previous decade.[87]

But in 1890 Windthorst's mind was not fixed on social legislation. He continued to be concerned about the growth of the Social Democratic movement and its agitation, but he accepted the government's decision to abandon Bismarck's methods against the party—methods that Windthorst had never been warm to. Much against his will he had to go along with the foundation in the late summer of a new Catholic mass organization, the "Peoples' Association for Catholic Germany." Two of his influential episcopal supporters, Felix Korum and Paul Haffner, the bishops of Trier and Mainz, respectively, had agreed with Felix von Löe and Karl zu Löwenstein that the establishment of the Evangelical League called for a Catholic counterpart. But Windthorst insisted that it be primarily an association to defend existing society against Socialist ideas and that its chairman should be his industrialist friend, Franz Brandts.[88]

It was characteristic of Windthorst that he was more interested in the government's presentation to the Landtag of a Prussian school bill meeting the expectations of the Prussian hierarchy and clergy than he was in the Imperial government's proposals for protection of workers. We cannot know whether Caprivi made an explicit promise to the Center leader that Heinrich von Gossler, the Prussian minister of public worship and education, would shape a bill to Windthorst's wishes, but Windthorst undoubtedly had that end in mind when he fought to save the first army measure.[89] Though in his remarks to the Catholic Congress in August, 1890, he was cautious about the prospects of such a bill, he was probably optimistic. It was painful and embarrassing to him when the bill turned out to be a confirmation of the status quo, though it stressed the responsibility of officials to consult with church representatives about the appointment of teachers and the materials they would use in religious instruction.[90]

Windthorst's legislative activities in the last two months of his life were a final demonstration of his realism and his commitment to the survival of his party. He undermined his health by a vigorous campaign against the Gossler school bill in the Landtag and made it clear to Caprivi that there could be no peace between the Center and the government until the bill was withdrawn.[91] He probably also demanded Gossler's removal, since Caprivi dismissed the minister shortly before Windthorst's death. But he was firm, though diplomatic, in dealing with the rampant emotionalism of both the Center parties in the Reichstag and Landtag. Knowing how passionate was William II's feeling for the navy, the members of the Reichstag Center wanted to take vengeance on Caprivi and the emperor by slicing the naval budget. At a rough session of his party on March 7, 1891, Windthorst was finally able to convince his associates that the Center should seek a compromise with the government on the naval budget.[92] His death occurred within the next week.

2. THE TRIUMPH OF THE POPULAR CENTRISTS

It [Windthorst's death] is the worst blow which could have struck the German state at this time.
Caprivi, March, 1891.[1]
I said to Count Ballestrem: Herr Count, you wish then to be the shepherd who leads the flock, and that I be the sheepdog who keeps the flock together behind you.
Lieber, 1891.[2]

The sudden passing of Windthorst, like Bismarck's departure from office a year earlier, was an event of national importance. Monarchical officials and the Cartel parties would now have to find out whether the government could secure reliable majorities without the use of Bismarckian electoral methods or the recall of the old chancellor to office. They would learn soon. The important legislation of the Caprivi government—the conclusion of new commercial treaties with several foreign states, the further reformation of the Prussian financial system and above all the major expansion of the army—all lay in the immediate future. The chancellor and Johannes Miquel, the Prussian minister of finance, the most influential member of the Prussian ministerial council, worried over the ability of Windthorst's successors to preserve the unity of the Center and discipline over their colleagues.[3] Although they were later to find the causes for apprehension relieved

---

[87] Ritter, *Volksverein*, p. 161; also Gunther Kriegbaum, *Die parliamentarische Tätigkeit des Freiherrn C.W. Heyl zu Herresheim* (Meisenheim, 1962), p. 222.

[88] Ritter, pp. 139–145.

[89] Lieber, Journal, June 16, 1890.

[90] Hess, *Kampf um die Schule*, pp. 37, 55.

[91] Adolf Marschall von Bieberstein, Diary, January 15, 1891. Notes in possession of David R. King.

[92] Lieber memorandum, "Windthorst," Lieber Papers, Wrocław, 177.

[1] Remarks made by the chancellor to a prominent Center deputy shortly after Windthorst's passing: Ernst Lieber, Journal, March 17, 1891.

[2] Bachem, *Zentrumspartei* 5: p. 242.

[3] After learning from Karl Bachem of Windthorst's death, Miquel pleaded excitedly that the Center should remain united; Bachem, "Meine Erlebnisse bei Windthorsts Tod," March, 1891. Karl Bachem Papers, File 63.

by more cheering signs, events in the winter of 1892 and 1893 justified their original fears.

In his funeral eulogy of Windthorst, Bishop Georg Kopp confessed that the members of the Center were themselves uncertain they could keep the party unified.[4] His remark was broadly true but it reflected more precisely the state of mind of the leading Centrist aristocrats, friends of Kopp, than that of their prominent middle-class colleagues. Franz von Ballestrem, the chairman of the Reichstag Center, his close friend, Karl von Huene, both Silesians, and members of their aristocratic circle, hoped to fill the vacuum in command by converting the chairmanship into a position of leadership for themselves and their class. In the last year of Windthorst's life, Ballestrem, Huene, Konrad von Preysing, the leading Bavarian nobleman in the Reichstag fraction, Clemens von Heereman, the chairman of the Prussian Center, and Franz von Arenberg, an ex-diplomat from the Rhineland had been more frequently in Windthorst's company than were any other Center dignitaries. Only they could have taken over the responsibilities of negotiating with the government and its other parliamentary allies, especially the Conservative and Free Conservative parties. Their contacts with William II through their attendance at court functions and Huene's friendship with Caprivi which dated from their joint service in the Franco-German War of 1870–1871 reinforced what was already a strong political position.[5]

But the position of Ballestrem and Huene was all the stronger because they enjoyed the patronage of Georg Kopp, prince-bishop of Breslau in Silesia. Of humble birth and small size, Kopp possessed an impressive personality, strong will, and diplomatic talent. He had been the most prominent ecclesiastical advocate of a compromise settlement of the Kulturkampf and, as we have seen, represented the Vatican in the negotiations which ended that conflict, probably at Bismarck's request.[6] To his great chagrin he failed to become the archbishop of Cologne, the most prestigous and influential see in the Prussian Catholic Church, apparently because of his unpopularity among the Catholic clergy and laity of the Rhineland who disapproved of his role in the settlement of the Kulturkampf.[7] Nevertheless he remained the favorite bishop

of Bismarck, Caprivi, and William II. And while the Vatican preferred the judgment of Philipp Krementz, the pious archbishop of Cologne on ecclesiastical appointments,[8] it usually took Kopp's advice on matters affecting relations between Church and state.

Ballestrem and Huene were not mediocrities who owed their parliamentary mandates or their influence in the Center to their wealth, which was considerable in the chairman's case, or their social status. The quick-tempered Ballestrem was a man of marked ambition, commanding presence, administrative ability, and keen wit. He was to serve as the president of the Reichstag in the period 1898–1906 with distinction and popularity.[9] But Huene was undoubtedly the dominant partner in their relationship, for he had the more concentrated personality, the greater political skill, and probably the stronger urge to lead the Center. His middle-class colleagues found him too reserved for their liking but they thought him to be of ministerial caliber. If it can be said that the Center had a leader in the period between the death of Windthorst and the angry party debates over the major army bill of 1892–1893 it was certainly Huene.[10]

Ballestrem and Huene went to work gathering their power immediately after Windthorst's death. The biggest decision facing the chairmen and executive committees of the two Center fractions in Berlin was the disposition of Windthorst's seats in the Landtag and Reichstag. The needs of party unity should have dictated their division between a nobleman and a Centrist of the middle class. Instead Ballestrem boldly recommended to the two executive councils that the Landstag and Reichstag mandates be offered, respectively, to himself and to Georg von Hertling. Apparently eager to avoid an embarrassing or divisive debate, the middle-class Centrists in the two committees approved the Ballestrem proposals.[11]

While governmental policies were favorable to the conservative leadership of the Center by aristocrats the social changes going on in the Reichstag Center were not. In fact, the leaders found it increasingly difficult as the Kulturkampf faded more deeply into the past to replace both the aristocratic and bourgeois members of the original leadership groups who had died or retired.[12] But the decline of the number of aristocrats in

---

[4] Majunke, "Windthorst," p. 217.

[5] On the Caprivi-Huene relationship: Generalleutnant August Keim, *Erlebtes und Erstrebtes, Lebenserinnerungen* (Hanover, 1925), p. 55.

[6] On Kopp see Rudolf Morsey, "Georg Kardinal Kopp, Fürst-bischof von Breslau (1887–1914)," *Wichmann-Jahrbuch für Kirchengeschichte im Bistum Berlin* **21–23** (1967–1969): pp. 42–65.

[7] *The Holstein Papers* **2**: pp. 237–238. But it is conceivable that Bismarck may have wanted from the beginning to secure Kopp's appointment to Breslau. Silesia had a large Polish population and the Prussian government had always used extreme care in approving the selection of a bishop for that diocese who would be a reliable supporter of the state's interest there.

[8] According to the well-informed Catholic nobleman, Count Bogdan von Hutten-Czapski, *Sechig Jahre Politik und Gesellschaft* (2 v., Berlin, 1936) **1**: p. 210.

[9] Obituaries: *Berliner Tägeblatt* and *Kölnische Zeitung*, December 24, 1910. Bachem, *Zentrumspartei* **5**: pp. 219–231.

[10] *Ibid.* **4**: pp. 288–289. Lieber, his rival, had high praise for his expertise on matters of military organization: Journal, December 15, 1892. On his leading role in the Center: Spahn, *Lieber*, p. 27.

[11] Lieber, Journal, April 9, 1891.

[12] On the problem of adequate replacements: Hertling, *Erinnerungen* **2**: pp. 139–140; Ernst Lieber to Luschberger, April 18, 1891. Lieber Papers, Speyer, L, 188.

the fraction was undoubtedly most painful to the Ballestrem circle. In 1889 aristocrats had held forty-one of the Reichstag's Center's ninety-eight mandates, but after the elections of 1890 only thirty noblemen sat in a fraction of one hundred six members.[13] There were probably two general causes for the reduction of aristocratic numbers. Some were apparently bored with the dullness of parliamentary routine and life in Berlin which kept them from their estates.[14] Still others were probably retired by local electoral committees who found them less acceptable to their constituencies than they had during the Kulturkampf. Hans Delbrück, the editor of the *Preussische Jahrbücher,* wrote shortly after Windthorst's death that the mandates of Centrists like Ballestrem, Huene and Preysing would be in danger at the next election since most of the Center's supporters really longed for a "democratic, particularistic, clerical and agrarian" party.[15]

Ballestrem and Huene did not feel comfortable in the post-1890 Reichstag Center once Windthorst was gone. They were at home in the Prussian Landtag where their natural social allies, the Conservatives, possessed such a strong position. In the year following Windthorst's death the Prussian Center led by Huene collaborated effectively with the Conservatives in forwarding the financial reforms of Johannes Miquel which shifted much of the weight of state taxes from the shoulders of the landed classes onto those of the well-to-do middle classes of the cities who normally supported the Radical party. Huene and Ballestrem wanted to deepen and strengthen the ties linking the Conservatives and their own party. They argued that the Landtag would be more important for the Center's interests in the immediate future than the Reichstag.[16] Apparently Lieber agreed with them or found it impossible to controvert their argument. The Center and the Conservatives had worked together on social legislation in the past and planned to provide majority support for the school proposals of Robert Zedlitz, Gossler's successor as Prussian minister of public worship and education, which would stress the confessionality of the school system.

But the Caprivi administration desperately needed the decisive assistance of the Center in the Reichstag, above all on the bill calling for the major expansion and reorganization of the army and the program of commercial treaties with foreign governments. In the Reichstag Center fraction discipline was likely to be looser than in its parent party of the Landtag since the Bavarians did not have to be as concerned about the needs of the Catholic Church as the Centrists in the Landtag party. The burdens of political responsibility

in the Reichstag Center were greater, too, because the expenditures of the Imperial government had to be met by a combination of indirect taxation which weighed heavily on the lower classes, contributions from the states and loans which created a steadily growing national debt. Since they had not wanted to promote Ernst Lieber's succession to Windthorst's position in the Reichstag, Ballestrem and Huene had thought of Georg von Hertling as the most suitable candidate for their purpose.

Hertling may have been the best known Catholic layman in western and southern Germany after Windthorst's death. He had been closely identified with the old leader for many years; in addition he was the founder and president of the *Görres Society,* the national Catholic learned association. Born in Hesse and later a resident in the Rhineland where he had taught at the University of Bonn he had become a Bavarian citizen during the Kulturkampf. Though he was proud of his aristocratic status and used it to advance his political career in Bavaria, his family's straitened finances, his academic profession, and personal preference had accustomed him to a bourgeois culture. He was unlike most of his aristocratic colleagues in his firm commitment to economic liberalism and his dislike of tariffs and compulsory guilds, views which made him comfortable in the company of Windthorst to whom he bore a physical resemblance.[17] Through an old university friendship with Hermann Cardauns, the managing editor of the *Kölnische Volkszeitung,* he had ties with the Rhineland Center. He also continued to maintain friendly contact with Lieber after his own withdrawal from the Reichstag in 1890. Unlike Huene, Ballestrem, and Preysing, he was an excellent speaker, clear, logical, and graceful, if a little cold in expression.[18]

Hertling made the decision, however, not to return to the Reichstag. But he could not have solved the problems of the aristocratic leadership in the Center. His political position in Bavaria, which rested solely on the patronage of Preysing and some other noblemen close to the court, long remained insecure, though the combination of his natural abilities with favorable circumstances eventually led him to the leadership of the Reichstag Center (1908–1912) and to the German chancellorship (1917–1918) as well, over the route of the Bavarian minister-presidency (1912–1917). An aristocrat, academician, and economic liberal, he was too remote from the economic concerns of most Bavarian Catholic voters, chiefly peasants and craftsmen, to achieve any real influence over the state Center party and the Bavarian contingent in the Reichstag.[19] In 1905 he was to consider seriously the advisability of

---

[13] From my analysis of the names of the Center deputies in the Reichstag between 1887 and 1893: Schwarz, *MdR Biographisches Handbuch der deutschen Reichstages,* pp. 251–506.

[14] Hertling, *Erinnerungen* 2: p. 139.

[15] *Preussiche Jahrbücher* 67 (1891): p. 401.

[16] Spahn, *Lieber,* pp. 27–28.

[17] For his economic views see his *Erinnerungen* 2: pp. 18–48.

[18] Prince Bernhard von Bülow, *Memoirs* (4 v., London, 1931–1932) 1: p. 196.

[19] See his *Erinnerungen* 2: p. 54; also Bülow, *Memoirs* 1: p. 296.

emigrating from Bavaria because of his political un-popularity.[20]

Though he pleaded the heavy demands of his professorship as the reason for refusing the offer of the Reichstag Center to campaign for Windthorst's seat, Hertling's decision was undoubtedly the product of a sober and carefully weighed political judgment. Before the end of March, 1891, Ernst Lieber and Julius Bachem let Hertling know in indirect fashion that they were opposed to Ballestrem's plan of making him the leader of the Reichstag Center. In a personal letter Lieber urged him to return to the Reichstag but insisted that there would have to be "a leisurely search" for a successor to Windthorst and that the successor could not be a single individual.[21] At approximately the same time, Bachem's article "Windthorst im Zentrum" appeared in the *Historisch-politische Blätter*. Bachem briefly concluded that Windthorst was irreplaceable but that there were enough talented men in the party who, acting together, could lead it competently.[22]

It was unfortunate for himself and his party that Julius Bachem was not to be one of them much longer. He may have been the most talented of Windthorst's former pupils, though the old leader had omitted his name when he referred to his probable successors at the Münster Catholic Congress of 1885.[23] As a parliamentarian, speaker, and editor, he demonstrated marked political intuition and judgment, a warm personality and force.[24] Tied down part of the week to his editorial chair at the *Kölnische Volkszeitung* from which he directed the Rhineland Center, Bachem had to restrict his parliamentary activity to the Landtag and the Cologne city council. Nevertheless, the liberal middle-class Centrists expected him to be an important member of the leadership group in Berlin. But barely two months after Windthorst's death Bachem announced his responsibility in a paternity case and had to relinquish his mandate.[25] Bachem's parliamentary career was at an end.

In contrast to Bachem, Lieber had earlier expected to succeed Windthorst. Most likely he still had the hope of doing so at some later time despite his explicit statement to Hertling that there should be a division of labor in the party. But in March, 1891, it appeared

to him that he could expect to achieve influence in the shaping of policy only if the leadership was collectively shared by prominent members of the Center inclusive of Ballestrem, Huene, Preysing, Bachem, Hertling, himself, and some other Centrists. As the leader of the party after 1893 he was to be hostile to the committee idea, but willing to draw other prominent members of the Reichstag and Landtag fractions into the shaping of the Center's policy on major issues. If he was not consistent in his views on the nature of the post-Windthorst leadership in the party, Lieber was probably sincere in his earlier statements that he had found Windthorst's "sole mastery" to be unbearable.[26]

Lieber was a sensitive man who took considerable pride in his family and in his own person. Moritz Lieber, his father, had become a national Catholic figure through his prominent role in the protest movement of 1837 against the Prussian government after its arrest of Archbishop Droste-Vischering. Two prominent Germans of the earlier nineteenth century, Philipp Veit, the son of Dorothea Schegel, and a noted painter himself, and Karl Ernst Jarcke, the political journalist, were the baptismal patrons of Ernst Lieber. He distinguished himself in his university studies, taking a double doctorate in law *summa cum laude* at Heidelberg.[27] His special parliamentary assets were political sense, a penetrating analytical mind, rhetorical prowess, and an iron self-discipline in his work habits. The strains he imposed upon himself and the frustrations he suffered to achieve recognition in his own party may have caused the serious stomach ailment that often incapacitated him and eventually caused his death. Self-centered, touchy, humorless, and inclined to irony, Lieber was not actually popular but he was highly respected by most of his colleagues and regarded by many middle-class Catholics as an uncompromising guardian of their interests.[28]

It is harder to define Lieber's complex political personality. He came out of a pious Catholic home and continued its traditions and spirit in his own large family. Unlike Windthorst and most other northern Center leaders Lieber had responded enthusiastically to the influence of the idealistic and clerical Catholicism of nearby Mainz and the southwest. Sometimes cuttingly critical of churchmen he had a romantic view of the church itself. Though he never lost his own feeling of attachment to Windthorst, despite their strained relations in 1890–1891, Lieber felt spiritually closer to Mallinckrodt, the epitome of Catholic idealism and piety in politics. Even as a mature parliamentarian Lieber was disconcerted by Windthorst's use of the political lie.[29]

---

[20] I treat his later political difficulties in Bavaria in chapter 8, p. 24.

[21] Lieber to Hertling, March 20, 1891. Lieber-Hertling correspondence, Lieber Papers, Camberg.

[22] J. B., "Windthorst im Centrum," 107 (1891): p. 52.

[23] See chapter 1, p. 12. But his cousin Karl wrote a friend many years later that in 1889 he heard others quote Windthorst as saying that he had "two capable aides and potential successors: Julius Bachem and Felix Porsch." Karl Bachem to Herr Ass, July 2, 1932. Bachem Papers, File 107. Lieber was in Windthorst's disfavor by that time.

[24] Martin Spahn, "Julius Bachem," *Hochland* 15 Jg. (1918): pp. 18–21.

[25] Lieber, Journal, May 30, 1891.

[26] Lieber to Hertling, March 20, 1891. See above fn. 21.

[27] Spahn, *Lieber,* p. 5.

[28] *Ibid.,* p. 4.

[29] Lieber, undated notes on Windthorst, Porsch Papers, File 1a9.

Nevertheless, Lieber was not a Catholic integralist, though the Center deputies of that persuasion looked to him as leader in the first years after Windthorst's death. He was born and raised in Nassau which, like the regions of the Rhine valley to the west and southwest, had no tradition of a strong landed nobility. Liberal Frankfurt, the great commercial city, was the cultural center of Lieber's own region. His social status, environment, education, and not least his intense personal pride predisposed him to liberalism rather than to conservatism. It is no doubt significant that the closest friend of his youth, Lujo Brentano, who left the Catholic Church in 1870 and later became a leading German liberal economist and academician, never lost his personal regard for Lieber.[30]

He had only supported Windthorst in his shift to the right with considerable reluctance and even then with the bitter complaint that the old leader was turning the Center into "a court party."[31] An "involuntary Prussian" like Windthorst, Lieber had an intense dislike for Prussian Conservatism, its sense of superiority and monopolistic position in the state. Not long after Windthorst's death he commented privately that he "would rejoice over anything that brings this society into disrepute."[32] During the early and mid-1880's he had speculated on the coming of a long liberal regime under the future Frederick III and called himself a "democrat."[33] The extent of his dislike for the Conservatives and his disappointment over Crown Prince Frederick's mortal illness were apparent in his hefty collision in the Landtag with the leaders of that party in February, 1888, during a debate over a National Liberal motion to extend the length of the legislative period. Upset by heckling from the Conservative benches, Lieber turned on his opponents and said they were elected to the Prussian government as representatives of the people, that in his opinion an annual parliament was the best kind and that every politician knew that monarchs and parliaments were at odds with each other throughout the world. But as a prominent representative of a party which stressed its monarchical allegiance Lieber was unable to defend himself effectively against the Conservatives' counterattack which quickly followed in what Martin Spahn later cited as the worst experience of Lieber's parliamentary career.[34]

In the period 1888–1891 Lieber's relations with Windthorst lost some of their old intimacy and finally became strained. Floundering in his career and somewhat at loose ends Lieber suddenly took up an interest in the problems of the Catholic German-Americans in the United States who were in conflict with the leading Irish-American bishops over their claims for separate German parishes and schools as well as equal representation in the episcopacy itself. Lieber's close friend and Centrist colleague, Paul Cahensly, a well-to-do merchant and head of the St. Raphael Association, a German emigrant society, had become deeply involved in the conflict and the whole movement for German Catholic parity in the Church was later called "Cahenslyism" by its opponents. Windthorst was upset over Lieber's insistence on speaking before the German Catholic Congresses of 1888 and 1890 in the United States and apparently with some reason since Lieber told the Congress of 1890 that German-Americans had the right to be both American citizens and German.[35]

In the year following Windthorst's death, Lieber had occasional doubts that he could supplant Ballestrem and Huene as the leaders of the Center. But his basic mood was one of conviction that they would stumble when faced with the task of leading the party over a major hurdle, presumably the major army program.[36] Prior to March, 1891, his journal had been filled with emotional statements that Windthorst was ruining the Center. After the old leader's death which, he said, came just in time to save Windthorst's reputation,[37] Lieber brought his emotions under control. He gave loyal support to the party leaders but he also preserved his independence from them. Lieber politely refused Ballestrem's invitation to sit in Windthorst's old chair in the Landtag or at the chairman's right in the sessions of the Reichstag fraction.[38] He found ready excuses for not accompanying his aristocratic associates to court functions, though he finally met William II at a private semi-official social affair.[39] He made no more trips to the United States prior to 1898; he had settled down to the business of seeking the leadership of the Center.

During the first year after Windthorst's demise, the leaders and Lieber found numerous important reasons to work in harmony. Lieber's personal relations with Ballestrem were good; the chairman had long been an intimate member of the Windthorst circle. Both wanted to keep any other competitors for the leadership out of the running, to consolidate Caprivi's position and ensure the passage of the Prussian school bill.

---

[30] Brentano, *Mein Leben,* p. 71.

[31] Lieber, Journal, February 26, 1891.

[32] *Ibid.,* June 1, 1891.

[33] Hertling claimed that Lieber still preferred to call himself "a democrat" when he, Hertling, returned to the Reichstag in 1896. *Erinnerungen* 2: p. 180. But Lieber was embarrassed by that reputation in the early 1890's and referred to "the falsity of my reputation as a 'Democrat,'" Journal, April 30, 1892.

[34] Spahn, *Lieber,* p. 22.

[35] The most thorough study of the conflict in the American Catholic church is essentially sympathetic to Cahensley himself: see Colman J. Barry, *The Catholic Church and German Americans* (Washington, 1953), pp. 177–182. For Lieber's remarks to the Congress of 1890: *ibid.,* p. 124.

[36] In December, 1891, when his own relations with Caprivi were good, he made the cryptic remark that "despite all efforts we will not find the bridge." Journal, December 9, 1891.

[37] *Ibid.,* March 15, 17, 1891.

[38] *Ibid.,* April 7, 1891.

[39] *Ibid.,* February 14, 1892.

If aristocratic solidarity had been an overriding conviction with Ballestrem and Huene they would have brought back Burghard von Schorlemer to the Landtag and Reichstag and drawn him into their intimate circle. The old agrarian leader was still an impressive and popular speaker at Catholic assemblies and congresses. He had returned to the Reichstag in 1890 and served according to his own words as "a simple soldier" in the Center's ranks [40] but had early tired of that role. As Lieber suspected, the Prussian ministry and the royal advisers would undoubtedly have preferred to see Schorlemer at the head of the Center than Ballestrem and Huene. Probably they felt more confidence in him than in the Silesian noblemen through his insistence in the later 1880's that his colleagues should abandon the Center and join in the formation of a new Christian Conservative party and his lack of intimacy with church leaders. [41] How high he stood in royal favor was evident in the fall of 1891. William II nominated him to the Prussian House of Lords where he joined Bishop Kopp and somewhat later the ruler approved the election of Florian von Stablewski, Schorlemer's intimate friend, as the first Polish archbishop of Posen since the early Kulturkampf. [42] Ballestrem and Huene refused, however, to revive his political career and he was, as he put it, thrown "onto the scrap heap." [43]

But a far more serious development involving the Center's relations with the monarch himself and those of the Catholic minority with the rest of the nation required a front of solidarity among the old and new leaders of the party. Leo XIII had finally awakened in the fall of 1888 to the reality that Bismarck would not endanger the alliance of Germany and Austria-Hungary with Italy by putting pressure on the Italian state to restore papal temporal power. In the half-year between the last months of Windthorst's life and the late summer of 1891 the Vatican took two meaningful steps, both highly embarrassing to the Center party. Though he did not issue his controversial encyclical to

the French episcopacy in favor of the republic in France until February, 1892, Leo XIII indicated his approval of it in February, 1891, when he praised Cardinal Lavigerie for his earlier toast to the republic. Four months later Germany and Austria-Hungary renewed their alliance with Italy and within weeks after that act the French and Russian governments moved toward an entente. Between June and August the Vatican press, led by the *Observatore Romano,* the leading papal journal, and the *Moniteur de Rome,* a paper edited by French clerics, initiated an angry press campaign against the Triple Alliance. It was the beginning of a much longer campaign which was to last throughout the 1890's and to be a continuous source of discomfort to the Center party. Cardinal Rampolla, the papal secretary of state, and Leo XIII himself apparently believed that the German and Austro-Hungarian governments would prefer to lose Italy as an ally than to alienate their Catholic populations through their alliance with the state that had taken possession of the papal territories. Despite the stature of the two churchmen as diplomatists they could not have misjudged more the attitude of those Catholic peoples nor appreciated less the embarrassment it created for the Catholic minority in Germany. [44]

The national liberal press and reviews welcomed the opportunity provided by the new orientation of the Vatican to embarrass the conservative leadership of the Center. The views expressed by the prestigious *Preussische Jahrbücher* were undoubtedly typical in this respect. In late August, 1891, Hans Delbrück, its editor, claimed that the Papacy's approval of the Republic would strengthen the French state, would enable it to undertake "great and dangerous enterprises," and weaken the confidence and approval of the German Catholics in their own emperor. [45] A month later he charged that the new entente between France, Russia, and the Papacy was conceived in the Vatican itself, perhaps with the collaboration of French cardinals. [46]

While Caprivi and Marschall von Bieberstein, the secretary for foreign affairs, were undoubtedly perturbed over the Vatican's new course, the Center leadership had to be mainly concerned with the severe emotional reactions of William II. One can only conclude that great waves of royal heat emanated from the palace afflicting ministers or other personages having relations with the Center. The emperor and his advisers were convinced that there was an anti-German conspiracy in the Curia to which Rampolla, Cardinal Ledochowski, the former archbishop of Posen and the Jesuits belonged. [47] It was characteristic of his response

[40] *VGVkD zu Coblenz* (Coblenz, 1890), p. 83.

[41] On Schorlemer's proposal that the Center be dissolved: Karl Bachem, Notes dated March 16, 1890, Bachem Papers, File 63.

[42] Lieber initially interpreted the royal nomination of Schorlemer to the Prussian House of Lords as a move to impose him as leader on the Center; he later recognized it was a reward for Schorlemer's public statements of loyalty to the Hohenzollern monarchy when the Vatican press was attacking the Triple Alliance: Lieber, Journal, September 21, 1891. On the Schorlemer-Stablewski friendship: Bachem, *Zentrumspartei* 5: pp. 25–26. The election of Stablewski has been a continuing puzzle to historians who have approached the question from the Polish side: see for example: Lech Trzeciakowski, "The Polish State and the Catholic Church in Prussian Poland, 1871–1914," *Slavic Review* 26, 4 (December, 1967): p. 632; also Harold Rosenthal "The election of Archbishop Stablewski," *Slavic Review* 28, 2 (June, 1969): pp. 264–275.

[43] Schorlemer to Hermann Cardauns, September 4, 1892, Karl Bachem Papers, File 14.

[44] See Bachem, *Zentrumspartei* 9: pp. 26–34.

[45] *68* (1891): pp 431–432.

[46] *Ibid.,* pp. 578–579.

[47] William II's excitement, his suspicions of a curial anti-German conspiracy and the discomfort of leading Catholics who had to treat with him at the time were all evident in an undiplomatic letter which Kopp wrote to the pope later in the

to the Vatican's pro-French diplomacy, however, that William II was most upset by the pope's intervention in the internal affairs of France and his advice that French Catholics should accept the republic. Years later he told a shocked nuncio in the Near East that Cardinal Rampolla was "the nefarious churchman who would be fatal to the Papacy" and "through him the Holy See had propagated anti-dynastic ideas destructive of order." [48]

The pope's efforts to change the political loyalties of French Catholics posed therefore a thorny problem for the Center's leaders and revived painful memories of Leo XIII's abortive intervention in the Septennat conflict. Ballestrem and Huene undoubtedly found themselves in a position where they could not say anything on the subject which would not offend either the ruler or the pope. But before or at the Danzig Catholic Congress of September, 1891, Ballestrem, Schorlemer, and Lieber made public statements to the effect that their monarch was in Berlin. [49] Almost a year later the *Kölnische Volkszeitung,* probably speaking for the Centrist leadership, asserted that French Catholics would be wise to revise their traditional stand on the republic if they wished to deprive their political opponents of an argument for "the de-Christianization of France." But the Center newspaper strongly implied that the pope could hardly require French Catholics to follow his directions in their basic political convictions. [50] Several years later Lieber was to say publicly that the French republic, in existence a quarter-century, had the right to require acceptance from its citizens. [51]

The leaders of the Center had no doubts what their response to the attacks of the Vatican press on the Triple Alliance should be. To remain silent while the *Observatore Romano* and the *Moniteur* fulminated against that alliance was to make the Catholic minority vulnerable to the charge that its leaders cared more for the restoration of the pope's temporal power than for the security of their country. At the Danzig Catholic Congress, Ballestrem used language which a Catholic audience had never heard from Windthorst when he took up the issues of the Triple Alliance and the Roman Question. Ballestrem spoke of the "brazenness" of the *Observatore Romano* in its campaign against the alliance of Germany and Austria-Hungary with Italy and voiced the "sense of outrage" of German

Catholics against the Vatican newspaper. [52] At the Mainz Catholic Congress of 1892 the Center's leaders refused to honor a papal request that they pass over the Triple Alliance in silence. [53]

German Catholic leaders were never able to accept the Vatican's friendship with the new Franco-Russian Entente and Alliance nor the campaign against the Triple Alliance with equanimity. They tried to maintain the fiction for a while that Leo XIII had nothing to do with the new policies but abandoned that argument after a few years. By the summer of 1892 they had learned how to handle the problem of affirming their responsibilities to their own country while claiming that the pope could only be independent if he had some territory of his own. Though they were firm in their refusal to honor Leo XIII's request to pass over the Triple Alliance in silence at the Catholic Congress of 1892 they sought to placate the pope and his secretary of state by insisting, as Windthorst had earlier done, that the Triple Alliance would be stronger if the Italian government satisfied its Catholic population with a restoration of the Papacy's temporal power. Only then, Ballestrem claimed, could the pope be free enough to function as an ideal arbiter of the differences between nations. [54]

As the leading figure on the Center's left wing and also the most popular member of the Reichstag fraction among Catholic integralists, Lieber's support was indispensable to Ballestrem in the delicate situation created by the Vatican's new course. An ultra-conservative French monarchist could not have been more critical of Leo XIII and his pro-French policies than Lieber in his private remarks. He was unenthusiastic about the revival of papal temporal power and deeply disliked, as a Catholic idealist, the Vatican's subordination of other aims to the diplomacy of its recovery of the temporal power in Italy. [55] Lieber had never got over the pope's attempts to intervene in the Septennat struggle and his concessions to Bismarck in the settlement of the Kulturkampf. Leo XIII had undoubtedly alienated Lieber still further when he rejected a memorial presented to him in 1891 by Cahensly on behalf of a recent congress of German emigrant societies which petitioned the pope to permit Catholic ethnic groups in the United States to set up their own parishes and schools and to have more bishops of their own

year. Kopp repeated the emperor's charge of a conspiracy and added that William II insisted that he, Kopp, be made a cardinal. Kurt von Schlozer, Prussian minister to the Vatican, December 29, 1891, GFM, NA Microcopy T-149, Roll 204; Leo XIII to William II, January 4, 1892. *Ibid.*

[48] Paul Cambon, ambassador to Constantinople, to minister for foreign affairs, October 26, 1898. *Documents diplomatiques Français* (1871–1914), first series (1871–1900) **15**: p. 711.

[49] *Correspondance de Monsieur le Chanoine Jacques-Ignace-Simonis,* Albert Schaffler, ed. (2 v., Colmar, 1947) **2**: p. 263.

[50] *Kölnische Volkszeitung,* June 18, 1892.

[51] *Duisburger Volkszeitung,* May 6, 1895.

[52] Bachem, *Zentrumspartei* **9**: pp. 34–35.

[53] *Ibid.,* p. 36.

[54] *VGVkD zu Mainz* (Mainz, 1892), pp. 429–430.

[55] Baron Cetto, the Bavarian minister to the Vatican, claimed in June, 1892, that Lieber had said publicly that the temporal power was superfluous for the Church. Cetto memorandum, appended to report from C. Pückler, Munich, to Caprivi, July 20, 1892, GFMA, Microcopy T-149, Roll 24. In a letter of December 30, 1893, to an unnamed correspondent, Lieber stressed his regard for the Triple Alliance, and his lack of enthusiasm for the concept of papal temporal power and his insistence on the right of German Catholics to be Germans: Lieber Papers, Speyer, Envelope *Briefe,* 1892–1893.

nationality.[56] But Lieber could not admit that there was another cause for his resentment against Leo XIII. Despite his long service to the German Catholic community he had never received any award from the Papacy.[57]

Ballestrem, Huene, and Lieber were also able to work in close harmony in asking their party to approve Caprivi's new commercial treaties with Austria, Italy, and Belgium in the early weeks of the Reichstag session of 1891–1892. The chancellor looked upon their early passage as a matter of the highest political importance. Faced with the imminent prospect of a Franco-Russian alliance he undoubtedly wished to strengthen Germany's ties with her allies, Austria and Italy. But Lieber was to state a few years later that Caprivi favored the new commercial agreements and their lower grain rates as defensive weapons in the struggle of the monarchy against Social Democracy.[58] The existing five-mark duty on wheat and inflation made German grain prices the highest in Europe. After riots had taken place in some Berlin districts the Social Democrats and Radicals had initiated a hard-hitting campaign against protectionism.[59] Caprivi was in a hurry to win approval for the new pacts, which provided for a three-and-a-half mark rate on wheat and rye, to relieve the political pressure from the leftist parties on the government and to neutralize Bismarck's attacks on the new treaties and his own person.

The agreements with Germany's allies and Belgium posed no serious problems for Ballestrem and Huene and none at all for Lieber. The political careers of the two Silesian noblemen were intertwined with Caprivi's and the chancellor had undoubtedly pledged the government's all out support for the Zedlitz school bill if the Center helped to secure the passage of the commer-

cial pacts. But they were undoubtedly worried for a brief period that the Center's support for the treaties would antagonize their Conservative allies.[60] Fortunately for them the Conservatives were divided among themselves over the merits of high tariffs and the legitimacy of opposition to the monarchical government.[61] Lieber welcomed the pacts and the collaboration between his party and the liberals in the debates on them. He responded readily to the opportunity to spite Bismarck and the high protectionist agrarians by speaking at a Center caucus in favor of Caprivi's request that the Reichstag vote on the agreements without preliminary committee hearings.[62] All three bills became law on December 18, 1891, after a bare week of debate. Ballestrem and Huene were now able to focus all their enthusiasm, energy, and hopes on the new Zedlitz school bill before and after its introduction to the Landtag in late January, 1892.

Caprivi and Zedlitz, a minister of strong personality, had rammed the new measure through the Prussian state ministry. They had experienced some initial opposition from their colleagues and especially from Johannes Miquel, the old National Liberal. But the minister-president and Zedlitz enjoyed the support of William II and knew that they would find a comfortable majority for the school bill in the Landtag where the Center and most of the Conservatives were expected to welcome it.

The Zedlitz proposals were a response to the old Center demand that a comprehensive law regulate all aspects of lower education in the Prussian schools. The Gossler bill of 1890–1891 had been limited to matters of religious education whereas the Zedlitz measure sought to regulate local school committees and teacher training institutions in addition to religious instruction, the most difficult issue. The new minister of education did not propose the waiving of the sole sovereignty of the state over the schools, its final right to determine the competency and appointment of teachers or the abandonment of the existing interconfessional schools. But his bill stipulated that the local school committees, the teacher-training institutions, and the teachers of religion had to be of the same confession as the majority of their students. The Church was to enjoy the right to participate in the examination of the individual teacher candidates in religion and of protest against appointments. And local pastors could visit the classrooms during religious instruction, correct the teacher, and even take over classes themselves on occasion if they chose.[63] Since one teacher taught all subjects in the primary schools, the Zedlitz proposals vir-

---

[56] On that memorial see: Barry, *The Catholic Church and German Catholics*, p. 134–15. Lieber made no reference in his journal to the pope's response to the memorial but he later described Archbishop John Ireland, Cahensley's leading opponent, as a "Free Mason" and "Darwinist." Journal, November 17, 1892.

[57] Some years later he was to say that "no Vatican cock had ever crowed for him" despite all of his long years of wearying work for his church. Lieber to Georg von Hertling, July 22, 1898. Lieber-Hertling Correspondence, Camberg.

[58] J. Alden Nichols appears to put somewhat greater stress on Caprivi's desire to use them as a means of strengthening Germany's alliance system than on the chancellor's wish to counter Socialist agitation against protectionism: *Germany after Bismarck* (Cambridge, Mass. 1958), pp. 138–142. The Lieber statement about Caprivi's actual motivation is to be found in undated notes in his handwriting, Envelope *Umsturzvorlage*, Lieber Papers, Speyer. I think a careful review of Caprivi's speeches during the spring of 1891 would reveal a serious concern over the Socialist exploitation of the issue of high food prices.

[59] Kenneth D. Barkin, *The Controversy over German Industrialization 1890–1902* (Chicago, 1970), pp. 44–45. This is a most useful study on an important debate in German politics in the late nineteenth century. The Center was not deeply involved in it, but the author's treatment of its stand on certain economic legislation is the weakest part of his book.

[60] Lieber complained in a journal entry about *Germania*'s "heartless Junker policy." Journal, May 31, 1891.

[61] Barkin, *German Industrialization*, p. 56.

[62] Lieber, Journal, December 2, 1891.

[63] Hess, *Kampf um die Schule*, pp. 67–69; Nichols, *Germany after Bismarck*, pp. 160–161; and Röhl, *Germany without Bismarck*, pp. 79–84.

tually provided for the restoration of the Churches' control over them.

Ballestrem and Huene were aware that the Zedlitz bill and consolidation of the Center-Conservative relationship in the Landtag would lead to a violent parliamentary struggle with the liberal parties. But in fact they welcomed and provoked the polarization of the Landtag in the interest of their design to tighten the alliance with the Conservatives and the government. They refused to make any concessions to their liberal critics. In the initial debates Huene and Felix Porsch made the extreme charge that the parliamentary struggle was between the advocates of a Christian and of a purely secular education; the opponents of the bill wanted, they claimed, to eliminate Christianity from the schools. To the bitterness of some Free Conservatives and liberals, Caprivi, in the excitement of the debates, made the mistake of stating that the choice confronting the Landtag was between "religion and atheism."[64]

Before the introduction of the bill, Bishop Kopp had indicated a lack of confidence in its prospects. His judgment proved sound.[65] Miquel made an effort to resign several days after the beginning of the debates on the measure and the National Radical party put itself at the head of a broad leftist opposition in and outside the Landtag. The liberal and Social Democratic press, Free Masons, Jewish groups and university professors attacked the Zedlitz bill. A struggle ensued between Caprivi and Zedlitz and the personal advisers of William II and, like Bismarck before them, the minister-president and the minister of public worship and education lost the contest. The government had withdrawn the bill from committee examination in early February and William II ordered its abandonment about six weeks later.[66]

The debacle was a bitter and humiliating experience for the leaders of the Center. They learned finally what the relative weights were of the National Liberal and Center parties on the monarchy's scales. Huene expressed the state of mind of the leaders when he said afterwards: "we are permitted to serve as the lead team but not to sit on the coachman's box."[67] The monarch's decision had other painful results. Zedlitz refused to continue any longer in his ministry and Caprivi resigned his office of minister-president, an act

which substantially reduced his influence over the powerful Prussian cabinet. Although the new minister-president, Count Botho zu Eulenburg, and Zedlitz's successor, Robert Bosse, were both close to the Conservative party, the leaders of the Free Conservative party now became favored parliamentary allies of the Prussian monarchy. The influence of its leaders, Baron Karl von Stumm-Halberg, the Saar industrial magnate, and Wilhelm von Kardorff, a prominent agrarian, was to be early noted in the rapid slackening of the government's interest in social reform. In May the Cartel parties rejected other bills in the Landtag of significant interest to the Center, one a proposal on behalf of miners, another a modest reform of municipal suffrage laws.[68]

The ill wind that chilled Ballestrem and Huene's hopes favored Ernst Lieber's leadership prospects. Lieber had not participated in the debates on the school bill nor had he sought a seat in the committee to which it had been submitted. He complained that he lacked the freedom and time to participate in the parliamentary proceedings on the Zedlitz measure. His most substantial excuse for not taking a place in the school bill committee was the heavy commitments he had outside Berlin, chiefly speaking engagements. In addition to serving in communal, county and provincial legislative bodies in Nassau, he was also active in promoting the cause of the new Peoples' Association throughout Catholic Germany. His extensive speechmaking trips on its behalf widened his contacts with local party leaders and the clergy and undoubtedly made him the best informed member of his fraction on broad Catholic feelings about issues.[69]

But the most logical explanation of Lieber's failure to seek a leading role in his party's activities on behalf of the Zedlitz bill is that he wanted to avoid involvement in a bitter conflict with the liberal parties. While Ballestrem and Huene welcomed such a contest, Lieber dreaded it. His fears were similar if not identical to those of his old political friend, Johannes Miquel. The Prussian minister of finance, as Bismarck had acutely observed, had regretted the presentation of a school bill which could only bring the Center and National Liberals into conflict and harm his efforts to promote collaboration between the Center and the Prussian government.[70] Lieber was plainly uncomfortable over the way that the school question dominated political discussion in Berlin in January, 1892. At that time

---

[64] Hess, *Kampf um die Schule*, pp. 105–106, 115, 129.

[65] In the late 1880's Kopp had not been enthusiastic about the concept of a school law since the Prussian government had not interfered with the Catholic clergy's control over the schools in Silesia. Kopp made his doubts about the Zedlitz bill known to a Free Conservative deputy who passed them on to Miquel: Hans Herzfeld, *Johannes Miquel* (2 v., Detmold, 1938) 2: p. 303. For this reason Lieber claimed later that Kopp was responsible for the school bill debacle: Journal, April 3, 1892. See also Baronin Spitzemberg, *Das Tagebuch der Baronin Spitzemberg*, R. Vierhaus, ed. (Göttingen 1960), p. 312.

[66] Nichols, *The Caprivi Era*, pp. 168–191.

[67] Lieber, Journal, April 3, 1892.

[68] On the new influence of the Free Conservatives with the monarch: *ibid.*, May 6, 1892. For the defeat of the bills: Spahn, *Lieber*, pp. 30–31.

[69] For his references to his commitments outside the capital: Journal, December 5, 1891; January 27, 30, 1892. Ritter stresses his contributions to the new Peoples' Association as a speaker: *Volksverein*, pp. 175–176.

[70] Bismarck explained Miquel's dislike of the Zedlitz bill in these terms although Miquel undoubtedly had ideological and other political objections to it as well. See Hans Herzfeld, *Miquel* 2: p. 295.

he complained that Eugen Richter's broadsides against the measure could only strengthen Zedlitz's position and,[71] one may assume, the ties between the conservative leadership of the Center and that of the Conservative party.

But Lieber did not maintain his position of reserve after the fiasco had occurred. Neither his party's sagging fortunes in Prussia nor his own career would permit it. He felt that the Prussian Center needed to use sharper language and to show more independence toward the state and the middle parties.[72] The deep resentments in his own party, evident in the attack that the Reichstag Center made on the naval budget in late March, needed an outlet. The Silesians, Ballestrem, Huene, and the more articulate Felix Porsch, felt incapable of attacking those who were responsible for the Center's humiliation. In late April, Lieber gave a major speech in the Landtag on the earlier school-bill crisis in which he made a delicate but overt criticism of both William II and Miquel. He also warned the liberal parties, especially those of the right-center, that any attack on the constitutionality of the confessional school would drive the Conservatives and Center together. The speech found an immediate response in the Prussian Center and its press and made Lieber its most influential member.[73] In addition to other parliamentary duties, he took on the negotiations with the new minister-president and the minister for public worship. It was most likely he who worked out secret agreements with Prussian officials which gave the Church a *de facto* veto power over appointments of teachers in the Catholic confessional schools.[74]

Nevertheless, Lieber did not press forward to seek the actual leadership of the Center in either the Landtag or the Reichstag. He preferred to let Ballestrem and Huene assume the responsibility of dealing with Caprivi and other Imperial officials in the pre-Reichstag discussions of the problematic plan for the expansion and reorganization of the army. His two Silesian colleagues knew they had come to the crossroads of their political careers and they readily shouldered their responsibility, though certainly in no light frame of mind. The Center aristocracy also demonstrated its knowledge or intuition that the debates over the army bill could be decisive for their influence in the Center and in Catholic society at large. When the Reichstag fraction met in November, they pressed together in the front and middle rows of the hall. Whether they were responding to a sense of victory or the lemming instinct is not evident. But there was tension in the air, especially when aristocratic members met Lieber who had refused to commit himself and who had even been critical of the government in public speeches on the army bill prior to the caucus of the Reichstag Center on the measure.[75]

During the summer of 1892 Ballestrem extended himself to win a commitment from Lieber in favor of the bill or a compromise measure. Both the local and permanent committees of the Catholic Congress had intended to keep Lieber from making a major speech at the Mainz Congress of that year, but Ballestrem exercised his full authority in successfully demanding that Lieber be invited to address the gathering on the Jesuit question.[76] In mid-October both Prince-Bishop Kopp and Ballestrem entertained him at their residences in Silesia. Lieber insisted, however, on retaining his tactical independence. At the Mainz Congress he had gone out of his way to underscore the fact that Caprivi, during the school bill debates, had affirmed that the Prussian government would not vote in the Federal Council for the return of the Jesuits while praising him for his remarks in support of the Zedlitz measure.[77] He apparently continued to speak in that ambivalent strain throughout the early fall. Although Bishop Kopp laid stress in his meeting with Lieber on the value to the Center of his being able to inform the monarch that there was unity between the "aristocracy and democracy," Ballestrem and Lieber apparently agreed to be in friendly disagreement about the immediate tactics to be followed regarding the army bill.[78]

Unlike the later Tirpitz naval programs there was much that could be said in favor of Caprivi's plan for the reorganization and expansion of the army by over eighty thousand draftees. The chancellor was no militarist; he feared for the security of his country faced with the possibility—for him a probability—of having to fight a war on two fronts with France and Russia. Their combined forces were then larger than those of Germany and Austria-Hungary. He had waged a long and unpleasant struggle with the emperor to offer the Reichstag the long desired concession of two-year service for all recruits. Nevertheless, the army bill was weighed down with serious political handicaps. The addition of eighty thousand men to the army would mean the virtual introduction of universal military service which Windthorst, in his resolutions of 1890, had claimed would bring unbearable financial burdens with it. Since the author himself was dead, no one could confidently say that his resolutions would apply to the costs of the new program. But it was undeniable that the new taxes to be raised in support of the proposed army program, especially those on beer, brandy, and tobacco would be felt most heavily by the lower classes and the economically weaker parts of the

[71] Journal, January 27, 1892.
[72] *Ibid.,* May 14, 1892.
[73] *Schlesische Volkszeitung,* April 30, 1892; also Spahn, *Lieber,* p. 29; Lieber, Journal, May 30, 1892.
[74] On the agreements: Dr. Julius Siben: *VGVkD zu Mainz* (Mainz, 1892) p. 333.

[75] Lieber, Journal, December 9, 1892.
[76] *Ibid.,* July 18, 1892.
[77] *VGVkD zu Mainz* (Mainz, 1892), pp. 367, 371.
[78] Lieber, Journal, October 9, 10, 1892.

empire, the south German regions.[79] The timing of the bill was also unfavorable since Germany was, like much of the western world, in the grip of a major economic depression.

The Catholic reaction to the bill was worst, as to be expected, in Bavaria where Caprivi was faced by Bavarian hatreds against an army establishment dominated by a Prussian general staff and Ministry of War. Almost two-thirds of the Bavarian Centrists had resisted Windthorst's pressure and voted against the little army bill in 1890, a year of prosperity. In 1892–1893 the growing agricultural depression weighed heavily on the Bavarian economy and created new resentments among the owners of large and middle-sized peasant holdings against the Berlin government. Josef Sigl, the editor of the particularist journal *Vaterland* and an ex-Centrist, exploited these feelings and blamed the fall of farm prices on the commercial treaties which Bavarian Centrists had helped to pass in the previous Reichstag session. In September, Georg Orterer, the leading middle-class Bavarian member of the Reichstag Center, suddenly laid down his mandate, ostensibly to accept an academic appointment[80] but more likely with the view of avoiding the oncoming political storm over the army bill. In a widely publicized by-election at Kelheim, Bavaria, in October, Sigl only narrowly failed to defeat the Centrist candidate.[81] The leaders of the state Center party, facing general Landtag elections in 1893, became increasingly emphatic in their oral and written opposition to the Caprivi proposals before and after their introduction to the Reichstag.

Huene and Ballestrem, both former army officers, were convinced of the necessity of the large-scale expansion and reorganization of the army. They also believed that their party should approve the army bill on political grounds and that Windthorst would have done so if he were still living. It is likely that they expected to have no serious difficulty with their north German colleagues. The reactions of the Centrist newspapers in the north to the proposed measure indicated that they would desire substantial reductions in the military estimates but were eager to avoid a conflict with the government. Nevertheless, Huene and Ballestrem concluded after a session with their south German colleagues in mid-November that they should ask Caprivi to cut his demands for new draftees and taxes by half.[82] The chancellor refused, however, to consider any compromise on his program and the Center's leaders found themselves in a hopeless tactical position when the Reichstag held its caucus in the first days of December. Lieber and his friends presented a proposal which called for the approval of twenty-seven thousand recruits, the number needed to maintain the peace strength of the army after the introduction of the two-year military service. Huene and his associates were unable to offer a motion of their own and the caucus had no other choice than to approve the Lieber proposal. The fraction did agree to permit Huene to carry on further negotiations with the chancellor, but its more decisive action was its commitment to the Lieber motion.[83]

While the initial reaction of the Silesian noblemen to the outcome of the caucus debates was one of pessimism,[84] Huene consented after a plea from the chancellor to renew his work of trying to win his party for the Caprivi bill. Throughout the first months of the army-bill crisis which extended from December to early May, 1893, he had reason to believe that he could win enough Center votes to ensure the passage of a compromise measure. The north German aristocracy desperately hoped that the Center would achieve an understanding with the government and the leaders of the Silesian and Westphalian parties were from that class. After years of exclusion its members wished to achieve acceptance at the court and in social circles dominated by the Protestant nobility of the Conservative party in addition to sharing some of the administrative benefits given to members of the ruling class.[85]

The middle-class leaders of the Rhineland Center also looked for a compromise between the Reichstag Center fraction and the chancellor on the army question. Along with the Conservatives and the right wing of their own party, Julius Bachem and Hermann Cardauns had welcomed the Miquel financial reforms which permitted the Prussian cities to impose certain taxes on their inhabitants earlier reserved for the state and which shifted much of the incidence of taxation from the backs of the lower classes onto those of the possessors of mobile capital. But the new taxes worked politically to the advantage of the National Liberals and Free Conservatives, the Center's major rivals in the Rhineland and the nearby industrial areas of Westphalia, since their bourgeois supporters were more heavily represented in the first and second classes of

[79] Nichols, *The Caprivi Era,* pp. 229–235. Goebel, *Die Militärvorlage 1892–1893,* p. 50.

[80] He was to complain during the crisis that Windthorst had used extreme pressure to prevail on some Bavarians to vote for the little army bill in 1890. *Ibid.,* pp. 54–55. On his resignation, Bachem, *Zentrumspartei* 5: p. 130.

[81] Philipp zu Eulenberg, the Prussian minister in Munich to Caprivi, October 15, 23, and 25, 1892, GFMA, NA Microcopy T149, Roll 28.

[82] Franz Arenberg to Hermann Cardauns, November 26, 1892: Bachem Papers, File 66c.

[83] Undated notes, Lieber Papers, Speyer, Envelope *Militärvorlage,* Lieber Journal, December 15, 1892. Huene and Lieber in the Reichstag: *Verhandlungen,* December 10, 1892: p. 233; December 14, 1892: pp. 327 328.

[84] After the caucus Huene and Ballestrem told Caprivi that the situation was hopeless: Johannes Werdemann, *Die Heeresreform unter Caprivi,* (Ph.D. diss., University of Greifswald, 1928), p. 96.

[85] Undated memo, apparently written by Lieber, Porsch Papers, File 1a9.

voters than they had been before.[86] Urban suffrage in Prussia was now glaringly plutocratic. In return for the Prussian Center's support of his financial program, Miquel had promised to bring about the introduction of a bill for urban electoral reform.[87] An earlier measure had fallen victim to the change of party alignments after the school bill debacle, but the Prussian government planned to introduce a new measure after the Christmas holidays. Understandably Julius Bachem and Cardauns were not pleased that Lieber had committed his Reichstag party to a position on the army bill which the government could not accept.[88]

Nevertheless, Huene and his friends undoubtedly felt that they could only confidently hope to win enough Center support to ensure the passage of a compromise measure if the government pledged them a major concession of broad significance to Catholics. Such a concession would make legitimate a decision of pro-government Centrists to separate from the rest of their colleagues at the second and third readings of the army bill. The Huene group evidently regarded a repeal of the anti-Jesuit law as the most practicable and useful objective in its negotiations with the government since its existence was an affront to Catholics throughout the empire and was of serious concern to the Vatican. In the first days of the new Reichstag session the leaders of the Center had introduced a motion calling for the revocation of the law.[89] As the army bill remained stuck in committee hearings throughout January and February, there was speculation in the press, chiefly in Social Democratic journals, that the Center was attempting to reach an agreement with the government on the basis of a withdrawal of the anti-Jesuit law.[90] But high government officials declared in February that there could be no concession to the Catholic Church and that the Center should approve the bill out of patriotism.[91]

By refusing to accept a cut in the number of new draftees or to revoke the anti-Jesuit law Caprivi and William II had barred two of the three possible approaches to a compromise with the Center. Miquel, the Prussian minister of finance closed the door to the third. The government, aware that indirect taxes were unpopular with the lower middle and working classes, had postponed the submission of a plan for the financ-

ing of the army expansion till the next year, but it had indicated that there would be new levies on beer, brandy, and the stock exchanges. In his speech at the first reading of the army bill Lieber implied that the government would do better to introduce a national income tax.[92] He did not actually pursue that idea further since the states were jealous guardians of their traditional right to levy direct taxes; instead he proposed to Miquel that the Imperial government should present a plan calling for contributions from the states raised through supplements to their existing income or property tax. But the finance minister had been moving in his thinking on taxational and wider financial questions for some time in a different direction. He wanted to relieve Prussia and other states from the responsibility of coming to the empire's financial assistance in the future, but also to permit them to take part of the income from new indirect taxes. He refused to enter into discussions of Lieber's proposal.[93]

Lieber did not welcome the army-bill crisis of 1892–1893, but he intended to exploit it for his own purposes. He had already foreseen in December, 1891, that there would be a profound disagreement between his party and the government over that measure.[94] Lieber had been acquainted for a long time with the dislike of many Centrists for new indirect taxes and with Miquel's financial thought; shortly before the first reading of the Caprivi proposal he affirmed that there would be a storm in the Center fraction when its members learned that Huene had virtually committed himself to Miquel's tax plan.[95] A few days after the first reading, he prophesied the defeat of the army measure and Caprivi's dismissal.[96]

It was actually Lieber's intent to use the army-bill crisis for the purpose of overthrowing Huene, Ballestrem, and the whole Center aristocratic wing from their positions of power in the party.[97] The Center stood in serious danger of losing its Bavarian contingent if it entered into a compromise with Caprivi based on a substantial acceptance of his proposals and the Miquel tax program. The defection of the Bavarian Centrists would have seriously weakened the popular wing of the party and deprived Lieber of many of his own supporters in his bid for the leadership. During the long drawn-out debates on the Caprivi measure he sought to justify his own stand by a reference to the fate of the first Prussian Center which had been caught in the middle between the government and the liberal

---

[86] The number of electors in the first and second classes was reduced, respectively, by one-half and one-fourth: *Kölnische Volkszeitung*, April 16, 1893.

[87] Herzfeld, *Miquel* 2: pp. 243, 310–312. Bachem, *Zentrumspartei* 5: p. 150. And see below chapter 3, p. 8ff.

[88] Alois Fritzen, the senior Rhineland Centrist in the Reichstag Fraction, said later that a compromise could and should have been reached on the bill. *Kölnische Volkszeitung*, August 21, 1916.

[89] Goebel, *Die Militärvorlage*, p. 59.

[90] *Niederrheinische Volkszeitung*, February 25, 1893.

[91] General von Löe to Caprivi, February 24, 1893. GFMA, NA Microcopy T149, Roll 12. *Echo der Gegenwart*, February 25, 1893.

[92] *Verhandlungen des Reichstages*, December 14, 1892: p. 330.

[93] Spahn, *Lieber*, p. 32.

[94] See above, p. 23, fn. 36.

[95] Journal, November 14, 1892.

[96] *Ibid.*, December 15, 1892.

[97] Several years later he was to say sardonically to a friend that he "had blown up" Huene and Ballestrem with the aid of "vulgus profanus": letter to Nicolas Thoemes, October 19, 1896. Lieber Papers, Wrocław, File 131.

opposition in the conflict over the army reform and expansion of the early 1860's.[98] The situation of the German Center in the winter of 1892–1893 did not correspond, however, to that of the original Prussian Center thirty years earlier. The Prussian wing of the German Center was strong enough to ensure the passage of the Caprivi measure if its members approved of a compromise. Because of the Kulturkampf it possessed more solidarity and influence and a larger Catholic press than its unfortunate Prussian predecessor. The Caprivi bill was unpopular in the north but active opposition to it or a compromise followed Lieber's declaration at the first parliamentary reading that his party would not approve the measure or a substantial part of its proposals.

In the weeks and months that followed the first reading Lieber demonstrated remarkable skill as a political strategist and tactician. His aim was to keep a tight hold on the leadership of the Center and to prevent Huene from winning open support in the Reichstag fraction and the regional Center parties for a compromise with Caprivi. The following excerpt from a speech he gave in his constituency of Montabaur on December 27, 1892, demonstrated his determination to identify Huene publicly with the position taken by the Center at the first reading of the Caprivi proposal.

If government organs should perhaps hope that the aristocratic members of the Center fraction, following their inclination as former military men, will help the proposal to a victory, they make a fundamental mistake. These gentlemen have to a much higher degree a heart for the welfare of the people and they adhere to the standpoint that the people cannot bear the burdens any more. . . .[99]

Huene openly complained over Lieber's tactics but his anger testified to their effectiveness.

On the other hand Lieber did not want to put too great a strain on the loyalty of the aristocracy to the Center. He feared that its defection might have incalculable consequences for the party's unity and strength, its rapport with the monarchy and its acceptance by the Papacy and German bishops. Lieber had put a high assessment on the services of Georg von Franckenstein, the earlier chairman, in keeping the Catholic nobility and the Bavarians in the party after the Kulturkampf[100] and he hoped that Ballestrem, despite his fervent monarchism and friendship with Huene, would put the unity of his party above those commitments. The Lieber group was even willing to speak of the chairman as "the leader" of the Center to keep him in line.[101]

Lieber's desire to exercise decisive influence over Ballestrem and to keep the aristocracy in his party

was evident in his handling of a disputed election in Olpe-Merschede, Westphalia, which won increasing attention in the Catholic and secular press throughout Germany in the middle and later phases of the crisis. The affair itself reflected, as Julius Bachem perceptively noted, the effects that hard times had upon small businessmen, craftsmen, and peasants and bore an obvious relationship to the earlier closely contested election in Kelheim, Bavaria.[102] The debates in the press over the army bill brought their deeper economic discontents to the surface. In early 1892 an ad hoc committee of noblemen, senior pastors, and other dignitaries had nominated an aristocratic agrarian for the succession to the seat of Peter Reichensperger who had died in December. A few days later a group of small businessmen, artisans, and peasants proposed as their candidate Josef Fusangel, a newspaper publisher, long known for his promotion of popular causes. Fusangel, in a frank and hardhitting campaign rarely waged in safe Centrist districts, emphasized his close association with the people and acquaintance with their needs. In addition to identifying himself as a "left-standing candidate," he also claimed that there was a democratic awakening in the clergy. Fusangel clearly thought he was providing local support for the Lieber position on the army bill by his statements that there were a right and left wing in the Center and that a further strengthening of the "juristic-bureaucratic" element in it was dangerous for the party.[103]

The widely publicized Fusangel affair was highly useful for Lieber's purposes. It demonstrated among other things the undercurrent of popular dissatisfaction with the government's army demands and with the Center's aristocratic elements. But Lieber was also able to use it for his tactic of asserting party unity. On February 22 the executive committees of the Center parties of the Reichstag and Landtag issued a joint declaration denying Fusangel's charge that there were two wings in the party and that it was under bureaucratic control.[104] Despite the opposition of some thoughtful leaders in the region, in particular Julius Bachem, Lieber and Porsch insisted on speaking in the Olpe-Merschede constituency on behalf of Fusangel's opponent who was unable to say much for himself.[105] Though Fusangel won the election by a margin of over three to one, the executive committee of the

[98] I have relied here on a memorandum written by either Lieber or Felix Porsch on January 25, 1893, for Cardinal Kopp. Porsch, then Lieber's close friend, acted as his deputy in communications with Kopp. Porsch Papers, Wrocław, File 1a9.

[99] Goebel, Die Militärvorlage 1892–1893, p. 57.

[100] Journal, January 21, 1890.

[101] Germania, January 19, 1893.

[102] HpB 111 (1893): pp. 449–452.

[103] Germania, February 28, March 1, 3, 25, 1893; P.M., "Die Verfall der Alten Parteien," HpB 111 (1893): pp. 63–64.

[104] Porsch sent a copy of the declaration to Cardinal Kopp in Rome for the purpose of acquainting him with the "weathersigns in North Germany." Lieber regretted Porsch's failure to point out to Kopp that "two left-standing" Centrists had sounded the alarm and called for action, and that he had then composed the declaration. Lieber's notes on back of a copy of the declaration. Lieber Papers, Wrocław, File 61.

[105] Niederrheinische Volkszeitung, March 14, 1893; Julius Bachem to Karl Bachem, March 9, 1893. Lieber Papers, Speyer, File B, 45.

Reichstag party refused to admit him to its membership.[106]

Since the opposition in Centrist regions to the Caprivi bill was extensive by mid-February, 1893, it is difficult to explain why the chancellor and the emperor thought that the measure had some prospect of success. William II, even more naïve in political matters than Caprivi, counted heavily on the ability of the Centrist aristocrats to influence the votes of their colleagues. But both the chancellor and the ruler assumed that the pope would help them by directing the Center to vote for the army proposals.

The celebration of Leo XIII's fiftieth anniversary as a bishop in February, 1893, provided the German government with the opportunity to use a number of agents, ordinary and extraordinary, in efforts to convince the pope that he should direct the Center leaders to support the army bill or permit part of their fraction to do so. There was of course a Prussian minister to the Vatican but he did not figure as an important factor in the special diplomacy of the Jubilee period. Caprivi chose to rely more on Prince-Bishop Kopp and Archbishop Stablewski of Posen as special advocates for the Center's support of the army bill at the Vatican since they were in Rome for the ceremonies in honor of Leo XIII. Stablewski successfully enlisted the assistance of his close friend, Cardinal Ledochowski, the prefect for propaganda.[107] The emperor also sent General Walther von Löe, the leading Catholic officer in the army, to the Jubilee as his personal representative, and in late April paid a personal visit to the pope. Behind the backs of Caprivi, his foreign secretary, Kopp, and Rampolla, a small circle of German officials, probably directed by Friedrich von Holstein, and acting with William II's approval, sought to bribe the papal nuncio to Austria, an old Windthorst opponent, and the pope as well.[108] But the net results of the extensive courting of Leo XIII by the German government were not impressive.

Rampolla believed that the German government had not given sufficient consideration to political and financial conditions when it made up the army bill.[109] But he and Leo XIII were influenced in their judgment of the Center's role in the crisis by Kopp and Stablewski who warned that relations between the monarchy and the Catholic church could be seriously impaired if the bill were rejected. On his arrival in Rome, General von Löe confirmed their judgment of the situation. William II, he said, had told him shortly before his departure that the monarchy and the Center would be separated for fifty years if it voted against the army proposals.[110] Shortly afterwards Ballestrem, apparently at Kopp's suggestion, was called to Rome. The pope told him that "wisdom" was better than "unity" and that he should heed the advice of a wise churchman on a question that lay in the mixed area between pure politics and ecclesiastical affairs. The churchman was, of course, Cardinal Kopp.[111] But Leo XIII's tactfully phrased directive to Ballestrem was a mild attempt at papal intervention in the affairs of the Center compared to his two appeals to Windthorst during the Septennat debates of 1887.

The pope had several reasons for not trying to apply higher pressure on the Center. He had been embarrassed by the rebuff he had received from Windthorst six years earlier. While Leo XIII hoped that there would be a peaceful division in the Center on the army-bill issue, he did not want to endanger the party's unity. But the pope might have been willing to approach Lieber directly if the German government had offered some compensation to the Vatican. Leo XIII was eager to bring about the early return of the Jesuits and the other banned religious orders to Germany; Kopp had apparently convinced him, however, that William II would be seriously offended if the pope approached him on that subject.[112]

Ballestrem turned out to be anything but an enthusiastic bearer of the papal message to his party. He had not changed his view that the Center would only support the Caprivi bill if the government took action on the anti-Jesuit law and he made his convictions to that effect known at the Vatican. Neither before nor during the decisive fraction caucus did Ballestrem present the pope's wishes with any conviction.[113] Cardinal Kopp had recognized at an early date, of course, that Lieber was the key to the solution of the army bill crisis and he sought to influence Lieber's decision

---

[106] *Germania*, April 18, 1893. He entered the Center later in the year.

[107] Bachem, *Zentrumspartei* **5**: pp. 281–282. Kopp to Porsch, January 20, 1893. Porsch Papers, la9.

[108] There is adequate coverage only of the German side of this affair. See Norman Rich, *Friedrich von Holstein* (2 v., Cambridge, 1965) **1**: p. 399; J. G. H. Rohl, *Historical Journal* **9** (1966): p. 395 and by the same author, *Germany without Bismarck*, pp. 107–108. A German representative, Prince Hohenlohe, a later chancellor, apparently gave a sizable sum of money to Galimberti, the nuncio to Vienna, but Leo XIII's representative broke off contact with another German representative when he stated that the gift would be made after the passage of the army bill. The genesis of the affair lay in Leo XIII's efforts before his fiftieth episcopal jubilee to secure grants of money from governments in place of the more traditional gifts presented to popes on their important anniversaries. Kopp and Rampolla tried to discourage German officials from responding to Leo XIII's request. Otto von Bülow to Caprivi, December 7, 1892, GMFA, NA Microcopy T-149, Roll 12; Kopp to Caprivi, December 16, 1892, *ibid.* And see Bachem, *Zentrumspartei* **5**: pp. 282–283.

[109] Löe to Caprivi, February 24, 1893. See fn. 89 above.

[110] Kopp to Lieber, February 20, 1893. Porsch Papers, File la9.

[111] Karl Bachem, notes dated August 25–29, 1895. Bachem Papers, File 66c.

[112] Kopp, notes on an audience with Pope Leo XIII, dated March 2, 1893. Kopp Papers, File 34.

[113] Ballestrem told other persons in Berlin that the Pope hoped that the army bill would be passed but did not wish to become directly involved in the debates over the measure. Löe to Cardinal Kopp, March 9, 1893, *ibid.*

through letters to Porsch, Lieber's close friend who was also the party manager in Silesia, and finally in a communication to the party leader himself. He asked Lieber to take a long-range view of the interests of the Catholic community and not to act on the basis of temporary circumstances. Kopp warned him that Catholics would suffer from a conflict with the monarchy over the army measure and a lost war.[114] Lieber apparently refused to write directly to the cardinal since Kopp later complained that the party leader was ignoring him.[115]

Despite Ballestrem's lack of conviction in his mission, most of his colleagues took a grim view of the efforts of Cardinal Kopp and Leo XIII to influence their voting on the army bill. They listened in silence and without approval when he made his report on his February audience with the pope.[116] But Martin Spahn and Karl Bachem have overemphasized the extent to which extensive resentment against Kopp and Leo XIII over their meddling in the internal affairs of the Center informed the attitudes of many Centrists toward the army bill. It was true, of course, as Lieber said after Ballestrem's report, that the Center could not afford to act on a purely political measure at the pope's direction.[117] But the Center could have preserved the fiction of its independence on such legislative issues and avoided a conflict with the government by accepting the Huene compromise measure which called for eleven thousand fewer recruits than the original Caprivi proposal.

Some weeks after the defeat of the Huene bill on May 6, August Bebel, the well-informed Social Democratic leader, insisted that the Center would have approved the compromise if its leaders had not been afraid that their party's support for the bill would cost the Center its Bavarian wing.[118] Indeed their Centrist colleagues in Munich, then facing early state elections and the agitation of Josef Sigl's new Bavarian Peasants League against their own party, were frantic with worry that the Center would enter into a compromise with the chancellor. The long delay before the second reading of the army bill, their awareness of the pope's advice to Ballestrem, Schorlemer's lobbying for the measure in the corridors of the Reichstag,[119] and finally the rumors in late March of Huene's preparation

of a compromise proposal appeared to point to a major effort by some prominent Prussian Centrists to avert a break between the government and their party over the army program. The leaders of the Bavarian Center decided to use shock tactics on their colleagues in Berlin. On or about April 10 they sent a formal communication to the leaders of the Reichstag Center with the message that their own state party would secede from the parent party if even a few Centrist deputies voted for the army bill.[120] In their public speeches at home they made violent attacks on "Prussian militarism."

Lieber's concern over the near collapse of the Center's popularity in Bavaria was evident enough: it led him to make extreme statements which were to be embarrassing to him in later years. On April 3 he spoke at a Center assembly in Aschaffenburg, Bavaria. His speech was a response to an earlier address made by Schorlemer in which the prominent Westphalian agrarian had praised the Hohenzollern dynasty and its army for their services to Germany and to peace. Lieber referred to himself as "an involuntary Prussian" and claimed that the dynasty had violated laws in the past. In the further course of his remarks he made the statement that "the existence of a party like the Center was more important for the empire than the passage of the military bill and even if all its demands were politically and militarily justified."[121] Lieber's worries were shared by many of his colleagues. At a special caucus covering the period April 14–18, the Bavarians and the members of the Huene-Ballestrem group engaged in angry debates over the question of the army bill. Near the end of the caucus Felix Porsch reported to Cardinal Kopp that an apparent majority of the Reichstag Center would probably be opposed to a compromise measure like Huene's proposal because of the fear that it would cause a secession from the party.[122]

At the final fraction caucus of May 2 and in the Reichstag voting on May 6 the Rhineland Centrists, twenty-eight in all, controlled the balance in the fraction. Julius Bachem, the leader of their provincial party, probably determined the fate of the army bill. In later years he, Karl Bachem, and Alois Fritzen adhered to their original conviction that Lieber should have sought an early compromise with the government.[123] They undoubtedly believed that Caprivi and other high officials would have made a successful effort to save the Prussian government's municipal suffrage bill if the Center had supported a compromise army measure. In early March Bachem still hoped that Lieber would permit his colleagues in the fraction to

[114] Kopp to Lieber, February 20, 1893. Porsch Papers, File 1a9.

[115] Lieber to Porsch, March 29, 1893. Kopp Papers, File 37.

[116] Karl Bachem, notes dated August 29, 1895. Fn. 104 above.

[117] Neither Bachem nor Spahn gives the date of the caucus at which Ballestrem spoke about his meeting with the pope: Bachem, *Zentrumspartei* **5**: p. 286; Spahn, *Lieber*, p. 34.

[118] *Briefwechsel mit Engels*, p. 683.

[119] A Bavarian friend wrote Porsch that regional Centrist leaders became nervous every time they read that Schorlemer had been visiting in the Reichstag: Goertz to Porsch, January 24, 1893. Kopp Papers, File 34.

[120] Porsch to Kopp, April 18, 1893. *Ibid.*

[121] Schulthess *Europäischer Geschichtskalender* **34** (1893): p. 54.

[122] Fn. 120 above.

[123] Julius Bachem: "Das Centrum angesichts der Neuwählen," *HpB* **113** (1893): p. 801; *KVZ*, August 21, 1916.

act freely in the final voting on the army proposal.[124] During the second half of April a committee of the upper house of the Landtag revised the suffrage bill along plutocratic lines. Two days after the final Center caucus and on the eve of the Reichstag voting on the Huene measure the Cartel majority in the Prussian House of Deputies approved the suffrage measure sent down from the House of Lords.[125] On the next day all but two of the twenty-eight Rhineland Centrists voted against the Huene proposal.

During the long crisis over the army bill Julius Bachem and the *Kölnische Volkszeitung* had actually followed a diagonal course. While they had desired a compromise solution of the conflict, Bachem and Hermann Cardauns, his managing editor, had shown marked if discreet sympathy for Josef Fusangel in his differences with the leaders of the Reichstag Center. Bachem and Cardauns were not interested in Fusangel because he was a fellow Centrist editor. Even prior to Windthorst's death in 1891 Bachem had been impatient to convince his prominent colleagues in Berlin that they should take early action to secure the allegiance of Catholic workers in western Prussia and wider Germany against the agitation of the Social Democratic party. In the late 1880's Fusangel, possibly with Bachem's encouragement, had made an abortive effort to establish an interconfessional miners' union in the Ruhr.[126] During the army-bill crisis the priest chairman of a group of Christian worker associations in Gelsenskirchen, the large Ruhr city, publicly announced his support of Fusangel in his effort to win admission to the Center fraction.[127]

Julius Bachem's decision that his Rhineland colleagues should support Lieber in the crucial caucus on the Huene bill did not only reflect his fear that the Center might injure its reputation with Catholic labor if it voted for that proposal. During and after his election campaign Fusangel had become the symbol to wide sectors of the Prussian Center press and apparently to the clergy as well of the popular opposition to the Huene-Ballestrem army bill.[128] Bishop Korum of Trier had already warned Kopp in mid-April that the Center would become a "Fusangel party" if it decided to vote for the army proposal without some pledge of a concession from the government.[129] Julius Bachem was too

realistic a politician to think of affronting the lower clergy and numerous Catholic voters in order to secure his own prize, a more liberal municipal reform bill.

The debates on that bill at the second reading were actually anti-climactic. Caprivi had accepted the Huene bill in place of his own measure in part because he wanted to use its author's name in the forthcoming election campaign. Expecting the defeat of the army proposals in the existing Reichstag, William II had signed the order for the dissolution of the parliament before leaving for Italy on April 25.

Lieber entered the special election of June, 1893, with considerable trepidation, despite the reassuring precedent of the Center's success in the Septennat elections of 1887 and the extensive evidence of the army bill's unpopularity in Catholic areas. He was badly shaken by Ballestrem's resignation of the chairmanship the day before the second reading of the Huene proposal in the Reichstag, an action he had striven to prevent since December, 1892.[130] Among the other nine Centrists who had voted with Ballestrem and Huene for that measure were Felix Porsch, one of Lieber's closest friends, and Franz von Arenberg, the prominent Rhineland deputy. Lieber was afraid that the split in the leadership group of the Center would be beneficial to Catholic anti-Centrist candidates. But his worries proved to be unjustified. Ballestrem and Porsch found that Catholic opinion in Silesia was so critical of their conduct they decided not to be candidates for reelection. Against his better judgment but at Caprivi's request Huene chose to do so.[131] He was soundly defeated in three constituencies. Though the Center lost eleven seats, it polled almost two hundred thousand more votes than it had in the elections of 1890. With ninety-five mandates the Center could expect to regain its pivotal position in the Reichstag.[132]

But it was fortunate for Lieber that the government was able to scrape together a temporary majority of Conservatives, National Liberals, dissident Radicals, anti-Semites, and Poles for the Huene bill during the short parliamentary session in July. If the new Reichstag had also rejected the army measure, Ballestrem and his friends might have become, as Kopp had told them earlier, the natural mediators between their party and the government.[133] However, Caprivi found his majority and the crisis over the army reform and expansion came to an end.

The Center fraction which returned to the Reichstag for the special July session was in its social composition an approximation of the "Catholic peoples party"

---

[124] The *Kölnische Volkszeitung* of March 1 carried a report from its Berlin correspondent to the effect that further debates on the subject of the army bill would not affect either those who favored the measure or those who were against it.

[125] *Schlesische Volkszeitung,* April 21, 1893; Spahn, *Lieber,* p. 34.

[126] See chapter 6 below, p. 77.

[127] Porsch to Kopp, March 31, 1893. Kopp Papers, File 37.

[128] At the Center caucus of April 14 Lieber, Porsch and Heereman had complained at length about the support which the Center press had given to Fusangel in his differences with the leadership of the party: Porsch to Kopp, April 18, 1893. Kopp Papers, File 37.

[129] Korum to Kopp, April 20, 1893, *ibid.* Ballestrem complained to Kopp a few weeks later about "the tyrannizing

and undisciplined press." Letter of May 3, 1893, Kopp Papers, *ibid.*

[130] Porsch to Kopp, May 3, 1893, *ibid.*

[131] Ballestrem to Kopp, May 3, 1893; Ballestrem to Kopp, May 29, 1893; Huene to Kopp, June 2, 1893, *ibid.*

[132] Bachem, *Zentrumspartei* 5: p. 294. If one includes the four Hanoverian guest members the actual strength of the Center was one hundred deputies.

[133] Ballestrem to Kopp, May 29, 1893. Kopp Papers, File 37.

of which Lieber had so often spoken in the past. The German government had anticipated a change in the social complexion of the Center after the elections and it asked Leo XIII in May to bring about the readmittance of Ballestrem, Huene, and Porsch to the party at a later date.[134] But the Center's executive committee had already issued a directive on May 15 to the effect that no one could be accepted as a candidate of its party who intended to vote for the army bill and it sent word to the pope that the three Silesians could not be readmitted on political grounds.[135] After the elections there was no longer an aristocratic wing of any strength in the Center since the number of noblemen in its ranks had declined from approximately thirty to eleven.[136] The willingness of a prominent Rhenish aristocrat, Count Alfred von Hompesch, to succeed Ballestrem, and of Clemens von Heereman to remain in office as chairman of the Prussian Center veiled only slightly the substantial changes in the social character of the two parliamentary fractions in Berlin.

Ernst Lieber was able at the end of the summer of 1893 to look back on the struggle with the government and the Huene-Ballestrem group with considerable satisfaction. He had saved the unity of his party and its substance. The triumphal acclaim which the participants at the Würzburg Catholic Congress accorded him in early September undoubtedly strengthened his belief in the validity of the course he had followed in the previous winter and spring. However, Lieber's period of contentment was not to last much longer. Within a few months he would learn that a peoples party does not respond to new taxes and other unpopular legislation any more readily under a bourgeois leader than it does under an aristocrat. Fortunately for his composure, he was unable to foresee how difficult his tasks were going to be.

3. THE CENTER AND THE CATHOLIC AGRARIAN MOVEMENT

The effort on behalf of the creation of interest groups [in the parliamentary party] is completely incompatible with the program of the Center which provides for the spiritual and material well-being of all national classes because the Fraction is based more than any other on the members of all classes of the population.
                    Julius Bachem, March, 1893.[1]

We had to prove that we are not the democratic party of naked sterile opposition far more to Fulda [the Conference of Prussian Bishops] and to Rome than to the Royal Palace and the Wilhelmstrasse [the Imperial Chancellery].
                    Ernst Lieber, April 7, 1894.[2]

Despite his long parliamentary career and careful study of Windthorst's methods, Ernst Lieber had to learn how to become an effective party leader the hard way. On his return to Berlin in the fall of 1893 he was in high fettle and optimistic regarding his party's immediate political prospects. Both the chancellor and Miquel, the Prussian minister of finance, now bitter rivals, were eager to win the Center's support for major programs which they were to present to the Reichstag in the new session.[3] Lieber found, however, that he could not readily convert his broad personal popularity among the Catholic electorate into disciplined control over the Reichstag Center which was sometimes more responsive to regional leaders and the press than it was to the leader himself. The absence of the once strong conservative right wing of the Reichstag fraction was not an unmixed blessing for a party which sought to support the government.

The confidence of secure leadership, the favorable political situation in Berlin and an apparent failure to appreciate the severity of the economic depression kept Lieber from properly anticipating the difficulties he would experience in a short time. That he did not do so was evident from his determination to seek the Center's approval of the Miquel finance program which called for extensive indirect taxation, although he and his party had essentially rejected the army bill because it was to be financed largely by levies on articles of mass use. It is less surprising that he did not perceive how much the authority of the party leadership and the Reichstag fraction, weakened by Windthorst's death, had been further eroded by the long army bill conflict of the previous year. Though Lieber stubbornly refused to accept the principle of a leadership committee, he was to agree finally to consult regularly with other prominent Centrists within and outside the fraction and to try to reach agreement on policies with them.

Despite Lieber's relative popularity, the position of the leader of the Reichstag and Landtag Center parties had lost some of its substance through the death of Windthorst and the open conflict between the chairman, Ballestrem, and the new leader, Lieber, in the spring of 1893. The local leadership groups, who controlled the electoral committees in the Prussian provinces or the south German states and sometimes the most prominent Center newspapers, were important centers of power. The leaders of the regional parties—Georg Orterer and Balthasar Daller in Bavaria, Theodore Wacker in Baden, Ballestrem, Huene, and Porsch in Silesia and above all Julius Bachem in the Rhineland were more important political personalities than the members of their state or provincial delegations in the Reichstag or Landtag. Lieber could not rely confidently upon the backing of the large Bavarian delegation, despite his friendship with Franz Schaedler, its

---

[134] Msgr. Johannes Montel to Kopp, May 17, 1893, *ibid.*

[135] Otto von Bülow, the Prussian minister to the Vatican, to Caprivi, July 18, 1893. GFMA, University of Michigan Microcopy T-149, Roll 110.

[136] From my count of the Center deputies listed in the *Handbuch des Reichstages* for the Reichstag period, 1893–1898.

[1] Vom Rhein. "Eine Ära von Schwierigkeiten, nicht zuletz für's Centrum," *HpB* 111 (1893) : p. 452.

[2] Lieber to Heinrich Otto, Karl Bachem Papers, File 67b.

[3] Lieber to Karl Bachem, October 4, 1893, *ibid.*, File 49. Spahn, *Lieber*, p. 36.

leading member, or on the Silesian contingent. For that reason the good will of Julius Bachem and his alter ego, Hermann Cardauns, were vitally important to Lieber and his successors as well since the Rhineland group in the Reichstag fraction averaged somewhat over a fourth of the entire Center membership throughout the 1890's.

The full influence of the Rhineland Center was incalculable since Bachem and Cardauns were also the editors of the *Kölnische Volkszeitung,* undoubtedly the most distinguished Catholic newspaper in Germany between the Kulturkampf and the outbreak of World War I. That it was far superior in that respect to *Germania,* the semi-official organ of the Reichstag and Landtag fractions, was due primarily to the talents of its two leading editors but also to the fact that the Cologne Centrist journal appeared in a densely populated Catholic region of Germany whereas *Germania* did not and therefore suffered financially.[4] Bachem and Cardauns were also the most influential members of the Augustine League, the Catholic press association, whose longtime chairman was their friend Heinrich Otto, the publisher and editor of the *Niederrheinische Volkszeitung* of Krefeld.[5] The leaders of the Rhineland Center also took pride in their close ties with the new Peoples' Association whose headquarters was at nearby München-Gladbach. Though there was no formal connection between the party and the new movement Karl Trimborn, Julius Bachem's chief aide, the deputy-chairman of the Peoples' Association, was apparently the contact between his party superiors and Franz Hitze, the leading social theorist of the Reichstag Center and the Peoples' Association.[6] Of all the regional Centrist parties the Rhineland Center had a distinct elan, believing that it was the intellectual center of modern German Catholicism by its commitment to constitutionalism, responsible capitalism and social reform.

Lieber recognized the importance of establishing and maintaining a closer relationship with Julius Bachem, the Rhineland Center, and the *Kölnische Volkszeitung* for the success of his immediate and long range aims. He respected Bachem's abilities as a politician and leader and knew that their views on basic issues were substantially alike.[7] No doubt he was correct that they would not have fallen out with each other, and at Lieber's expense, if the prominent Rhineland editor had been able to resume his political career in Berlin.[8]

Bachem had believed in the spring and summer of 1893 that the serious rifts caused in the Center by the army bill conflict provided an ideal opportunity for his return to the Landtag and the inner circles of the two Center fractions. The authoritative, confident and moderate manner in which he expressed his views on the issues confronting and dividing his party in the later period of the crisis made that belief apparent. He posed as a party statesman who anticipated the problems the Center would face in the future because of the rising social unrest which he saw as the true cause of the disputed elections in Catholic regions. In the early spring of 1893 he prophesied correctly that the Center was entering "a period of difficulties" and that it would have to be concerned with the growth of anti-Semitism and Social Democracy.[9] But his immediate aim was to appear as the voice of moderation between Lieber and Huene, each of whom, in his implicit view, had taken an extreme position and endangered the unity of the party. Bachem tried unsuccessfully to prevent Lieber from assuming a stand of sharp confrontation in his election conflict with the aristocrats around Huene and Ballestrem,[10] possibly with the hope of staving off a south German ascendancy under Lieber's leadership. But the facts of the general political situation and Bachem's own career dictated a rapprochement with Lieber before the elections and the two men apparently met for that purpose when the new party leader spoke at a mammoth rally in Cologne in late May. It was undoubtedly the occasion when Lieber told the Bachems he "hoped, even wished" that Julius Bachem could return to political life. But Heereman, the chairman, and the Executive Council of the Prussian Center decided otherwise and Bachem apparently recognized the hopelessness of any further appeal.[11]

---

[4] In the late 1880's Windthorst had thought of putting *Germania* under the control of the *Kölnische Volkszeitung* because of its editorial inadequacies. Lieber and his friends opposed the establishment of such a relationship in the spring of 1894 when *Germania* was nearly bankrupt because they were engaged in a feud with the Bachems. Paul Cahensly, Lieber's merchant friend, secured enough money from well-to-do Catholic business and professional men, to restore the journal's solvency. Lieber to Adolf Gröber, May 15, 1894, Lieber Papers, Wrocław, File 41; the same to Nicolas Thoemes, May 17, 1894, *ibid.;* and Gröber to Lieber, June 20, 1893, Lieber Papers, Speyer, File G, 24. Lieber's letter to Gröber indicates that Ballestrem, the wealthiest member of the Center, still owned a large number of *Germania's* shares. Soon after the defeat of the Huene army bill Cardinal Kopp spoke of "ruining *Germania* financially." Morsey, *Wichmann-Jahrbuch für Kirchengeschichte im Bistum Berlin 1967–1969,* p. 51. He probably meant that if he chose to do so, he could prevail on Ballestrem to withdraw his funds from the journal.

[5] Johannes Kisky, *Der Augustinus-Verein zur Plege der katholischen Presse von 1898 bis 1928* (Dusseldorf, 1928).

[6] There is a slender biographical study of Trimborn by Hermann Cardauns, *Karl Trimborn. Nach seinen Briefe und Tagebuchern* (München-Gladbach, 1921).

[7] He said in 1891 that Bachem's withdrawal from parliamentary life would be a severe loss to his own orientation in the party: Journal, June 1, 1891.

[8] On that issue as the cause of their political conflict: Lieber to Gröber, May 15, 1894. Lieber Papers, Wrocław, File 41; Lieber to Thoemes, May 17, 1894, *ibid.*

[9] *HpB* 111 (1893): pp. 448–457: "Das Centrum und die Neuwählen, *ibid.,* pp. 803–804.

[10] *Ibid.,* pp. 801, 803.

[11] Lieber claimed in 1891 that many Centrists thought Bachem had blocked his own way to a return to parliamentary life by his public statement regarding his responsibility in the paternity case which forced him out of the Landtag. On his later encouragement to Bachem and the refusal of the Execu-

That decision was final but it did not end Bachem's determination to share in the leadership of the party. He was to speak later of a party "directory," [12] though it is not clear whether he thought of a small group of Center dignitaries embracing members of the two fractions in Berlin and prominent regional leaders like himself holding occasional meetings or an intimate circle of the two fractions in which his cousin Karl Bachem and Alois Fritzen, a senior Rhineland Centrist, would act for him. There was no place, however, in Lieber's mind for any kind of supreme party council, though he did not want to restore the Windthorst dictatorship. Even if they had not differed on a substantial issue in the Reichstag session of 1893–1894 and on other matters, major and minor, in the future, marked differences were inevitable between the two politicians. By reason of his authority over the Rhineland delegation in the Reichstag Center and possibly even more his wide influence as an editor Bachem was able to make Lieber feel the weight of his opposition.

The substantial question on which they strongly disagreed in the fall and winter of 1893–1894 was the Miquel financial reform which was intended to provide sixty million marks for the reorganization of the army and forty million marks for the annual use of the states. The plan revealed its author's political shrewdness since it appealed to the concern of the Center for the financial well-being of Bavaria and the other German state governments. Because of the reduction in the income of the Reich through the effects of the Caprivi commercial treaties and the inevitable increase in its expenditures on the army and navy, the states faced the prospect of having to contribute more to the Reich in the form of matricular contributions than they received from it under the working of the Franckenstein clause. Miquel's reform plan was doubly sweet to the other finance ministers since it proposed that the states would receive annually forty million marks from the empire and also be free of all financial responsibility to it.[13]

Miquel and Arthur von Posadowsky-Wehner, the secretary of the Imperial Treasury, believed they could make a strong case for their proposal by stressing the actual needs of the Reich and the validity of the taxes. The empire was deeply in debt and likely to depend even more heavily on loans if the new program was not approved in full since the states were seemingly incapable of enabling it to balance its budget. Both officials were convinced that they could demonstrate the justice and potentialities as a source of rich income

of the major levy in the proposals, a tax on the tobacco industry. They claimed that their countrymen paid lower taxes on the tobacco they smoked than any other people in western and central Europe. They also pointed out that the German tobacco industry was far larger than that of France, the second largest continental producer of the crop, both in the acreage under cultivation and in the number of workers employed on a full or part-time basis in the industry. Miquel and Posadowsky also defended a tax on wine on the grounds that it was proper to impose a levy on the drink of the more affluent classes since there already were taxes on beer.[14] The financial program also provided for taxation on the stock exchanges, freight ladings and certain types of receipts.

Lieber knew well the unpopularity of the Prussian minister of finance in the Rhineland and that Julius Bachem and his colleagues might want to reject the whole plan.[15] Miquel had given them a promise that he would promote a reform of the Prussian municipal suffrage in return for the support of his major reorganization of the Prussian financial system. The defeat of the bill on electoral reform in May, 1893, had been excruciatingly painful to the Bachem group because it not only left their provincial party in a worse political situation than it had been prior to the Miquel reforms but also made them appear as "dupes" of the Prussian finance minister.[16] That Miquel, the only liberal in the Prussian or Imperial governments, may not have been able to save the electoral reform bill because of his dependence on his own party or the limits of his actual influence in the Ministry did not appear to be an adequate explanation to Bachem and his friends. Julius Bachem and Cardauns were determined to ruin Miquel politically. A desire to promote the integration of their own provincial party may have been a secondary consideration in their anti-Miquel campaign. They had recently prevailed upon Felix von Löe, the aristocratic leader of the Rhineland Peasant Association, and his friends, to stay in the Center but their relations with the Rhenish agrarians and the integralist Catholic newspapers who resented the influence of the *Kölnische Volkszeitung* remained tender at best.[17] For the integralists and many other Catholics, Miquel was the official who had contributed significantly to the defeat of the Zedlitz school bill.

It is not clearly evident why Lieber committed himself to the support of Miquel's proposal when he knew that it would be so unpopular with the Bachem circle and

tive Committee of the Prussian Center to approve Bachem's return to the fraction: Lieber to Gröber, May 15, 1894, Lieber Papers, Wrocław, File 41; Lieber to Thoemes, May 17, 1894, *ibid.*

[12] *Kölnische Volkszeitung*, March 27, 1894.

[13] See Herzfeld, *Miquel* **2**: pp. 356–362; Nichols, *Germany after Bismarck*, pp. 278–289; and *Verhandlungen des Reichstages*, January 11, 1894: pp. 568–576.

[14] *Verhandlungen des Reichstages*, January 11, 1894: pp. 568–577; *ibid.*, January 19, 1894: pp. 919–921.

[15] Lieber to Karl Bachem, October 4, 1893. Bachem Papers, File 49.

[16] *Kölnische Volkszeitung*, February 5, 1894.

[17] I treat their relations with Löe and his association later in this chapter. Lieber was angry that the Rhineland Centrists had become reconciled with Löe, one of his political enemies, without any previous consultation with him: Lieber to Karl Bachem, October 4, 1893. Fn. 15 above.

substantial numbers of Catholics in the Rhineland, probably elsewhere as well. He was also reversing his stand on the question of indirect taxation. In his public remarks he argued that there was an obvious need for a major financial reform and that the Center should participate in the shaping of it so that the taxes would actually fall on the users and consumers of the more expensive tobaccos and wines.[18] But there was no indication that Miquel was willing to provide for a complex list of differentiated tax schedules and the likelihood was that the main incidence of the taxation would fall directly or indirectly on large numbers of small tobacco and wine producers.[19]

Some of Lieber's associates later assumed that he had been the victim of Miquel's dazzling personality and persuasive powers.[20] Miquel was undoubtedly the most impressive of all the ministers in the Prussian or Imperial governments after Bismarck. Of both French Catholic and German Protestant ancestry he was a man of rare charm and brilliant conversation. He and Lieber became closely acquainted in the 1880's when Miquel served as mayor of Frankfurt. The minister of finance had begun to cultivate Lieber more seriously in the months following the Zedlitz bill debacle which had so injured his own reputation among many Catholics.[21] In the fall of 1893, however, Miquel still had faith in his own political future. He probably expected to become minister-president of Prussia at some later date if he achieved a major success with the Imperial reform bill and to exercise decisive influence on the course of Imperial affairs as well.[22]

The more logical explanation of Lieber's commitment to the Miquel program is that he felt an urgent need to produce early successes as the Center's leader. Though he never referred to the subject of his relations with the ruler, Lieber certainly recognized that his decisive opposition to the army bill of the previous year must have antagonized the irascible young emperor and that his leadership of the Center was offensive to the ruler. That was indeed the case. William II's resentment against Lieber and his party confirmed the warning that both Cardinal Kopp and General von Löe had given the Vatican in the previous winter.[23]

Lieber had no patrons among the Prussian bishops or at the Curia and he felt a need to demonstrate to high church officers in both the Prussian state and the Vatican that his leadership of the Center was no serious impediment to the improvement of the Catholic Church's position in Prussia and the wider Reich.[24] His own enthusiastic confidence in the combined ability of Miquel and Caprivi to secure concessions for the Church from the Prussian state and the Federal Council was evident in his plea to the Bachem group that they should not oppose "a reasonable financial reform" and his confident assertion that "our wheat is blooming." [25]

Lieber's plea fell on deaf ears; Julius Bachem and Cardauns were implacable in their determination to humiliate the Prussian finance minister and to impose a different financial policy on the government. It is apparent that they were more concerned about party and social interests than they were about the return of banned religious orders or a new Prussian school law. The real emphasis of the Rhineland Center after the spring of 1893 was on social legislation for artisans and workers and parity in government service for the educated middle classes of the Catholic faith.[26] Their views on financial policy, expressed in the electoral pronouncement of their regional party or in the *Kölnische Volkszeitung* undoubtedly reflected their intention to adopt a common front with the old allies of the Radical party against the Cartel. They indicated that they would not look favorably upon new taxes, the plan to free the states from their financial obligations to the Imperial government or extensive expenditures for the army and navy.[27]

At an early date in the new parliamentary session of 1893–1894 Lieber had a premonition that he and Miquel would suffer at least a partial defeat on the question of financial reform. The electoral pronouncement of the Rhineland Center, the statements of the *Kölnische Volkszeitung* and the cool reaction of the Rhineland Catholic press to his major speech in support of the Miquel program at Krefeld on October 22 were undoubtedly revealing to him.[28] He was unprepared, however, for the massive attack which the young Karl

---

[18] *Kölnische Volkszeitung*, October 24, 1893.

[19] Miquel did abandon special taxes on the finer and luxury tobaccos based on their value: Herzfeld, *Miquel* **2**: p. 362. The governments of several southwestern states later opposed the wine tax successfully.

[20] *Kölnische Volkszeitung*, August 21, 1916; also Nichols, *Germany after Bismarck*, p. 309.

[21] Lieber, Journal, April 3, 4, 1892. It is impossible to tell whether Miquel was responsible for Lieber's appointment to the chairmanship of the press committee for the World's Columbian Exposition at Chicago, established by the Imperial Ministry of the Interior. *Ibid.*, April 26, 1892.

[22] Herzfeld, *Miquel* **2**: p. 340.

[23] William II was to cut Lieber ostentatiously at a court ball in February, 1895. See chapter 4, p. 52. His hostility to the post-1893 Center was pronounced enough and provided considerable material for discussion in political circles. The well-

informed *Kölnische Zeitung* later claimed that Lieber had uncomfortable thoughts about the criticisms he had made of the Hohenzollern dynasty during the army bill crisis: issue of April 10, 1894, nr. 297.

[24] See the second quotation on page 1 of this chapter. His own bishop, Karl Klein, was close to Cardinal Kopp; Lieber's only episcopal patron was the archbishop of Freiburg in Baden who could not really help him politically. Lieber, Journal, January 26, 1892.

[25] Letter from Lieber to Karl Bachem, October 4, 1894. Fn. 15 above.

[26] See my treatment of its influence on the Center's proposals for social reform in this chapter, pp. 45–46 and in chapter 6.

[27] *Kölnische Volkszeitung*, October 7, 1893; also the *Dürener Anzeiger*, October 10, 1893.

[28] On the reaction of the Rhineland Center press to Lieber's speech: *Kölnische Zeitung*, October 24, 1893.

Bachem made on the proposals at the first caucus of the Reichstag Center in mid-November. Both humiliated and enraged, Lieber immediately resigned his mandate and only agreed to return to the Reichstag after several days.[29] After that brief capitulation to his emotions he decided to fight against his opponents within the party and to carry out his commitment to Miquel. And he did defend the principle of a tobacco tax throughout the session of 1894–1895 insisting that his south German friends, Gröber and Schaedler, do the same.[30] But he and Miquel had both undergone an overwhelming and deeply embarrassing defeat since Lieber had already found it necessary in January, 1894, to oppose the basic reform which would have changed the financial relationship between the Reich and the states.[31] At the second reading in April the Reichstag finally approved only twenty-four million marks in taxes instead of the desired one hundred million.

Despite his long years in parliamentary life, Lieber's difficulties with his own party over the Miquel reform had been a learning experience for him. He came to a heightened appreciation of the power of the press. The claim of some Social Democratic journals that the tobacco tax would destroy fifty thousand jobs was an important factor in its eventual defeat.[32] The *Kölnische Volkszeitung's* criticism of his views on the wine tax shook Lieber enough to make him desire to abandon his feud with the editors since there were large numbers of small vintners in his traditional sphere of influence in the southwest.[33] Though he kept his pledge on the question of a tobacco tax for a year, Lieber was never again to let his name be associated with a major indirect tax on the needs and pleasures of the lower classes.

Unlike Miquel, whose career lost considerable momentum through his major setback,[34] Lieber was able to complete the session of 1893–1894 with an important legislative victory which obscured his earlier failure. In some degree his original optimism about his party's prospects was justified since he had not been forced to invest all his political capital in Miquel's cause. Caprivi's commercial treaties, especially his major agreement with Russia, progressively absorbed the attention of the political parties and the press before and after the Christmas holidays. The emotionalism of the agrarian campaign against the treaties, Caprivi and Adolf von Marschall von Bieberstein, the secretary of state for foreign affairs, who presented the new measures to the Reichstag, created an atmosphere of tension and drama in the debates on them that was relatively absent from those on Miquel's plan.

Lieber was eager to assist both the chancellor and the secretary of state for foreign affairs in a struggle which could determine their future in government. Marschall had been a political ally of Rudolf von Buol, a Centrist deputy in Baden politics in the 1870's;[35] he and Franz von Arenberg moved in the same social circles.[36] The secretary of state for foreign affairs had stood aside from the efforts of Caprivi and Kopp to involve the Papacy in the army bill debates and Kopp did not regard him as a political friend.[37] Marschall was probably responsible for the early change in the attitude of Foreign Office officials toward Lieber. It was he who effected a reconciliation between Caprivi and the Centrist leader in the late summer of 1893.[38] Though he was heavily dependent upon Friedrich von Holstein, the senior councilor of the Foreign Office, in diplomatic affairs, Marschall was an official of high character, competence, and resourcefulness.

In offering to support the last commercial treaties, particularly the Russian pact, Lieber appeared to be capricious. The most serious economic problem of the period 1892–1897 was the continuing fall of agricultural prices. The following table which gives prices in marks for one hundred kilograms of wheat at the Breslau and Cologne grain exchanges between 1891 and 1896 reveals the extent of the declivity[39]:

	Breslau	Cologne
1891	21,5	22,1
1893	13,9	15,5
1895	14,0	14,0
1896	15,1	16,2

Agrarian spokesmen generally attributed agriculture's problems to the earlier Caprivi trade treaties which had reduced the tariff on foreign wheat imports from five marks to three and a half per two hundred-weight. It was to be expected, therefore, that most agrarians looked upon Caprivi's last trade treaties with Rumania and Russia, the largest grain producer on the continent, with the massive hostility and early organized themselves to bring about their defeat in the session of 1893–1894.

The hard core of the campaign against the last commercial agreements and Caprivi was located in the east and not in the Catholic west or southwest, although

[29] Karl Bachem notes, undated, Bachem Papers, File 67b.

[30] Lieber to Schaedler, June 9, 1894. Lieber papers, Speyer Envelope, *Briefe 1892–1897.*

[31] Lieber's rejection of the basic reform plan: *Verhandlungen des Reichstages,* January 29, 1893: p. 912.

[32] Herzfeld, *Miquel* 2: p. 362.

[33] Lieber to Hermann Cardauns, December 29, 1893. Bachem Papers, File 66b.

[34] Herzfeld, *Miquel* 2: p. 362.

[35] Bachem, *Zentrumspartei* 5: pp. 124–125. Before Marschall became state secretary for foreign affairs in March, 1890, Buol had campaigned for him in the Reichstag elections: C. von Wedel, *Zwischen Kaiser und Kanzler* (Leipzig, 1943), p. 58.

[36] Spitzemberg, *Tagebuch,* pp. 336–337.

[37] Röhl, *Germany without Bismarck,* pp. 107–108. Kopp to Porsch, January 30, 1893. Lieber Papers, Wrocław, File 61.

[38] Lieber to Arenberg, July 12, 1895. Lieber Papers, Wrocław, File 95.

[39] Franz X. Pichler, *Centrum und Landwirtschaft* (Cologne, 1897), p. 57.

most of the regional peasants' associations had been in existence since at least the early 1880's. The leading organizations in the assault on Caprivi's economic policy were the Agrarian League established by Prussian Junkers in February, 1893, and, to an appreciably smaller degree, the Bavarian Peasants' League established by Josef Sigl two months later. The economic crisis was undoubtedly more severe in the eastern areas where the land was poorer, the yield smaller and the debts larger than in the west. The collective psychology of the founders and leaders of the new agrarian leagues was different from that of their counterparts in the peasants' associations. They had created a political organization for the specific end of promoting the interests of big agriculture. One of their founders called upon agrarians "to scream until people listened," and "to pursue ruthless and undisguised interest politics." The peasants' associations, regionally circumscribed, were supposed to be purely educational and social in their objectives and to stay out of politics. And as their name indicated, they were intended to serve the needs of the peasantry, not of the aristocratic estate owners who led them.[40] But it was inevitable that the combination of the severe agricultural depression and the massive agitation of the Agrarian League would have an effect upon the thinking and conduct of the big landowners who led the Christian peasants' associations.

The leaders of the Christian peasants' associations in Prussia were almost uniformly aristocrats, except for an occasional priest director like Georg Dasbach in the Trier region of the Rhineland. It is understandable therefore that prominent Centrist politicians claimed that the opposition of the Catholic agrarians to their policies was basically political rather than economic.[41]

Their thesis was true to some extent, but it was not an adequate explanation of agrarian dissidence. After all the Center had devoted itself more assiduously to the economic interests of this group in the 1880's than it had to those of any other class, a fact somewhat obscured by its primary concern with church questions and its more widely publicized support for social legislation for workers. And from Windthorst's death to the winter of 1892–1893 aristocratic agrarians had led the party.

Lieber's accession to the party leadership represented a triumph of a bourgeois Centrist over his aristocratic colleagues, Ballestrem and Huene, but also the victory of a liberal free-trader over agrarians. The political weakness of the agrarians in the Center party organizations had already been demonstrated shortly

before the last Reichstag elections. In late May, 1893, the Westphalian Center had rebuffed Schorlemer when he demanded that the provincial electoral committee set aside four places on its candidates' list for the elections on the grounds that its approval would create a precedent that would permit other vocational groups to insist that they be given quota representation. Like other prominent Centrists before and after them, the Centrist leaders in Westphalia undoubtedly believed that the representation of interest groups in the Reichstag Center would loosen the party's unity and lead possibly to its collapse.[42] But the fact that Schorlemer, the former chairman of the Prussian Center and of the Westphalian Center itself, could be treated so cavalierly in a Catholic region which was heavily agricultural in its economy demonstrates how little influence agrarians had in their own party.

Lieber's enthusiasm for the continuation of Caprivi's liberal trade policy was evident and natural enough even though it was undoubtedly intensified by his need to win a legislative victory. He and his party or at least his wing of the Center could not afford to let Caprivi and Marschall von Bieberstein be driven out of office and to see them replaced by officials connected with the Conservative party. The treaties provided Lieber with a valuable opportunity to work intimately with both the National Liberals and the Radicals at the expense of the Conservatives. An assiduous representative of his province he was also interested in securing lower tariff rates on the admission of Nassau mineral water to the Russian market.[43]

In committing himself to the support of the last commercial treaties, Lieber appeared to gamble with the unity of his party. Before the submission of the Rumanian treaty to the Reichstag in December the Christian peasants' associations of the Rhineland and Westphalia, the Bavarian Center party, and the *Kölnische Volkszeitung* all took a public stand against the Rumanian and Russian pacts. A somewhat larger number of Centrist deputies, led by Schaedler, the Bavarian, cast ballots against the Rumanian agreement than of those who supported it. After its passage, Lieber chose to continue on the same course in his approach to the Russian bill which came up for debate in late February and early March, 1894. The Center split again in the balloting on that treaty but a few members from agrarian districts did move over onto Lieber's side. The margin of the treaty's success in the Reichstag was a comfortable fifty-four votes.[44]

---

[40] On the differences between the older essentially Catholic peasant associations and the newer agrarian leagues see: Blondel, *Études sur les populations rurales*, pp. 233–240.

[41] This was the central argument of a long memorandum by Hermann Cardauns on the subject, dated 1896. Bachem Papers, File 66c.

[42] Ferdinand Jacobs, *Von Schorlemer zur Grünen Front. Zur Abwertung des berufständischen und politische Denkens* (Düsseldorf, 1957), p. 28 ff.

[43] Lieber to Marschall von Bieberstein, December 22, 1893. Lieber Papers, Speyer, Envelope *Personliche Angelegenheiten, I.*

[44] Sarah R. Tirrell, *German Agrarian Politics after Bismarck's Fall* (New York, 1951), p. 212 ff. Klaus Müller, "Zentrumspartei und Agrarische Bewegung im Rheinland 1882–1903," in *Im Spiegel der Geschichte-Festgabe für Max Brau-*

The dangers of either a defeat to Lieber and the government or of a serious split in the Center were not real. Schorlemer had finally expressed his own approval of the Russian trade bill and his friend, Heereman, joined Lieber and his group in backing it. There was a lack of tension between the two halves of the fraction in the voting on both the Rumanian and the Russian treaties. Before the second reading some deputies made assertions that the government would dissolve the Reichstag if the measure was defeated because of the importance of a successful agreement for Russo-German relations.[45] Lieber was to boast later during an inner-party conflict that he had saved the Center since it could not have survived an election campaign in which agriculture and industry, peasant and worker, would have been pitted against each other.[46] But the size of the majority vote indicated that there could have been little fear of the bill's defeat and of the possibility of a Reichstag dissolution. One can only assume that Schaedler and the other opponents of the Russian treaty realized that the Center could not afford to prejudice the passage of a major treaty, especially one affecting relations with a great power after it had blocked the initial approval of the army bill and then made a broad assault on the government's program for financial reform. Lieber was apparently able to rely upon the assistance of the bulk of the Rhineland Centrists for the additional reason that the treaty would be beneficial to north Germany's coal, iron, and electrical industries.[47]

In fact all the Centrist leaders knew that the agrarian opponents of the treaties were in a weak debating position. After granting Austria and Italy favorable treatment in the treaties of 1891, Caprivi could hardly have afforded to deny it to Russia or Rumania.[48] Lieber realized that the leaders of the agrarian movement considered the true panacea for their problems to be the introduction of cheaper money through a bimetallic standard.[49] The German market was already open to surpluses of several major agricultural countries, the United States among them, through earlier favored-nation agreements and both Russian and Ru-

manian exporters could send their wheat into Germany via Austria if they so chose.[50]

After the successful second reading of the Russian treaty in late March, Lieber was in a state of marked self-satisfaction which bordered on euphoria. In return for his support of the treaty he had prevailed upon Caprivi to abandon the graduated rates on the Prussian railroads which had permitted eastern Prussian agrarians to transport their grain to the markets of western and southern Germany at low cost. In his own words he had brought home "the golden fleece" to the Center agrarians in Prussia's western provinces.[51] Sensitive to the charge that he had not been concerned enough in the army bill debates to Germany's security needs, Lieber took marked satisfaction from the belief that the Russo-German treaty would improve their diplomatic relations and benefit European peace. He now expected the leading members of the wider Center party and its press, inclusive of the leaders of the Rhineland Center and Catholic editors of the province, to recognize his accomplishments and to end their criticisms of his leadership.

During the last weeks of March, Lieber had carelessly engaged in brief but polemical exchanges with critics of the Russian treaty. In a rebuttal to an opponent who had compared the passage of the treaty to Napoleon's defeat of Prussia at Jena, he said that it was actually like the great victory of the German armies over France at Sedan.[52] It was more embarrassing for some regional Center leaders, especially those in the Rhineland, that Lieber and Felix von Löe, still a member of the executive council of the Prussian Center, argued publicly over the Russian treaty, though the party leader was essentially defending himself. In a major speech at Frankfurt-am-Main on March 26, Lieber compared Löe's competence as an agricultural expert unfavorably with Schorlemer's.[53] Numerous Centrist newspapers, the Bachem press bloc in the lead, criticized both dignitaries for quarreling publicly.

The criticism from the *Kölnische Volkszeitung* and its Rhenish press bloc was both profoundly painful and disconcerting to Lieber. He may have hoped that the renewed tension between the Rhineland Center leaders and the leading peasants' association of their province would work to his benefit. The newspaper and the agrarian circle around Löe had collided very heavily over a Prussian agrarian legislative issue in the period when the Russian trade treaty was under debate in the Reichstag.

During the debates on the Russian agreement Bachem and Cardauns, to Lieber's disappointment, aligned

bach, Konrad Repgen and Hans Skalweit, eds. (Münster, 1965), p. 834. Count Kanitz, the agrarian Conservative: *Reichstag Verhandlungen,* November 13, 1893: p. 31. Forty-six Centrists voted for the Russian treaty, thirty-nine against it, which meant that ten must have abstained.

[45] Rudolf von Buol of the Center wrote a friend: "It is absolutely certain that the Reichstag will be dissolved if the Russian treaty were rejected." Buol to Albrecht von Stötzingen, February 8, 1894. Copies in possession of Professor Josef Becker, University of Augsburg. Lieber to an unnamed friend, June 2, 1894. Lieber Papers, Wrocław, File 41.

[46] Lieber to Heinrich Otto, April 7, 1894. Bachem Papers, File 66b.

[47] On its value to industry: *Kölnische Volkszeitung,* February 5, 1894.

[48] Spahn, *Lieber,* p. 37.

[49] Lieber to Mallinckrodt, December 23, 1893. Lieber Papers, Speyer, File L, 48.

[50] Heereman developed this argument at some length in the Reichstag during the debates: *Reichstag Verhandlungen,* March 16, 1894, Lieber to Thoemes, May 20, 1894. Lieber Papers, Wrocław, File 41.

[51] Lieber to Otto, April 7, 1894. Fn. 43 above.

[52] *Reichstag Verhandlungen,* March 16, 1894: p. 1911.

[53] Reported in the *Frankfurter Zeitung,* March 27, 1894.

their newspaper with the agrarian opposition. But it is unlikely that Löe and his followers could have taken much satisfaction from the stand of the *Kölnische Volkszeitung* since Karl Bachem and most of the Rhineland Center delegation had voted in favor of the last trade treaties. It was not substantial opposition and the paper did not express disappointment over the treaty's approval.[54] Löe had seen through Bachem's and Cardauns's game; the three men did not come into sharp conflict over the question of the Russian pact, however, but over an issue on which they were ideologically divided.

Despite his reconciliation with the Rhineland Center in the fall of 1893, Löe had earlier decided to help revive the Catholic corporatist movement and a priest friend, Peter Oberdörffer, then prominent in the Catholic worker association of the Rhineland, had been at work drafting a program since the summer of that year.[55] The combined activities of Oberdörffer and Löe worried local and national leaders of the Center because they apparently feared that the old corporatist idea of vocational representation might become popular in a time of severe economic distress. They were also perturbed over the manner in which the corporatists insisted on calling their proposals "the Catholic social program" and on linking them with Leo XIII's social encyclical *Rerum Novarum*.[56] Löe and his friends were encouraged by the decision of the Prussian government, probably at Miquel's instigation, to introduce a bill to the Landtag in January, 1894, establishing agrarian chambers in each Prussian province. The government proposal did not call for the granting of the actual legislative powers that the corporatists desired, but the chambers were to have the right to discuss agricultural questions and to make reports and recommendations to the government. Though most of the Rhineland Centrists probably did so with marked reservations, the whole Prussian Center announced its support for the bill at its first reading.[57]

During the committee hearings on the new measure and after them the *Kölnische Volkszeitung* and a majority of the Prussian Center took a position of hostility toward the bill. When it was evident that the Reichstag would approve the Russian treaty the Prussian government insisted that the Conservatives should seek an agreement with the National Liberals on the structuring of the suffrage and membership requirements for the chambers. The revised bill reserved election to them to the larger landowners and virtually disenfranchised the middle and small peasants who

made up the bulk of the members of the peasants' associations. Though Löe and his friends wished to vote for the bill, they were forced by the attacks on the measure by the Bachem press bloc and the imposition of party discipline to oppose it in late March.[58] The Catholic agrarian leaders in the Rhineland were bitter over the whole affair and met in March to discuss the possibility of establishing their own newspaper. Therefore, Lieber's Frankfurt speech on March 27 with its deprecatory remarks about Löe was embarrassing to Julius Bachem and Cardauns because of the crisis in their own provincial party.

Early in the second week of April, German Catholics were shocked to read in the press that Lieber had announced his intention to withdraw from parliamentary life. One of Lieber's editor friends, Nicolas Thoemes, had printed a copy of the letter dated April 7, which Lieber had written to Heinrich Otto announcing that decision and protesting against the ungenerous treatment he had received in Otto's newspaper and in the *Kölnische Volkszeitung* because of his Frankfurt address. The letter was a detailed eulogy of his recent accomplishments and services as party leader in the debates on the trade treaties. The climax of his apologia was a claim that his critics had failed to understand the basic motivation behind his action. He had not been concerned in the first instance to win the approval of the ruler or the chancellor—there was no reference to Miquel—but to prove to the Prussian bishops and the Vatican the Center was not now a "democratic party of naked sterile opposition."[59] A few days later, however, Lieber announced his intention to continue his parliamentary career and returned to Berlin.

Lieber's letter to Otto carried overtones of strong feeling against his press critics because of their lack of objectivity and fairness in balancing his legislative performance against his recent slips in the debates on the Russian treaty. But Lieber had reacted less to their criticism than he had to his own belief that Julius Bachem was determined to exercise a decisive influence on the Center's course through his leadership of the Rhineland Center press if he could not do it more directly. To his acute discomfort, the *Kölnische Volkszeitung* had affirmed on March 17 that there was a bitter struggle for office going on in Berlin between Caprivi, who was popular with many Catholics, and Miquel and that one official would inevitably fall from power.[60] But Lieber's letter of April 7 to Otto was

---

[54] *Kölnische Volkszeitung*, March 17, and March 29, 1894.

[55] Müller, *Im Spiegel der Geschichte*, pp. 837–840. Ritter, *Volksverein*, pp. 203–204.

[56] *Ibid.* The encyclical did put stress on the formation of vocational associations though not on corporatism itself, so Centrist leaders had to be careful in their reactions to the proposals of Oberdörffer.

[57] Herzfeld, *Miquel* 2: p. 331.

[58] During the committee hearings on the measure Count Wilhelm von Hoensbroech, Löe's close friend, charged that the reports in the *Kölnische Volkszeitung* "sought to discredit the sound core of the proposal": letter to Hermann Cardauns, March 9, 1894. Karl Bachem Papers, File 66. Some non-Center papers charged later that the government had been able to modify the proposals because it knew that the Prussian Center was divided on them: *Germania*, June 21, 1894.

[59] Lieber to Otto, April 7, 1894. Fn. 43 above.

[60] Lieber had protested to Karl Bachem some days later that it was dangerous for the *Kölnische Volkszeitung* to make such

inspired most of all by Bachem's editorial statement in the newspaper of March 27 that there was no "statesman" successor to Windthorst in the Center and that he had personally hoped for the establishment of a "directory" in the party.[61]

Lieber was determined to break his opposition once and for all. He rebuffed Julius Bachem's gestures of apology and reconciliation[62] and refused to attend meetings of the Catholic press association where he would have had to meet the Rhenish Catholic editors on their own ground. Lieber intended to defer any reconciliation with his Rhineland opponents until some date after the Catholic Congress which was to meet in Cologne in late August.[63] He clearly expected the Congress to uphold his leadership. His confidence that it would do so was undoubtedly strengthened by two major political victories in the later spring and summer. The Reichstag for the first time passed by a comfortable majority a Center motion to revoke the anti-Jesuit law. The Federal Council ignored the Reichstag's action but approved the exemption of the Redemptorist and Holy Ghost religious orders from its provisions. That concession to the Catholic Church was undoubtedly a payment for Lieber's services to Caprivi and to his continuing commitment to Miquel's tobacco tax.[64]

Bachem and his friends apparently thought that Lieber left them no choice but to engage in a test of strength with him over the leadership of the party. They attempted to bring about the defection of some of Lieber's regional supporters by telling them the party leader would try to win backing for Miquel and the tobacco tax at the next session of the Reichstag.[65] They hoped to create a broad political front based on the Huene-Ballestrem group in Silesia and on whatever backing Georg von Hertling, now a severe critic of Lieber, could drum up in Bavaria.[66] Their trump card appeared to be their ability to award all the choice speaking at the Cologne Catholic Congress and the presidency of the session to their friends through their control over the local arrangements committee.

But Lieber's belief that the Congress would express confidence in his leadership was fully justified. Huene did not attend and Lieber received an enthusiastic reception whenever he spoke. Georg Orterer, the Bavarian president of the Congress, referred openly to the rumors circulating in the hall that he was going to help "lift one friend out of the saddle and others into it."[67] Several of the most prominent speakers, Orterer, Schorlemer, who had only recently returned to the Center party, and Auxiliary Bishop Schmitz of Cologne who spoke for the cardinal archbishop of that city, all dilated on the single theme of unity.[68] That was the major theme of the Congress. Afterwards Hertling and Cardauns acknowledged it had only produced "petty results" for their efforts.[69]

Their failure is not difficult to explain. Most of the rank and file Centrists, whether they were local leaders, editors, or prominent pastors, did not want to be confronted with a threat to the unity of the party. They came to the Congress to hear good news and to see evidence of collaboration, not strife, among the leaders. That was their natural state of mind but it must have been strengthened by their recollection of the conflict in the party over the army bill in the previous year.[70] The stress upon unity in the speeches of Orterer, Schorlemer, and Bishop Schmitz, and the absence of Huene warrants the conclusion that both the Prussian bishops and the government, possibly the Vatican as well, had informed prominent Centrists that they did not want a struggle for power to break out in the Center.

Once it was clear to both parties that he enjoyed a position of superior strength, Lieber was willing and even eager to negotiate with his Rhineland rivals. He made it clear that he wanted nothing to do with a party "directory"[71] and the *Kölnische Volkszeitung* made no further reference to such an institution. But Lieber offered significant concessions to the Bachem group on questions of financial policy. Karl Bachem was to speak for the Center at the first reading of the budget in December and to underscore his party's demand for economy. Lieber also formally abandoned his support of the principle of a tobacco tax and was to call for systematic reduction of the national debt in the next Reichstag session.[72]

---

an influential minister like Miquel run the gauntlet: letter dated March 23, 1894. Bachem Papers, File 66b.

[61] This was evident in a letter Lieber wrote to an unidentified friend: June 2, 1894. Lieber Papers, Wrocław, File 41.

[62] Lieber comments on a second Bachem note dated April 25, 1894, *ibid.*

[63] Lieber to Lambert Lensing, May 26, 1894, *ibid.*

[64] Despite statements from some of his colleagues to the contrary, Lieber told the Reichstag in mid-April, 1894, that his party had not abandoned the tobacco tax permanently; *Westfälische Volksblatt*, April 19, 1894. And see Bachem, *Zentrumspartei* 5: p. 350.

[65] Lieber to Gröber, June 14, 1894. Lieber Papers, Speyer, L, 243.

[66] Julius Bachem spoke of Huene as the "statesman intellect" in the Center after Windthorst at a meeting of the Augustine League in early June: *ibid.* Hertling to Hermann Cardauns, April 19, 1894. The late Ernst Deuerlein of München was generous enough to permit me to see his copies of the Hertling letters to Cardauns.

[67] *VGVkD zu Köln* (Köln, 1894), pp. 116–117.

[68] *Ibid.*, pp. 148–149, 166.

[69] Hertling to Cardauns, September 15, 1894. Hertling-Cardauns correspondence.

[70] A Lieber supporter had written him in early May that most of the Centrist editors and politicians at an Augustine League meeting wanted a common front against Baron von Löe and opposed any other action that could split the party: Phillip Wasserburg to Lieber, May 7, 1894, Lieber Papers, Speyer, File W. 169.

[71] At a regional meeting of the Augustine League on October 18 in Freiburg: Kisky, *Augustinus-Verein*, p. 168.

[72] I treat the statements of Karl Bachem and Lieber on financial policy in the Reichstag sessions of 1894–1895 in the next chapter, p. 52.

Nevertheless, the political conditions in Berlin and in Catholic rural areas in October, 1894, must have led Lieber and Julius Bachem to conclude that they should end their feud. They watched helplessly while the Bismarckian press and the Conservatives created a political crisis which finally led to Caprivi's fall from office on October 26. Prominent Catholic agrarians had already begun a new campaign of criticism against the Center party because of its economic policies earlier in the month.

The chancellor's enemies, frustrated by their failure to shake William II's support of Caprivi on the trade treaties, had found a new issue to use against him. In the early summer of 1894 anarchists had assassinated President Carnot of France and wounded other prominent governmental personalities in Europe. Bismarckian and Conservative journals declared that social revolutionaries were threats to the safety of William II and his family and the stability of German society; they insisted that the government should introduce a new anti-Socialist bill with severe punishments for revolutionary agitators. Caprivi and the Center favored instead a somewhat milder measure based on general legal principles.[73] While their immediate objective was the replacement of Caprivi by Count Botho zu Eulenburg, the Prussian minister-president, an old Bismarck dependent, the chancellor's opponents hoped to provoke a conflict between the monarchy and the Reichstag and to bring about a conservative revision of the suffrage. The emperor was initially favorable to their proposals, but drew back from their acceptance when he encountered resistance from the National Liberals and some south German governments. He finally dismissed both Caprivi and Eulenburg and appointed Prince Chlodwig von Hohenlohe, a Bavarian aristocrat, conservative liberal and anti-clerical Catholic to the chancellorship and Prussian ministry-presidency. Hohenlohe was seventy-five, Bismarck's age when he was dismissed in 1890. He appeared to be a stopgap appointee to the highest Imperial and Prussian governmental offices and the Conservatives hoped that they could dislodge him too.[74]

The other development inducing the Center leaders to resolve their quarreling occurred within Catholic agrarianism. On October 1, Felix von Löe founded a new agrarian newspaper, *Der Rheinische Volksstimme*, which immediately began to campaign against the Rhineland and Reichstag Center parties. Long acquainted with Löe, Lieber and Julius Bachem knew they had to contend with a difficult opponent. Patriarchal in appearance, with long white hair and beard and a big hooked nose, and dogmatic in his convictions, he was less flexible than Schorlemer or Huene on economic questions.[75] Löe apparently believed German agriculture was facing the fate suffered by its British counterpart some decades earlier;[76] he may have been afraid too that the Agrarian League would attract some of the members of his own Rhineland Peasants' Association if he did not take an advanced stand on agricultural issues. Despite the rigidity of his beliefs, Löe was probably a shrewd enough tactician. Even though the founding of his newspaper was a gesture against the Rhineland Center, Löe was astute enough to retain his formal ties with the party and to keep his seat on the executive council of the Prussian Center. By staying in he made it more difficult for the Center press to attack him as vigorously as the editors some times desired.[77]

Over the course of the next year or more Löe's activities became a cause of increasing worry to Julius Bachem and to Lieber, though the party leaders also had serious concerns in Berlin. As they expected, Löe's example encouraged prominent Catholic agrarians in other regions to attack the Center for its supposed lack of attention to agriculture. Grain prices were lower in remote Silesia than in the west. Silesia was also part of the sphere of operations of the Agrarian League and, as the activities of Ballestrem, Huene and Cardinal Kopp had earlier demonstrated, a history of collaboration existed between the aristocratic agrarians of the Conservative party and those of the Center. Silesian Catholic agrarian leaders were even more brutal in their criticism of the Center than Löe himself. Count Strachwitz, a one-time Center deputy from Silesia, told an assembly of agrarians at Breslau in February 1895 that "the Center would either be agrarian or it would not be."[78] In Bavaria the *Historisch-politische Blätter* claimed that agrarians were fighting for their existence and they should be free to act as they pleased on economic questions.[79]

The leader of the Rhineland Peasants' Association was also sharply divided from his Centrist critics on the principle of party organization. Beneath that argument lay a disagreement on economic policy. In keeping with his corporative beliefs and his disaffection with the Rhineland Center, Löe wanted the governing group in the Prussian Center to accept the principle of vocational representation, which meant, basically, more mandates for prominent members of peasants' associations and craftsmen's organizations. In the early months

[73] On the Center and the early discussions of a new anti-revolution measure: Zechlin, *Staatsreichpläne*, pp. 197, 220–223.

[74] For the most recent account of the chancellor crisis of 1894 see Rohl, *Germany without Bismarck*, pp. 110–117.

[75] On Löe and the Center in this period: Blondel, *Études sur les populations rurales*, p. 16; Müller, *Im Spiegel der Geschichte*, pp. 834–836; Kisky, *Augustinus-Verein*, pp. 191–198.

[76] *Rheinische Volksstimme*, September 24, 1895.

[77] Karl Bachem said in October, 1895, that at least one-third of the members of the Landtag fraction would oppose any effort of the leaders to take disciplinary action against Löe. Bachem to Lieber, October 2, 1895. Lieber Papers, Speyer, B, 238.

[78] Franz Arenberg to the papal nuncio in Munich, May 27, 1896. Bachem Papers, File 66b.

[79] *HpB* **111** (1895): p. 450.

of 1895 his new journal, *Die Rheinische Volksstimme,* criticized leading Rhineland Centrists like Franz Hitze [80] who had voted for the Russian trade treaty even though they represented essentially rural constituencies. That campaign frightened the leaders of the Rhineland Center, since many of the members of the provincial delegation in the Reichstag fraction had some agrarian constituents. They were not certain that those urban middle-class deputies who owed their regular re-election to the Reichstag or Landtag to their fight against the Kulturkampf legislation could compete favorably against advocates of extensive agrarian and artisan programs.

Löe's opponents in the Rhineland Center also assumed that he wanted to dismantle the Center party, which he called "an association of Catholic pastors." [81] It is likely, however, that he really set for himself a more practicable goal: a recognition of the right of agrarian and artisan representatives in the fraction to vote in accordance with their beliefs on legislation affecting their constituents, and therefore in alliance with the Conservatives and the various agrarian parties. Those Catholic representatives would be required to act together with the other members of the Center only on matters affecting the Catholic Church. The acceptance of Löe's proposals regarding representation and the freedom of deputies in their decisions on secular legislation would have made the Center politically impotent and cost it the support of its labor electorate in the large cities of the west and northwest. Löe coolly dismissed this danger by saying that most of the industrial working class was already lost to Social Democracy.[82]

Löe's position on basic economic issues was still more extreme than his views on the proper representation of Catholic agrarian associations in the Center and was of one piece with his fundamental hostility to liberal parliamentarism. His doctrinaire cast of mind, his sincere concern over the future of German agriculture, and his need to keep his own association competitive with the Agrarian League led Löe to espouse the maximal program of the League: the plan of Count Kanitz, the noted agrarian Conservative, for the nationalization of all imports of grains and the setting of their prices by the states, the introduction of bimetallism and the abolition of all speculation in futures at the grain exchanges. In December, 1895, at a general assembly of the Rhineland Peasants' Association at Neuss near Cologne, the Löe group called for the extension of state controls over domestic wheat production as well as over imports; the states would delegate their legislative powers in this regard to the provincial agricultural chambers. Löe and his friends sought by the advocacy of that transfer to overcome the basic argument against Kanitz's proposal that it was too socialistic and to use the Kanitz measure for their own corporatist program.[83]

It was easy enough for Lieber and his associates to reject Kanitz's plan out of hand, since it was too much of an attack on capitalism for Schorlemer, the government, National Liberals, and the Free Conservatives to swallow. In December, 1895, the Reichstag refused to give the proposal a committee hearing. Lieber did speak favorably on the subject of bimetallism, but his remarks were tactical in character, for Wilhelm von Kardorff, the leader of the Free Conservatives with whom he had been trying to establish a political relationship, was an ardent advocate of a double standard.[84] But the future of bimetallism really depended on the attitudes of the British and American governments and they were opposed to its introduction. In the Reichstag session of 1895–1896 the Center, with some reluctance, did promote the passage of a bill to abolish speculation on grain futures.[85] The Conservative party and the agrarian organizations had long claimed that the speculation in the grain exchanges was an important factor in the low prices of wheat. Between 1894 and 1897 the Center also initiated or supported other legislation of a more modest character to aid the agrarians and peasants. It helped to secure the establishment of an agricultural bank in Prussia, the building of grain warehouses for domestic crops, restrictions on similar structures for foreign grains in transit, higher taxation on margarine, lower taxes on production of sugar, and a subsidy for its export.[86]

In the early and mid-1880's debates in the Center and wider Catholic circles over agrarian questions had usually been linked with consideration of the difficulties and grievances of artisans. Chaplain Oberdörffer in his program of 1894 had stressed equally the fundamental importance of the peasantry and the craftsmen to a restored corporative order. Löe's claim that the industrial working class was lost to Social Democracy implied that the Center and the Catholic Church would do better to treat the complaints of the artisans than to concern themselves with the needs of industrial workers.

While it is difficult to secure reliable and precise facts about the participation of Catholic craftsmen in the artisan movement, most of those who were politically active in it apparently desired the restoration of the guilds' powers. During the later eighties and

[80] Müller, *Im Spiegel der Geschichte,* pp. 844–845.

[81] Karl Bachem, undated notes on Löe, Bachem Papers, File 14.

[82] *Rheinische Volksstimme,* September 24, 1895.

[83] Müller, *Im Spiegel der Geschichte,* p. 843.

[84] He, Kardorff, and Robert Friedberg, a National Liberal, recommended in February, 1895, that the government issue invitations to an international conference to deal with currency questions: Pichler, *Centrum und Landwirtschaft,* p. 32. On Kardorff and bimetallism see Barkin, *The Controversy over German Industrialization 1890–1902,* pp. 89–90.

[85] Pichler, *ibid.,* p. 28.

[86] *Ibid.,* p. 54–60.

early nineties, major debates had taken place among leading artisan federations over the questions of whether masters and journeymen should be required to join a guild and whether journeymen should pass a test of competence administered by a local guild. Some artisans' organizations believed that craftsmen would be better off in craft unions.[87] There were significant political indications to justify the conclusion that most Catholic master craftsmen adhered to traditional guild philosophy. The Bavarian Center had been committed for a long time to the principle of compulsory guilds[88] and the Rhineland Center gave vigorous support to Franz Hitze's efforts, between 1895 and 1897, to secure their introduction throughout the empire.

It is not surprising that most south German Centrists were committed to the concept of the compulsory guild membership and the proof of competence, since they came from regions of Germany which were predominantly rural. Hitze's passionate devotion to economic corporatism reflected his own Westphalian background and the dislike he carried as a priest for the economic warfare of free enterprise. But it was remarkable that Hitze, a member of the Rhineland Center, spoke for his party in the debates on legislation concerning the artisans in the period 1895–1897. And even though the leadership groups of the Rhineland and Reichstag Center parties were traditionally committed to industrial free enterprise, they supported, either substantially or formally, legislative measures intended to impose severe restraints on it. It is likely that they wanted to separate the master craftsmen from the agrarians, but there were other reasons for trying to placate them.

During the winter of 1892–1893 when the Centrist leaders realized that the army-bill crisis might lead to early parliamentary elections, they had become concerned over the revival of anti-Semitism in rural districts. There were residues of the old peasant antagonism toward Jewish moneylenders and cattle merchants, though the peasants' associations were progressively destroying the traditional nexus between Christians and Jewish merchants. But in the smaller cities and towns, the Jewish retailer, traveling salesman, and peddler competed against the indigenous Christian shopowners and craftsmen. The Christian shopkeepers and artisans, who were apparently trained in the old guild traditions, resented the commercial techniques of some Jewish competitors and thought them unethical.[89] No doubt anti-Semitism was widespread, for Lieber told a rabbi friend in 1894 that, if the Center were to dissolve, its rural electorate would turn to the anti-Semite parties.[90] At that time Karl Lueger was near success in his construction of a Catholic party in Austria based on the appeal of anti-Semitism to the Austrian *Mittelstand* of artisans and peasants.

There is no evidence, however, that after the elections of 1893 the Center retained a serious fear of competition from anti-Semitic parties. It lost no mandates to them in that contest and no Catholic politician sought to emulate Lueger's example. In March, 1894, the party leaders and *Germania* spoke out against the agitation of the anti-Semites and a year later Lieber said in the Reichstag that anti-Semitism was a "disgrace for Germany and worse than Social Democracy."[91] During the debates in which Lieber made that charge, Heereman, the leading aristocrat in the Center, defended, to the approval of the *Kölnische Volkszeitung*, the constitutional right of Jews to hold judgeships and other public offices.[92] Nevertheless, both Julius Bachem and Lieber had been concerned enough over hostility of Catholic retailers and artisans toward their Jewish competitors to call in 1892–1893 for legislation against "Jewish business excesses."[93] Although their provinces, the Rhineland and Hesse-Nassau, had almost the same number of Jews, Lieber, unlike Bachem, felt uncomfortable in that role. He may have been concerned about the danger of alienating his local Jewish supporters, whose votes in Landtag elections were weightier than they were in those for the Reichstag. But his correspondence reveals that he valued the reputation among Jews in his district of being a just man and able to respect himself.[94]

In the early months of 1895, Gröber and Hitze introduced a bill to the Reichstag calling for the imposing of restrictions on the amount of goods and wares that traveling salesmen and peddlers could bring into local markets. Artisan federations had long called for a ban against peddling and there was widespread antagonism on the part of local craftsmen and retailers against Jewish salesmen. It is not clear how the Gröber-Hitze bill would have affected the mass of peddlers and commercial travelers. Hitze insisted that he and his colleague had no desire to destroy the traditional peddler

---

[87] *Staatslexikon* (3rd rev. ed.) **2**: pp. 1102–1103.

[88] Hertling, **2**: p. 54.

[89] *Staatslexikon* **2**: p. 1470. Julius Bachem: *HpB* **111** (1893): p. 449. August Bebel was surprised by the degree of anti-Semitism he found among craftsmen and shopkeepers during the elections of 1893: *Briefwechsel mit Engels,* p. 698.

[90] Letter to Rabbi Horwitz, April 14, 1894. Lieber Papers, Wrocław, File 40.

[91] *Rheinischer Kurier,* March 7, 1895. Rudolf von Buol said that the Social Democrats were "gentlemen" compared with them: letter to Albrecht von Stötzingen, December 22, 1893. Buol-Stötzingen Correspondence.

[92] *Kölnische Volkszeitung,* February 17, 1895.

[93] Julius Bachem to Lieber, January 11, 1893. Lieber Papers, Speyer, B, 216. Pulzer, *Political Anti-Semitism,* pp. 274, 278.

[94] Lieber to Rabbi Horwitz, November 1, 1893. Lieber Papers, Wrocław, File 1b. Lieber to August Röhling March 11, 1895. Lieber Papers, Speyer, File L, 60. One of his daughters later recalled that he taught his children to have a deep respect for the Jewish religion and to recognize Christianity's relationship to that faith: Sister Hortulanar hl. Franciskus, typescript, recollections of her father, December 6, 1916. Camber. Lieber Papers, Camberg.

class, but were essentially concerned about peddlers who came with extensive wares from factory outlets.[95] The government did not respond favorably to the measure and approved it only in a modified form at a later date. In the Reichstag session of 1895–1896 the Center had more success with a bill against "unfair competition" whose actual author was Julius Bachem. That measure imposed severe fines on merchants who were guilty of false advertising.[96]

The Center's major effort on behalf of Catholic artisans was Hitze's proposal for a law which would require all masters and journeymen to join a guild and would establish local handicraft chambers like those for merchants. Guild partisans claimed that compulsion was necessary if the guilds were to flourish. Only one-tenth of all the masters and journeymen did have membership in a guild at the beginning of 1895.[97] But the Imperial and state governments, capitalistic in economic orientation, were uncomfortable about the principle of compulsion and after over two years of debates and negotiations the Center had to accept a compromise measure which provided for limited obligatory guild membership on a democratic basis. The modified measure which became law in June, 1897, specified that seventy crafts would come under its application. The artisans engaged in those crafts would decide by majority vote in individual districts whether they wished to belong to a guild and be subject to its prescriptions. The results of the elections prior to 1900 appeared to validate the claim of the guild advocates: the number of compulsory guilds and their membership grew appreciably after the introduction of the new law. But even the general triumph of the principle would not have provided adequate protection against the economic power of big industry which satisfied needs far beyond the reach of the handicrafts.[98]

In its insistence on a compromise measure the government knew that the Center leadership was not united on the principle of compulsory guilds. Both Lieber and Georg von Hertling, who had returned to the Reichstag in June, 1896, were opposed to a law making guild membership obligatory. The two men had made up their personal differences in 1895 and Lieber welcomed the return of a colleague who would give him support in his inner-party struggle with Hitze over questions of economic freedom.[99] The *Kölnische Volkszeitung* was not pleased over Hertling's reelection and

noted that the artisan federations in his region had opposed it.[100] Hertling apparently owed his success in the election to his recent defense of peasants involved in a controversy with an aristocratic landowner and possibly to the intervention of high church authorities.[101]

After the passage of the craftsmen's bill in 1897, the artisans were not a serious political problem for the Center. Felix von Löe's death in May, 1896, the slow improvement of grain prices in the same year, and the Reichstag's agrarian legislation also reduced significantly the agrarian pressures on the leaders. They may have overestimated the danger of the Catholic agrarian movement to the Center; Löe and the other heads of peasants' associations would not have been able to lead their followers arbitrarily. The Catholic clergy had contributed significantly to the organizing and growth of the associations and the agrarian leaders could not lightly disregard their views. The bishops and priests were essentially concerned with the preservation of the unity and effectiveness of the Center. When Schorlemer, after his resignation from the party in May, 1893, founded his own newspaper, he soon came under systematic attack from his pastor, and the Westphalian nobility showed a curious lack of interest in helping to keep his new journal in existence.[102] The priest secretary-general of Löe's peasants' association openly disagreed with his superior's course of action.[103] The majority of the small landowners were more likely to follow their pastors and the priests in the peasants' associations than they were their aristocratic leaders.

Nevertheless, the reaction of the leadership to the disaffection of the agrarians and the artisans in the mid-1890's did reveal the extent to which the Center depended on those social elements of the *Mittelstand*. The Catholic agrarians in particular had given Lieber and his colleagues a serious scare. Soon after his election, Hertling told a Bavarian audience that domestic economic legislation for the next decade would be primarily concerned with agrarian questions.[104] The Center's determination to placate the landed classes was to be evident in all of the later Catholic Congresses and finally in its response to the major tariff bill of 1902.

4. THE YEARS OF UNCERTAINTY, 1894–1897

The unfavorable attitude of the emperor to the party was . . . the most vulnerable place in its public es-

[95] *Deutscher Reichs-zeitung*, February 4, 1895.

[96] "Gesetz zur Bekampfung des umlauteren Wettbewerb," *Reichsgesetz Blatt*, 1896: p. 145.

[97] From statement made by the secretary of the interior, Heinrich von Boetticher, in January 1895: Schulthess, *Geschichtskalender* (1895), p. 18.

[98] For the Center's views on craft guilds see the *Staatslexikon* (3rd rev. ed.) 2: pp. 1102–1104, 1385–1390.

[99] Hertling took the first step in the restoration of their old friendship by inviting Lieber to address the annual meeting of the Görres Society at Munich: letter to Lieber, July 2, 1895. Lieber Papers, Wrocław, File 151.

[100] *Kölnische Volkszeitung*, June 15, 1895.

[101] Hertling, *Erinnerungen* 2: pp. 171–175. In his interviews of 1893 and 1895 with Cardinal Rampolla, the papal secretary of state had expressed regret that Hertling was no longer in the Reichstag: Hertling to his wife, October 21, 1895. Hertling Papers, Bundesarchiv, Koblenz, File 11.

[102] Jacobs, *Schorlemer zur Grünen Front*, pp. 27–28.

[103] Müller, *Im Spiegel der Geschichte*, p. 850.

[104] *Niederrheinische Volkszeitung*, September 17, 1895.

teem; its national effectiveness like that of the Reichstag was diminished by it.

Martin Spahn [1]

. . . we do not wish to hunt after the phantom of an erroneous Weltpolitik by which a once great imperial dynasty was ruined and with it the strength and glory of the old German Reich.

Alois Fritzen, November, 1896. [2]

The first years of the Hohenlohe chancellorship were a period of insecurity and anxiety for Lieber and his colleagues. While the agricultural depression and the extremism of some Catholic agrarian groups contributed to that mood, the poor relations between their party and the monarch were more responsible for it. The Center's leaders had been severely shaken by Caprivi's dismissal, coming as it did after a session in which they had helped him to win a major victory in the passage of the last trade treaties. [3] William II's decision to drop his second chancellor demonstrated his lack of respect for the Reichstag and its leading party. Since the emperor intended to initiate policies under Caprivi's aged successor, his attitude toward the parliament and their party was a matter of grave concern to Lieber and his associates.

Nevertheless, the Centrist leadership found some reason for hope in the outcome of the chancellor crisis. William II had not appointed a Prussian Conservative to the chancellorship or to the minister-presidency. At the time of his appointment Hohenlohe's political views and associations were known only to a few persons in high government circles, but his profile was to become clearer in the winter of 1894–1895.

The new chancellor was not a typical Catholic nobleman, although his brother Gustave was a cardinal in residence at the Vatican. But Cardinal Hohenlohe was hardly a conventional high churchman since he had been willing to become the Prussian minister to the Vatican in the early 1870's, then remained silent during the Kulturkampf and later flaunted his sympathy for the Italian state in Leo XIII's face. The chancellor himself was essentially a Whig politician, interested in a successful governmental career, hostile to ecclesiastical restraints on individual thought and conduct and devoted to the ideal of a strong German national state. While minister-president of Bavaria in 1869 he had attempted unsuccessfully to block the proclamation of papal infallibility by the first Vatican Council; a few years later as a Free Conservative deputy in the Reichstag he promoted the introduction and passage of the anti-Jesuit law. [4] In the mid-1870's, however, he left

parliamentary politics, becoming first the German ambassador to France and then governor-general of Alsace-Lorraine. He apparently adapted himself in the eighties to the changes in the status of the Catholic Church and the Center party in German affairs. During his decade of service in Alsace-Lorraine he had no serious differences with the Catholic clergy and made a warm friend of the French rector of the major seminary at Strassburg. [5]

Lieber and Julius Bachem chose to adopt a reserved attitude toward the chancellor during his first month or so of office. Because of the circumstances surrounding the Caprivi crisis they were more concerned over Hohenlohe's constitutional views than they were about his anti-clericalism. Hohenlohe did not look like a conflict chancellor; his mind was still keen and his enjoyment of office was to become increasingly evident, but he was highly aged, stooped in body and mild in temperament. Nevertheless, he had either kept in office or appointed Prussian ministers who were hostile to the Reichstag's electoral system. They included General Walter Bronsart von Schellendorf, the Prussian minister of war, [6] Ernst von Köller, the new minister of the interior, and Miquel. After the completion of the governmental changes in Berlin, the *Kölnische Volkszeitung* implied that it was more concerned about Köller's record than Hohenlohe's since the new minister of the interior had the reputation of being "decisive." [7] And Lieber hinted in late November or early December that Miquel would welcome a conflict between the government and the Reichstag over an anti-revolution bill in the hope that a new parliament would approve an extensive tax program. [8]

By the time that the Reichstag opened on December 6 the leading Centrists were more confident about the good intentions of the new chancellor. The royal advisers responsible for his appointment, Friedrich von Holstein of the Foreign Office and Friedrich, the grand

---

[1] Spahn, *Lieber*, p. 45.

[2] *Verhandlungen des Reichstages,* November 30, 1896: p. 3599.

[3] Schulthess, *Geschichtskalender* **36** (1895): pp. 169–170; and also *Denkwürdigkeiten des General-Feldmarschalls Alfred Grafen von Waldersee,* Heinrich von Meisner, ed. (2 v., Stuttgart and Berlin, 1925) **1**: p. 330.

[4] Windthorst once complained that no prominent Catholic family had "harmed" the Catholic Church so much by its conduct during the Kulturkampf as the Hohenlohes: letter to the

papal nuncio in Vienna dated November 19, 1879, *SaML* **83**: p. 15. On the brothers, Chlodwig and Gustave, in that period: *Denkwürdigkeiten des Fursten Chlodwig zu Hohenlohe-Schillingfurst* Friedrich von Curtius, ed. (2 v., 1907) **2**: pp. 1–70; Georg Franz, *Kulturkampf* (Munich, 1954), *passim;* and Schmidt-Volkmar, *Kulturkampf,* pp. 98–103.

[5] There are numerous letters from the rector, the Abbé Dacheux, to Hohenlohe in the last volume of his memoirs: *Denkwürdigkeiten,* K. von Müller, ed. (Stuttgart, 1931), *passim.*

[6] Notes by Karl Bachem, dated June, 1898. Bachem Papers, File 88. But he criticized William II to his face in February, 1895, after the ruler insulted Lieber and questioned the loyalty of Catholic army officers: Röhl, *Germany without Bismarck,* p. 133.

[7] *Kölnische Volkszeitung,* October 28, 1895.

[8] *Amerika* of St. Louis, Mo., December 20, 1894. Lieber did not refer to Miquel or to any other high official but said simply that newspaper editors thought the anti-revolution bill was simply a device that the government would use to secure a Reichstag favorable to its financial program. But he undoubtedly knew that Miquel had been initially in favor of a stiff repressive measure which could bring on a conflict with the parliament.

duke of Baden, had helped to undermine Bismarck's position in 1890 because they assumed that his negotiations with Windthorst would promote particularism in Germany. Four years later they believed that steady collaboration between the monarchy and the Reichstag led by the Center, the Free Conservatives, and the National Liberals was vital to the stability of the empire. Hohenlohe had revealed their intentions and his own when he insisted on retaining Marschall von Bieberstein as secretary of state for foreign affairs, although William II had an intense dislike for Marschall.[9] The secretary had been the major link between the Caprivi administration and the Center. Hohenlohe also invited Lieber to read and to amend the speech that he intended to deliver to the Reichstag at its opening session. At Lieber's suggestion he later told the parliament that his earlier anti-clerical activities had no relevance to the current political situation.[10] The old chancellor disliked both confessional parties and universal suffrage but he feared what the results of a conflict between the crown and the Reichstag could be for the popularity of the monarchy and for the unity and security of the Reich.[11]

Hohenlohe's assumption of the chancellorship and the Prussian minister-presidency marked another stage in the political decline of the conservative Centrists. Cardinal Kopp and Ballestrem had enjoyed close relations both with Caprivi and Eulenburg and had probably hoped that those two officials would compose their differences over the anti-revolution bill.[12] The cardinal was deeply disturbed over the outcome of the chancellor crisis and his later failure to establish a personal relationship with Hohenlohe.[13] His frustration and humiliation were complete when he learned that the chancellor preferred to use Franz Xaver Kraus, the noted liberal priest scholar and friend of the grand duke of Baden, as his prime source of information about the Vatican rather than Kopp himself.[14]

Lieber was grateful to Hohenlohe for his reserve toward Kopp. Nevertheless, he recognized that the policy of excluding the cardinal from the Center–government relationship and negotiations could be politically dangerous to his wing of the Center and the chancellor. Botho zu Eulenburg, eager to overthrow Hohenlohe, told Kopp in January 1895 that the chancellor, a Catholic, could not intervene on behalf of the Jesuits, whereas he, Eulenburg, a non-Catholic, could and would be able to secure the revocation of the anti-Jesuit law.[15] Over the course of the next year or more Lieber was to suspect that Ballestrem and Kopp were engaged in discussions with prominent Conservatives or persons close to the Prussian court over a proposal whereby the Catholic Church would approve the abandonment of universal and equal suffrage in Reichstag elections in return for the restoration of the Jesuits and the granting of other benefits to the church. There is no hard evidence that Kopp actually presented such a plan to the Prussian hierarchy or to the Vatican.[16] He may have been reluctant to assume any responsibility for a decision which would have stripped the Catholic minority of its influence in national politics. But Lieber's fears about Kopp's political activities were substantial and they heightened his desire to prevent a serious conflict between his party and the government which could lead to Hohenlohe's dismissal from office and his replacement by Eulenburg or a general.

It was no easy task for the Center and the government to get through the legislative session of 1894–1895 without significant disagreement. In settling his differences with the Rhineland Centrists Lieber had apparently committed himself to a policy of governmental economy and fiscal responsibility.[17] It was difficult, however, to reconcile that kind of a financial policy with the budget demands made by the government in December, 1894. William II, finally freed of a military chancellor who had been interested only in Germany's continental security, insisted that Hohenlohe should make greater demands on the Reichstag for naval ex-

---

[9] Franz Arenberg urged the Kölnische Volkszeitung to refrain from criticism of the new chancellor because Hohenlohe had shown his good will toward the Center by his retention of Marschall and his recommendation that Marschall be given a Prussian ministry without portfolio. Letters dated October 28 and November 1, 1894. Bachem Papers, File 16.

[10] Karl Bachem notes, dated June 16, 1900. Ibid., File 72.

[11] For an informed and detailed interpretation of Hohenlohe's views in his chancellorship years see: Karl A. Müller, "Der dritte deutsche Reichskanzler. Bemerkungen zu den 'Denkwürdigkeiten der Reichskanzlerzeit' des Fürsten Chlodwig zu Hohenlohe-Schillingfurst," Sitzungsberichte der Bayerischen Akademie der Wissenschaft (Philosophisch-historisch Abteilung) 4 (1932): pp. 1–60.

[12] The Associated Press reported in late August that Ballestrem might enter the Prussian ministerial council and Miquel might leave it if William II succeeded in reconciling Caprivi and Eulenburg: N. Y. Staatszeitung, August 26, 1894.

[13] On his mood in early 1895: Lieber to Arenberg, July 12, 1895; Lieber Papers, Wrocław, File 95.

[14] Kopp finally complained to the chancellor in February, 1896, over his use of Kraus on a special mission to the Vatican: Hohenlohe, Reichskanzlerzeit, pp. 182–183.

---

[15] Lieber to Marschall von Bieberstein, entry dated February 21, 1895. Marschall Diary. From notes taken by Professor David R. King. According to Lieber, Eulenburg, then Prussian minister of the interior, had discovered Kopp when he was the vicar-general of his home diocese. Lieber to Arenberg, fn. 13 above.

[16] Lieber did say in a letter of March 15, 1896, to Karl zu Löwenstein that he had heard "a reliable report" that "one" had approached the Vatican with such a proposal. He used strong language to frighten Löwenstein, a confident of the pope and of the leading Catholic artistocrats, claiming that if the Vatican approved that plan it would experience a repetition of the losses of the sixteenth century. On March 25 he wrote Löwenstein that the Vatican would be sacrificing the highest political rights of an economically depressed Catholic minority and the defense of the Catholic Church against Social Democracy if it offered up popular suffrage for incidental concessions to the church. Copies of the original letters in the Löwenstein Archiv in Wertheim am Main in my personal possession.

[17] See below, pp. 52–53.

pansion and colonial administration. Since the government still carried a large debt, Miquel and Posadowsky, the Imperial secretary of the treasury, wanted substantial new taxes, inclusive of a tobacco levy, which would eliminate the need for new financial contributions from Prussia and the other states.

The most dramatic and sensitive measure to be considered by the Reichstag was the so-called anti-revolution bill. While he was under the influence of Botho zu Eulenburg and other advisers close to the Conservative parties William II had committed himself in a speech on September 6, 1894, to a new campaign against revolutionary agitators in defense of "religion, morality and order."[18] Even though Eulenburg fell from office seven weeks later, the monarch was ready to assume the primary responsibility for the suppression of the Social Democrats, the actual targets of his attack. William II was incapable of steady application to any governmental task, but his own resentment against the Social Democrats for their republicanism and the steady pressures exercised by the Prussian Conservatives on court personnel and ministers of state kept the idea of a repressive law against the Socialists in or near the forefront of the ruler's thinking till 1900.

The new bill, unlike the Bismarckian anti-Socialist law or Eulenburg's proposal, was based on general law and did not contain provisions for the expulsion of persons found guilty of revolutionary agitation. It called for a sharpening of certain articles in the Criminal Code, the Military Code, and the press laws and for substantially stiffer penalties for their violation. The proposals did depart sharply from traditional juridical norms since the planned revision of article 111a of the Criminal Code called for the arrest and punishment of persons who "glorified" or "praised" actions which were criminally illegal under article 111 or other articles of the new measure.[19] The main aim of the bill was the more effective defense of the monarchy, the government, the army, and capitalist society against Social Democratic criticism and ridicule, although the omnibus article 130 of the Criminal Code also offered the same protection to religion, marriage and the family. Adolf Bebel, the Social Democratic leader, said that his party's editors would have one foot in jail all the time if the measure became law.[20] Many years later Karl Bachem finally admitted that it was a "disguised anti-Socialist bill."[21]

William II and his ministers were initially confident about the prospects of the new bill. The ruler, Caprivi, or some other governmental representative had received promises of support for such a measure from high

Catholic churchmen and Center leaders in the summer of 1894.[22] The Vatican undoubtedly hoped that the Center would vote for it. Leo XIII had been upset in 1879 when Windthorst and his whole party opposed the passage of Bismarck's severe anti-Socialist bill[23] and his social encyclical of 1891, *Rerum Novarum,* revealed that he still feared the activities of the Social Democrats among the working classes. In the summer of 1893 Rampolla had parried the complaints of the German government over the exclusion of Ballestrem and Huene from the Center with the assertion that the Catholic Church would unite with the German Reich in a campaign against Socialism.[24]

The Centrist leaders did not require any prodding from the Roman Curia on the advisability of supporting restrictive legislation against Social Democrats.[25] Unlike many of their voters who regarded liberal Protestantism, the Jewish merchant, or big business as the main threat to Catholicism or their personal security, they believed that Social Democracy would be the greatest rival of their church and party in the future. They also wanted to help Hohenlohe pass his first major political test and to show William II and the leaders of the Cartel parties that the Center was a reliable ally. The *Kölnische Volkszeitung* was willing to give cautious support to the new anti-revolution measure. Julius Bachem had apparently changed his mind on the subject of legislation aimed at the Social Democrats since he had insisted in 1891 that the Center should not let the government use it as a "party of order."[26] He had become concerned no doubt over the vigorous manner in which the Social Democrats had responded to their failure to capture any seats from the Center in the Rhineland and Westphalia in the elections of 1893. In 1894 they founded a new Social Democratic newspaper in Cologne, the *Rheinische Zeitung,* and provided that journal with a highly competent staff and large sums of money for its operations.[27]

Lieber and his colleagues did not assume that the new government would cripple the Social Democratic movement nor did they want it to do so. The presence of a Social Democratic fraction of respectable size in

---

[18] Bachem, *Zentrumspartei* **5**: pp. 361–363.

[19] In his first speech to the Reichstag on the bill Adolph Gröber, one of the Center's leading jurists, stressed the novel character of article 111a: *Verhandlungen des Reichstages,* January 9, 1895: p. 219.

[20] Letter to Engels, *Briefwechsel mit Engels,* p. 792.

[21] Bachem, *Zentrumspartei* **5**: p. 386.

[22] F. Hellwig, *Carl, Freiherr von Stumm-Halberg* (Heidelberg, 1936): Zechlin, *Staatsreichpläne Bismarcks,* pp. 197, 222, Kraus, *Tagebücher,* p. 623.

[23] Schmidt-Volkmar, *Kulturkampf,* p. 229.

[24] Rampolla Memorandum, dated July 14, 1893, GFMA, Microfilm Copy, University of Michigan, Roll 110; Otto von Bülow, the Prussian minister to the Vatican to Caprivi, August 2, 1893, *ibid.*

[25] The Bavarian representative in the Federal Council, Count Lerchenfeld, warned his own government that the Center would resent any attempt by the Vatican to influence its decision: Peter Rassow and Born, Karl E., *Akten zur staatlichen Sozialpolitik in Deutschland, 1890–1914,* Historische Forschungen, No. 3 (Wiesbaden, 1959): p. 58.

[26] *HpB* **108** (1891): p. 835.

[27] Gerhard A. Ritter, *Die deutsche Arbeiterbewegung in der Wilhelminischen Epoche, 1890–1900* (Berlin, 1965), p. 69.

the Reichstag was necessary for the Center if it wished to control the balance in the chamber and to demonstrate its usefulness to the government as an ally.[28] But Lieber and his colleagues did have a personal interest in legislation which would restrain the agitational activities of a potentially dangerous rival. They learned, however, at an early date in the parliamentary session of 1894–1895 that substantial parts of the Catholic press did not share their views on the subject.

The long struggle between the Huene-Ballestrem and Lieber groups for the leadership of the Center had weakened the authority of the Reichstag party over Catholic editors. As Ballestrem recognized, the press had contributed significantly to the defeat of the army bill and to Lieber's triumph over his own aristocratic wing of the party. In the following year, however, Centrist journals, led by the Bachem bloc in the Rhineland, had delivered a painful setback to Lieber on the Miquel finance plan. It is likely that integralist Catholic newspaper editors thought they could achieve the same kind of victory against the new anti-revolution proposal. In early December, a full month before its introduction to the Reichstag, the *Deutsche Reichs-zeitung* of Bonn made a severe attack on the proposed measure, claiming that it was aimed against opposition rather than revolution. The editors added that the government would do better to draft a new bill which would focus on the universities, the basic source of revolutionary thought.[29] They did not expect a government led by an old anti-clerical Catholic to take their advice. Their undoubted aim was to create as much embarrassment for him and the National Liberals as they could.

The bishops and lower clergy were undoubtedly disappointed in the provisions of the new Hohenlohe bill against revolutionary agitation. That proposal contained an article which provided for the protection of religious practices, marriage, and the family against insults and revilement. But the main emphasis of the governmental measure was on the protection of the state and existing society.

High Catholic churchmen were for the most part not immediately concerned with the growth of the Social Democratic movement. They worried more about the decline of religious belief, traditional morality, and ecclesiastical authority in a liberal culture. At their annual Fulda conference in August, 1894, the Prussian bishops had written a letter to Caprivi in which they expressed "deep concern" over the increase and dissemination of literature "destructive of religion and morality" and over the influence of "positivism and materialism" in society.[30] The more conservative bishops looked upon the universities as the primary danger to traditional religion because philosophical positivism was the dominant *Weltanschauung* in them. But it is inconceivable that any informed church dignitary thought that the Prussian government would consider interference with the intellectual freedom of its universities of which it was so proud. Attacking the universities was a crude sport in which some Catholic editors and politicians engaged when they wanted to arouse or appease the provincial clergy or middle classes for a political end.

Caprivi had not answered the Fulda letter of the Prussian bishops, but they undoubtedly believed that William II was responding to them when he, in his widely quoted speech of September 8, called for a campaign in defense of "religion, morality and order." With the probable exception of Kopp and his friends, most of the Prussian and other German bishops did not know that the emperor's remarks on that occasion reflected the influence of Conservatives like Eulenburg who wanted to win the approval of the Catholic Church for an attack on the Reichstag and universal suffrage. Consequently, they were either disappointed or aggrieved at the government when Hohenlohe's proposal became known to the press in the late fall of 1894.

There is circumstantial evidence that two prominent conservatives in the Prussian hierarchy, Korum and Kopp, either initiated or encouraged the efforts of integralist Catholic newspapers to kill the anti-revolution bill by insisting that it be aimed against the universities.[31] The *Deutsche Reichs-zeitung* had long represented Korum's views on legislation in its columns and editorials and the *Mainzer Journal,* its ally, was the mouthpiece of the bishop of Mainz, Paul Haffner, Korum's friend. On January 6, 1895, *Germania,* in an editorial which undoubtedly reflected Kopp's thinking and demands, stated flatly that the government bill would be unacceptable to Catholics unless it made specific reference to the defense of two religious doctrines, the belief in the existence of a personal God and the immortality of the individual soul.[32]

The Centrist leaders were conscious at an early date in the Reichstag session of 1894–1895 that they might find themselves in opposition to the government in the later course of the deliberations on the Hohenlohe proposal.[33] They used tactics which they hoped would

---

[28] There were virtually no Social Democrats in the Prussian Landtag. At some time in the mid-1890's the Center leaders discussed the suitability of a suffrage reform which would ensure the Social Democrats about one-third of the mandates in that body. Undated notes, apparently in Lieber's handwriting, Lieber Papers, Speyer. Envelope: *Umsturzvorlage 1895.*

[29] *Deutsche Reichs-zeitung,* December 11, 1894.

[30] Printed copy of letter from the Prussian bishops to Caprivi, dated August 22, 1894, Lieber Papers, Wrocław, File 24.

[31] After the government's proposals ran into Centrist opposition in April 1895, William II was to express resentment against Bishop Korum and Cardinal Rampolla and to express uncertainty about his relationship with Kopp. Franz Xaver Kraus, *Tagebücher* (Cologne, 1957), p. 623.

[32] *Germania,* January 6, 1895.

[33] Rudolf von Buol wrote a friend in late November, 1894, to the effect that the Center would accept the bill only on its own terms which included, among other things, articles of censorship on prostitution, indecent exposure, and the like:

reassure the Catholic critics and opponents of the anti-revolution bill but not cause Hohenlohe and William II to doubt the Center's reliability as a supporter of the monarchy's policy on revolutionary agitation. In early January Lieber, speaking at a Catholic rally attacked the intellectual liberalism which was "the parent of socialism." But he stressed the fact that he was not attacking political liberalism.[34] The Center chose Gröber, probably at Lieber's request, to speak for the party at the first reading of the bill on January 9. A master of both subtle and massive polemic, Gröber devoted minimal attention to a Socialist threat to the state and society; instead he criticized the government for its failure to remove the special legislation against the banned religious orders and then dilated at considerable length on the damage done by university professors to religious belief.[35] But only a few days later he, Peter Spahn, and Karl Bachem, all skilled jurists, voted in committee for the controversial elastic article 111a.[36]

If anything, Lieber's desire to achieve a compromise with the government on the anti-revolution measure grew during the months of February and March. He had learned in early February that he was still outside the circle of William II's favor, probably because of his decisive role in the initial defeat of the army bill in 1893. At a court ball the emperor rebuffed Marschall when the secretary of state attempted to present Lieber to him; instead William II chose to speak at length with an ex-Jesuit who was making a career out of attacks on his former order and the Catholic Church. Marschall was already deep in the ruler's bad graces because of his earlier opposition to a strong anti-Socialist law and his intimacy with the Centrist leadership; William II was eager to use the incident with Lieber as an excuse to get rid of him. Thanks to Marschall's success in winning the Center's approval for four new cruisers which the emperor ardently wanted and to some other achievements the secretary for foreign affairs managed to hold on to his position.[37] But even though William II was enthusiastic over the passage of the naval budget the Center's failure to bring the anti-revolution bill to a second reading before the end of April intensified the emperor's hostility toward it. In the next two years it was to become increasingly evident that the more serious cause of William II's resentment against the Center was not the

recollection of Lieber's earlier conduct but the party's failure to assure his personal government a safe and reliable Reichstag majority.

The editors of the *Kölnische Volkszeitung* also took a sober view of the monarch's marked dislike of their party, though they felt obvious pleasure in reporting the incident at the court ball.[38] They justified the conduct of the three Centrist deputies in the special committee on the anti-revolution bill who had voted for article 111a and who had soon come under heavy fire from conservative Catholic newspapers for it. They claimed the government attached more importance to that article than to any part of the bill.[39] Julius Bachem and Hermann Cardauns were apparently nervous over the possible consequences of a Reichstag rejection of a compromise on the measure. The Bismarckian, agrarian, and Conservative newspapers were advocating the acceptance of the Kanitz bill and attacking the Reichstag for its delays on the anti-revolution proposals. The editors of the *Kölnische Volkszeitung* warned that their defeat could lead to a dissolution of the Reichstag and to an electoral campaign in which the Center's enemies would make the Kanitz bill the major issue. Those opponents would also be able to charge that the Center had refused to provide security for the ruler and the empire.[40]

Julius Bachem and Hermann Cardauns wanted in addition to avoid a confrontation with the new administration over the anti-revolution measure because they expected the Center to take a hard line on the budget and financial reform. They intended to persist in their old vendetta against Miquel and their demand that the government pursue a course of economy. Speaking for his party at the first reading of the budget in early December, Karl Bachem warned the government against excessive spending.[41] In mid-February, 1895, Lieber implied that the Center would not approve the tobacco tax which the government still desired.[42] Richard Müller-Fulda, the party's financial expert, had convinced his colleagues that the income of the Imperial Treasury would substantially increase in the budget year 1895–1896 and that the government could get along with a more modest tax program.[43]

The Center also roundly refused to accept a government plan for new financial relations between the Im-

---

Buol to Albrecht von Stötzingen, November 30, 1894. Buol-Stotzingen Correspondence.

[34] *Germania*, January 6, 1895.

[35] *Verhandlungen des Reichstages,* January 9, 1895: pp. 213–214.

[36] Spahn and Gröber were both judges and Karl Bachem had been trained in law. They were Lieber's chief legislative aides after 1894.

[37] Röhl, *Germany without Bismarck*, pp. 132–136.

[38] They said that the emperor had wanted to talk with Lieber but had no time to do so because of his long conversation with Paul Hoensbroech, the ex-Jesuit, and others: *Kölnische Volkszeitung,* February 12, 1895.

[39] Quoted in the *Deutsche Reichs-zeitung,* February 4, 1895.

[40] *Kölnische Volkszeitung,* March 19, 1895.

[41] *Ver handlungen des Reichstages,* December 11, 1894: pp. 33 ff.

[42] *Ibid.,* February 15, 1895: p. 914–915.

[43] The *Niederrheinische Volkszeitung* claimed on January 7, 1895, that the government would only need to raise three million marks more than a tobacco tax would produce for its whole budget because of the improvement in its regular receipts.

perial and state governments. The proposed reform was both modest and sensible; it asked simply that the Reich and the states balance out their financial obligations to each other. In the future the Reich would retain all of its surplus income for the reduction of the large national debt, except for the returns from taxes on brandy and stamps which would go to the states. Lieber was honest enough to acknowledge the theoretical merits of the plan and to say that the matricular payments were "a blood tax" upon states' savings. But he doomed the plan when he said in mid-February, 1895, that his party would insist upon the maintenance of the Franckenstein clause for both constitutional and financial reasons.[44]

Nevertheless, the Reichstag Center had become increasingly apprehensive about the campaign of the conservative Catholic press against the anti-revolution bill. By late January, several Prussian and Hessian journals had mounted a broad attack on the proposals on the grounds they constituted a threat to Catholic liberties. Some of them singled out the three Centrist deputies who had approved article 111a in committee for special chastisement.[45] While the Catholic press leadership against the bill came from the north, there was considerable opposition in the south as well, south Germans were accustomed to a less severe restraint on their freedom than their Prussian neighbors and probably regarded the bill as an essentially Prussian creation. Catholics in the south also resented the Pulpit Law, a Kulturkampf measure, which the liberal Bavarian government had initiated in the Federal Council for the purpose of keeping priests from making political addresses during church services. The Center was to insist on its removal as a partial concession for its support of the official anti-revolution proposals.[46]

Throughout the long committee deliberations on the bill, Lieber apparently refrained from making any public revelations of his views and intentions regarding it. Karl Bachem stated some years later that Lieber finally accepted the decision of the fraction to reject the measure.[47] Bachem did not identify the prominent members of the fraction who insisted on its rejection nor did he indicate at what point Lieber capitulated to the will of his colleagues. According to Bachem the turning point in the party's attitude toward the bill was the decision of its members in the special Reichstag committee to permit Viktor Rintelen, a leading Centrist

ultra-conservative, to present a supplementary motion to the bill. The Rintelen proposal constituted a threat to the freedom of German universities and science and was obviously intended to put the Center onto a collision course with the National Liberals and the government, as well as the left of the Reichstag. It stipulated that any person or persons who attacked or denied the existence of God, the immortality of the soul, the religious and moral character of marriage and the family should be subject to a fine or imprisonment. Rintelen introduced his motion at the end of February; his colleagues later substituted a weaker measure for it which stated that a person or persons could be fined or imprisoned for using demeaning expressions or ridicule about God, Christianity, or the doctrines, institutions or ceremonies of the Christian churches in a manner dangerous to the public peace. The authors of the newer proposal intended to aim it against Socialist agitators rather than university professors; nevertheless, it was also offensive to the government and liberal parties.[48] Bachem claimed that the other Centrists who supported the Rintelen motion in the first place did it with the intent of blowing up the whole anti-revolution bill.[49]

The Centrists who were apparently responsible for the decision to replace the Rintelen motion with a modified version were Karl Bachem, Peter Spahn, and Adolf Gröber. Bachem was the source of the information regarding the genesis of the Rintelen proposal. He, Spahn, and Gröber also overrode Lieber in late March in the politically delicate issue of whether the Reichstag should approve a birthday greeting to Bismarck. In order to prevent any further strain in its relations with the old chancellor and the Conservatives, Hohenlohe and Marschall wanted the Center to permit the passage of the Cartel motion calling for the sending of a greeting on his birth date, April 17. Lieber and Franz von Arenberg vainly sought to persuade their fraction to act in this sense but then abandoned their effort and went along with Bachem, Spahn and Gröber.[50]

One could not conclude from reading the notes compiled by Karl Bachem, probably at the time of the incident, or from his history of the Center written a full generation later, that there was any connection between his party's stand on the anti-revolution bill and on the question of the greeting to Bismarck. In his later years Bachem was apparently embarrassed by the Center's initial willingness to collaborate with the government on the repressive measure and he sought to present its later modifications to the bill as an attempt to make it applicable to elements in the educated upper classes as well as to those from the working class.[51]

[44] Spahn, *Lieber,* p. 45.

[45] The *Deutsche Reichs-zeitung* and the *Mainzer Journal,* February 4, 1895; the *Volksfreund,* February 15, 1895.

[46] August Bebel indicated in the crucial phase of the debates on the anti-revolution bill that there was considerable opposition to it in the south: *Briefwechsel mit Friedrich Engels,* p. 801. On the Center and the Pulpit Law: Rudolf von Buol to Albrecht zu Stotzingen, November 30, 1894. Buol-Stotzingen Correspondence. Hohenlohe, *Reichskanzlerzeit,* pp. 60–61.

[47] Karl Bachem to Julius Bachem, May 12, 1902. Bachem Papers, File 154.

[48] For the texts of the original and modified Rintelen motions: Bachem, *Zentrumspartei* **5**: p. 414.

[49] Karl Bachem, letter to Julius Bachem, May 12, 1902. See fn. 36 above.

[50] Spitzemburg, *Tagebuch,* p. 336.

[51] Bachem, *Zentrumspartei* **5**: pp. 387–389.

On the other hand Bachem took intense pride in his own role in persuading the Center to defeat the Cartel motion in honor of Bismarck. He argued that neither he nor his party were motivated so much by antagonism to the old chancellor as they were by their belief that they had to get rid of Albert von Levetzow, the Conservative president of the Reichstag, who stood under Bismarck's influence. Levetzow, whom the Center had always supported in elections for the presidency, had threatened to resign his office if the Cartel proposal were defeated.[52] It was true that Levetzow was under Bismarck's thumb and that a Conservative was an anachronism in the Reichstag presidency in view of the strong negative or even hostile feelings held by members of his party toward universal suffrage.[53]

Nevertheless, the conclusion is undoubtedly warranted that the decisions to make the anti-revolution bill intolerable to the government and its closest Reichstag allies by illiberal Center modifications and to deprive Bismarck of a Reichstag greeting on his anniversary were intimately related. Karl Bachem, Spahn, and Gröber had suffered painful exposure through their initial support of the controversial article 111a and were eager to restore their injured reputations as reliable Center representatives.[54] What better ways were there to restore them than by causing the defeat of the anti-revolution bill and in denying an honor to the hated Bismarck?

How widespread that feeling about the first chancellor was in Catholic circles had been clear enough to the Center leaders since early January. At that time Julius Bachem had apparently decided to test the feelings of northern Catholics on the subject of later honors for Bismarck. The city council of Cologne voted to send a gift to him on his birthday and Romanus Braubach, a Centrist member of the council and of the Reichstag, sided with the National Liberal majority in favor of the proposal. Poor Braubach immediately found himself in the eye of a press storm and the *Kölnische Volkszeitung* was isolated when it tried to defend Braubach by pointing out that the pope himself had once given Bismarck a high papal decoration. Though the worst attacks came from the integralist journals, the most significant aspect of the assault on Braubach was that editors near the middle of the Center spectrum, Lambert Lensing of Dortmund and Eugen Jäger of the Palatinate joined in the criticism.[55]

Braubach did not return to the Reichstag in the next session of 1895–1896[56] and the Center leaders learned a political lesson from the experience. In fact, Lieber's habit of attacking Bismarck in popular Catholic assemblies was to be an irritant in the relations between himself and the Free Conservative party with which the first chancellor had been so closely identified in the 1870's and 1880's.[57]

After the Center had caused the defeat of the Cartel motion to send Bismarck a formal greeting on his birthday, Levetzow had resigned his office. The Center, supported by the left side of the Reichstag, proceeded then to elect one of its own south German members, Rudolf von Buol, to the presidency. Buol was the son-in-law of Karl von Savigny, the first chairman of the Center, and was, despite his long-time friendship with Marschall von Bieberstein, welcome at the Prussian court.[58]

No doubt Lieber saw some political advantages in the replacement of a Conservative in the presidential chair by a member of his own party. In view of his own old dislike for the Conservatives and Levetzow himself, he must have taken some personal satisfaction in that action. The Center could not have afforded to elect a National Liberal in Levetzow's place because of the unpopularity of that party among the Catholic electorate. By assuming the presidency the Center combined its actual responsibility and power in the Reichstag with its most expressive symbol, the presidency, and made it easier for south German Catholics to identify themselves with the national parliament in Berlin.

The newest strain on the Center's relations with the monarch, the government, and the middle parties made Lieber eager to reach a compromise with Hohenlohe on the anti-revolution bill. His desire to justify a settlement with the government at the second reading in early May was evident in a speech that he gave in the Ruhr less than two weeks before that debate. He acknowledged that most Catholics, either for ideological or class reasons, still regarded right wing liberalism as the prime enemy, not Social Democracy. Lieber insisted that liberalism as an ideology was a danger but not political liberalism which was actually finished as a force in politics. The Social Democratic movement he added was not merely a political threat and the Catholic Church had been forced to found the Peoples' Association in 1890 to counter it. He recalled that August Bebel had repeatedly said his party sought three goals, the republic, socialism, and atheism.[59]

---

[52] Karl Bachem, undated notes, Bachem Papers, File 73.

[53] Lieber had complained a few years earlier about the unconstitutional conduct of Levetzow in the presidential chair: letter to Karl Bachem, May 28, 1892. Bachem Papers, File 67b.

[54] Gröber was later to make a bitter complaint about the abuse he and his two colleagues had suffered from some Catholic journals in the previous January. See below p. 55.

[55] The *Deutsche Reichs-zeitung* dealt with the incident in considerable detail on January 10 and 11, 1895. It chose to call Braubach's conduct "a scandal."

[56] Schwarz, *MdR Biographisches Handbuch der deutschen Reichstages*, p. 278.

[57] Wilhelm von Kardorff, *Verhandlungen des Reichstages*, November 16, 1896, p. 3281.

[58] Bachem, *Zentrumspartei* 5: pp. 401–403. His correspondence with Albrecht von Stötzingen reveals that William II cultivated him.

[59] At Laar: *Duisburger Volks-zeitung*, May 6, 1895.

Nevertheless, Lieber did not make an effort to secure an agreement between his party and the goverment in the course of the crucial reading on May 11, 1895. The reasons are obscure. Many Centrists from the Rhineland and various south German delegations favored the outright rejection of the bill and most likely some members from other regions were of the same mind.[60] The *Schlesische Volkszeitung* of Breslau stated two months earlier that the great majority of the Catholic people were, at least in its judgment, opposed to the anti-revolution bill.[61] On the other hand August Bebel, Marschall von Bieberstein, and Franz von Arenberg all believed that two Prussian ministers, Köller, the minister of the interior, and Schönstedt, the minister of justice, had prevented a compromise by their severe criticisms of the Reichstag and the Center during the second reading.[62] They were probably right, but Bebel pointed out that a compromise would have put a tremendous strain on the unity of the Center.[63] One can assume that such an agreement would have required the restoration of some of the sharp teeth in the original government bill and the abandonment of the modified Rintelen proposal. Because of the earlier activity of the conservative Catholic press, the acceptance of such a compromise would have been highly unpopular in Catholic circles. It was evident from statements made by Centrist leaders later in 1895 that most middle class Catholics and the clergy wanted to hear criticism of liberalism more than they did of Social Democracy.[64]

It was for the purpose of reestablishing the political authority of the Reichstag fraction over Center policies and tactics that the leaders apparently asked the officers of the Catholic press association to hold a special meeting in Berlin on May 20–21, 1895. Lieber did not attend but Heereman and Gröber undoubtedly presented his views; Julius Bachem was also absent but Heinrich Otto, Franz X. Bachem, the publisher of the *Kölnische Volkszeitung,* and Franz Hitze of the Rhineland Center probably spoke for him and the liberal editors of the Bachem press bloc. Karl Hauptmann,

whose *Deutsche Reichs-zeitung* had led the campaign against the anti-revolution bill, was the spokesman for the integralist and other conservative journals.[65]

Gröber was the chief speaker at the conference and gave a long position paper on the roles of the Reichstag fraction and the Center press in Catholic politics. His own bitterness over the abusive treatment he, Spahn, and Karl Bachem had experienced in certain conservative journals was markedly evident in his repeated reference to that experience. In his talk, however, he sought mainly to demonstrate the differences between the functions of the Center fraction and the press. Only the fraction and its leaders, Gröber insisted, adequately understood the compromises the Center, a minority party in a position of parliamentary leadership, had to make with the government and other parties in order to achieve its own goals and to carry out its responsibilities. The task of the press was to provide a theoretical treatment of political issues and to enlighten its readers. The press should support the fraction rather than make difficulties for it. Gröber's speech was both a reasoned statement of the leaders' conception of the correct roles of the fraction and Centrist newspapers in politics and a critique of the conduct of the conservative Catholic press in the recent debates on the anti-revolution bill.[66]

The earlier attacks on Karl Bachem, Spahn, and Gröber had been severe violations of Center etiquette and no one attempted to defend those newspapers in which they had appeared. But both conservative and liberal Catholic editors rejected Gröber's interpretation of the legitimate role of the press. Karl Hauptmann of the *Deutsche Reichs-zeitung* claimed that his newspaper had opposed the anti-revolution bill because of the large number of readers who wrote to the editors against it. And Heinrich Otto, an old foe of Hauptmann, insisted that the Center press was no longer in "its infant stage" since it possessed numerous editors schooled in higher politics. Otto also read a letter from a "veteran editor," most likely Julius Bachem, warning against any attempt to chain the Catholic press.[67]

The leading Center deputies wanted to improve relations with the Centrist and wider Catholic press but there were definite limits to the concessions they were willing to make to editors to achieve a healthier relationship between the party and the press. They were apparently afraid of any changes that could bring the party under the control of Julius Bachem and his press bloc. Heereman agreed that there should be more contacts between deputies and press representatives and that it was also desirable to strengthen the Center press bureau in Berlin. But he was emphatic in his insistence

[60] Bebel, *Briefwechsel mit Engels,* p. 801. Also the *Allgemeine Zeitung,* May 11, 1895. I doubt, however, that this prominent National Liberal journal was right in claiming that Gröber, one of Lieber's closest friends, had organized the Catholic opposition in the south to the bill.

[61] *Schlesische Volkszeitung,* March 12, 1895. This Center newspaper had turned overnight into a supporter of the Caprivi army bill in 1893, so I suspect that it reflected Cardinal Kopp's views on the anti-revolution bill. Viktor Rintelen, a deputy from Trier, probably expressed Bishop Korum's position on the measure. For William II's loss of confidence in them, Kraus, *Tagebücher,* p. 623.

[62] Spitzemberg *Tagebuch,* p. 337; Bebel, *Briefwechsel mit Engels,* p. 801.

[63] *Ibid.*

[64] Karl Bachem at the Munich Catholic Congress: *VGVkD zu München* (Munich, 1895), pp. 223–224. Lieber before a Catholic assembly at Stuttgart in mid-September, 1895. See fn. 74 below.

[65] Brochure, *Augustinus-Verein zur Plege der katholischen Presse,* ausserordentliche Versammlung, Berlin, May 20–21, 1895.

[66] *Ibid.* Kisky, *Augustinus-Verein,* pp. 168–169.

[67] Brochure, *Augustinus-Verein,* May 20–21, 1895.

that there could be no "press directory" in that city through which all information from the party to the press would have to flow. Some of his colleagues, undoubtedly at his insistence, flatly refused to approve Franz Hitze's proposal that a representative of the Augustine League be permitted to attend party sessions.[68] Nevertheless, the temper of many editors toward the party leadership must have improved as a consequence of the meeting since they cheered Lieber when he appeared for the first time at their Conference in May 1896.[69]

The year between the defeat of the anti-revolution bill and that reception was a cheerless period, however, and Lieber's mood was sometimes somber. His reconciliation with George von Hertling in the early summer of 1895 temporarily lifted his spirits since Hertling had been close to both the Silesian and Rhineland Centrists and the Bavarian royal family.[70] But the Center had not gained any ground in establishing a confidential relationship with the emperor and the middle parties nor had it strengthened the positions of the ministers friendly to it. Lieber was keenly aware that his continuation as leader would depend on his ability to influence key Prussian ministries, like the Ministry of Public Worship and Education and the Ministry of the Interior which controlled administrative appointments. He was obsessed with the belief that Cardinal Kopp was waiting for him to fail so that he could try to secure the appointment of an aristocratic conservative to the leadership of the Center.[71]

By the early fall of 1895 Lieber had become increasingly depressed over the difficulties that his party faced in trying to bridge the gap between itself and the emperor. William II had been undeterred by the defeat of the anti-revolution bill and Hohenlohe was too weak a chancellor to insist that a new legislative campaign against the Social Democrats was inadvisable. In the summer of 1894 Bismarck had taken the initiative in calling for an anti-Socialist legislative program and William II now wanted to take the sole credit for a new attempt of that nature. He and his privy advisers did not intend to risk a second defeat in the Reichstag but planned instead to take the apparently safer route through the Prussian Landtag where they expected to win the support of the Conservatives and the National Liberals. As he had done a year earlier, William II

issued a new call for a crusade against the Social Democrats who "were not worthy to bear the German name."[72] Sure of the ruler's enthusiastic support, Köller, the minister of the interior, intended to present the Prussian cabinet and then the Landtag with a bill which would permit the police to dissolve Social Democrat associations and prevent members of that party from holding assemblies.

Lieber's reaction to the announcement of a new anti-Socialist campaign was clear and emphatic. Two days after William II made his Sedan Day statement he wrote to Lujo Brentano "the Center is not going with the government through wind and litter and will not . . . so long as I amount to anything. It will be better to let the signals stand at renewed division."[73] In a public speech at a Catholic assembly on September 16, Lieber was more restrained in expression but his position on new extraordinary legislation against the Social Democrats was clear enough. He announced that his party was ready to participate in a campaign against revolutionary activity but that it would not deviate from constitutional principles. He and his associates had learned from the fiasco of the anti-revolution bill that many Catholics were unlikely to look favorably upon legislation aimed against the Social Democrats alone and in his speech he pointedly stressed the contribution of liberalism to modern revolutionary trends.[74] But the type of legislation which Köller and William II had in mind was dangerous to the basic civic liberties of all parties and hence intolerable to the Center.

In early December, Köller was suddenly dismissed from office. There was no apparent connection between that event and the Center's antagonism to his anti-Socialist plans; shortly afterward a prominent Centrist claimed that the minister's fall had come as a surprise to his party.[75] It was seemingly due to a disagreement between Köller and his colleagues in the Prussian Cabinet over the question of public court martials which Hohenlohe and the other Prussian ministers wanted William II and the Federal Council to introduce throughout the army. Köller revealed to some intimates that he had been the only minister to oppose the reform of court-martial procedure. Though the emperor was hostile to that reform and deeply attached to Köller, he bowed to the insistence of the other ministers that the minister of the interior be dismissed for breaching the secrecy of the Cabinet proceedings.[76]

The resentment of the ministers against their colleague may have been the actual cause of Köller's dismissal. But it is undoubtedly significant that the

---

[68] *Ibid.*

[69] Brochure, *Augustinus-Verein*, ausserordentliche Versammlung, Berlin, May 4–7, 1896. But Lieber may have owed the enthusiastic reception he received to the fact that he and the editors had vigorously opposed a few months earlier William II's sudden plans to expand the navy. See p. 58 below.

[70] See above ch. 3, p. 47.

[71] Lieber to Franz von Arenberg, July 12, 1895. Lieber Papers, Wrocław, File 95. He made it clear to Arenberg that Kopp was his rival for actual control of the Center. About a year later he wrote a Jesuit priest that the Curia was being led to believe, apparently by Kopp, that "Lieber achieves nothing." Lieber to Nix, October 18, 1896. Porsche Papers, IaN9.

[72] Hohenlohe, *Reichskanzlerzeit*, p. 92; Röhl, *Germany without Bismarck*, p. 138. Schulthess, *Geschichtskalender* **36** (1895): p. 178.

[73] September 4, 1895, Lieber Papers, Wrocław, File 93.

[74] *Niederrheinische Volkszeitung*, September 17, 1895.

[75] Buol to Albrecht zu Stotzingen, December 29, 1895. Buol-Stötzingen Correspondence.

[76] Röhl, *Germany without Bismarck*, pp. 142–146.

three most active members of the opposition to Köller in the Prussian Cabinet, Miquel, Marschall, and Walter Bronsart von Schellendorf, were close either to the National Liberal or Center parties. Like the Center, the National Liberal party was embarrassed by Köller's plans for a new anti-Socialist law which could endanger general civil liberties and its leaders had briefly considered the possibility in the early fall of introducing their own new anti-revolution bill.[77] Köller's going was undoubtedly as great a relief to Rudolf von Bennigsen and his colleagues as it was to Lieber and his leadership group.

Nevertheless, the removal of Köller from the government scene did not provide the Center with more than a brief breathing spell. Beginning with the advent of the Hohenlohe administration, William II's interests had fluctuated between a governmental assault on the Social Democrats and the expansion of the navy. On January 18, 1896, approximately six weeks after his dismissal of the Prussian minister of the interior, he made his historic *Weltpolitik* speech in which he announced that Germany's future lay on the water.

After becoming leader of the Center Lieber had recognized the crucial importance of the naval question in the relations between his party and the monarch. In early 1894 he took over the position of reporter for the budget committee on the naval budget.[78] He found he had a major task to perform in changing his party's essentially negative attitude toward the navy. In contrast to the army, the navy had no physical or sentimental association with the west or south where most Catholics lived and it was, unlike the army, a strictly Imperial institution whose officers were solely subject to the emperor in Berlin. Unable to make meaningful economies in the army's budget, Centrist deputies imposed them on the navy prior to 1894. Alois Fritzen, the financial expert of the Rhineland delegation and the then Reichstag reporter for the naval budget, had said in November, 1892, that no party had "fewer naval enthusiasts among its members" than the Center.[79] In theory the party was willing to support a navy capable of defending the national coasts and breaking through a blockade, in practice it had refused to accept the responsibility of providing for the regular replacement of obsolete ships for that purpose. Lieber's first triumph as reporter for the naval budget was to convince his party and the Reichstag in March, 1894, that it

should accept the principle of regular substitution of new ships for those no longer fit for active service.[80]

From 1890 to 1894 Caprivi, obsessed with Germany's need for military security in central Europe, had restrained the naval ambitions of the emperor and the naval high command. Under the weaker Hohenlohe, William II found more scope for his own naval and colonial ambitions. In the Reichstag the National Liberals and the Free Conservatives, the so-called "national parties," fretted over Caprivi's lack of interest in colonial acquisition and a wider world role for the Reich. Therefore, Hohenlohe's first budget called for the building of four new cruisers and additional responsibilities for the navy. It was to protect German commerce and citizens abroad and show the flag in remote parts of the world.[81]

The size of the naval budget and the navy's new missions posed uncomfortable problems for the Center. Lieber and the Rhineland Centrists had agreed to stress economy in the forthcoming budget. The Center had earlier acknowledged that the navy, in addition to the defense of the home coasts and harbors, should protect the colonies and the economic interests of German businessmen in a few scattered areas where there was no strong governmental authority. By comparison with them, the new functions of the navy appeared to be open-ended. Before the opening of the Reichstag session of 1894–1895 the *Kölnische Volkszeitung* warned "we cannot send a fleet of armored cruisers to foreign seas. . . . We have to limit ourselves to the defense of our coasts and build up our army." [82]

Unlike the editors of the *Kölnische Volkszeitung*, Lieber was willing to approve both the naval budget and the new policy. He kept his actual views to himself but in his report to the Reichstag on the debates in the Budget Committee over the naval budget he attached high importance to the remarks that the secretary of state for foreign affairs had made to that body. Marschall had "demonstrated convincingly" how dependent the German nation was on the security of its import and export trade. The Centrist leader added that neither the Foreign Office or the Naval Secretariat felt that it could take the responsibility for the safety of German commerce unless the navy were strengthened.[83] The likelihood was, however, that Hohenlohe, Marschall, and Lieber had more compelling political reasons for advocating the course on naval policy they favored. There had been a bittter rivalry throughout 1894 for the confidence of William II between moderate

---

[77] The *Kölnische Volkszeitung* on September 11, 1895, and *Germania* on September 28, 1895, both reported that the National Liberals were then thinking of introducing their own anti-revolution bill: quoted in the *HpB* **120** (1897) : p. 388.

[78] Alois Fritzen, the previous reporter for the naval budget, was apparently critically ill at the time that Lieber replaced him: Lieber Journal, February 6, 1894.

[79] *Verhandlungen des Reichstages*, February 27, 1892; p. 4420.

[80] Hans Hallmann, *Der Weg zum deutschen Schlachtflottenbau*, Beiträge zur Geschichte der nachbismarckischen Zeit und das Weltkrieges. **14/15** (Stuttgart, 1935) : p. 95.

[81] From Lieber's report to the Reichstag: *Verhandlungen des Reichstages*. March 1, 1895: p. 1180.

[82] *Kölnische Volkszeitung*, November 2, 1894. Fritzen had delivered the same warning in the Reichstag over a year earlier: *Reichstag Verhandlungen*, March 3, 1893: p. 1494.

[83] *Ibid.*, March 1, 1895: p. 1180.

navalists like Admiral Hollmann, the secretary of the navy, and certain high naval officers, among them Captain Tirpitz, who called for the construction of a battleship navy which would operate on the high seas and enable Germany to act as a great maritime power. Lieber was convinced that his party had to support the course advocated by the Imperial ministers if it did not want to be confronted with the more extreme policy. Either he or one of his closest colleagues told Hollmann during the session of 1894–1895 that his party would never approve a battleship navy "to be used for offensive ends."[84]

Nevertheless, it was remarkable that the Center voted for all four of the cruisers in the budget and even William II was pleasantly surprised that it did so. Most members of the party knew that the Center's relations with the emperor could not deteriorate any further since William II had ignored Lieber at the court ball in early February, 1895. The debates on the naval budget took place in early March when it was evident that the Center would not support the anti-revolution bill in the form which the government and the National Liberals desired.[85] By accepting the whole naval budget, the Center hoped to soften the resentment the ruler would feel against it if the party eventually rejected the anti-revolution measure. That calculation was certainly realistic enough. But neither the Center's approval of the naval budget in March, 1895, nor its rejection of the anti-revolution bill a few months later were to dissuade William II from his crusade against the Social Democratic movement. The Center's inability to support the emperor in that undertaking was to have some influence on its response to the ruler's naval programs.

In the next three years the Center was faced with a new situation where naval policy was concerned. Despite Hollmann's success with the naval budget in March, 1895, the emperor became impatient with the gradualness of the program of naval expansion dictated by the Center's control over expenditures. The German government had intervened with Russia and France in the settlement of the Sino-Japanese War in the spring of 1895 with a view to the eventual acquisition of a naval base on the coast of China. In the fall of the same year it had sided with the Boer states of southern Africa, the Transvaal, and the Orange River Colony in their differences with Great Britain, their suzerain. William II, profoundly upset by the abortive attempt of British imperialists to overthrow the government of Transvaal brought on a serious crisis with the British government through his telegram of January 3, 1896, to President Krüger of the Transvaal which affirmed Germany's recognition of the sovereignty of the two Boer states.

After Germany's involvement in Far Eastern affairs the emperor demonstrated renewed frustration over the

relative weakness of the navy. His resentment deepened as relations between the German and British governments became more tense during the late fall and early winter of 1895. But he was also eager to exploit the sudden explosion of anti-British feeling among the German middle classes to convince the pro-government parties they should approve a large-scale building program of cruisers to be financed by loans and to be undertaken after the passage of the regular naval budget. At a conference which Hohenlohe held with representatives of the Center, Conservative, and National Liberal parties on January 13, the parliamentarians were unenthusiastic about the ruler's plan. Fritzen, the Center's envoy, was firm in his insistence the Center would have enough to do to bring about the acceptance of the budget because of the forthcoming parliamentary elections of 1898.[86] William II decided then to employ the tactic he had used in introducing the earlier campaigns against the Social Democrats; he appealed directly to public opinion as a means of putting pressure upon the Reichstag parties by making his widely publicized *Weltpolitik* speech of January 18.

Lieber, his leading Reichstag associates, and the *Kölnische Volkszeitung* were alarmed over the ruler's assumption of personal and public leadership in the formulation of naval policy. In the previous Reichstag session Lieber had tried to reassure his colleagues regarding the government's naval plans with the confident statement that "all limitless plans for the future are private music."[87] He assumed prior to January, 1896, that the Reichstag would have to do nothing more than approve a conventional naval budget. But it was evident to the Centrist leader and his colleagues, as he stated in the Budget Committee after the ruler's speech, that William II was listening to other advisers than his ministers. Those persons were "intriguing" to bring about the replacement of the present ministers so that they could commit the government to adventuresome plans in foreign and domestic affairs.[88] Nevertheless, Lieber restricted his critical remarks to the Budget Committee and to conversations with government officials. The *Kölnische Volkszeitung* and leading Rhineland Centrists recognized the threat of the new *Weltpolitik* to the Center's traditional course on naval policy and attacked it vigorously, directly, and publicly.[89]

The restraint of the Centrist leader may have been rooted in profound concern about the basic political situation in Berlin. William II's preference for personal rule had become evident in the previous year in

84 Hallmann, *Weg nach Schlachtflottenbau*, p. 155.
85 See above p. 53.

86 Hohenlohe, *Reichskanzlerzeit*, p. 137.
87 *Verhandlungen des Reichstages*, February 28, 1895: p. 1175.
88 Apparently made in January, 1896: *HpB* **119** (1897): p. 229.
89 The *Kölnische Volkszeitung* remarked on January 25, 1896, that the pursuit of *Weltpolitik* could be the worst thing that could happen to Germany. Fritzen compared the *Weltpolitik* of a nation with the "serious delusions" of an individual. *Verhandlungen des Reichstages*, March 18, 1896: p. 1537.

his encouragement of Köller's plans for new anti-Socialist legislation and his stubborn opposition to the reform of court-martial procedures. His insistence in January, 1896, in accelerating naval construction was further evidence in that direction. There were signs that some advisers and other persons around the emperor desired a confrontation and conflict between him and the Reichstag. Courtiers, prominent generals, ministers like Miquel and General Bronsart von Schellendorf, and leading Conservatives all advocated the abolition of universal suffrage in Reichstag elections. Lieber's and Gröber's speeches in the parliament in January, 1896,[90] and the leader's correspondence with Karl zu Löwenstein in March of that year [91] revealed their fear that high persons in the ruler's Prussian entourage with the connivance of conservative Catholic dignitaries like Ballestrem and Löe would attempt to do away with popular franchise.

The crisis between the Center and the government over the naval question was seemingly resolved during the budget debates. The key to its resolution was apparently Lieber's success in convincing his Rhineland colleagues that the responsible ministers were in possession of William II's confidence once again. Marschall had come into the Budget Committee in February and made the assertion that the government had no ambitious naval plans in mind. Fritzen expressed the confidence of his party in the person of Admiral Hollmann, but made it clear that it was based on the Center's assumption that the secretary of the navy would commit the government to a modest plan for further naval building and not confront the Reichstag with new surprises. The Center, he stated, had decided itself, however, that the best way to save the parliament from "limitless plans" was to approve what was indispensable for the navy.[92]

That harmony owed much, however, to successful collaboration between the Center, the middle parties, and the government on the passage of the new civil law code which had been in preparation for twenty years. In the 1870's the Center under Windthorst had opposed the initiation of the work on the Code whereas the National Liberals had been enthusiastically in favor of it.[93] Lieber and his colleagues decided they had to take both a positive stand on the Code and the leading position in the Reichstag deliberations on its provisions. To the disappointment of the National Liberals, the Center insisted that the most eminent jurist in its own ranks, Peter Spahn, should be the chairman of the special committee which drafted the final version for the Reichstag's consideration.[94] It was an opportunity for the Center to demonstrate to the emperor and the "national" middle parties that it was capable of taking responsibility for legislation which was unpopular in some Catholic circles.

The most sensitive issue for the Center's leaders in the Reichstag deliberations on the Code was that of the introduction of obligatory secular marriage. To Catholics marriage was not simply a contract of a very special kind but a sacramental relationship which could not be dissolved. It was painful for some of them, uncomfortable for others, that members of their church had to appear first for a civil marriage ceremony before the religious rites. On the other hand Catholics in the Prussian Rhineland had been accustomed to the institution of civil marriage since Napoleonic times and those in the rest of Prussia since the passage of the civil marriage law of 1875. Though the Windthorst Center had voted against that measure, the bishops had always instructed members of the Church to obey the laws on civil marriage. According to Lieber the Catholic Church recognized the validity of the civil marriage ceremony in mixed marriages between Catholics and non-Catholics.[95] The question in 1896 was whether the Catholics of the Center should take responsibility for its incorporation in the new Civil Code and application in other parts of the Reich.

In mid-May, 1896, Lieber was uncertain whether the highest officials of the Catholic Church in Germany and Rome would permit the Center to approve the codification of civil marriage.[96] The bulk of the Conservatives had refused to go along with a proposal of some of its members that it collaborate with the Center to make civil marriage voluntary. After that failure the Center had moved into negotiations with the National Liberals on the question of the acceptance of civil marriage as the norm. Leading conservative Catholic journals, like the *Deutsche Reichs-zeitung* and the *Mainzer Journal*, supported by Löe's *Rheinische Volksstimme* violently opposed such an agreement.[97] It is likely they represented the views of the bishops of Trier and Mainz, Korum and Haffner. If such was the case, Cardinal Kopp may have contributed significantly to securing a favorable decision from the Vatican in favor of the agreement since he advocated its acceptance.[98]

In return for the Center's concession on the institution of obligatory civil marriage the government, the National Liberals, and the Free Conservatives were

---

[90] Gröber, *ibid.,* January 29, 1896: pp. 607–608; *ibid.,* pp. 612–614.

[91] See above p. 49, fn. 16.

[92] Fritzen also expressed confidence in Hollmann saying that he knew the secretary of the navy would not pull any surprises on the Reichstag. March 18, 1896: p. 1536.

[93] Bachem, *Zentrumspartei* 5: p. 424.

[94] Hermann Oncken, *Rudolf von Bennigsen. Ein deutscher liberaler Politiker* (2 v., Stuttgart, 1910) 2: p. 398.

[95] Lieber to Lujo Brentano, September 4, 1896. Lieber Papers, Camberg.

[96] Lieber Journal, May 4, 1896.

[97] Lieber to Brentano, September 4, 1896. Fn. 81 above. He told Brentano he became a "deliberate heretic" to wide circles in Mainz.

[98] Bachem, *Zentrumspartei* 5: pp. 446–447.

willing to make some of their own to the Center and its church. Under existing law women separated from their husbands but not divorced were denied a share of their common property, a legal provision which worked hardship on Catholic women who had left their husbands' homes. The new Civil Code stipulated they would now be entitled to part of the joint property.

There was also a compromise involving a revision of the laws of association which would in the future provide religious societies with the same legal rights as those existing for a social or economic purpose. And finally the government and middle parties agreed to a proposal which permitted the churches to receive financial gifts up to five thousand marks without government approval.[99]

The Centrist leaders and Cardinal Kopp had undoubtedly hoped for a more generous recognition of the Center's contribution to the success of the Civil Code legislation. On two earlier occasions a Reichstag majority made up of the Center and the left of the chamber had passed a Centrist motion asking for the revocation of the anti-Jesuit law. During the debates on the Civil Code the leaders of the National Liberals and the Free Conservatives agreed to support a more modest Liberal proposal calling for the deletion of the second or expulsion article from that law. The Imperial government, aware of the extensive Protestant opposition to any change in the status of the religious orders affected by the law and the opposition of most of the state governments to any revision, chose to ignore the Reichstag's action.[100]

Despite that setback, Lieber was in high spirits at the closing of the Reichstag in late June, 1896. His party and the Reichstag had been able to log two positive accomplishments of political importance in the previous parliamentary session—the passage of the budget, inclusive of the parts on the navy, and the Civil Code. Its critics could not honestly claim that the Reichstag led by the Center was a "do-nothing" parliamentary body. But part of his satisfaction came from the successful collaboration with the National Liberals and Free Conservatives on both important legislative measures. The leaders of the Free Conservatives, Karl von Stumm-Halberg, the prominent Saar industrialist, and Wilhelm von Kardorff, a prominent agrarian, had considerable influence at court. The National Liberals had less influence with the ruler and his entourage but the more responsible advisers of William II had always been sensitive to their views. The leaders of that party, Rudolf von Bennigsen and Friedrich Hammacher, were also more reliable on basic constitutional questions than their allies of the Free Conservative party. Both parties, representatives of the well-to-do Protestant bourgeoisie, were keenly aware that they faced increas-

ing difficulties at Reichstag elections and wanted to win the Center's help in the elections of 1898.[101]

To Lieber's acute disillusionment the parliamentary session of 1896–1897 proved to be the worst of his brief career as the Center's leader. William II had become increasingly impatient with the budgetary conservatism of the secretary of the navy and insisted that the new budget be substantially larger than that of the previous year. Nor was Hollmann able to present a plan to the Reichstag which he had promised the parliament in the spring. There is widespread evidence that William II was ready for a showdown with the Reichstag which would either enable him to impose his own will on the parliament in naval matters or justify his dismissal of Hollmann, Marschall, and other ministers who he thought were too accommodating to the Center party.[102] But at the first caucus of the Center in late November, Lieber was confronted with rebellion in his own fraction when it discussed the budget and especially its naval parts.[103]

Julius Bachem and Hermann Cardauns had watched the growth of monarchical personal government and the ruler's emphasis on naval expansion with marked concern. They were looking ahead to the elections of 1898 and to a new test of strength with the Social Democrats. They did not want the Center to be burdened with the responsibility for added indirect taxes on the lower classes. Bachem and Cardauns were in a particularly sensitive mood about naval policy during the session of 1896–1897 because William II's schemes, such as they were, threatened to undermine the Center's plans to secure greater economy in government operations and to continue the passage of additional legislation to reduce the national debt. Alois Fritzen had called for such a reform in November, 1893, and the government and the Reichstag had approved a Center motion for the reduction of the debt in the session of 1895–1896.[104] The Rhineland Centrists thought the government should give priority to the legislative management of the social problem rather than expend large sums of money on unclear plans for naval expansion.[105]

There is no concrete evidence that the Rhineland Centrists were in league with Friedrich von Holstein,

---

[99] *Ibid.*, pp. 434–435, 442.
[100] *Ibid.* **8**: pp. 289–290.

[101] Wilhelm von Kardorff had begun negotiations with the Center in an effort to win its support in some western constituencies in the elections of 1898: S. von Kardorff, *Wilhelm von Kardorff*, p. 319.
[102] See Röhl, *Germany without Bismarck*, pp. 182–199.
[103] Hallmann, *Weg nach Schlachtflottenbau*, p. 215.
[104] Fritzen: *Verhandlungen des Reichstages*, November 23, 1893; for the so-called "Lieber laws" of debt reduction of 1896 and 1897 see Spahn, *Lieber*, pp. 49–51; also Bachem, *Zentrumspartei* **9**: pp. 215–220. Bachem says that Fritzen's first demand for a policy of debt reduction dated from 1895; his first initiative was actually part of the Rhineland Center's assault on Miquel's financial program of 1893–1894.
[105] Karl Bachem, *Verhandlungen des Reichstages*, March 20, 1897: pp. 5214–5215.

the forceful senior councilor of the Foreign Office, who was trying to create a united front of Prussian ministers and Imperial secretaries of state against William II's attempts to exercise personal government. But Franz von Arenberg, the Rhineland Centrist deputy, and Marschall von Bieberstein were close friends, and Arenberg visited the Foreign Office from time to time.[106] That there was an alignment of fronts between the *Kölnische Volkszeitung* and the left-wing liberals and their leading organ, the *Frankfurter Zeitung,* was undoubtedly true since they were both severely critical of the new trends in naval and foreign policy and the heightened expenditures to which they led.[107] The *Frankfurter Zeitung* was widely read in the Catholic areas of the southwest and south,[108] probably even more than the *Kölnische Volkszeitung* itself. Like Eugen Richter and other left-liberals the Rhineland and Bavarian Centrists were also unhappy over the new anti-British and pro-Russian trends in German foreign policy. During the Anglo-German crisis of January, 1896, the *Historische-politische Blätter,* a stern critic of the Hohenlohe administration, had quoted with marked approval an earlier statement from the *Kölnische Volkszeitung:*

Austria and England are the great states with whom we feel ourselves most related; and an alliance with Russia is unsympathetic; but what comes even more into consideration, we hold it to be impossible.[109]

In mid-November, 1896, revelations by Bismarck regarding the earlier secret treaty of 1887–1890 between Germany and Russia set off a debate in the Reichstag in which the left-liberals attacked the current pro-Russian diplomatic orientation of the Reich. That debate imposed a severe strain on Lieber's oratorical acrobatics. In earlier public assemblies he had sharply attacked Bismarck, an easy target in any popular Catholic gathering, but then defended the government's foreign policy in the Reichstag. The *Kölnische Volkszeitung* tactfully chose to say something affirmative about both the Center and the left-liberal speakers.[110]

A new coolness had suddenly sprung up between the editors of the *Kölnische Volkszeitung* and Lieber in the mid-summer of 1896. Several weeks after the Reichstag had closed its doors the Cologne journal carried a lead article on the contributions of numerous prominent Centrists to the approval of the new Civil Law Code. Lieber was the only leading member of the Reichstag fraction who was not mentioned, a fact that caused him considerable distress.[111] The probable cause of the new breach between the editors and Lieber was the widely publicized visit of the Center leader to the naval dockyards with the naval secretary and the leading budget specialist of the Conservative party.[112] Some weeks before the opening of the Reichstag, Julius Bachem sent a "friendly counsel" to Lieber that he should follow Windthorst's example of not exposing himself too much to the public.[113]

The course of the Reichstag session of 1896–1897 demonstrated clearly that Julius Bachem hoped to shove Lieber into a corner in the naval debates. The attack on the naval budget at the first Center caucus in late November was somewhat reminiscent of the harsh assault that Karl Bachem and Fritzen had made on Miquel's finance plan of 1893–1894. At both the first reading of the budget shortly afterward and again in the early spring of 1897 Fritzen and Karl Bachem made it clear they were directly attacking the emperor's own policy of *Weltpolitik* as they had done in the first months of 1896. It would be difficult to find any more severe critique of the new foreign and naval policy after its inception than Fritzen's statement regarding the Center's policy:

We do not wish to chase after the phantom of an erroneous *Welpolitik* by which a once great imperial dynasty was ruined and with it the strength and glory of the old Reich.[114]

Indeed Fritzen's warning was more prophetic than he could have realized. Although William II aggravated his already bad relations with the Reichstag still further in the early months of 1897, the most important step that Julius Bachem wanted his party to take followed logically from the stand the *Kölnische Volkszeitung* and prominent Rhenish Centrists had assumed since the emperor's first advocacy of *Weltpolitik.* On March 15 Bachem urged his party colleagues in Berlin to make a formal protest in the Reichstag on behalf of the people against the Emperor's abuse of his constitutional powers. They advised him, however, that such an act would only add to the ruler's dislike for Catholics.[115]

Despite his original pessimism over the initial reaction of his fraction to the naval budget Lieber continued in the session of 1896–1897 to pursue his own traditional strategy. He hoped to demonstrate to William

[106] Röhl, *Germany without Bismarck,* pp. 118–199; Rich, *Holstein* 2: chapters 35–38. Holstein once quoted an offensive remark which William II had made in Arenberg's presence about the Reichstag in the summer of 1896: *Holstein Papers* 3: p. 657. And see Hohenlohe, *Reichskanzlerzeit,* pp. 11, 26.

[107] The *Historisch-politische Blätter* referred in its early issues of 1897 to the criticisms that the two newspapers and left liberal politicians had been making of William II's actions: **119** (1897): p. 229 ff., 464 ff.

[108] Gröber: speech to the Augustine League, May 20, 1895. See above fn. 53.

[109] *HpB* **117** (1896): p. 138.

[110] *Kölnische Volkszeitung,* November 17, 1896.

[111] *Kölnische Volkszeitung,* July 30, 1896. Karl Trimborn to Lieber, August 6, 1896, Lieber Papers, Speyer, T 15. Trimborn, Bachem's longtime aide and Lieber's friend, tactfully wrote the Center leader that he did not know why he had been ignored in the article.

[112] *HpB* **118** (1896): p. 202.

[113] Lieber to Thoemes, October 19, 1896, Lieber Papers, Wrocław, File 131.

[114] See fn. 1 above.

[115] Röhl, *Germany without Bismarck,* p. 216.

II that the Center was a friend of the navy and to prove that the Emperor could secure the bulk of his demands by relying upon his ministers, who had the confidence of the Center, and upon the usual mechanisms of the Budget Committee and the Reichstag. He undoubtedly used the argument with his colleagues that it was in the Center's best interest to support Hollmann and Hohenlohe by passing most of the naval budget. But the ruler's conduct only served to strengthen the opposition to Lieber's course in the Center.[116] In attempts to sway its decision on the budget, he threatened on several occasions to dissolve the Reichstag and to establish a Cartel coalition if the budget were not approved. And during the deliberations the hapless secretary of the navy sought to save it by claiming that the government really wanted a navy capable of taking the offensive on the high seas. All things considered it was not surprising that the Center and the Reichstag deleted the funds for two cruisers from the budget and that Lieber blamed the crisis caused by that action on the emperor himself. The crisis was artificial to a substantial extent since the parliament had actually doubled the amount of money it had approved for the navy in the previous session.[117]

But Lieber and the other Center leaders, inclusive of the Rhineland Centrists in the fraction, recognized the political weakness of their own position. Lieber's colleagues had wanted to teach William II a lesson in constitutional government and to impress upon him the wisdom of relying upon his ministers; they intended to give him his two cruisers in the next session if he did so.[118] The presence in office of moderate ministers was the front line of the Center's defense, though hardly one that provided security. The attachment of the Center to ministers like Hohenlohe, Marschall, and Bötticher, the Imperial secretary of the interior, was evident in its leaders' response to a painful incident that occurred on April 24. On that date William II sent a telegram to his brother, Admiral Prince Henry, in which he spoke of the "unpatriotic fellows" in the Reichstag, by whom he meant the members of the Center party. Prince Henry read the telegram to his officers and crew. Lieber advised Marschall that his party would interpellate the government on the incident. But he readily dropped the matter when Hohenlohe told him that it would lead to his dismissal and

that of other ministers friendly to the Center.[119] If the chancellor fell, Lieber apparently assumed that Eulenburg was likely to take his place. Eulenburg's appointment would lead to the restoration of Cardinal Kopp's influence.

Nevertheless, Lieber and his party were unable to avoid a direct conflict with their ruler. On February 20, William II had issued a call for a new legislative campaign against the Social Democrats, the opponents whose organized existence was a constant affront to him. During the debates on the Civil Code, Hohenlohe had promised the Reichstag that he would introduce a more liberal law of association to the Prussian Landtag eliminating old restrictions on political societies. Instead he presented a reactionary measure which virtually contained only provisions against associations and assemblies which the police deemed to be dangerous to the state. They could readily dissolve and prevent political meetings. The Center felt that it could not compromise with the Prussian government on questions of fundamental civil rights. Fortunately Rudolf von Bennigsen and his associates in the National Liberal party were of the same mind; the two parties stood shoulder to shoulder in concerted opposition to the bill, causing its defeat in late May.[120] It was to be the last governmental effort to strike directly at the Social Democratic political organization itself.

But Lieber must have wondered in the early summer of 1897 whether the triumph of the Center in the struggle against the ruler's anti-Socialist campaign was not a Pyrrhic victory. It was one thing for the National Liberals to fight against the Prussian monarchy over one of the two major issues of serious concern to William II, another for the Center to do so. The National Liberals remained in some degree a part of the state establishment to which the Center did not and probably could not belong under the Hohenzollern dynasty. They had helped to defeat the association bill, but had identified themselves with the cause of naval expansion while the Center had collided with the monarch over both policies.

What the cost of that opposition might be had become evident to Lieber between the end of March and the last days of June. Admiral Hollmann had to leave office after the naval debates in the Reichstag and was replaced by Admiral Tirpitz. Then after a hiatus of over two months William II disposed of Marschall von Bieberstein and Heinrich von Bötticher, old Center friends, who were succeeded by Bernhard von Bülow, an earlier Bismarck subordinate, and Arthur von Posadowsky-Wehner, the former secretary of the treasury. Hohenlohe remained but he was increasingly ineffective as an influence on the monarch. Even though Botho zu Eulenburg remained out of high office, the German

116 After the heat of the final debates on the budget the *Kölnische Volkszeitung* pointedly remarked that the Center was no longer willing to make sacrifices to keep Hohenlohe: April 8, 1897, quoted in the *HpB* 119 (1897): pp. 844–845.

117 Hallmann, *Das Weg nach Schlachtflottenbau*, pp. 227–232; Jonathan Steinberg, *Yesterday's Deterrent. Tirpitz and the Birth of the German Battle Fleet* (New York, 1965), pp. 110–114. On the amount approved by the Reichstag: Müller-Fulda, *Verhandlungen des Reichstages*, March 18, 1897: p. 5159.

118 Arenberg to Princess Radziwill: Marie Princesse de Radziwill, *Lettres de la princesse Radziwill au general de Robilant, 1889–1914* (4 v. Bologna, 1933–1934) 2: p. 73.

119 Hohenlohe, *Reichskanzlerzeit*, p. 332.

120 Röhl, *Germany without Bismarck*, pp. 225–229; Steinberg, *Yesterday's Deterrent*, pp. 118–119.

monarchy appeared to be moving to the right. It is little wonder that Lieber turned to his old foe, Cardinal Kopp, and spoke gravely "of the heavy and fateful crisis in which we [German Catholics] now stand." [121]

5. THE CENTER AND THE FIRST NAVAL BILL OF 1898

It was the profound tragedy of the German Empire that the decisions which determined its domestic and external positions in 1914 were concentrated from 1897 to 1902 and the contemporaries of this colossal crisis were not conscious of its ultimate importance.
Eckart Kehr [1]

. . . this Reichstag is confronted with one of the most serious, weightiest decisions imaginable which could ever concern a German Reichstag.
Lieber, December, 1897 [2]

The debates on naval budgets between 1894 and 1897 had demonstrated the increasing significance and sensitivity of the naval question for the relations between the monarchy and the Center. The parliamentary session of 1897–1898 was to be crucial for those relations. The Center's record on the budgets in the mid-1890's had been good, but it had been hostile to any program stressing the building of battleships and uninterested in any plan to elevate Germany to the status of a first-class naval power. Its leaders, under prodding from the Rhineland Centrists and secular left-liberals like Eugen Richter, had insisted that the government should present a binding plan for naval construction; the Center itself wanted, however, to hold onto its right of modifying the annual budget. In the fall of 1897 Admiral Tirpitz, the new secretary of the navy, presented a bill to the Reichstag which put particular emphasis upon battleship construction and on a legal commitment from the Reichstag to fund the program over a period of seven years. Like Ballestrem and Huene in 1892, Lieber and his intimates were confronted with a major defense measure which was difficult to approve or reject.

Throughout the summer and fall of 1897 the Center press reacted unfavorably to the reports concerning the nature of the proposed Tirpitz bill.[3] The more experienced members of the Imperial and Prussian governments, Hohenlohe, Posadowsky, and Miquel, did not believe that the Center would ratify the bill in its original form. The old chancellor was particularly aware of the nervousness among some Centrists, probably those from the Rhineland and industrial Westphalia, about the forthcoming parliamentary elections of 1898.[4] Un-

like the costs projected by the Caprivi army proposals of 1892 and 1893, those defined in the Tirpitz program were not an inflammatory issue in the Centrist press discussion of the measure. The German economy was now in a period of new prosperity and the Imperial government enjoyed enough of a surplus to support the projected new building from the Treasury reserves. The critical issue was the provision in the bill that the Reichstag should bind itself to the execution of the building proposals through a Septennat. There seemed to be no possibility of a compromise between the Center and the secretary of the navy on that point. The Center's influence depended primarily on its control over the budget; it was not in its interests to sacrifice the right to approve or disapprove naval expenditures, especially at a time when the government planned significant expansion of the fleet.

In the summer of 1897 Lieber made a serious effort to secure the deletion of the Septennat provision from the Tirpitz plan.[5] He and Miquel apparently worked out an agreement whereby the Center would provide assistance to the Free Conservatives and the National Liberals in the national and Prussian parliamentary elections of 1898 in return for Miquel's support for the Center's views on the naval plan. Lieber was undoubtedly hopeful that the emperor's longtime respect for Miquel's judgment would give the Prussian finance minister greater influence over William II on that issue than Tirpitz wielded. Hohenlohe, Posadowsky, Philipp zu Eulenburg, the ruler's friend, and apparently Bülow as well were all in favor of a compromise on the naval bill which respected the particular concerns of the Center.[6]

Miquel's commitment to the Center on the troublesome question of the Septennat was undoubtedly serious enough, for he greatly wanted the party's help for the Free Conservatives and the National Liberals in the next elections. Relations between the Conservatives and the National Liberals had been seriously strained by their differences over the Caprivi commercial treaties and more recently over the abortive Prussian bill of associations. Miquel hoped to restore their old electoral alliance by underscoring their mutual antagonism to the Social Democrats and left-liberals in a policy of *Sammlung* or concentration. But he knew that the Cartel parties were not popular enough in the west and southwest to do well in the elections without the aid of the Center, and he wanted that party to become a partial and silent partner of the Cartel's electoral alliance.[7] There were to be indications in June,

---

[121] Lieber to Kopp: June 14, 1897. Lieber Papers, Speyer, File 219.

[1] *Schlachtflottenbau und Parteipolitik, 1894–1901* (Historische Studien, Heft 197) (Berlin, 1930), p. 207.

[2] *Verhandlungen des Reichstages,* December 7, 1897: p. 82.

[3] For the reaction of the Center press to the bill: Kehr, *Schlachtflottenbau,* pp. 75–84.

[4] Hallmann, *Weg nach Schlachtflottenbau,* pp. 268, 275.

[5] On the prime importance that prominent Centrists and the Center's press attached to the Reichstag's retention of its annual budget right: Kehr, p. 84; Hallmann, p. 268.

[6] Hallmann, *ibid.*

[7] On Miquel's policy of *Sammlung* see Röhl, *Germany without Bismarck,* p. 246. Röhl and other historians who have dealt with it are unaware of the Center's modest involvement in that plan.

1898, that Lieber had made agreements with leaders of the Free Conservative and National Liberal parties to provide support to some of their members.[8]

In the past the *Kölnische Volkszeitung* and the Rhineland Center had adhered firmly to the old Windthorst tradition that the party should not support either National Liberals or Free Conservatives in elections because of their prominent roles in the Kulturkampf. But the hostility of many Conservatives to the Reichstag and the backing they gave to the repressive Prussian associations bill had made a definite impression on Julius Bachem and Hermann Cardauns as did the efforts of the National Liberals to uphold constitutional government in the Reich and Prussia. They now acknowledged that the Center could throw support in elections to National Liberal candidates when the conditions were appropriate.[9] It is likely that they expected Miquel to bring about a major modification of the Tirpitz bill in return for the pledge of Centrist assistance to some National Liberal or Free Conservative candidates in the elections of June, 1898.[10]

By the later part of August it was clearly evident that Miquel had less influence with William II on the navy question than Tirpitz and Admiral Senden, the emperor's personal naval adviser and a rabid navalist. The Prussian minister of finance had made a determined effort to live up to his end of the agreement with Lieber. He told Captain Capelle, Tirpitz's deputy on political affairs, that the naval bill could not pass in face of the Center's opposition and he himself wrote against the measure in the *Norddeutsche Allgemeine Zeitung,* the organ of the Prussian government. But Miquel had probably weakened his own position in advance by telling Tirpitz and the emperor that the government would not need to ask the Reichstag for new taxes to fund the naval program. In late August, William II forbade him to write any more articles on the bill and in early September a conference of high Imperial and Prussian officials over which the ruler presided approved the Tirpitz plan.[11]

Lieber was ready for such a contingency. He had not anticipated at any time the possibility of pitting his person and party against the emperor on the naval bill, but he had hoped the chancellor, Miquel, and their colleagues would prevail over Tirpitz on the objectional issue of the Septennat. During his August talks with Miquel, however, Lieber had expressed a willingness to talk with Captain Capelle.[12] On October 15 he wrote

Capelle that he would meet with him in Berlin. Lieber affirmed his positive attitude toward the naval bill, saying that he would demonstrate "my good will in general without committing myself to the details." But he made it evident that he would come to Berlin to negotiate and not simply to learn Tirpitz's desires regarding the passage of the bill. Lieber warned Capelle that "among other things his decision whether to remain as reporter for the naval budget would depend on the talks" in Berlin.[13] And in the course of his conversations with Capelle and Tirpitz he was to reject their request that he commit himself firmly to the bill.[14]

The reasons for Lieber's decision to reach an understanding with Tirpitz which would involve the acceptance of the basic features of the first naval bill are still unclear. He had been willing, of course, to go along with William II's inchoate plans of a cruiser fleet providing a German presence and defending German commerce around the world if the ruler respected the Reichstag's budgetary and legislative rights. But Lieber knew from his reading of the initial draft of the Tirpitz measure that the new secretary of the navy hoped to make Germany into a first-rate naval power. He wanted to give her a fleet which could assume an offensive against an enemy and attack its ports, functions which far exceeded the older primary naval aims of defending the coasts and breaking an enemy blockade.[15] Lieber had understood since 1896 that the advocates of a big German navy wanted to compete with Great Britain, the greatest naval power in the world.

Lieber actually viewed the whole movement for heightened naval expansion with informed skepticism. He noted down on the first draft of the Tirpitz bill in October, Hohenlohe's statement that there would have been no agitation for the navy if either William I or Frederick III were still ruling. The young emperor was the initiator of the efforts to promote the navy's growth and naval officers naturally responded enthusiastically to his encouragement in that regard.[16] Over the course of the three years that he had served as reporter for the naval budget Lieber had become a learned amateur in naval affairs. He was intimately acquainted with the numerous changes that had taken place in naval technology in the nineteenth century and was doubtful that they had come to an end. In his early opposition to Tirpitz's demand for a Septennat budget he had been influenced by his conviction that the continuing revolution in naval technology made it impossible to plan naval building on a long-term

[8] See below p. 72, fn. 77.

[9] *Kölnische Volkszeitung,* July 12, 1897.

[10] After learning that Miquel had recently visited with Lieber, Karl Bachem wrote an enthusiastic letter on August 22, 1897, to his party leader saying "so the old fox came into your hole." Lieber Papers, Speyer, File B, 183.

[11] On Miquel's relations with the Center leader and his abortive efforts to block the Septennat: Waldersee, *Denkwürdigkeiten* 2: p. 239; Herzfeld, *Miquel* 2: p. 525; and Hans Hallmann, *Das Weg nach Schlachtflottenbau,* pp. 268–299.

[12] *Ibid.,* pp. 279, 283.

[13] Lieber to Capelle, October 15, 1897. Lieber Papers, Wrocław, File 59.

[14] Lieber, undated notes on back of a letter from Capelle to Lieber of October 13, 1897, *ibid.*

[15] Lieber notes in margin of original draft of the first naval bill, *ibid.*

[16] Lieber notes on back of the original draft of the first naval bill. Lieber Papers, File 59.

basis.[17] But Lieber's reactions to Tirpitz's aims were grounded in his concern for their financial implications and nothing else; hence political expediency dictated his ultimate response to the first naval bill.[18] His friend, Martin Spahn, was undoubtedly right when, in his short biographical sketch of Lieber published in 1906, he said that the Centrist leader was ready to accept the Tirpitz proposals if a suitable agreement for their financing could be worked out. Spahn's claim that Lieber had a deep personal interest in the navy and also wished to aid his government in its efforts to make Germany attractive as an ally to Russia through its building of a large navy can be discounted.[19]

Center historians and biographers including Spahn were correct in stating that Lieber feared the consequences of a conflict with the government over the Tirpitz measure. Such a confrontation could have led to the Center's loss of its decisive position in the Reichstag.[20] The Center had been able to impose economies on the navy in the past because government could not afford to dissolve the parliament and hope to wage a successful campaign against the Center and the left-liberals over a naval budgetary issue. But the government had gone confidently to the middle-class electorate in 1887 and 1893 over major army bills and secured the majority for its proposals through the elections. If the Center lost an election over the naval Septennat, it would be out of power in the Reichstag for at least five years, possibly more. That was likely to be the case since Tirpitz and some of his subordinates were highly skilled in the art of devising propaganda about the navy and its importance for Germany's defense and influence.

Some analysts at the time thought, however, that Lieber's motives were not essentially defensive. Two prominent editors of the day, Hans Delbrück of the *Preussischer Jahrbücher* and Franz Mehring, the prominent Social Democrat, assumed that Lieber considered the naval bill highly important for his party's future relations with the goverment:[21] his aim was to demonstrate the Center's reliability on the so-called national issues. Eckart Kehr adopted a similar view of Lieber's motivation. In his impressive study *Schlachtflottenbau und Parteipolitik,* which appeared in 1930, Lieber, he argued, intended to improve the Center's position in the Reichstag by associating it successfully with the government's attempt to create a strong navy. The Center would then become the "hegemonial" rather than just the "decisive" party in the Reichstag.[22] Kehr disapproved of the Center party itself because he thought it refused to accept the normal responsibilities of a secular political party. He was impressed by Lieber's political intelligence, skills, and knowledge, but inferred that Lieber was unduly influenced by Tirpitz's confident personality and the intellectual appeal of a detailed rational plan of naval construction.[23]

Kehr had to rely solely upon the Center press and the Reichstag speeches of its members; therefore, he was inadequately aware of the strains within the party over the naval question and of their causes. Since he did not concern himself with the Center's policies on other issues, he did not see the reaction of Lieber and other Centrist leaders to the naval question in relation to their responses to the government's economic and anti-Socialist policies. But his thesis was sound enough, at least up to a point. After he took over the party leadership in 1893 Lieber had extended himself to prove to the government that the Center was a "state-supporting party." The stands that he took on the Russian commercial treaty, the anti-revolution bill, the Civil Legal Code, and individual naval budgets provided evidence that he was willing to offend elements in his own electorate to show the government and the monarch that the Center was reliable and responsible in the exercise of its decisive influence in the Reichstag.

Two later works on the genesis of the Tirpitz program did not contribute any further enlightenment on Lieber's motivation. Hans Hallmann's *Der Weg nach deutschen Schlachtflottenbau,* appearing in 1933, the year that Hitler came to power, presents the thesis that the party leaders who advocated the approval of the first naval bill did so for patriotic reasons. It is a useful supplement to Kehr's study nevertheless, since Hallmann fills out the Center's record in the parliamentary debates on the navy and shows that Miquel sought in the summer of 1897 to get the Imperial government to abandon the plan for a Septennat.[24] The more recent work by Jonathan Steinburg on Tirpitz's planning to 1898 is captious in its treatment of Lieber and attributes his support of the first bill to vanity.[25]

---

[17] During the later debates on the Tirpitz proposal, August Bebel recalled that Lieber had opposed Admiral Hollmann's surprise plan for extensive naval construction in March, 1897, on the grounds that the continuing changes in naval technology made long-range planning unwise: *Verhandlungen des Reichstages,* December 11, 1897: p. 157. There is an undated Lieber memorandum in his papers in Wrocław in which he detailed many of the changes that had taken place in the construction, machinery, fire power, and armoring of naval vessels in the nineteenth century: *ibid.*

[18] In commenting on the naval enthusiasm of William II and his marine officers, Lieber's only complaint was that the poor taxpayers would have to finance the expansion. See fn. 14 above.

[19] Spahn, *Lieber,* p. 52.

[20] *Ibid.* Hermann Cardauns, "Ernst Lieber," *Staatslexikon* 3: p. 857. Bachem, *Zentrumspartei* 5: p. 474.

[21] *Preussicher Jahrbücher* 91 (1897): p. 184: Franz Mehring, *Politische Publistik 1891-bis 1904,* v. 14 of *Gesammelte*

Schriften Thomas Höhle, Hans Koch and Josef Schleifstein, eds. (Berlin, 1964), p. 196.

[22] *Schlachtflottenbau und Parteipolitik,* p. 148.

[23] *Ibid.*

[24] See above pp. 63–64.

[25] *Yesterday's Deterrent* (New York, 1965), p. 191.

The extensive Lieber papers do not provide evidence which disturbs the Kehr thesis. But they reveal that Lieber became increasingly concerned between 1895 and 1898 over his need to produce results for his church and the Catholic minority and over the strained relations between the Center and the monarch. He was obsessed by the conviction that Cardinal Kopp was seeking to undermine whatever confidence the Vatican had in his leadership of the Center by saying that he was too close to the liberal Hohenlohe government and had produced nothing substantial for the Church.[26] Lieber was sensitive about his inability to secure even a partial modification of the anti-Jesuit law.

Lieber was undoubtedly perturbed and sometimes deeply discouraged in the year 1897. All his efforts to overcome the emperor's old hostility to the Center by demonstrations of its friendliness toward the navy and the new *Weltpolitik* had been seemingly vitiated by the conflict between the ruler and the party over the budget in March. Then only a few months later he had to provide vigorous leadership for the Center in its joint campaign with the National Liberals against the Prussian association bill. In a relatively short space of time the German Center fraction had come into opposition with the monarch over the expansion of German naval power and the Prussian Center had clashed with his plans for the destruction of the Social Democrats' political organization; these were the two issues that had most engaged the emperor's thought and emotions since Caprivi's dismissal. Lieber wrote Kopp in mid-June that the Catholic minority was confronted with a serious crisis in their relations with the monarchy.[27] He was to be all the more certain of that fact in the late summer of 1897.

In the course of the previous year the Vatican had become impatient over the absence of any change in the legal status of the Jesuits and the other banned religious orders.[28] It is not evident why the Curia assumed that the German monarchy would take any steps to revoke or modify the anti-Jesuit law, for the strain in the relations between the Vatican and the Triple Alliance powers was acute in the mid-1890's. Leo XIII had symbolized their state in June, 1896, by

bestowing a decoration on the Abbé Colbus, a Reichstag deputy from Alsace who was a critic of German rule in his province.[29] But the Curia had approved the Center's stand on obligatory civil marriage shortly before that event and probably assumed that it deserved some compensation in return. It was aware that a majority of the Reichstag had voted twice in favor of the Center's motions calling for repeal of the anti-Jesuit law and that a far larger majority had twice approved another motion to delete the expulsion paragraph from the law. In February, 1897, the Curia suddenly notified the chairman of the Center, Hompesch, that his party should take up the Jesuit question with the government. If there were serious talks between high government officials and Center representatives, they led nowhere. Hohenlohe and Miquel expressed a willingness to advocate the abolition of the anti-Jesuit law in return for the Center's willingness to support a more conservative suffrage system for Reichstag elections. But each side found the other's price too high for the concession it sought.[30]

There was undoubtedly a direct connection between the failure of the Vatican's initiative on the Jesuit question and the Canisius Encyclical of August 1, 1897, which was highly offensive to German Protestants in general and to the emperor in particular. The apparent author of the papal letter, though it appeared under Leo XIII's name, was Cardinal Steinhuber, a German Jesuit. The encyclical, which was issued to honor the forthcoming four hundredth anniversary of the death of Peter Canisius, the leading figure of the German Counter-Reformation and a Jesuit, contained a number of phrases concerning Protestant reformers and their doctrines characteristic of the polemical Catholic style of the sixteenth century. For a brief period William II insisted that he would recall the Prussian minister to the Vatican.[31]

No prominent Catholic, clerical or lay, was more shaken by the Canisius Encyclical and the furor it caused in high court and other Protestant circles than Kopp. He came more into contact with William II than other prominent Catholics and knew at first hand how low the emperor's boiling point was. Kopp had already suffered considerably because of the new Vatican press campaign against the Triple Alliance and the sharp differences between the Center and the monarch. But even after William II expressed his satisfaction with Rampolla's comments on the Canisius Encyclical, Kopp did not recover his confidence. He remained

[26] Lieber to Pischel. November 8, 1897. Lieber Papers, Wrocław, File 95: Hohenlohe, *Reichskanzlerzeit,* p. 397. A year later Kopp was to write a high Prussian official that "Hertling alone had a wide view" and that "Lieber and Karl Bachem have neither goals nor principles." Nachlass Althoff, Deutsches Zentralarchiv, Merseburg, File XCVI. Copy in possession of Rudolf Morsey. Lieber's relations with the archbishop and auxiliary bishop of Cologne were good: Lieber to Auxiliary Bishop Schmitz, November 11, 1897. Lieber Papers, Wrocław, File 95.

[27] Letter to Kopp, June 14, 1897. Lieber Papers, Speyer, File L, 217.

[28] Kopp's notes on an audience with Leo XIII dated February 25, 1896. Kopp Papers, Wrocław, File 67. The pope wanted to write a personal letter to William II requesting his intervention on behalf of the Jesuits, but was persuaded by Kopp not to do so.

[29] From the French newspaper *La Libre Parole,* June 12, 1896. It reported that Colbus had spoken in the Reichstag of his love for France. Marschall von Bieberstein attributed the awarding of the decoration to Colbus to "the silly unfriendliness of the Curia toward us." Letter to the Prussian minister to the Vatican, June 26, 1896, GFMA, T149, ACP 24.

[30] See Hohenlohe, *Reichskanzlerzeit,* pp. 298–299; Herzfeld, *Miquel* **2**: pp. 462–463.

[31] Bachem, *Zentrumspartei* **9**: p. 306.

nervous over the possibility that some new incident in the relations between the Catholic Church and the German monarchy would lead to a serious explosion against his church.[32]

In mid-September, 1897, Kopp suddenly turned on Lieber and charged in a letter to the Centrist leader that the party was not interested in doing anything for the Jesuits. He claimed that a prominent Polish deputy had made an open statement to that effect and that the Center had introduced its last two Reichstag motions on behalf of the Jesuits only at the Vatican's insistence.[33] While his motives were not evident, Kopp probably sought to put pressure on Lieber to approve the new naval plan. It is likely that for pastoral reasons but even more out of eagerness to demonstrate his reliability to the Vatican, he wanted Lieber to use the promise of Center support for the bill as a counter for the return of the Jesuits.

The Center leader did not need any direction from Cardinal Kopp regarding the stand he should take on the new naval program. But the combination of the conflict with the monarch over the Prussian associations bill, the ruler's angry reaction to the Canisius Encyclical, and Kopp's pressure on him over the Jesuit question all helped to harden his conviction that the Center could not afford to oppose the naval measure. The Center was at a crossroads in its relations with the monarch and Lieber believed there was only one road that his party could afford to take. But he refused to press the Jesuit issue after Hohenlohe said that the Canisius Encyclical made it impossible to consider even the deletion of the expulsion article.[34] Instead he wrote directly to the general of the Jesuits in Rome, explained the difficulties that the Center, a minority party, faced in its efforts to secure the revocation of the law and warned against any policy of opposition which would "break the porcelain."[35]

Before his talks with Capelle and Tirpitz in Berlin between October 22 and 24, Lieber had adequate opportunity to study the first draft of the new naval bill. He was impressed by the clarity, the precision, and above all, the organic character of the plan.[36] The navy was to have a definite scheme of organization;

the home fleet, its main core, was to be divided into two squadrons of eight battleships each, one for service in the North Sea, the other for the Baltic Sea. The home fleeet would also contain a flagship and two other battleships for reserve purposes, eight coastal defense ships already in service, and six large and eighteen small cruisers. The overseas elements of the navy were to be kept within modest limits, numbering in all three large cruisers, nine small cruisers, and four gunboats, with six cruisers serving as a reserve. To bring the navy up to this planned strength, the Secretariat of the Navy would have to build eleven battleships and nine cruisers, some of them replacements, between 1898 and 1905. The first naval bill also stipulated that the battleships should be automatically replaced after twenty-five years, the smaller ships at an earlier time.[37]

At the sessions with Capelle and Tirpitz, Lieber repeated his favorable disposition toward the bill, but he refused again to commit himself to it as the naval officials desired.[38] Lieber was a hard negotiator. The secretary of the navy was discomfited and deeply disappointed over the outcome of the talks and feared that the concessions he had been asked to make could weaken his position with William II. He later complained that "the whole plan had lost greatness and decisiveness as a result of their talks."[39]

Lieber did not attempt to negotiate with the secretary of the navy over the program of naval construction itself, which was not unusually ambitious. He hoped that he could secure concessions from Tirpitz on the annual extraordinary expenditure for shipbuilding, reducing them from fifty-eight million to approximately fifty million marks. He also wanted to separate the requests for the battleships from those for the cruisers to be used on foreign service; he would remove from the latter the legal requirement that they be built within a specific time. A more tender question in the talks between the Center leader and Tirpitz was Lieber's proposal that the Septennat be replaced by a flexible building period of either six to eight or five to nine years.[40] It is not evident whether Tirpitz was also upset over Lieber's request that he accept a settlement based on a lower ceiling of annual expenditure and a separation of the ships to be built for the home fleet. But the secretary of the navy was seriously disturbed over Lieber's suggestion that he accept a modified scheme for the completion of the building program.[41]

Nevertheless, Lieber was able to impress his own point of view on Tirpitz on an issue of overriding po-

---

[32] Kopp to an unnamed prelate at the Vatican, November 14, 1897. Kopp Papers, Wrocław, File 49. Earlier in the year Kopp had told the Badenese representative to the Federal Council that he would "like to disappear." E. von Jagemann, *75 Jahre des Erlebens und Erfahrens, 1849–1924* (Berlin, 1924), p. 149.

[33] Kopp to Lieber, September 20, 1897. Lieber Papers, Wrocław, File 97. The Polish deputy made a vigorous and convincing denial of the validity of Kopp's statement: P. Wawrzyniak to Lieber, September 25, 1897. *Ibid.*, File 96.

[34] Hohenlohe, *Reichskanzlerzeit*, p. 397.

[35] Lieber to the general of the Jesuits, November 9, 1897, Lieber Papers, Wrocław, File 95. One of Lieber's two brothers was a Jesuit priest in Sweden.

[36] He praised those qualities in his first Reichstag speech on the first naval bill: *Verhandlungen des Reichstages,* December 7, 1897: p. 85.

[37] Steinberg, *Yesterday's Deterrent*, pp. 144–147.

[38] Undated Lieber notes, written on final draft of Tirpitz bill, Lieber Papers, Wrocław, File 59.

[39] Tirpitz notes, dated November 24, 1897, Bundesarchiv-Militararchiv, Freiburg. Nachlass Tirpitz (N253), pp. 182–183. Copy in possession of Patrick J. Kelly.

[40] Lieber's notes on original draft of the naval bill: Lieber Papers, Wrocław, File 59.

[41] Footnote 39 above.

litical importance, the strategic functions of the navy. For all his vaunted reputation for being an astute manager of parliamentarians, Tirpitz and his advisers showed incredible ignorance of the Center's aversion to any naval plan calling for a fleet which would assume anything but a defensive role, except for a breakthrough of a blockade. The first draft of the bill seen by Lieber referred to the memorandum on those aims written in 1867 for the new North German government by General Roon, at that time the Prussian secretary of war. Tirpitz's quotations from the Roon statement revealed that the naval secretary would not be satisfied with a modest strengthening of the home fleet so that it could provide a better defense of the coasts. Roon had assigned numerous responsibilities to the navy, but he had insisted above all that it should be capable of taking the high seas and of destroying the enemy's sea trade and his coasts and harbors. Lieber left no record of what he said to the secretary of the navy about the legitimate goals of the navy, but it can safely be assumed that he told Tirpitz the inclusion of the quotations from the Roon memorandum would doom the first naval bill.[42] The second and final draft of the bill contained no references to Roon's ambitious strategic objectives for the navy, but referred only to the more modest memorandum of 1873 prepared by admiralty chief, General Admiral von Stosch, which affirmed simply that the navy should be able to take the offensive but proposed no more than fourteen front-line ships.

From the face of things it appeared as if Lieber was confronted with highly unfavorable odds in his efforts to win his party for the new bill. There was no prospect of even a partial modification of the anti-Jesuit law. While the Prussian Ministerial Council had voted in favor of the return of two small religious orders, the Lazarists and the Sisters of the Sacred Heart, the Imperial government did not make a commitment to take any action on their behalf.[43] Economic conditions were undoubtedly better in southern Germany than they had been in 1893, but Bavarian politicians complained about the shortage of agricultural labor. They were also resentful of the Imperial government's efforts to centralize the administration of military justice in Berlin and to make Germany a major naval power. In the summer of 1897 some of them wanted their state Center party to break away from the Reichstag Center party in Bavaria.[44] The main contrast, however, between the reaction of regional Center parties to the Caprivi bill of 1892 and 1893 and their response to the Tirpitz proposals of 1897 was to be found in the atti-

tude of the Rhineland Center and the *Kölnische Volkszeitung.*

The basic position of the Rhineland Centrists on the new naval proposals was that the Reichstag could approve the expenditures required for the first year of the building program in a regular budget but must reject the Septennat.[45] Their leaders suspected that Lieber might abandon his earlier opposition to a binding law and might not intend to keep his leading colleagues informed about his own plans. On September 25 Karl Bachem attacked the Tirpitz bill in a public speech without consulting Lieber in advance about its text and later pleaded illness as the reason for not accepting Lieber's invitation to visit his home.[46] At some point in October the Center leader learned that Müller-Fulda planned to leave the Reichstag before the elections of June, 1898. Lieber was so concerned about the threat that he made a special trip to Fulda to change Müller's mind and to ask the bishop of the diocese to work on him to the same end. Lieber was relieved to find out that Müller's only demand regarding the naval bill was that the Center, meaning the leader, should not commit itself or oppose the measure in advance.[47]

The caucus debates in early December clearly reflected the hostility of the Centrist electorate toward the first naval bill. Only Lieber and Gröber, his faithful deputy, spoke explicitly or implicitly in favor of it and Gröber sought to cover his embarrassment in doing so by putting heavy emphasis upon the need for a national income tax to cover any future costs, though he admitted that such a levy could only be used as a threat.[48] While Georg von Hertling also thought that the Center had to approve the Tirpitz proposals to prove its reliability on national issues, he chose discreetly to continue his university lectures until after the conclusion of the caucus.[49] Hertling's view was atypical in the Bavarian Center contingent since he had his hopes fixed on a ministerial career in his state.

In the fraction debates from two to four Centrists each from the Bavarian, Westphalian, and Rhineland delegations spoke. No one from the Silesian or Baden contingents addressed the fraction.[50] Despite differences of nuance and emphasis, the speeches con-

---

[42] See footnote 39.

[43] William II was to veto in May, 1898, a proposal of Tirpitz and some of the other Imperial officials that the government take action on behalf of the two religious societies: Hohenlohe, *Reichskanzlerzeit,* p. 444.

[44] Buol to Stötzingen, July 7, 1897. Buol-Stötzingen Correspondence.

[45] Kehr, *Schlachtflottenbau,* p. 42, fn. 30; pp. 83–84, fn. 44. And see below p. 70.

[46] Kehr, p. 137. Kehr appears to confuse Karl Bachem and Julius Bachem. On Karl Bachem's supposed indisposition: letter to Lieber, October 25, 1897. Lieber Papers, Wrocław, File 95.

[47] Lieber notes, dated November 5, 1897, on a letter from Müller-Fulda of November 3, 1897. *Ibid.*

[48] Hertling states in his memoirs that Lieber spoke for two hours at the caucus and infers that he did so in favor of the measure: *Erinnerungen* 2: p. 197. Lieber took notes of the remarks made by his colleagues but left no record of his own. Possibly he gave essentially the same long speech at the caucus that he later delivered to the Reichstag on December 7, 1897. The Lieber notes are in his papers at Wrocław, File 59.

[49] Hertling to Lieber, November 25, 1897. *Ibid.*

[50] Lieber notes on the Center caucus. *Ibid.*

tained the same objections and reservations about the naval bill. The suspicion of Tirpitz's ambitions was evident in the insistence of both Fritzen and Schaedler that the army was primarily responsible for the defense of Germany and that naval expansion had to be in accordance with Germany's means. The doubt that the government would adhere to the Septennat was repeated several times and most speakers complained that the binding of the Reichstag through a law would restrict the exercise of its powers. There was a general insistence that if the government needed new sources of supply for the program it could not turn to new indirect taxes at the expense of the lower classes, though there was no agreement how the government could raise funds by direct taxation without violating states' rights.[51]

Nevertheless, the results of the caucus debates were not a defeat for Lieber. There was no outcome like that of the debates of early December, 1892, when the fraction committed itself to a Lieber motion which it knew the government would not accept. An oppositional alliance between the Bavarian and Rhineland Centrists would have hamstrung Lieber in his efforts to secure a compromise with the government but despite the close similarity between the speeches of Fritzen and those of Schaedler, Lieber's friend, that coalition did not come into being. The prominent Rhineland Centrist proposed that the fraction "refuse the bill for the time being," though he said he had no objection to its consideration by the Budget Committee.[52] But even though Schaedler frankly stated that the complete rejection of the Tirpitz measure would be the most popular course for the party, he and Arenberg said that the proposals should not be rejected outright. Peter Spahn summed up the debates for the fraction, saying that there was agreement that the bill should be sent to committee and that it should be kept there as long as possible.[53] The implication in his remarks was that the leaders should have time to find a compromise with the government.

Lieber's long speech to the Reichstag at the first reading of the naval bill on December 7 reflected the outcome of the earlier debates in the fraction caucuses. He did not make any remarks that could commit his party in any way to the support of the measure and he detailed at some length the Center's reservations about it. Lieber underscored the fact that the government wanted to impose a control upon the parliament while it refused to accept any restraints upon itself in the naval program. He also expressed the Center's concern about future handling of additional costs. Lieber pointed out that the government had not taken any steps to remove the archaic state laws banning the

union of political associations, to introduce public court martials or even to remove article two of the anti-Jesuit law.[54]

But the Center leader had sent signals in the clear to Tirpitz and other government officials which were reassuring to them. He referred solemnly to the historical significance of the decision confronting the Reichstag, praised the organizational character of the new naval plan and concluded his speech with the wish that the Reichstag would produce an effective navy. During the debates on December 7 he conversed readily with federal officials sitting at the table of the Federal Council. At the end of the day government representatives and reporters concluded that the Center would finally approve the bill.[55]

The situation in the Center had not changed, however, over the course of a few days. It was at least six weeks after Lieber's speech before his influence in the fraction became evident. At that time he was to win a test of strength with his opponents in the wider Center party and the outcome indicated what the final decision of the fraction would be. During the long interval between the first reading in early December and the commencement of the hearings in the Budget Committee during the last week of February, 1898, Lieber abandoned the semi-collegial system of fraction leadership that he had introduced in the fall of 1894. He was able to meet legitimately with Tirpitz and other relevant Imperial officials in secret session because he was the reporter for the naval budget. But behind the cover of that position he tried to work out a compromise with the secretary of the navy that would be acceptable to his party. He kept his thoughts to himself or confided only in a few intimates. By the time that he and his eight colleagues in the Budget Committee met with the rest of the fraction for the second reading of the bill he was apparently ready to commit himself on all but the question of how future naval building would be financed.[56]

Lieber's *modus operandi* was disconcerting at an early date to some of his colleagues inside the fraction and in the wider Center party outside. On January 9 Adam Schmitt, the leader of the Mainz Center party and an enthusiastic backer of Lieber in the early 1890's, attacked him at a public assembly in Mainz for his speech on the naval bill in the Reichstag.[57] Schmitt's action undoubtedly reflected the discontent among Catholic integralists over the Center's course since the passage of the Civil Legal Code and the failure of the Imperial government to make any significant change in the status of the banned religious orders. One of the leading integralists in the Prussian Center fraction,

---

[51] *Ibid.*
[52] *Ibid.*
[53] *Ibid.;* Spahn, *Lieber,* pp. 52–53; Hertling, *Erinnerungen* **2**: pp. 196–199.

[54] *Reichstag Verhandlungen,* December 7, 1897: pp. 83–85.
[55] *Allgemeine Zeitung,* December 9, 10, 1897; *Preussischer Jahrbücher* **91** (1897): p. 164.
[56] On Lieber's tactics: Spahn, *Lieber* p. 53; Kehr, *Schlachtflottenbau,* p. 139.
[57] *Ibid.,* pp. 136–137.

Chaplain Georg Dasbach, a deputy from Trier and a prominent agrarian leader and newspaper publisher, had been eager to succeed to Müller-Fulda's seat if he did not run in the 1898 elections.[58] Lieber preferred to keep Müller-Fulda in the fraction and to leave Dasbach out.

Nevertheless it was Müller-Fulda who was responsible for the most serious shock that Lieber and Tirpitz experienced before the fraction's second reading of the bill in early March. Around the middle of January the Bachem press in Cologne published a brochure by the Center's financial expert on the recent history of German naval budgets. Müller-Fulda did not identify himself as a Centrist deputy, but his brochure appeared as one of the Center's publications in its new series on legislative issues. The author's aim was to demonstrate that the Reichstag had provided enough funds for the navy's needs through the annual budget method of appropriation, especially in the period 1893–1898. He did not develop that argument in detail but said simply that he was interested in presenting the facts from which his readers could draw their own conclusions. He volunteered no prophecy about the prospects of the Tirpitz bill but ended the pamphlet with the phrase *Quien Sabe* in large type.[59]

There is no concrete evidence that Julius Bachem was the actual instigator of the Müller-Fulda sortie against the Septennat, but it is likely that he was. For all his impressive financial expertise, Müller was not an independent politician. Julius Bachem and his close associates were angry over Lieber's silence about his plans regarding the naval bill; they knew that he would expect the Rhineland delegation in the fraction to supply the decisive votes. During the caucus debates of December, Fritzen had complained that if the Center brought about the passage of the Tirpitz measure it would do so "three months before our deaths" in the Reichstag elections of 1898 when the Rhineland Centrists would have to face the Social Democrats.[60] The leaders of the provincial party were irked that Lieber had not sought a concession favorable to them in return for the Center's support of the naval bill. Their immediate desire was not for the revocation of the anti-Jesuit law or the introduction of a second Prussian school law, but for a new promise of a reform of the communal suffrage which could bring their party into power in the western municipalities.[61]

Still the tactic of Müller and Bachem proved to be a complete failure, although Lieber and Tirpitz were both alarmed over it.[62] They apparently feared that it would set off a series of explosions in the Catholic west and south. Lieber and Gröber insisted on the fraction's informing the Catholic press that the Müller brochure was not an official publication of the party. The other leaders apparently rallied around them and even Karl Bachem complained mildly to his family that Müller had been tactless.[63] If anything Lieber's position was strengthened by the affair, since the fraction's decision amounted in effect to the approbation of his leadership.

In the first two sessions of the second reading of the bill in the Budget Committee, those of February 24 and 26, Lieber committed himself to the acceptance of its contents and then to the principle of a legal regulation for the period of construction.[64] Although he had insisted that his party stood under no obligation to follow him, Eugen Richter complained bitterly at the second session that any further debates on the bill were now useless.[65] There was considerable truth in Richter's charge, for the government, the Free Conservatives, and the National Liberals were hardly likely to let the bill fail for lack of an agreement over the method by which future costs would be met, which was the critical issue for the Center.

During the initial sessions of the Budget Committee Tirpitz expressed a willingness to accept or to consider certain Centrist proposals modifying or supplementing the bill. Both he and the Center thought Müller-Fulda's motion calling for a naval Sextennat rather than a Septennat would be beneficial to the navy and to the Reichstag. He did not oppose Lieber's proposal that the government accept a limit on the amount of money that could be spent for building in any one year. But it was far more difficult to come up with an agreement on the taxes to be levied by the government if the Secretariat of the Navy ran out of money. This was a crucial question for the Center because it was a party of the Catholic *Mittelstand* and the working classes.[66]

Lieber may have believed that he would win his party's support for the Tirpitz bill if he were able to demonstrate to the Center that he had reconciled the building of a new navy with his party's social conscience. His immediate concern was undoubtedly to

[58] On Müller-Fulda's threat of resignation: Lieber's notes, dated November 5, 1897: Lieber Papers, Wrocław, File 95. Kehr says that of all the Center journals the *Märkische Volkszeitung*, the newspaper published by Dasbach, and the *Deutsche Reichs-zeitung* of Bonn used the sharpest and harshest language against the naval bill: *Schlachtflottenbau*, p. 138, fn. 95.

[59] *Kölnische Volkszeitung*, January 18, 1897.

[60] Footnote 50 above.

[61] Karl Trimborn was to complain later to Karl Bachem about Lieber's failure to demand that the government offer compensation to the Center for its support of the naval bill

in the form of a reform of the Prussian municipal suffrage: letter of September 8, 1898. Bachem Papers, File 106.

[62] Kehr, *Schlachtflottenbau*, pp. 140–141.

[63] Karl Bachem to Fridolin Bachem, January 20, 1898. Bachem Papers, File 84. If Hertling can be believed, Müller-Fulda was somewhat disconcerted by the disturbance he had caused: Hertling to his wife, January 20, 1898. Hertling Papers, Bundesarchiv, Koblenz, File 78.

[64] Kehr, *Schlachtflottenbau*, pp. 151–152.

[65] *Bericht der Kommission für den Reichshaushalt-Etat*, February 26, 1898: p. 19; Kehr, pp. 151–152.

[66] *Ibid.*, pp. 153–155.

make it possible for the Rhineland Centrists to vote for the naval bill and hence to ensure its passage. On March 3, five days before the Center fraction began debates on the Tirpitz measure, he had proposed to the Reichstag Budget Committee that any further financial shortage for the naval program should be met by a direct income tax imposed by the states on all taxable income of ten thousand marks or more. Lieber knew that if his measure failed of acceptance by the government he could fall back upon a proposal made by Rudolf von Bennigsen, the National Liberal leader, which stipulated that if expenditures in any year on the navy exceeded one hundred seventeen million marks additional appropriations could not be approved which would increase the amount derived from indirect taxes.[67]

The course of the Center caucuses between March 7 and 9 essentially confirmed Eugen Richter's pessimistic prophecy about the Center's final decision on the naval bill. Lieber's health broke down under the strain of the responsibility he had borne in the previous months and he was present for only part of the first session of March 8. He and then Gröber at a later session confronted the fraction for the first time with the stiff warning that political necessity dictated approval of the Tirpitz measure.[68] The danger that the Rhineland Centrists, the Bavarians, and the integralists might build a strong opposition bloc evaporated, although they apparently approved Fritzen's proposal for the removal of the provision in the naval bill for the automatic replacement of all ships after a certain age limit. But the automatic substitution of new ships for older vessels of a specific age was crucial for Tirpitz's building plans and by threatening to resign from his position he prevailed upon the Center to abandon Fritzen's motion.[69] The Bavarians persisted in their strong opposition to the naval bill but Lieber had a majority of the fraction behind him before the caucus ended.[70] Those of his colleagues who supported Lieber apparently agreed that he should not commit the Center to an approval of the Tirpitz measure until the government and the Cartel parties had agreed to a tax plan satisfactory to the Centrist leadership.

Nevertheless, the further course of the deliberations on the naval proposals was anti-climactic. The German state governments, in particular Bavaria, were not willing to ratify Lieber's motion of a supplement to their income taxes to help in the financing of naval construction. Lieber then recommended to the Budget Committee on March 16 that it approve the Bennigsen pro-

posal with the modification that the phrase "taxes which burden mass consumption" be substituted for the reference to "indirect taxes."[71] The committee accepted the Bennigsen measure with Lieber's modification. Except for Müller-Fulda all the Center members of that body voted for the amended naval bill.[72] A week later the Reichstag voted at the second reading on the modified naval bill. Fifty-five of the ninety-six Centrists supported the government; twenty-six went into opposition. They included twenty-three Bavarians and two prominent integralists, Heinrich Roeren and Adam Schmitt. Some fifteen deputies had apparently been absent from the Reichstag on that day, half of them from Bavaria alone.[73] But their conduct on March 23 was less significant than the fact that a majority of the fraction voted favorably for the first time on a major defense measure. The contrast with their performance on the Caprivi army bill of 1893 was marked.

Lieber's reasons for preferring a compromise which represented the virtual acceptance of the government's views are probably evident enough. But why did the bulk of the Silesian, Westphalian, Rhenish, and Badener Centrists follow him in the voting? Important negative factors were helpful to Lieber in his effort. Economic conditions had continued to improve, though agriculture was still a softer area in the economy than industry and trade. Unlike Huene and Ballestrem five years earlier, Lieber did not have to contend with an articulate and gifted opponent of his course. It was in part because he was a relatively popular middle-class leader and not an aristocrat that Lieber had been able to take the political risks he did. But in the final analysis the decisive factor in the decision made by the members of the majority who did not belong to the intimate Lieber circle or were not government types like Arenberg and Hertling was a fear of conflict with the government. This was evident in the conduct of Alois Fritzen and Karl Bachem, the leading Rhineland Centrists in the fraction. Though they had been consistently critical of the first naval bill from the summer of 1897 to the near completion of its course through the Reichstag they had not dared to demand that their party reject the Sextennat.[74]

The passage of the first naval bill was seemingly a

[67] Ibid., pp. 156–158; Steinberg, Yesterday's Deterrent, pp. 187–188.

[68] Spahn, Lieber, p. 53; Porsch to Kopp, March 12, 1898, Kopp Papers, File 49.

[69] Steinberg, Yesterday's Deterrent, p. 190.

[70] Kehr, pp. 161–162. After the caucus Porsch expressed a restrained confidence about the success of the bill: letter to Kopp, fn. 65 above.

[71] Kehr, p. 163.

[72] Bachem, Zentrumspartei 5: p. 476.

[73] Ibid., p. 477.

[74] Karl Bachem later claimed that he and many of his colleagues had been influenced in their eventual response to the Tirpitz bill by the possibility of the government's doing away with the Reichstag's system of universal equal suffrage if the parliament rejected that measure. Karl Bachem notes, dated June 24, 1898, Bachem Papers, File 88. While that consideration may have influenced the thinking of Bachem and some other Centrists, I believe that they were more concerned over the response of church dignitaries toward the Center itself if its leaders created a crisis between the party and the government by defeating the Tirpitz proposals.

turning point in Lieber's career and in the development of his party. The Center's acceptance of the Tirpitz measure and its approval by the Reichstag was a personal triumph for the party's leader. William II's longtime enmity toward him was apparently at an end. Through a personal representative, the emperor offered Lieber a decoration and a high governmental office, probably the superior presidency of Hesse Nassau, both of which he turned down. Lieber did attend a court dinner, talked with William II, and requested the monarch's picture.[75] Tirpitz wrote him a long and flattering letter in which he called Lieber "the godfather" of the new navy and asked him to stand by its side with further counsel and assistance. He added that the Center, by its support for the naval bill, had destroyed the old belief that Catholics were opposed to the progress of the Reich and had helped to open up a new future for the German nation.[76] The outcome of the elections of June, 1898, was a further reassurance to Lieber that he had made the right decision in linking up his party's fortunes with the naval proposals. He had reason enough to be concerned about their outcome, for the Center had supported a major military measure for the first time and had done so without any concession to the party or its church. If the Center had suffered a serious setback in the elections as the Rhineland Centrists had earlier feared, a committee system of leadership would have come into existence. The Social Democrats did score a modest though meaningful success in the contest, expanding their seats in the Reichstag from forty-four to fifty-six. But they had done so at the expense of the liberal parties, since the Center increased its number of mandates from ninety-six to one hundred and two.[77]

Lieber's mood in the summer and early fall of 1898 was one of triumph and confidence. It was evident in two incidents. When ill health prevented Rudolf von Buol, the Centrist president of the Reichstag, from presenting himself as a candidate for reelection to the parliament, Ballestrem and Hertling became interested

in succeeding to Buol's position. Even though Lieber was closer to Hertling and had received a request for support from him, the party leader told his Bavarian colleague that Ballestrem's earlier distinguished service in the vice-presidency of the Reichstag gave him the better claim.[78] Lieber had probably concealed his real motive in preferring Ballestrem to Hertling, which was to weaken the conservative alliance between Ballestrem and Cardinal Kopp. In the fall the Center supported Ballestrem's candidacy and he was elected to the vacant position. Between the time of his correspondence with Hertling over the Reichstag presidency and the opening of the parliament Lieber made his first trip to the United States in eight years. He went for the purpose of addressing a congress of the German Catholic Central-Verein at Milwaukee. The friction between the Irish-American bishops led by Archbishop John Ireland and the German-American clergy was then intense and a nervous papal nuncio to Munich had asked Lieber to postpone his American visit.[79] In his remarks to the congress Lieber called on his auditors to remain united and pointedly recalled that the Center had been attacked from behind in the Septennat crisis of 1887,[80] a scarcely veiled reference to the abortive papal intervention in that affair.

Lieber's slighting reference to the Papacy in Milwaukee reflected the tension between the Center and the Vatican over an international issue in which Leo XIII and Rampolla found themselves caught between Germany and France. In the early fall of 1898 William II had begun preparations for a visit to Palestine and to Constantinople, where he hoped to increase Germany's political influence with the Ottoman government and to win railroad concessions for German business groups. It was an embarrassment to the German government and to William II that France, under the terms of a treaty concluded with the Sultan's government in 1740, still claimed the right to be the protector over all Latin Christians, including German Catholics, in the Ottoman Empire. Despite official German demands that the Vatican recognize its right to assume that role for German Catholics, the Curia in its fear of antagonizing the French government upheld the arrangements of the treaty of 1740. To shake the Vatican loose from its pro-French stand on the question of the protectorate, the German government apparently called upon the Center party to affirm a strong national point of view on the question.[81] During the

---

[75] Bachem, *Zentrumspartei* 5: p. 482. According to a note Bachem wrote after Lieber's death in 1902, both the deceased leader and his widow had indicated that a representative of the emperor had offered him a high governmental office, presumably the superior presidency of his own province: Karl Bachem notes, dated January 1, 1899, Bachem Papers, File 154; same to Julius Bachem, April 10, 1902, *ibid.* Karl Bachem notes, dated May 5, 1902, *ibid.*

[76] Tirpitz to Lieber, April 23, 1898, Lieber Papers, Speyer, T61.

[77] Bachem, *Zentrumspartei* 5: p. 486. Lieber apparently ran into serious difficulties in trying to carry out his earlier *Sammlung* electoral agreements with the National Liberals and the Free Conservatives. Instead of supporting National Liberal candidates as Lieber desired, Theodor Wacker entered into an alliance with the Social Democrats in Baden during the elections of 1898: *Konstanzer Zeitung*, September 28, 1889. The Essen Center party refused to support the candidacy of Friedrich Krupp, a Free Conservative: *Kölnische Volkszeitung*, August 21, 1916.

[78] Hertling to Lieber, July 20, 1898, Lieber Papers, Wrocław, File 151. Lieber to Hertling, July 22, 1898. Lieber-Hertling Correspondence, Lieber Papers, Camberg.

[79] Hertling to Lieber, July 20, 1898. Lieber Papers, Wrocław, File 151.

[80] Printed protocol of the Congress, Lieber Papers, Speyer, Envelope *Amerika (1898)*, *Milwaukee*.

[81] Marschall von Bieberstein, German ambassador to the Ottoman Empire since June, 1897, wrote the Foreign Office that the Vatican's enthusiasm for its French friends would cool if it knew that the German bishops and the great majority of

course of his Near Eastern trip William II purchased a small church built on land associated by tradition with Mary, the mother of Jesus, and then turned it over to a German Catholic society.

The leaders of the Center welcomed an opportunity to prove their patriotism to the emperor and to annoy Cardinal Rampolla for the embarrassment and concern they had suffered from the Vatican press attacks on the Triple Alliance. A prominent Centrist deputy, probably Arenberg, an old friend of von Bülow, had written in *Germania* in early October that Germany would protect her citizens in the Turkish Empire by force if necessary.[82] On December 12 Fritzen, at the first reading of the general budget, affirmed the desire of German Catholics to be protected by their own government and not by an anti-German and anti-clerical foreign government.[83] Three days later Lieber stepped forward in the Reichstag to express his own approval of Fritzen's speech. He claimed that German Catholics wanted the right "to be both German and Catholic."[84] The zealous papal nuncio in Munich complained to Hompesch, the chairman of the Center, about Lieber's speech and forwarded a formal statement rebuking the Centrist leader which he asked Hompesch to publish in the name of the Reichstag Center fraction.[85] Hompesch took no action, but Lieber later made his own trip to Canossa during a journey of convalescence to Italy and France in 1900.[86]

Lieber's mood of exultation did not survive the first days of the new Reichstag session. Many of his associates had come back from their constituencies in an unhappy mood anyway and then found on their return that the government would present to the Reichstag a new army bill, though one of modest proportions. In his remarks on December 12 Fritzen had carefully distinguished between the agreement reached by the Center and the government concerning the Palestinian protectorate from the dissatisfaction within Germany over domestic affairs. The government had disregarded the Reichstag's wishes on the rights of association and the Jesuits.[87] The loyal Gröber, while insisting that Lieber should not become upset over the coldness in the fraction toward his person, said that those members of the Center who preferred "a sharper manner of speaking" would be sure to get the upper

hand if the party approved large demands for the navy and army and then found the remnants of the Kulturkampf still in existence. The emperor's gift to Catholics of a church in the Holy Land was a handsome expression of his personal attitude toward them, Gröber added, but it was hardly an adequate substitute for the removal of laws of persecution against them.[88]

It was unfortunate for Lieber that the new army bill followed the first naval proposals by only a year. While the measure called for a modest increase in the number of draftees, approximately twenty-seven thousand, its extraordinary expenditures were to double those of the bill of 1893, which had initially called for the addition of eighty-four thousand effectives to the army. The relatively pronounced increase in costs was probably because the bill called for the expansion of artillery and cavalry units.[89] The extensive opposition in the Center and its press to the army proposals was embarrassing and annoying to Lieber. It interfered with his efforts to create a new image of his party and he undoubtedly thought it useless to mar that image by insisting on even a modest reduction of the number of troops.[90] That was no easy undertaking since he also had to take a firm stand against the desires of both the emperor and Tirpitz to replace the first naval bill with a new measure.

Lieber and his colleagues had suspected during the early deliberations over the first Tirpitz proposals that it would not reach its legal conclusion. But it must have been acutely embarrassing for them to hear rumors—perhaps we should say accurate reports—that the government was already planning a new naval proposal before the initial measure was a half-year old, and at a time when the Reichstag was reacting unhappily to a new army bill.

The secretary of the navy had been determined from the beginning to maintain an annual construction tempo of three battleships or large cruisers but under the provisions of the law of 1898 that building program would end after 1900. In December, 1898, the emperor gave his approval to Tirpitz's plan to request approval from the Reichstag for a second double battleship squadron and supporting vessels before the Sextennat ran out in 1903. Tirpitz and William II were undoubtedly convinced by the relative ease with which the secretary of the navy had brought his first proposal through the Reichstag that they would not experience serious difficulty in winning parliamentary approval for a second naval bill.[91] Recent developments in international affairs appeared to demonstrate the importance of sea

Catholics stood on the side of their government: letter of September 11, 1898; *Der Grosse Politik der europäischen Kabinette* **12**: p. 606.

[82] Below-Rutzau, Prussian chargé d'affaires of the Prussian mission to the Vatican, to the Foreign Office, October 1898, *ibid.*, p. 623.

[83] *Reichstag Verhandlungen*, December 12, 1898: p. 25.

[84] *Europäische Geschichtskalender* **39** (1898): p. 185.

[85] Copy of the nuncio's letter to Hompesch, dated December 19, 1898. Porsch Papers, Ia9.

[86] Ballestrem sought unsuccessfully in 1899 to win a Vatican decoration for Lieber: Otto von Bülow, the Prussian minister to the Vatican, November 11, 1900. Foreign Ministry Archives, University of Michigan, Microfilm, Roll 113.

[87] *Reichstag Verhandlungen*, December 12, 1898: p. 24.

[88] Gröber to Lieber, December 10, 1898. Lieber Papers, Camberg, *Briefe 1898*.

[89] Bachem, *Zentrumspartei* **6**: pp. 10–11.

[90] Lieber later complained to Cardinal Kopp that his party still insisted on making its traditional demand for a deletion of a part of each military proposal: letter of March 19, 1899. Lieber Papers, Speyer, L, 172.

[91] Berghahn, *Der Tirpitz-Plan*, p. 163 ff.

power. The United States had relied heavily on its navy in its defeat of Spain and Great Britain had been able to force France to back down in their diplomatic contest over the Sudan because she controlled the sea lanes of the Mediterranean. Germany's own maritime impotence was to become apparent in March, 1899, when serious differences between Great Britain, the United States, and herself over Samoa ended in a seeming setback for German interests.

Because of his party's bad mood in the early winter of 1898–1899, Lieber found it imperative to secure a denial from the government that it intended to replace the naval Sextennat in its early stages with a new bill. In December, 1898, and again in the following January, Lieber interpellated the government on the subject in the Reichstag and received the answer that it had no plans to bring an early end to the first naval law.[92] That response was an untruth since Tirpitz was to tell Hohenlohe in May, 1899, that he expected to bring a new naval proposal to the Reichstag in 1901.[93] But Lieber undoubtedly preferred the lie to the truth since the tenuous relationship between the Center and the government in the session of 1898–1899 could not have borne the weight of the news that Tirpitz planned to ask the Reichstag for a new naval law in the early future. By the same token Lieber knew that the Center could not afford to make serious difficulties for the government's army proposal if it refused to consider a replacement of the first naval law by a new proposal.

Nevertheless, Lieber became seriously worried about the opposition in the Center to the army bill and did not attempt to circumvent its critics. A strong majority, opposed to the bill as it stood, undoubtedly contained both the Bavarian and Rhineland contingents. The *Kölnische Volkszeitung* had stated on January 14 that a cause of its own disaffection with the proposal was the government's lack of consideration for the Center's desires, among them a reform of communal suffrage in Prussia. Behind the scenes Lieber moved quickly in February to secure a commitment from Miquel that the Prussian government would present a new bill for such a reform at an early date.[94] But the fraction continued to insist that the government had to make some concession on the bill itself and in mid-February Gröber announced that the Budget Committee had voted for a reduction of seven thousand recruits from the measure.[95] By that date the debates over the army bill had turned into a full-bloom crisis. Hohenlohe and Lieber's other friends in the government were seemingly unable to help the Center leader in his predicament. William II was adamantly opposed to any concession to the Center and the Reichstag majority.

The crisis was not due only to the resentments of many Centrists over the government's failure to make a specific concession to their party and church. The Prussian Conservatives and some of the National Liberals in the Landtag hoped that the army-bill crisis would lead to a conflict between the monarchy and the Reichstag and they used their influence to prevent a settlement of the differences between the government and the Center on the proposed bill. They continued to nurse hopes that the Imperial government would devise some way to replace universal equal suffrage with a more conservative electoral system.[96] Miquel, Lieber's earlier political ally, was apparently involved in the efforts of the Center's foes to bring on a major political crisis over the army measure.[97] But they were to be frustrated, however, by Lieber's resourcefulness in securing William II's acceptance of a compromise measure.

Lieber was proud of his proposal. It stipulated that the number of effectives would be cut by seven thousand but that the Reichstag would later approve them if the government demonstrated the army's need for them. Hohenlohe won over William II for the compromise proposal by pointing out that the government could scarcely hope to wage a successful campaign against the Center over the elimination of seven thousand effectives from an army bill.[98] After he and the chancellor had resolved the crisis Lieber took high satisfaction in his achievement. He wrote Cardinal Kopp that he had never undertaken anything more difficult, "the naval law included," and that he "had only found a solution at the last moment."[99]

Despite the satisfactory settlement of that crisis the Reichstag session of 1898–1899 ended on an unpleasant note for Lieber. The emperor and the leaders of the Cartel parties were determined to secure the passage of the controversial anti-labor Prison House bill. Since Posadowsky, the secretary of the interior, was unable to offer any concession to the trade unions to offset the deep unpopularity of the measure in working-class circles, Lieber and his party refused to permit its submission to a Reichstag committee after its reading in late June, 1899. By taking that action, however, they had saved the proposal from a decisive defeat at a second reading and enabled the government to postpone further parliamentary action on it till the next fall. Lieber hoped that Hohenlohe and Posadowsky would be able to exercise a moderating influence over the ruler and make him more disposed to reasonable collaboration with the Center. But Lieber was to be profoundly disappointed in his hopes. The period from August to late December was to be full of frustration for him and the strains he experienced in its course were to cause the complete breakdown of his health.

[92] Kehr, *Schlachtflottenbau*, pp. 171–172.

[93] Hohenlohe, *Reichskanzlerzeit*, p. 498.

[94] Cardauns, *Trimborn*, pp. 84–86; Herzfeld, *Miquel* 2: p. 561.

[95] Schulthess, *Geschichtskalender* **40** (1899): p. 50.

[96] See Spahn, *Lieber*, p. 65 ff; Bachem, *Zentrumspartei* **6**: pp. 11–12.

[97] Lieber to Kopp, March 19, 1899. Fn. 90 above. Bachem, *Zentrumspartei* **6**: p. 12.

[98] *Ibid.*

[99] Lieber to Kopp, March 19, 1899. See fn. 90 above.

6. THE CENTER AND LABOR, 1891–1901

*. . . for us social reform is not a question of tactics,
not a question of opportunism but a question of justice
and conscience.*

Gröber, August, 1896.[1]

*How nicely the Prison House Bill fell, you know.
That was the power of the Catholic worker who,
circumstances permitting, has more weight than the
craftsman of the Center.*

August Bebel, November, 1899.[2]

Adolf Gröber's statement to the Dortmund Catholic
Congress of 1896 implied the existence of a significant
and active commitment on the Center's part to social
reform prior to that date. It was true in a broad sense
since the party had provided decisive support for programs beneficial to the *Mittelstand* of peasants, craftsmen, and small shopkeepers and had sought, though
unsuccessfully, to secure full rights of coalition and
related benefits for industrial labor. The Center's failure to aid urban workers was due in the first instance
to the stubborn mentality of Imperial advisers and the
Cartel parties whose thinking was geared to repression
rather than to reform. But concern for the industrial
working class did not enjoy a high priority in the
Reichstag Center and its leaders did not challenge the
government on that subject prior to the turn of the
century. Its most important achievement for labor—
Catholic and Social Democratic—was its refusal in
1899 to approve the unpopular Prison House bill, a decision which led the monarchy to change its course from
repression to moderate social reform.

The Center's reluctance to prod the monarchy on labor's behalf reflected the sharp change in course taken
by the ruler and his advisers in 1890–1891 while the
government's legislative program for worker protection was in passage through the Reichstag. During
his struggle with Bismarck in late 1889 and early
1890 William II had appeared as the protector of the
German working classes. Under the influence of officials like Hans von Berlepsch, a former district president in the Rhineland and the new Prussian minister
of commerce, Heinrich von Bötticher, the Imperial
secretary of the interior and certain other advisers, the
emperor had issued his noted February decrees on the
theme of social reform. In them William II affirmed
the state's responsibility for the protection of workers
and their right to equality with other classes. But the
ruler appeared to reach out most sympathetically to
German labor when he stated that workers should be
able through their elected representatives to participate
in the regulation of their common affairs and to carry
on negotiations with employers and with governmental
agencies. Berlepsch and labor leaders interpreted this
statement to be an approval of trade unions and work-

ers' councils though William II may have been thinking
only of labor-management works committees which the
Prussian government had established in its own state
coal mines in 1889.[3]

The emperor's concern with the needs and aspira-
tions of industrial workers was shortlived, however,
since it had been in substantial degree a product of his
conflict with Bismarck. He and his advisers were
distrustful of organized labor and also acutely sensitive to the views of the leading industrialists of the
Free Conservative party, "King" Stumm and Friederich
Krupp, who treated their own workers well but refused to let labor organizers pass beyond their factory
gates. Although Stumm was frustrated in his hopes
that the monarchy would do away with universal suffrage he was to exercise a virtual veto on any plans for
industrial social legislation from 1891 to 1899.[4]

Lieber had mixed feelings about the government's
sudden abandonment of industrial social reform and
the ascendency of Stumm and Krupp as its advisers on
social questions. His own party had won additional
prestige through the government's adoption of its program for worker protection and its dependence upon
Hitze's advice in the shaping of its proposals. It appeared then that Berlepsch, Bötticher, and other high
officials would continue to rely on Hitze and the Center for the formulation and passage of additional legislation for labor.

But Lieber's regrets over the setback to his party's
prospects were balanced by his relief over the sudden
turn of the political wheel which depressed Hitze's
fortunes.[5] He had not rejoiced in 1890 over William
II's conversion to the cause of social reform and made
morbid prophecies about the government's continuance
of Bismarck's "State Socialism" with Schorlemer "as
its pilot" in the Reichstag.[6] The likelihood is that
Lieber secretly feared that a serious governmental
commitment to social legislation would strengthen the
position of the conservative wing of his party and en-
hance its efforts to create a Center-Conservative coalition which would identify itself with the ideals of a
"Christian social order and culture." In fact Ballestrem had insisted on taking the chairman's position in

[1] *VGVkD zu Dortmund* (Dortmund, 1896), p. 418.

[2] Viktor Adler, *Briefwechsel mit August Bebel und Karl
Kautsky, sowie Briefe von und an I. Auer und E. Bernstein,*
F. Adler, ed. (Vienna, 1954), p. 332.

[3] Berlepsch was responsible for the drafting of William II's
decrees and hence knew their intent, but the ruler was only
briefly under his influence. On the debate: Karl von Stumm-
Halberg, *Reichstag Verhandlungen,* May 3, 1899: p. 2047.
Karl Born, *Staat und Sozialpolitik seit Bismarcks Sturz. Ein
Beitrag zur Geschichte der Innenpolitischen Entwicklung des
Deutschen Reiches 1890–1914* (Wiesbaden, 1957), p. 10 ff.

[4] Born insists that the emperor did not need advice from
Stumm since he and most of his advisers were not interested in
further social reforms. *Ibid.,* pp. 66–69, 113–114. But Lieber,
who was usually well informed on such matters, thought that
Stumm had considerable influence with the monarch. Journal,
May 6, 1892. And see Bachem, *Zentrumspartei* **5**: pp. 416–417.

[5] Lieber to Lujo Brentano, May 17, 1892. Lieber-Brentano
Correspondence, Camberg.

[6] Lieber to Hertling, March 3, 1890. Lieber-Hertling Correspondence, Camberg.

the committee on the worker protection program in 1890.[7] Once Ballestrem and Huene had been overthrown in 1893 Lieber did not find it difficult to join with Hitze in presenting various motions on behalf of labor. Neither deputy expected to achieve anything meaningful in the way of new social reform in the immediate future and Hitze, no seeker after personal power or prestige, was content to adapt himself to the existing political situation.

Nevertheless, Lieber and Hitze thought it desirable and necessary to urge governmental action in two directions. The Center was morally committed to the principles of worker protection; its leaders felt an obligation to supervise the administration of the legislation passed in earlier years and to seek its expansion. Because of his own dislike for Berlepsch's approach to social reform, Lieber took pleasure in harassing the impotent minister of commerce with complaints about insufficient security arrangements in individual factories.[8] Hitze who was actually closer to Berlepsch called for the appointment of more factory inspectors in Prussia.[9] Lieber had no interest in going further along the route of government regulation of industry. Aside from his own exaggerated fears of "state socialism" he undoubtedly had compelling political reasons for rejecting such a course. The Cartel parties disapproved of new government controls over business and there was no evidence for serious support for such a policy in the Center itself.

Hitze's most important contribution to his party's program for industrial labor was his advocacy of the granting of full legal rights to trade unions and the establishment of workers' industrial councils. His interest in unions and workers' councils derived naturally from his vision of a corporative society based on institutions representing different vocational groups rather than from the liberal concept of association and representation. Hitze also thought that actual experience had demonstrated the usefulness of trade unions. He believed that workers would be less inclined to engage in wasteful and violent strikes if they were organized in strong unions whose leaders could negotiate with employers. Indeed the great Ruhr strike of 1889, which was essentially the work of unorganized groups of disaffected miners, should have demonstrated the validity of this thesis in that respect. Hitze was also convinced that there would be more harmony between employers and workers if the employees were drawn through their representatives into the internal management of their factories as they were in the textile mill of Franz Brandts at München-Gladbach.[10]

Despite his ideological differences with Hitze, Lieber's succession to the party leadership in 1893 led to an early identification of the Center with the cause of trade union rights and worker's councils. It is true that Hitze and Stötzel had expressed their fraction's will in April, 1891, in helping to defeat the efforts of the Cartel parties to curtail the legal strike powers of the unions contained in article 153 of the Industrial Code.[11] But Franz von Ballestrem, then the chairman of the Center, was a mine owner and a firm opponent of trade unionism.[12] At the end of the decade his episcopal patron, Cardinal Georg Kopp, was to become the leading ecclesiastical foe of the new interconfessional trade union movement, though his rejection of it was probably due to concern for his own authority and general church discipline than to Ballestrem's influence.

Lieber had always taken a certain amount of pride in his earlier role as a leading advocate of social reforms for the working classes in his party. His correspondence with Lujo Brentano, the most prominent German authority on British trade unionism, revealed his desire to appear as a friend of the German labor movement.[13] There was no passionate conviction, however, in his speeches about the intrinsic value of trade unions. His willingness to act in partnership with Hitze in presenting motions to the Reichstag calling for full rights on behalf of the unions and for workers' councils probably reflected the strong support Hitze enjoyed from his provincial party, the Rhineland Center, and the headquarters staff of the Peoples' Association at München-Gladbach. Hitze, August Pieper, the general secretary of the Peoples' Association, and Karl Trimborn, the chairman of the Rhineland Center, were a closely knit team and continued to be such after Trimborn entered the Reichstag in 1896.[14]

In the earlier and mid-1890's Hitze and Lieber knew that they were only speaking for the record in presenting motions beneficial to industrial labor.[15] At that time more meaningful developments were taking place within the Catholic labor movement itself. Leo XIII's encyclical of 1891 on the labor question, *Rerum Novarum,* had awakened the interest and enthusiasm of many young priests throughout western Europe in doing work among the laboring classes in the cities. In Germany, however, it had also provoked a debate between the corporatists and the Center's leaders about the forms that associations of workers should take and the validity of free enterprise. Between 1893 and 1896 the leaders of the Rhineland Center and the Peo-

[7] Bachem, *Zentrumspartei* 5: p. 134.
[8] Lieber to Brentano, fn. 5 above.
[9] *Deutsche Reichs-zeitung,* February 12, 1895.
[10] Ritter, *Volksverein,* pp. 131–132. Franziska Vincke, "Die Arbeitnehmer Sozialpolitik des Zentrums unter besonderer Berücksichtigung ihrer ideologischen Grundlagen" (Ph.D. diss., Münster, 1933), p. 68 ff.

[11] *Ibid.,* p. 67. Stumm in the Reichstag: *Verhandlungen,* February 7, 1895: p. 730.
[12] Karl Bachem, notes dated April 13, 1905, Bachem Papers, File 223.
[13] See below, p. 79, fn. 31.
[14] Cardauns, *Trimborn,* pp. 77–78.
[15] *Reichstag Verhandlungen,* February 6, 1815: pp. 690–693; *ibid.,* February 7, 1895: p. 715.

ples' Association were deeply concerned over the efforts of Peter Oberdörffer to win acceptance of his extreme corporative ideas from the Catholic workers' associations of the archdiocese of Cologne. He was then the editor of the publications committee of that group. But he was no match for Julius Bachem and his associates. In 1897 Cardinal Krementz, the archbishop of Cologne, appointed August Pieper to the chairmanship of the archdiocesan committee itself even though he came from a Westphalian diocese.[16] It was to be a position of considerable importance in the later development of the Catholic worker movement, since Pieper and his colleagues were to make their archdiocesan organization the nucleus of the Union of Catholic Workers' Associations in West Germany in 1904.

The Catholic workers' associations were not adequate substitutes for trade unions but they served a worthwhile purpose. They were ecclesiastical institutions whose first aim was to keep Catholic workers in their church. The chairman of the individual association was always a priest who was subject to his bishop. Nevertheless, they played a useful role in acquainting members with their rights under existing social legislation and with the prospects of further legislative benefits. Under the direction of the staff of the Peoples' Associations, which provided special courses for them, lay leaders became schooled in wider labor questions and methods of worker leadership. Some of them moved later into important offices in the Christian trade unions. The Catholic workers' association movement was in an organizational phase throughout most of the 1890's; in 1895 its total membership was about sixty thousand compared to the two hundred sixty thousand members of the Social Democratic unions.[17] In western and southern Germany, where they enjoyed considerable freedom under their episcopal superiors, they tended to be progressive in labor matters. While the Catholic workers' associations in the northwest came to take the primary place in the general movement, those in the south were not behind them in their own programs. Lorenz Huber, the priest chairman of the Munich federation and then only twenty-eight had presented a program to the Congress of the chairmen of Catholic Workers' Associations at Mainz in 1892 which advocated the complete legalization of trade unions, workers' councils, and labor offices among other proposals. And like the Cologne federation, its Munich counterpart was to support the cause of interconfessional trade unions in the later 1890's.[18]

It is a reasonable if unproven assumption that Julius Bachem and his intimates took the initiative in promoting the foundation of the first Christian trade union, although in the early 1890's Franz Hitze had appeared to favor further training of Catholic worker leaders in Catholic associations organized along craft lines.[19] But most priest chairmen of these Catholic organizations discouraged their members from making use of the strike. The secular unions associated with the Social Democratic party were not subject to such restraints and were increasing rapidly in their membership. There was a precedent, though it was of an unsuccessful effort, for the foundation by Centrists of an interconfessional union. In 1889 Gerhard Stötzel and Fusangel had tried to start a Christian miners' union in the Ruhr. August Brust, who had participated in that abortive undertaking, took the initiative in founding the new Union of Christian Miners at Essen in October, 1894.[20] With remarkable quickness, Hermann Schmitz, the auxiliary bishop of Cologne, publicly approved its establishment.[21]

Like the Catholic workers' associations, the Christian trade unions grew slowly. Since Catholic social reformers objected to the partisan character of the Social Democratic trade unions, Bachem and his friends could not logically affirm a relationship between their own party and the new movement. It is evident, however, that they wanted the annual Catholic Congress to pass a resolution in their favor. Both Brust and Hitze spoke to the Dortmund Congress of 1896 about the new labor organization, but Lieber apparently blocked a resolution to that purpose. He and Brust collaborated on another resolution which expressed regret over the lack of Christian influence in existing trade unions and called on workers to try to place them on a Christian basis.[22] At the same congress Gröber acknowledged that it was "difficult" and "painful" to form labor associations on a confessional basis but he stressed the unfortunate but deep division between the confessions.[23] Lieber's and Gröber's reserve was hardly due to confessional narrow mindedness; they were undoubtedly concerned about the reactions of the bishops and the clergy to the emergence of a new trade union movement in which they would have no influence. In 1898 the Krefeld Catholic Congress did approve a resolution which implicitly sanctioned interconfessional trade unions by stating that the foundation of unions on a Christian basis was a pressing necessity.[24]

Despite their desire to preserve the loyalty of the new Catholic labor leaders and the worker vote, the Centrist leaders did not display meaningful vigor in trying to push legislation for labor in the Reichstag session of 1893–1898. There were two major reasons for their reluctance to do so. It was clear that the Prussian monarchy and its allies in the Federal Council were

16 Ritter, *Volksverein*, p. 283.

17 Born, *Staat und Sozialpolitik*, p. 283.

18 *Ketteler Wacht*, November 1, 1966.

19 Peter Molt, *Der Reichstag vor der improviersten Revolution* (Cologne, 1963), p. 244; Ritter, *Volksverein*, pp. 291–293.

20 *Ibid.*, p. 215.

21 Ernst Deuerlein, "Der Gewerkschaftstreit," *Theologische Quartalschrift* 139 (1959): pp. 43–44.

22 *VGVkD zu Dortmund* (Dortmund, 1896), pp. 253–263, 374–375.

23 *Ibid.*, p. 423.

24 Ritter, *Volksverein*, p. 297.

still not interested in ending the long pause in social legislation. To the marked satisfaction of the Central League of Industrialists and several state governments Berlepsch was either forced or allowed to resign in June, 1896.[25] The government hoped to resolve the social problem by repression of the Social Democrats, the renewal of ties between the old Cartel parties and the social groups they represented, and *Weltpolitik*. In February, 1895, Hitze and Lieber interpellated the government at length on its position regarding the provision of full legal rights for trade unions and the establishment of labor chambers. Both deputies spoke with apparent feeling about the legitimate claim of workers to such institutions. But a Social Democratic opponent was undoubtedly right in claiming that Hitze and Lieber thought it tactically advisable to take the initiative at that time because their party was then virtually committed to the support of the anti-revolu-ion bill.[26]

Within their own constituency, Lieber, Gröber, and Julius Bachem were more concerned in the mid-1890's with the complaints of the Catholic agrarians and the *Mittelstand*. Those groups were in a nastier mood than many Catholic workers and better organized. The favorable outcome of the elections of 1893, especially in the industrial areas, had apparently convinced the Centrist leaders that they could rely on the loyalty of Catholic labor for the immediate future. Their stance in the debates over the Prison House bill of 1899 re-vealed, however, that they could not afford to partici-pate in the sacrifice of labor's legal goods in the interest of their high strategy of winning the confidence and approval of the monarchy.

The Prison House proposal was the last major effort of reactionaries and conservatives in the Prussian gov-erment, the court, the army, and the Cartel parties to lame the Social Democratic movement. Posadowsky, its author, was able to win the support of the National Liberal leadership for his bill because he did not intend to tamper with basic civic rights of assembly, associa-tion, free speech, or the Reichstag suffrage. Though the aim of the bill was to put restrictions on the ability of trade unions to carry out strikes, Posadowsky in-sisted that he wanted to preserve the right of the in-dividual worker to make his own free choice whether he would participate in such actions or not. In his first programmatic speech to the Reichstag in Decem-ber, 1897, on the question of labor's rights he made it evident that he did not belong to the group of officials, generals, and parliamentarians who wanted to get rid of universal suffrage.[27] He also hoped to convince the Center and some left-wing liberals that his proposals would not violate the concept of equality before the

law since some of its provisions applied both to em-ployers and to workers.

The new bill proposed changes in Article 153 of the Industrial Code. In some respects it stood in direct contradiction to earlier legislation or court rulings on permissible practices of corporations. The Prison House proposals stipulated that heavy penalties should be imposed on those who attempted to force other persons to join their economic association. But the Craftsmen bill of 1897 made it obligatory for artisans in certain crafts to join a guild if a majority of their co-workers agreed to do so. Some trusts and other business combinations imposed their wills on smaller firms without fear of punishment.[28] The Prison House measure also provided severe punishment for anyone who sought to make others join in a strike or lockout through violence, threats of injury, attacks on their reputation, or the like. The rights of unions to use picketing was reduced substantially to the point where it would be ineffective.

While the bill would have experienced difficulties in the Reichstag in any event, Posadowsky and William II were awkward or worse in their staging of its intro-duction. The minister of the interior was strikingly inept in stating to the Reichstag in December, 1897, that universal suffrage made trade unions superfluous. The emperor made a widely noted speech in Sep-tember, 1898, in which he made it clear that the new legislation would be aimed against labor alone and specifically those workers who strove to keep others from their jobs. The Social Democratic press quickly seized on William II's clumsy reference to the imposi-tion of severe prison terms on offenders and the pro-posal became popularly known as the Prison House bill from that point onward. After the emperor's speech Posadowsky and Miquel became discouraged over the prospects of the bill's approval in the Reichstag.[29]

Lieber conducted himself wth considerable skill and tact during the preliminary discussions of the measure. After Posadowsky had made his statement about the superfluous character of the trade unions, Lieber im-mediately inserted a notice in *Germania* justifying their existence and affirming the need for further social legislation.[30] In a Reichstag speech on January 20, 1898, he asserted that the growth of worker organiza-tions would reduce breaches of labor contracts. But he also indicated that his response to the Prison House bill might not be negative, since he added that his party would want to consult with the government if willing workers were threatened by terrorism. In the further course of his speech Lieber also emphasized the fact that the Social Democratic unions were "the ene-mies of our Christian workers' associations." Lujo

[25] Hohenlohe, *Denkwürdigkeiten*, p. 234; Born, *Staat und Sozialpolitik*, pp. 127–134.
[26] *Reichstag Verhandlungen*, February 7, 1895: p. 721.
[27] Born, *Staat und Sozialpolitik*, p. 144.

[28] *Ibid.*, pp. 151–152.
[29] *Ibid.*, pp. 147–148; Herzfeld, *Miquel* 2: p. 536.
[30] Born, p. 145.

Brentano, the leading advocate in university circles of trade unionism and Lieber's old friend, anxiously inquired of the Center leader whether he intended to support a legislative attack upon picketing. Although Lieber reassured Brentano that neither he nor Posadowsky wanted to destroy picketing,[31] Brentano's concern was undoubtedly justified.

Indeed Lieber's desire to satisfy William II and the Cartel parties was acute when the Prison House bill finally reached the Reichstag in June, 1899. During the early winter he had been forced to express his party's concern over the rumors that the secretary of the navy was at work on a second navy plan. Soon afterward the new army bill had led to a crisis between the government and the parliament. The Centrist leader was now eager to demonstrate to the ruler and the anti-labor parties that they could rely upon the Center's support for legislation which was necessary in their judgment for the maintenace of law and order in industrial affairs.

Nevertheless, Lieber could not expect his party to support the Posadowsky proposals without a meaningful concession to labor. The Center itself had opposed the sharpening of Article 153 of the Industrial Code at labor's expense in 1891 because the working classes were denied full rights of coalition. The Prison House bill was widely unpopular before its submission to the Reichstag and prominent left-liberals like Lujo Brentano had spoken out publicly against the measure. The Catholic press joined in the campaign and a leading place in it was taken by the *Westdeutscher Arbeiterzeitung,* the new organ of the Catholic Workers' Association of the Archdiocese of Cologne which began publication in April, 1898. Johann Giesberts, its first editor, proved to be an articulate and robust journalist, speaker, and politician. The fact that he had previously worked as an engineer at the plant of the *Kölnische Volkszeitung* probably warrants the inference that Julius Bachem was his patron and adviser.[32]

Before the first reading of the bill Giesberts attacked the government's claim that it wished to accord equal treatment to workers and owners in its proposed revision of Article 153. He noted that Posadowsky had not asserted the illegality of black lists. But Giesbert's main intent was to demonstrate that the solution to economic conflict could only be found in according workers more adequate rights of coalition, not through repression. He quoted official statistics to prove that while the number of strikes had increased in recent years the number of workers punished for violations of the law had been relatively low, approximately four per cent per one thousand workers. Giesberts attributed this fact to the growth of labor organizations and their influence. His conclusion was that the govern-

ment would be better advised to drop the Prison House bill and to strengthen labor organizations instead.[33] Shortly after defeat of the bill in its first reading the editor of the *Westdeutscher Arbeiterzeitung* was to write:

A storm of indignation goes through the whole German working class . . . over this demand of the government which offers the stone of an exceptional law in place of the bread of the freedom of coalition.[34]

And in that view the bulk of the Center press had concurred.

Lieber tried hard to win a concession from the government and its coalition allies, the Free Conservatives, Conservatives, and National Liberals but without result. He knew before the presentation of the bill to the Reichstag that they would not give any ground on the extension of full rights of association to trade unions. Lieber and Hitze decided, therefore, to offer a motion for the establishment of works chambers in which both labor and management would be represented.[35] But Stumm, who apparently spoke for the official coalition, insisted that the only legitimate form of labor organzation was workers' funds societies and argued that all other labor organizations would come under Social Democratic control.[36] Therefore, the Reichstag had to vote on the Prison House bill by itself and the Center formed part of a large majority, inclusive of some prominent southern National Liberals, which refused to send the bill into a committee.[37] The Center and the left-wing National Liberals chose not to run the risk of antagonizing William II by proceeding to a decisive second reading which would have killed the measure.

The emperor's rigidity on the Prison House bill was a depressing revelation to Lieber of the influence that the Conservatives had over the ruler. But his spirits revived in the midsummer when a breach occurred between William II and the Prussian Conservatives. The monarchy, the National Liberals, and some Free Conservatives were eager to promote the building of a series of canals linking up the major industrial and commercial centers of the Ruhr with the Rhine and with the west, Berlin, and the east.[38] The agrarian Conservatives were hostile to the plan because it would benefit industry and trade and open up their own agricultural markets to competitors. Lieber was sympathetic to the canal plan itself and, as always, to most proposals which would enable his party to win William II's approval. He also thought that the relentless op-

[31] Lieber to Brentano, January 28, 1898. Lieber-Brentano Correspondence, Camberg.

[32] Ritter, *Volksverein,* pp. 287–288.

[33] *Westdeutscher Arbeiterzeitung,* June 17, 1899.

[34] *Ibid.,* July 22, 1899.

[35] Vincke, *Die Arbeitnehmerpolitik des Zentrums,* pp. 76–77. *Reichstag Verhandlungen,* May 3, 1899: pp. 2043–2045.

[36] *Ibid.,* pp. 2044–2045.

[37] On the collaboration between the southern National Liberals and the Center: Hellwig, *Stumm-Halberg,* p. 557.

[38] See Hannelore Horn, *Der Kampf auf den Bau des Mittel-land-kanals* (Cologne and Opladen, 1964), p. 36 ff.

position of the Conservatives to the proposal would lead to a break between the ruler and their party; the monarchy and the Prussian ministry would then have to depend upon the National Liberals and the Center as its chief supports both in the Landtag and in the Reichstag.[39] Hohenlohe had assured Lieber that William II, angry over the refusal of the Conservatives to follow their ruler on the issue, would dissolve the Landtag and call for new elections if the canal proposal were lost through the Conservatives' opposition.[40]

If anything, however, the outcome of the parliamentary debates and negotiations over the canal bill proved to be a greater disillusionment to Lieber than the emperor's stand on the Prison House bill. First of all Lieber had been unable to control his own party in the Landtag. Ballestrem and most of the Silesian Centrists were hostile to the measure.[41] The votes of the Rhineland Centrists, by far the most numerous regional group in the Prussian Center, were indispensable for the passage of the canal proposals. Their support hinged upon the willingness of the National Liberals to agree to a reform of the communal suffrage acceptable to Julius Bachem and his associates. After difficult negotiations the National Liberals agreed to such a reform proposal. The leading members of the Rhineland Center later held a caucus in their province on July 27 to discuss the tactics to be used by their colleagues in the Landtag during the second reading of the canal bill. The caucus decided that the Rhineland Centrists deputies should vote against the measure if it came to a vote before the proposal on the modification of communal suffrage. The justification for this policy was given by Julius Bachem and his intimates: that they did not want to be duped again as they had been in 1893 after their earlier support of Miquel's tax legislation.[42] The Conservatives succeeded in bringing the canal bill to a vote first on August 12 and the Rhineland Centrists joined with them in causing its defeat.

The failure of the bill was a severe and painful blow to Lieber and its effects were exacerbated by later developments connected with it. William II decided not to break with the Conservatives by dissolving the Landtag but insisted only that the county councilors who had opposed the canal proposals should be retired. He offered as his reason the government's need for Conservative support for the Prison House bill in the next Reichstag session.[43] The emperor's insistence on the importance of that collaboration between the government and the Conservatives in the parliament indicated,

as later developments proved, that he was still opposed to any benefits for working-class organizations which would offset the purely repressive character of the anti-labor measure. The Center would be confronted with a painful alternative; it would have to affront either the ruler or its own working-class electorate whose loyalty was crucial to the party's future. Lieber also learned that government might introduce a second major naval bill to the Reichstag in the winter.[44]

Lieber's disappointment over the defeat of the canal proposal turned to cold rage after he learned more about the circumstances connected with the monarch's decision not to dissolve the Landtag. Johannes Miquel had initially identified himself with the Conservative opposition to the canal bill; then he came out in favor of the measure when he saw how insistent William II was on its passage. Miquel had long recognized that his political career depended on his ability to get along with the Conservatives and he apparently sought to soften the ruler's anger toward them. A government official, probably Hohenlohe, told Lieber that Miquel had drafted the speech which William II read to the Prussian Crown Council rejecting its earlier proposal that he dissolve the Landtag. The same informant or another source informed the Center leader that Miquel in a conversation with the ruler blamed the defeat of the canal bill on the Center because it had coupled that measure with a proposal for electoral reform.[45] Even though the Prussian finance minister had visited him earlier that summer,[46] Lieber made a veiled attack on Miquel in late September in an address to the state rally of the Hessian Center party. To the undoubted surprise of his audience and newspaper reporters who knew of his longtime friendship with Miquel, he charged that "a very influential man in the Prussian state ministry wished to deprive the Center of its decisive position in the Reichstag" and had high hopes of being able to do so in the next parliamentary session when the Reichstag would consider the Prison House bill and possibly new military proposals as well.[47]

Lieber's conviction that Miquel, a minister with ready access to the ruler, had striven to undermine William II's confidence in the Center, fragile at best, was sufficient reason in his judgment to break publicly with his old political ally. But his relationship with Miquel had already been weakened by other differences and strains before the canal-bill fiasco.

In the course of the naval-bill debates of 1897–1898 Miquel had established a close relationship with Cardinal Kopp. After the failure of their joint effort to deprive Tirpitz of his Septennat in the late summer of 1897, Lieber refused Miquel's offer to serve as the mediator between the new secretary of the navy and

[39] Spahn, *Lieber*, pp. 71–72.
[40] Karl Bachem, notes dated June 1899. Bachem Papers, File 106.
[41] Hohenlohe, *Reichskanzlerzeit*, p. 517.
[42] Printed report of the caucus, dated July 29, 1899. Lieber Papers, Envelope *Mittelland Kanal*, Trimborn to Lieber, August 1, 1899, Lieber Papers, Speyer, File T, 20.
[43] Hohenlohe, *Reichskanzlerzeit*, p. 516.

[44] *Kölnische Zeitung*, September 25, 1899.
[45] Karl Bachem, notes dated October 10, 1899. Bachem Papers, File 106.
[46] *Freisinnige Zeitung*, April 2, 1902.
[47] See fn. 44 above.

the Center and negotiated in person with Tirpitz. Miquel was unwilling to be left out of the most important legislative undertaking of the later 1890's and he initiated his own negotiations with Kopp.[48] It is probably significant that the Prussian government began in the Landtag session of 1898 to introduce a series of legislative measures providing higher salaries for the pastors and lesser clergy of the Catholic and Evangelical Churches.[49] Though Lieber made no reference in the following year to any earlier collaboration between the cardinal and the minister of finance in his correspondence, his discontent with both Miquel and Kopp was real enough. He wrote the cardinal in mid-March, 1899, that Miquel was privy to the efforts of the Conservatives to cause a crisis over the Gossler army bill.[50] Shortly afterward he warned Robert Bosse, the Prussian minister of public worship, that Kopp was "a deceitful person."[51]

Nevertheless, Lieber had maintained his ties with the minister of finance through most of the summer of 1899. During that season Miquel called on him in either the Reichstag or in Camberg to ask if he would support a plan to modify the national parliamentary suffrage along conservative lines. At a later date Lieber implied to his associates that Miquel's proposal was an important factor in their estrangement from each other.[52] But Miquel's hostility to universal suffrage was probably well known to most of the Centrist leaders and the cause of Lieber's rage against him was undoubtedly the reports that the minister of finance had tried to turn the emperor against the Center after the canal-bill fiasco.

Despite the bitterness of his feelings toward Miquel, Lieber's public attack on the minister was not due only to his conviction that an old political ally had betrayed him. In August the editors of the *Kölnische Volkszeitung*, frustrated again in their efforts to secure a reform of the Prussian municipal electoral system, had begun a new campaign to bring about Miquel's dismissal from office. Since the Prussian bureaucracy prided itself on the integrity of its members, the *Kölnische Volkszeitung* charged that Miquel was "a minister without credibility."[53] While Lieber took some pleasure in punishing the minister of finance whom he had defended in Centrist debates of well over a half-decade, he was more interested in the establishment of a confidential relationship with his old foes, Julius Bachem

and Hermann Cardauns. Lieber assumed that the government might confront the Reichstag with both the Prison House bill and a second major naval proposal in the late fall. The outcome of the debates on those two unpopular measures would depend upon the votes of the Rhineland Center delegation in the Reichstag fraction. His friendy relations with Miquel had been a major obstacle to the reconciliation between Lieber and the leaders of the Rhineland provincial Center party in the past.

Lieber's assumption that William II and Tirpitz might make the decision to seek the Reichstag's approval of a second big naval bill before its predecessor was three years old was proven correct in the fall.

On October 9 war broke out between Great Britain and the Boer Republics. Most Germans, anti-British to begin with, felt intense sympathy for the small African states in their struggle with the British Empire. Encouraged by Admiral Senden, his naval aide, and by Miquel, William II decided to exploit the situation for his naval ambitions in a speech at Hamburg on October 18. As he had done so often in the past, he tried to bring the Reichstag under pressure from middle-class public opinion. With characteristic exaggeration he stated that the expansion of its navy was a "bitter necessity" for the German Empire. Though the ruler did not attack the Center directly, he did so implicitly by calling on the German people to put aside "narrow party tendencies" and to place the well being of the nation above party interest.[54] Several days later Tirpitz wrote an article for the *Norddeutsche Allgemeine Zeitung* expressing the need for further naval expansion without specifying the time when it should take place.

The leaders of the Center were both upset by William II's speech and embarrassed at the prospect of being confronted with a major naval bill within two years of the passage of the first Tirpitz proposals. Yet they realized that the emperor might be willing to pay a high price for their party's support. William II was in fact willing to do so. Miquel, hoping to rehabilitate himself with the Center, negotiated with "a Center leader" on the naval question and made wide promises, specifically that the clergy could control the appointment of religion teachers in Prussia and that the anti-Jesuit law would be withdrawn.[55] But some of the emperor's advisers had different views about the wisdom of antagonizing the Evangelical League and large segments of conservative and liberal Protestant opinion. Even Hohenlohe thought that the government could offer no more than the deleting of the expulsion paragraph in the anti-Jesuit law and the return of two minor religious orders.[56] In the end the government, confident that the Center would have to approve the bill, offered nothing for the religious orders.

[48] Herzfeld, *Miquel* **2**: pp. 449–451.

[49] In May, 1898, Robert Bosse, the Prussian minister for public worship, thanked Kopp for his assistance on the recent pastors' salary law: Bosse, Journal entry, May 17, 1898. Copy in possession of Rudolf Morsey.

[50] See above chapter 5, fn. 97.

[51] Bosse, journal entry, May 29, 1899. Fn. 48.

[52] Karl Bachem, notes dated October 10, 1902. Bachem Papers, File 106. Matthias Erzberger, "Die Bedeutung des Zentrums für das Deutsche Reich," *Zeitschrift für Politik* **2** (1908–1909): p. 222.

[53] *Kölnische Volkszeitung,* August 23, 1899.

[54] Schulthess, *Geschichtskalender* **40** (1899): p. 108.

[55] Hohenlohe, *Reichskanzlerzeit,* p. 538.

[56] *Ibid.,* p. 542.

Lieber was deeply upset and his health shaken by the course of events. After friendly Imperial and Prussian officials failed to secure the indefinite postponement of the new naval bill, he told Hohenlohe in mid-November that his party would not support the measure.[57] But his basic mood was one of discouragement rather than of opposition. On November 20 the parliament voted on the Prison House bill in its second reading. Posadowsky had apparently promised Lieber that he would try to persuade William II to pair concessions to the working classes with the anti-labor measure. The emperor was unwilling, however, to let his secretary of the interior do anything more than make vague promises about the later grant of full rights of coalition to labor unions and the establishment of labor chambers. Most likely the Prison House bill was dead before its second reading. Nevertheless, Posadowsky tried to save it by inviting the Center to make proposals to him regarding the establishment of labor chambers. But Hitze and Lieber were unable to reach an agreement on them before the Reichstag voted on the bill. Two other prominent Rhineland Centrists, Karl Bachem and Peter Spahn, were adamantly opposed to the Prison House measure and even Gröber, normally Lieber's faithful deputy, finally abandoned the leader. Lieber decided then to lead his fraction in its negative vote on the proposal.[58]

Had Lieber hoped to win his party's approval of the Prison House measure so that it could then proceed more confidently to oppose the second naval bill? William II and Tirpitz were apparently alarmed over Lieber's angry response to the government's failure to offer any *quid pro quo* for the Center's backing of the new naval proposals since they decided to hold back temporarily on the presentation of the projected bill to the Reichstag. But the Centrist leader was hardly inclined to sacrifice his party's reputation as a reliable national party by making serious difficulties for a second naval measure, above all at a time when German feeling was running high against Great Britain. Lieber's second attack on Miquel would appear to warrant that conclusion.

On December 12 Lieber addressed the Reichstag on the subject of the general budget. He stated that his party would want to study the naval proposals very carefully after the government introduced them to the parliament. Then Lieber made brief complaints about the emperor's Hamburg speech; he said that it was an unprecedented criticism of the German people in their own house and before the world and that the Reichstag was the right forum for the discussion of the naval question. Finally he launched into a violent assault on Miquel, apparently aiming to discredit the finance minister with the emperor and the Cartel parties. He brought out an old story of Miquel's youthful association with the Communist League and asserted that the Prussian minister was incapable of loyalty to a party—an apparent reference to his conduct in the canal-bill crisis. The attack was too personal and unrestrained to be effective and Miquel, possibly the most skilled speaker in German public life, was able to defend himself successfully some days later.[59]

While emotion flamed Lieber's speech against his old ally, it undoubtedly had design to it as well. Miquel's failure to carry out the pledges he had given to Lieber himself or some other Center dignitary when they discussed the possibility of Centrist support in early November for a new naval bill left the Center's leaders in the position of having to support the naval proposals without any hope of a major concession which they could show off to their electorate. Lieber hoped to assuage Catholic resentment by bringing about the sacrifice of an unpopular Prussian minister.

Nevertheless, it was a chastened and conciliatory Lieber who spoke again in the Reichstag on January 20, 1900. He was clearly intent on repairing relations with the monarch and the Conservatives, whom he had bitingly described as the "sham Conservatives" in his remarks to the Hessian Center congress in September, 1899.[60] He was probably afraid that William II and the Conservatives might have reacted violently to his criticisms of them and to the unceremonious manner in which the Center had disposed of the Prison House bill. In early January a British warship had stopped a German mailboat in South African waters on the grounds that it might be carrying contraband of war. Public opinion became even more hostile to Great Britain. It is likely that Lieber worried over the possibility that William II and the Conservatives might welcome a conflict with the Reichstag. Under the circumstances they could hope to secure the election of a Cartel majority which would keep the Center in isolation for five years and attempt to change the Reichstag suffrage along conservative lines. In his speech Lieber turned to Herbert von Bismarck and Wilhelm von Kardorff and recalled that it was Bismarck's father who had established the Reichstag on the basis of universal equal suffrage. Lieber added that there was no need for a conflict between the monarchy and the parliament.[61] Lieber was under severe strain when he spoke and a few days later he suffered a complete collapse. For the next several weeks his life was in danger.[62]

[57] *Ibid.*, pp. 545–546.

[58] Hohenlohe, *Denkwürdigkeiten*, p. 532; Born, *Staat und Sozialpolitik*, p. 160. The *Vörwarts* of November 15, 1899, reported that Ballestrem had spoken in a lifeless manner in opening the session. Karl Bachem, notes on fraction session of November 20, 1899. Bachem Papers, File 99; notes dated December 7, 1899, *ibid.*, File 104.

[59] On the whole incident: Spahn, *Lieber*, pp. 72–73; Schulthess, *Geschichtskalender*, 1899: pp. 173–174; Herzfeld, *Miquel* 2: pp. 556–557.

[60] *Kölnische Zeitung*, September 25, 1899.

[61] Spahn, *Lieber*, p. 73.

[62] Karl Bachem, undated notes, Bachem Papers, File 924.

Even though he was to return to the Reichstag in the fall, his active parliamentary career was over.

There is no evidence that William II and his ministers thought seriously in the winter of 1899–1900 of trying to do away with universal suffrage. For a variety of reasons, military, political, and economic, they wanted to exploit the state of public opinion to bring about the early introduction of the second naval bill. For several months the Navy League and other nationalist propaganda organizations had been carrying on a vigorous agitation for additional naval expansion. The economy was in a slump and heavy industry was desperate for armament contracts.[63] After the mailboat incident William II ordered Tirpitz to present his new proposals to the Reichstag within a few weeks and predicted that pressure from the people would force the Budget Committee "to make a favorable settlement." [64] It was a safe prediction, though the emperor, acting through Ballestrem, thought it advisable to assure the Centrist leaders that he would bring about the revocation of the anti-Jesuit law if their party voted for the new bill.[65]

The second Tirpitz measure proposed the addition of sixteen more battleships and supporting smaller vessels to the navy for home use and a foreign service component of thirteen cruisers. The new program of construction was to be completed in 1917. The government claimed, as it had done in 1897–1898, that it would not have to impose new taxes to fund the construction program but would make use of its surplus and loans. But the Center had to assume on the basis of experience that overruns would occur and that new taxes would be needed.

The concern of the Center's leadership with the financing of the bill and its pacifism were evident throughout the debates on it. The fraction's choice of Schaedler as its speaker at the first reading on February 8 was intended to reassure the party electorate, especially in Bavaria, that it would not capitulate outright to the government's demands. Schaedler was deliberately unpleasant in the manner in which Bavarian Centrists excelled when dealing with Prussian officials. The government, he noted, had not lived up to its own pledge that it would carry out the Septennat of the 1898 bill; he repeated the old warning that the Center would never approve the building of a navy strong enough to attack the enemy in his own waters, implying that the Naval Secretariat had such an ambition in mind. The Center would only provide support for naval forces that would defend Germany herself, her sea trade, and her colonies. But Schaedler stressed his party's commitment to the gradual development of a strong German navy, while making it clear that the

Center's reaction to the present bill would depend on how the government was willing to finance it.[66]

In contrast to their conduct during the debates on the first naval bill two years earlier, Julius Bachem and his colleagues in the Rhineland did not make any serious effort to halt the substantial approval of the second Tirpitz measure. The warning of the *Kölnische Volkszeitung* during the debates that the Center would reject the Tirpitz proposal if the government did not agree to a satisfactory funding of it was an unnecessary challenge [67] since the chancellor and the secretary of the treasury were determined to reach an understanding with the Center on that issue. Undoubtedly Bachem thought it politically dangerous for the Center to make difficulties for the naval bill at a time when popular passions ran strongly against Great Britain. But it is difficult to resist the conclusion that Bachem, the *Kölnische Volkszeitung,* and the Rhineland Center had been more concerned about the response of Lieber and the Reichstag Center to the Prison House bill than they were to its reaction to the second naval measure. The leading Rhenish Centrists would not have dared to insist on a peremptory rejection of the Prison House bill in November, 1899, if they had intended to fight against a naval bill at a later point in the session.[68] They undoubtedly believed that the government and their party were engaged in a major compromise which would be both beneficial and unpleasant to each side.

It was evident from the distribution of the Centrist votes at the second reading of the naval bill on June 6, 1900, how little satisfaction there was in the fraction over that proposal. A high majority of the party members looked upon its passage as a grim political necessity and only nine deputies actually answered no in the voice vote. But only thirty-five of the remaining ninety-one members answered yes. Fifty-six Centrists were absent from the chamber or the city, most of them without permission.[69] In March, 1898, fifty-five members of the fraction had voted in favor of the initial Tirpitz measure.[70] Nevertheless, the low number of negative votes cast by Centrist members on June 6, 1900, four of them north Germans, indicates that the party had additional reasons for desiring the passage of the measure besides its need to please the monarchy.

Eckart Kehr has called attention to the interesting fact that Müller-Fulda took the lead in pointing out

---

[63] Kehr, *Schlachtflottenbau,* p. 188 ff.

[64] Hohenlohe, *Reichskanzlerzeit,* p. 556.

[65] Bachem, *Zentrumspartei* **6**: p. 28. The Center's leaders undoubtedly understood that it was a meaningless gesture.

[66] *Reichstag Verhandlungen,* February 8, 1900: pp. 3959–3960.

[67] Gröber in the Reichstag: *Verhandlungen,* June 6, 1900: p. 5827; Kehr, *Schlachtflottenbau,* p. 196.

[68] Karl Bachem had earlier told Porsch that the Center did not dare to strain the loyalty of Catholic workers any further after the long popular agitation against the Prison House measure and at a time when the second naval bill was in sight, letter of November 20, 1899. Bachem Papers, File 37.

[69] *Verhandlungen des Reichstages,* June 6, 1900: p. 5839 ff. There were one hundred and one members of the fraction at the time but a new deputy had not yet taken his seat.

[70] Bachem, *Zentrumspartei* **5**: p. 477.

to the government during the naval-bill deliberations that agriculture was in a state of need. Though he was uncertain about the causes of the Center's interest in the agrarian question and higher tariffs, Kehr suggested that the primary reason was probably the Center's wish to secure the backing of the Conservatives for its cultural programs; in fact, the two parties did collaborate closely during the period January–June, 1900, on a censorship measure. He also assumed that the Center planned to propose at a later date that income from higher tariffs could be used to defray the expenses of social welfare programs and for further naval building.[71]

Kehr's insights were sound enough. The Center could not hope to secure the revocation or modification of the anti-Jesuit law or church control over religion teachers in the Prussian schools; but it had to demonstrate to the Catholic clergy and the laity that it had not supported a major naval bill for a second time without compensation to the Catholic Church and, as they had demonstrated in the earlier 1890's, the bishops wanted tighter controls over prostitution, pornographic materials, the theater, artistic exhibitions, and literature.[72] And in the later debates on the tariff bill of 1902, the Centrist leadership was to propose that the government finance benefits for widows and orphans from the new rates on foreign grains and other foodstuffs.

Yet the party's leadership group undoubtedly thought in the early months of 1900 that it had to make some conciliatory gestures to its own agrarians in return for their support of the naval program. Despite the upturn in agricultural prices after 1896, Centrist agrarians in the east, the west, and the south continued to make aggrieved and sometimes noisy complaints about their problems, the shortage of farm labor, and their need for higher prices. Bavarian Centrists appeared to make the loudest and most frequent complaints about their difficulties.[73] Since they did not offer a serious resistance to the second naval bill, we can only conclude that the Centrist leaders had reassured them the tariff bill of 1902 would go far to satisfy their needs.

Still, the Center was unable to end the session of 1899–1900 with a legislative political success. The in-

valid Lieber, probably out of consideration for the sensibilities of his National Liberal and Radical allies, did not show any interest in the new censorship bill.[74] His leading colleagues, Gröber, Karl Bachem, and Spahn, were glad to let Hermann Roeren, a Catholic integralist, pilot the measure through the committee hearings. The prospects for its success were favorable, for a majority of the Reichstag, including the National Liberals, passed it in its second reading. But between the second and third readings the Radicals and the Social Democrats, stimulated by the wide opposition to the bill from writers, artists, persons connected with the theater, and the liberal press, engaged in extensive obstruction to its proposals. The unwillingness of the National Liberals to aid in breaking the obstruction and the frequent lack of quorums in the Reichstag placed the bill in jeopardy. In mid-May Ballestrem brought the leaders of the Center, the Cartel parties, and the Radicals together and prevailed on them to work out a compromise. The result was a shell of a censorship measure stripped of all paragraphs imposing new restraints on the theater and the arts.[75] It was a painful demonstration to the Centrist leadership that its party's power in the Reichstag had definite limits.

In the judgment of both Lieber and his integralist colleagues the session of 1899–1900 was probably a disaster for their party. Julius Bachem was depressed over the relentless course of the race in armaments as demonstrated anew in the success of the second naval bill.[76] But the previous parliamentary session had not been completely fruitless for the Center. Its stand on the prison house proposal had put an end to the monarchy's long efforts to cripple the Social Democratic and labor movements by punitive legislation and led the Imperial government to choose the new course of positive social action. Compared with the triumph of the monarchy's naval programs it was a modest victory, but the Center and the crown were not parties of equal strength.

7. THE HAPPY YEARS, 1901–1905

. . . the Center and Caesar, personal government of the emperor and decisive parliamentary position of the Center party. This new period could only achieve full development under Bülow who came . . . from old holy Rome and, while he cited Kant, Fichte, and Goethe, smoothed the way to mastery for the Center.
Friedrich Naumann, January, 1905.[1]

It was impossible, especially after the elections of 1903, to conduct business without the help of the Center. The Imperial chancellor was compelled to seek its approval for the economic and national legislation for the

---

[71] *Schlachtflottenbau*, pp. 204–205.

[72] See chapter 4, p. 51.

[73] Hertling opposed a Hitze motion in March, 1897, which called for a sixty-three-hour week for industrial labor; Hertling argued that it would attract farm workers to industry: *Reichstag Verhandlungen*, February 11, 1897: p. 4614. In the following year Ballestrem petitioned the government to give Polish farm laborers permission to stay in Germany on a twelve-month basis since they were indispensable on the estates and farms of eastern Germany: *ibid.*, April 21, 1898: p. 2108. On the same theme of the scarcity of agricultural labor: *HpB* **123** (1899): pp. 220–222. The editor complained that the recent military legislation benefited industry and city at the expense of agriculture. At the Catholic Congress of 1899 a Silesian priest deputy stressed the Center's earlier tradition of putting agricultural interests ahead of those of industry and commerce: *VGVkD zu Neisse* (Neisse, 1899), p. 20.

[74] Karl Bachem to Julius Bachem, May 12, 1902. Bachem Papers, File 154.

[75] Bachem, *Zentrumspartei* **6**: pp. 63–81.

[76] *HpB* **126** (1900): p. 139.

[1] Friedrich Naumann, Werke, **4**, *Schriften zum Parteiwesen und zum Mitteleuropaproblem*, Thomas Nipperdey and Wolfgang Schieder, eds., (Cologne and Opladen, 1964): p. 58.

*best interests of the land. I deny that he ever sur-
rendered sovereign right or showed any weakness in
religious or cultural questions out of deference to the
Center.*

Chancellor Bülow, New Year's Eve, 1906.[2]

In October, 1900, Bernhard von Bülow, the secretary of state for foreign affairs, replaced Hohenlohe in
the chancellorship. The Centrist leadership welcomed
the change. In six years of office Hohenlohe had been
unable to secure a single concession for their party
which they considered worth while and he was clearly
without any influence on the definition and execution
of government policies near the end of his career. Informed parliamentarians had known for some time that
Bülow was "the Dauphin of Hohenlohe." [3] Over the
course of the next several years the new chancellor
was gradually to develop closer working relations with
the Center than either Caprivi or Hohenlohe and to
make its leaders feel that they and the monarchy were
now joined in an intimate political alliance.

Bülow approached his eventual succession to the
chancellorship with confident assumptions about his
ability to achieve a firm and reliable working relationship with the Center. Then in his early fifties, handsome, a master in the art of manipulating others and
unusually effective as a speaker, he was near the height
of his personal powers. Through a life-long friendship
with Franz von Arenberg, his marriage to an Italian
Catholic, and his long diplomatic service in Italy,
Bülow had developed sympathies for the Catholic minority in Germany. While still secretary of state for
foreign affairs, he initiated the practice of inviting
leading Centrists like Lieber, Gröber, and Müller-Fulda
to his office for political talks.[4] He also won Hertling's
personal attachment by approving and promoting his
mission to seek Vatican approval for establishing a
Catholic theology faculty at the predominantly Protestant University of Strasbourg. That proposal and
the decision of the Imperial government to appoint
Martin Spahn, the historian son of Peter Spahn, to
a professorship at the same university were probably
the work of Johann Althoff, a prominent official in the
Prussian Ministry of Education, but both proposals required Bülow's firm support since they ran into opposition in the Prussian government and in liberal university circles.[5] It is likely he told the leading Centrists that he had no personal objections to the return
of the Jesuits and other banned orders since he made
no secret of his views on that subject in the presence
of prominent Protestant courtiers who opposed that
action.[6]

During the years that Bülow had served as secretary
of state for foreign affairs, the Center had given him
firm support and sometimes high praise for his conduct
of foreign policy. He may have attached too much
significance to those facts since Lieber and his associates
had been reluctant to become involved in serious discussions of German foreign policy. No Centrist really
understood the possible complications that could flow
from the new *Weltpolitik.* Nor was there any relationship between the prominent Catholic aristocrats who
served in the German diplomatic corps, like the ambassador to Great Britain, Paul Hatzfeld, and his successor Paul von Wolff-Metternich, or Hugo von Rade-
lin, the ambassador to France, and the Center party
leadership. A Catholic nobleman who desired to have
a successful career in the foreign service would not
dare to be associated with the Center in any way. But
Lieber and his successors were determined in any event
to avoid offending the emperor by invading the one
sphere of government operations, the definition and
conduct of foreign policy, which was not subject to
some degree of parliamentary control. They were also
eager to demonstrate, in Lieber's words, that the Center was all "black, white and red" in matters regarding
Germany's relations with other powers.[7] It is difficult
to avoid the conclusion that the relative frequency with
which Centrist leaders began to deliver long speeches
on foreign affairs in the early Bülow years was in response to the chancellor's invitation. Unlike his own
airy orations, they were usually dull.

Nevertheless, Bülow was under a serious and prolonged strain for the first two years of his chancellorship. Prior to his return to Germany in June, 1897,
he had spent most of his adult life on diplomatic service outside of his country. William II expected him
to be a highly successful conductor of foreign policy
in the new era of *Weltpolitik.* But Bülow knew that
he could not afford to suffer a serious setback in domestic affairs, especially in his handling of the new
giant tariff bill for which the government had been
making preparations since 1897. Indeed success in
internal affairs was to become increasingly necessary
for his political survival since he proved to be incapable
of preventing the separation of the German and British
governments after August, 1901, which was to lead to
the formation of the Anglo-French entente in 1904.
And despite his personal relations with Arenberg,
Hertling, Lieber, and some other prominent Centrists,
he worried over the uncertainty of the party's response
to his administration in the first years of his chancellorship.

Bülow was unfortunate in the circumstances which
precipitated his appointment. He also learned at an
early date that the Center leaders were in a state of

---

[2] George D. Crothers, *The German Elections of 1907* (New
York, 1941), p. 249.

[3] Bachem, *Zentrumspartei* **6**: p. 95.

[4] Richard Müller-Fulda to Karl Bachem, September 18, 1930,
and January 21, 1931, Bachem Papers, File 99.

[5] On Hertling's mission and the Spahn appointment see
Hertling, *Erinnerungen* **2**: pp. 205–219, 223–232, 275–289.

[6] Waldersee, *Denkwürdigkeiten* **3**: p. 192.

[7] Lieber: *Verhandlungen des Reichstages,* February 22, 1897:
p. 4857; March 1, 1899: p. 978; Hertling, *ibid.,* January 13,
1899: p. 221. Spahn, *Lieber,* p. 52.

frustration over the monarchy's adamant refusal to consider the withdrawal or revision of the law against the banned religious orders.

The events which precipitated Hohenlohe's resignation and Bülow's succession had been especially painful for Lieber who was then convalescing from his near fatal attack of January, 1900. In mid-June the Boxer insurgents in China had assassinated the German ambassador, a nephew of Bishop von Ketteler, and threatened temporarily the security of all diplomatic missions in Peking. The emperor, after a telephone conversation with Bülow, first dispatched four battleships and marines and some weeks later an expeditionary force to China. He instructed that contingent to use the utmost force and severity in overcoming the insurgents and bombastically announced that no decision could be taken there by the powers without the approval of the German emperor. Though the whole intervention, which was accompanied by considerable cruelty to the Chinese and destruction of property and art treasures, was to cost one hundred fifty million marks, the government did not call the Reichstag into a special session.[8] Efforts by parliamentary leaders to bring about a meeting of the parliament were unsuccessful. In October, Hohenlohe knew that he would face severe questioning and criticism from the Reichstag and chose to resign.

Lieber was mortified and angry over some aspects of the intervention, though he was careful to approve of the action itself. He considered himself to be the leading member of the Reichstag and responsible for the defense of its rights and honor. In the past he and other Centrist dignitaries had rebuked ministers, Chancellor Hohenlohe included, when they said or did anything offensive to its dignity.[9] In the Reichstag debates on China in December, 1900, Lieber complained about the disregard for the legitimate rights of the parliament, the ruler's remarks to the troops regarding their treatment of their foes, and the acts of cruelty committed against them.[10]

But Lieber had always been most sensitive about his power and dignity as the leader of the Center; his earlier differences with Julius Bachem, Cardinal Kopp, and Miquel demonstrated that fact clearly enough. He probably suspected that William II had discussed his plans for an intervention in China with Ballestrem, the

Centrist president of the Reichstag. On July 2, *Germania* had referred to the "frightful crime" which called out "for revenge" and for a German policy of being "strong and harsh in China." At the end of the article the editors sought to circumscribe the implications of their remarks by saying that the government should not fail to act decisively as soon as "there was clarity about the identification of the guilty."[11] A few weeks later the government announced that the emperor had bestowed the personal title of "Excellency" upon Ballestrem.[12] Near the end of July, William II dispatched additional forces to China with the oral directive that they "should give no pardon and take no prisoners." The staging of the Chinese intervention was a profoundly disillusioning revelation to Lieber of his failure to win any recognition or respect for his person, the Center party, and the Reichstag from William II. Lieber informed Bülow by letter that he approved of the undertaking and apparently implied that he did not hold him responsible for the manner in which the Reichstag had been ignored.[13] But after he became chancellor, Bülow could not avoid a second unpleasant experience involving the monarchy, the Center party, and its leader.

Despite its decisive position in the Reichstag and its contributions to the passage of the second navy bill of 1900 the Reichstag Center had not made any substantial progress in achieving legislation pleasing to the Catholic clergy. The government had taken a silent but firmly negative stand on the question of even a partial modification of the anti-Jesuit law. The Center had also suffered a partial defeat with its censorship bill earlier in the year.[14] Lieber and his colleagues came to the Reichstag in the early winter of 1900–1901 determined to wrest some important concession from the emperor and the Federal Council which would demonstrate to the clergy and the Catholic electorate that the Center's decisive position in the Reichstag could produce results beneficial to Catholicism.

The Centrist leadership hoped to make headway on the difficult question of the religious orders in the next parliamentary year through the pursuit of another tack. Immediately after the opening of the Reichstag it introduced a general bill of toleration. The proposal contained two parts; the first called for the establishment of religious freedom and equality for all citizens throughout the empire, a provision that had particular relevance to some smaller states in central and northern Germany where there were severe restrictions on Catholics and other religious minorities. The second part contained provisions for the freedom of religious associations. They were to enjoy full rights of association

---

[8] On the whole affair: Bachem, *Zentrumspartei* 6: pp. 88–92; Rich, *Holstein* 2: pp. 618–619.

[9] Buol, then the Centrist president of the Reichstag, chided Chancellor Hohenlohe for insisting that the parliament should not be dilatory in its deliberations on the proposed Civil Code: *Verhandlungen des Reichstages* January 17, 1896: p. 390. A year later Lieber politely rebuked the colonial director and later secretary for foreign affairs, Richthofen, for asking that the parties leave politics out of consideration when discussing the colonial budget. He told Kopp, who tried to intercede for Richthofen, that it was important to show new ministers from the beginning how they should act toward the Reichstag: Lieber to Kopp, January 7, 1897, Lieber Papers, Wrocław, File 94.

[10] *Verhandlungen des Reichstages,* November 19, 1900: p. 16.

[11] Quoted in the *Kölnische Zeitung,* 2nd M. Ed.: July 3, 1900.

[12] Franz Mehring, *Gesammelte Schriften* 14: p. 350.

[13] Bülow praised Lieber for his "patriotism" in his telegraphic reply: August 6, 1900. Lieber Papers, Wrocław, File 50.

[14] See above chapter 6, p. 84.

and movement in Germany. If the tolerance bill became law it would either require the revocation of the anti-Jesuit law or supersede it.[15]

Understanding though he was of the Center's claims for complete religious freedom, Bülow must have felt profoundly unhappy that he had to try to cope with its new bill just after his accession to office. The governments of the smaller states in which there were still severe restrictions on the religious freedom of those individuals who did not belong to the state church were frightened by the furor that the passage of even the first part of the bill would create among their own clergy and laity. The larger states, not least Bavaria, were deeply worried over the possibility that the Imperial government might expect the Federal Council to approve the second part which would permit the return of controversial orders like the Jesuits and Dominicans. Their concerns were soon laid to rest.[16] William II took ironic pleasure in stressing his personal patronage of the Benedictines who had a highly decentralized structure and a benign reputation, but he was adamant in his resistance to the return of the other major orders.[17]

It was undoubtedly William II who was responsible for the manner in which Bülow had to address the Reichstag on the tolerance motion. Regardless of its prospects, the proposal was a prestige question for the Center. In sharp contrast to his reaction to the censorship bill, Lieber participated enthusiastically in the preparation of the new measure because it was an expression of the liberal principle of religious freedom.[18] In the past German chancellors had normally refrained from taking a negative stand on new parliamentary proposals at the first reading. Bülow appeared in the Reichstag on November 26 and stated that the Federal Council would not participate in the deliberations on the Center's bill. He justified that stand with the argument that the Council could not interfere with the constitutional rights of the individual states to regulate matters of church and state by themselves. Lieber countered Bülow's statement with the rebuttal that the Imperial government had initiated several laws against the Catholic Church in the 1870's, but Bülow and the other major representatives of the Federal Council remained away from the later committee hearings on the bill.[19]

The slights which he, his party and, in some measure, the Reichstag itself received left Lieber with feelings of smouldering resentment. He was in that emotional state when he addressed the Reichstag in mid-January on the cases of the three young candidates for reserve officers' commissions from Cologne who had been denied them because they refused to commit themselves to the use of the duel. In the mid-1890's the emperor had issued two decrees whose intent was to put severe restrictions on the practice of dueling in the army,[20] but it was well known in the officers' corps that the monarch would not insist on their rigid enforcement. Lieber spoke heatedly on the subject of dueling in the army and at the universities whose graduates helped to maintain the tradition in the middle-class reserve officers' ranks. After his speech he suffered a new and near fatal collapse.[21] It was his last appearance in the Reichstag before his death some fourteen months later. During that period Bülow was to have considerable reason to regret his absence from Berlin.

It was already evident by the first months of 1901 that the chancellor was vitally concerned about the prospects of the tariff bill which he was to introduce to the Reichstag in the following autumn. Bülow's vice chancellor, Posadowsky, was formally responsible for its development and the supervision of its movement through the parliament, but Bülow's interest in it was patently evident. He took over the decisive negotiations with the leaders of the parties in the government coalition and followed closely the newspaper coverage of the debates on the bill before and after its presentation to the Reichstag. Though he was to insist at different times that the government could always abandon the idea of a tariff law and negotiate separate trade agreements with other states,[22] it was politically necessary for the chancellor to satisfy the demand of all agrarian organizations and the Conservatives that there be a domestic tariff.

The political and diplomatic problems inherent in the planning of a major tariff bill were unusually difficult. The Caprivi commercial treaties had reduced the earlier Bismarckian rates on wheat and rye from five and a half to three and a half marks per two hundred weight. The Agrarian League and the new Confederation of Christian Peasants' Associations demanded a high tariff of seven and a half marks on the same grains.[23] But Bülow was to be absolutely rigid on his insistence that the government would not approvate rates over five and a half marks on wheat and rye. His stand

---

[15] Bachem, *Zentrumspartei* **6**: pp. 101–121.

[16] The Bavarian government was to express concern in 1907 when the Vatican insisted on naming a German Dominican as the nuncio to Bavaria. It accepted his appointment but imposed the condition that he could not ask for the return of his order: Rotenhan to Bülow, October 24, 1907, GFMA Microcopy T149, ACP24.

[17] He once appeared at a festive dinner at Cardinal Kopp's palace wearing a large and small medal each of which had been given to him by a Benedictine abbot: Radziwill, *Lettres* **3**: p. 97.

[18] Karl Bachem, undated memo, Bachem Papers, File 924; *ibid.*, letter to Julius Bachem, May 12, 1902. File 154.

[19] Bachem, *Zentrumspartei* **6**: p. 113.

[20] Matthias Erzberger, *Duell und Ehre* (Wurzburg, 1912): pp. 60–64.

[21] *Reichstag Verhandlungen*, January 15, 1901: pp. 708–709; Karl Bachem, undated memo, Bachem Papers, File 924.

[22] Karl Bachem, notes dated September 16, 1902, Bachem Papers, File 170; Bülow to Holstein, October 4, 1902, *Holstein Papers* **4**: p. 266.

[23] Müller, *Im Spiegel der Geschichte*, pp. 850–851.

then and later on that issue indicates that he felt an inability to compromise on it. The chancellor was concerned about the harmful effects that such tariffs could have on Germany's ties with Russia, a heavy exporter of agricultural products. At home he had to contend with the National Liberals and the industrialist wing of the Free Conservatives who feared that high agricultural rates would damage Germany's trade with foreign countries.[24]

Bülow was acutely aware at an early date that he could only hope to secure the passage of a moderate tariff measure if the Center agreed to support him. The chancellor felt that the Center was in essentially the same situation as the government: "both," he claimed, "wished to protect agriculture without ruining industry and trade."[25] In fact, the Center's political situation did approximate more closely that of the government than any other German party because of its varied electorate.

Ernst Lieber undoubtedly agreed with the chancellor on the tariff question. Still convalescing in Camberg from his last attack of illness, he made no statements on a suitable bill in 1901. But Müller-Fulda, now an intimate friend, wrote two articles on the tariff issue which appeared in *Germania* on August 17 and 18. They certainly reflected Lieber's views.[26] The Hessian Centrist claimed that the limited size of German farms, their high production costs, insurance payments for workers, and taxation dictated some protection for agriculture. The government planned to set the rates on wheat at five and a half marks and on rye at five marks. Müller-Fulda suggested that an average tariff of five marks on both grains would be justified by the needs of German agriculture, but warned his readers that the financial burdens created by the tariffs would not be born solely by foreign producers or middlemen. At the same time he sought to win wider support for the chancellor of his party.[27] Lieber was not interested, however, in reassuring Bülow about the prospects for his bill's success. Talks between Bülow and other Centrists in early 1901 had not produced any pledges of concessions to the Center from the chancellor in return for its support.[28] Lieber had probably hoped that the promise of Centrist backing for the tariff measure would bring a government pledge to revoke the whole or partial revision of the anti-Jesuit law. At the Cath-

olic Congress in late August, 1901, he remarked bitterly that "the ruling authorities would not trample on our backs if they were not so confident of our obedience under conscience."[29]

At the first reading of the proposed tariff in December, 1901, the Center's spokesman refused to take a clearcut stand which would reassure Bülow. In his remarks Peter Spahn stressed the importance of the agricultural parts of the tariff measure and added that his party would not have voted for the earlier Caprivi commercial treaties if it had foreseen their consequences for agriculture.[30] Though the tenor of his speech was pro-agrarian, he rebutted the argument of another deputy who had insisted that the costs of a high tariff on grains would not have a significant impact on food prices at home but would be borne by foreign producers and exporters.[31] Spahn's implication that his fraction favored a relatively high agricultural tariff or at least one with higher rates than those of the government proposals may have been nothing more than a purely tactical move, intended to soften up Bülow for the eventual Centrist demands for concessions. But it is also possible that he was unsure whether he and his associates could impose moderate rates upon their own agrarians and win adequate support from other segments of the party.[32]

During the long period from the early summer of 1901 to the early weeks of the Reichstag session of 1902–1903 Bülow felt continued uncertainty about the Center's ultimate decision on the tariff. He was keenly aware that the leaders of the Bavarian and Rhineland Center parties were hostile to him. The chancellor apparently assumed that he could not hope to change the attitudes of the Bavarian Centrists toward his person but he had made an unsuccessful attempt through Müller-Fulda to secure relief from the criticisms made of his administration by the *Kölnische Volkszeitung*.[33]

In October, 1900, just a few weeks before Bülow's first appearance before the Reichstag, the German government concluded an agreement with Great Britain to preserve commercial freedom in China. It was the beginning of a new effort to bring the two powers together in a closer diplomatic relationship which was to reach its emotional height in January, 1901, when William II visited his grandmother, Queen Victoria, then on her deathbed. In his speech on the German intervention in China to the Reichstag in late November of the previous year Lieber had expressed his pleasure over the Chinese accord between the German and British governments.[34] No doubt his remarks were the

---

[24] On the various proposals for a tariff: Bachem, *Zentrumspartei* **6**: pp. 129–134; Kenneth Barkin, *The Debate over German Industrialization* (Chicago, 1970), p. 220 ff.

[25] Bülow to Lieber, August 19, 1902. Lieber Papers, Wrocław, File 51.

[26] Müller-Fulda later claimed that he had spent at least one hour each week in Bülow's company from 1900 to 1905: letter to Karl Bachem, September 18, 1930, Bachem Papers, File 99. He made the financial arrangements for the attendance of Lieber's eldest son at a Berlin gymnasium: letter to Lieber, February 18, 1902. Lieber Papers, Speyer, File M, 86.

[27] Müller-Fulda to Karl Bachem, August 19, 1901. Bachem Papers, File 170.

[28] See below pp. 89–90.

[29] *VGVkD zu Osnabrück* (Osnabrück, 1901), p. 390.

[30] For those treaties see ch. 2, p. 26 and ch. 3, pp. 39 f.

[31] *Verhandlungen des Reichstages,* December 3, 1901: p. 2913.

[32] In his letter of February 18, 1902 to Lieber, Müller-Fulda said "nothing will actually come out of the tariff bill." Fn. 26 above.

[33] See fn. 27 above.

[34] See fn. 10 above.

expression of a sincere conviction since the whole Center had traditionally favored a pro-British orientation for German foreign policy before the introduction of Germany's *Weltpolitik*. The Bavarian Centrists because of their attachment to Austria-Hungary and their Russophobia had been opposed to the new *Weltpolitik* in the 1890's partly because they feared it could create differences with Great Britain. But in contrast to Lieber, Franz Schaedler chose to be disparaging and even insulting to the new chancellor and to the emperor in his own remarks to the Reichstag in March, 1901, on recent developments in German foreign affairs. He claimed the German people were still sympathetic to the Boers in their war with Great Britain, implied that William II had been led by his family connections with the British ruling house to seek an improvement in Anglo-German relations, and suggested that the government be cautious in its dealings with Russia because she was untrustworthy.[35] Bülow was apparently angered over Schaedler's offensive remarks and said that he did not need the Bavarian Centrist's advice.[36]

Schaedler's tactless speech had nothing to do with the temporary improvement in 1900–1901 in Anglo-German relations. Schaedler was intent on underscoring at the very beginning of Bülow's chancellorship how dissatisfied Bavarian Centrists were with the *Weltpolitik* of which he was the official symbol and which had led to a highly expensive German intervention in China in the previous summer.[37] Georg von Hertling, Bülow's staunch friend, was to become increasingly aware of his own isolation and the growing ascendency of Georg Heim, the agrarian, in Bavarian Centrist circles after 1900. In view of those circumstances it was a curious lapse in political judgment that led the German government to propose substantially lower tariff rates for barley which was a popular Bavarian crop than those it requested for wheat and rye which were grown more widely in the north.[38]

Nevertheless, the chancellor's concern over the attitude of the Rhineland Center toward his administration was much greater than it was over Bavarian hostility to his person. Posadowsky and Bülow had carried on negotiations with some of its most prominent members early in 1901.[39] The fact that their talks took place a full eight or nine months before the first reading of the tariff bill revealed how eager Bülow was to win the assurance of the Center's support for the government bill and especially that of its Rhenish members. But they had proven to be abortive by the beginning of the spring.

The first proposal that Karl Bachem made to Bülow was that the government pay expense accounts to all Reichstag deputies. The apparent reasons for this concession, long demanded by the Center and other parties, was that it was necessary to overcome absenteeism in the Reichstag and especially in the Center party itself. Through much of each parliamentary year there were rarely more than one-fifth of the members of the Center sitting in the Reichstag chamber. There were more members of the Center who held double mandates than there were in other parties since many of them felt the need to draw parliamentary allowances from a state legislature. The social changes that had taken place in the Center since the later 1880's had made it more of a people's party but had also impoverished it.[40]

The emphasis that the Rhineland Centrists put on this concession was probably due to an overt and concealed motive. It was embarrassing, occasionally crippling for the leading party to be represented in the national parliament by so few of its deputies for most of the parliamentary period. Centrist representatives were able to make a substantial argument to the government in favor of parliamentary allowances. Unless they were paid to deputies, there was no assurance that the government could find a favorable majority in the chamber which could outlast and overcome the certain Social Democratic obstructionism against the tariff bill. A similar hindrance had led to the serious if not complete setback which the Center and the Conservatives had suffered in their promotion of the censorship bill of 1900. But it is curious that it was the Rhineland Centrists who pushed hard for the establishment of parliamentary allowances and not the leadership of the Reichstag fraction. In all likelihood Julius Bachem may have stressed the value of the allowances that would permit the Bavarians to attend more sessions in the Reichstag.[41] If they did so, then the Rhineland Centrists would be able to influence the balance of power in the Reichstag fraction and in the Centrists' membership of the major Reichstag committees.

Bülow finally said, however, that the emperor would not approve such a concession to the Reichstag. Bismarck had deliberately refused to make provision for parliamentary allowances for Reichstag deputies on the grounds that they would lead to the growth of a class

[35] *Reichstag Verhandlungen,* March 5, 1901: p. 1695.

[36] Schulthess, *Geschichtskalender* **42** (1901): p. 49.

[37] In his memoirs Bülow was satisfied to be satirical at the expense of some of the Centrist leaders but he tried to destroy Schaedler's moral character as a priest. See Bachem, *Zentrumspartei* **6**: pp. 375–378.

[38] Hermann Renner, *Georg Heim, der Bauerndoktor* (Munich, 1960) p. 82.

[39] Karl Bachem, notes dated February 27, 1901, on Trimborn's meeting with Bülow, Bachem Papers, File 170; notes dated March 8, 1901, on Bachem's own talks with the chancellor, *ibid.*; and letter to Lieber, March 22, 1901, Porsch Papers, File 1a9.

[40] The Center's interest in parliamentary allowances dated from the 1870's: by 1895 the Reichstag had passed a motion in favor of them on ten occasions: *Deutsche Reichs-zeitung,* March 28, 1897. On Centrist absenteeism: Lieber to Heinrich Otto, April 7, 1894. Bachem Papers, File 67b.

[41] The government finally agreed in March, 1906, to grant allowances to deputies. Karl Bachem pointed out soon afterward that the leaders would have greater difficulty controlling the fraction because the Bavarians would be more regular in attendance: notes dated March 21, 1906. Bachem Papers, File 239.

of professional politicians. The argument that the grant of allowances would provide more quorums for the readier dispatch of legislation was certainly an argument that the government could appreciate, but the more frequent attendance of Bavarian and other south German Centrists was not likely to make them appealing to Imperial officials. It is evident in any event that Bülow's leading advisers, adhering to the old Bismarck tradition among the higher bureaucracy, insisted that he should not make such a concession and the chancellor followed their advice while choosing to attribute the decision to William II.[42]

A more crucial concern for the Rhineland Center was its need, if the Center were to approve the tariff bill, for some kind of a concession from the government which would give it protection in the elections of 1903 against the attacks from the Social Democrats that it was responsible for the increased cost of bread and meat for the workers. Bülow had been impressed by this argument when Karl Bachem presented it to him and by Bachem's stress on the number of important cities in which the Center was still the dominant political party.[43] On March 1, 1901, he told the Reichstag that the government would use some of the income from the tariffs for social purposes.[44] Some weeks later, however, he informed Karl Bachem that the government could not offer to make such a concession to the Center. The probable reason was that the serious financial problems of the government would not permit it to assume such a heavy financial responsibility.[45]

In the winter of 1901–1902 Bülow suffered again from a combination of unfortunate circumstances and the desire of some parts of the press and Centrists to harass him. The policies of the Prussian government toward the Polish minorities in its eastern provinces had always been a tender spot in the relations between the Center and the monarchy, except in the Caprivi era. On the recommendation of Miquel who wanted to reunite the Conservatives and the National Liberals by stressing national causes, the Prussian government in the later Hohenlohe years began to stiffen its already unsympathetic attitudes toward the Poles.[46] Most importantly it doubled the budget of the agency which had been set up in 1886 to settle German colonists in West Prussia and Posen. On his appointment to the minister-presidency in 1900 Bülow found that he was expected to promote the execution of old decrees regarding the use of German in the lower schools of the Polish provinces. In the late spring of 1901 an ugly incident occurred in Wretschen, Posen, when some school children refused to recite in German during their religious instruction. They were whipped and some parents were arrested after a confrontation with officials.[47]

The Prussian Center had always taken up the causes of the Poles and Alsatians because they were Catholics or predominantly so, useful allies, and minority peoples who could not defend themselves. Its leaders did not object in theory to the settling of Germans in the eastern provinces but they noted that the program denied legal equality to the Poles who were excluded from it. They also claimed that it was anti-Catholic since the Prussian government had only given land to a token number of Catholics by 1900. In their Landtag speeches on the Wretschen incident they did not question the right of the state to insist on the use of German as the language of instruction, but they claimed that children could learn their religion better through the use of their mother tongue. The Center spokesmen, Hermann Roeren and Alois Fritzen, both from the Rhineland, used the debates on the whole affair, however, to call into question the value of the government's anti-Polish policies.[48]

The Rhineland Centrists were interested in the Wretschen affair for other reasons than their party's traditional stand on the use of German in religious instruction in Polish schools. There were substantial numbers of Polish miners in the Ruhr who had consistently voted for the Center in earlier years; in Upper Silesia a majority of the Center's mandates derived from the votes of Polish peasants and workers. Just before the turn of the century, radical Polish nationalists had come into both areas and attacked the Center party on the grounds that it was not sufficiently attentive to Polish rights. Since the Prussian Center had to face state elections in 1903, Julius Bachem was deeply concerned with the danger of Polish Catholic disaffection in both areas and sought to promote agreements between local Center parties and moderate Polish leaders.[49] But talks between Westphalian Centrists and Polish representatives in the Westphalian Ruhr were to break down in 1903. In Upper Silesia, Felix Porsch and Ballestrem opposed such a compromise in the interest of maintaining the close ties between the

[42] Friedrich von Holstein and some other high officials were to dissuade Bülow from making this concession to the Center in November, 1902: *The Holstein Papers* 4: p. 272.

[43] Karl Bachem, notes dated March 8, 1901, of talk with Bülow. See above fn. 38; Karl Bachem to Lieber, March 22, 1902. Porsch Papers, File Ia9.

[44] Barkin, *Debate over German Industrialization*, p. 238.

[45] The Imperial secretary of the treasury was to put up a strong protest when the Center presented such a motion for the payment of pensions to widows and orphans in the Budget Committee: *Frankfurter Zeitung*, October 2, 1902. See below fn. 64.

[46] In March, 1898, Miquel called on the Center and Catholics to place themselves on the "national side" in the Polish question: *Verhandlungen des Reichstages*, March 3, 1898: p. 1104.

[47] See the excellent study by Richard W. Tims, *Germanizing Prussian Poland. .The H. K. T. Society and the Struggle for the Eastern Marches in the German Empire, 1871–1919* (New York, 1941), p. 83.

[48] Roeren, *Reichstag Verhandlungen*, December 10, 1901: pp. 3089–3091; Fritzen, *Stenographische Berichte der Verhandlungen der Abgeordnetenhaus der Preussischen Landtags*, January 13, 1902: pp. 94–102.

[49] Karl Bachem to Carl Trimborn, September 23, 1901, Bachem Papers, File 154.

Silesian Center, the Conservatives, and the government.[50] But the leaders of the Prussian Center were now keenly conscious of the Polish question. In their electoral pronouncement of 1903 they were to stress their party's intent to uphold the religious and cultural rights of the Poles while rejecting the aims of the nationalist "Greater Poland" movement.[51]

The Wretschen affair and the Landtag debates over it in the early months of 1902 were embarrassing to the chancellor. The Reichstag tariff committee had just begun its deliberations and Bülow was still uncertain regarding the stand that the Center would take on the government's bill, in particular its proposed rates on wheat and rye. Bülow was determined to continue the policy of Germanization in the Prussian Polish provinces. He had the characteristic Prussian contempt for the Poles and, in a rare moment of tactlessness, was to say in an interview that they multiplied like rabbits.[52] But he feared that the Catholic bishops and the Center would consider his Prussian policies as an attack upon their church. He also assumed that the Center's refusal to come out in support of his tariff plans reflected its church's dislike of the government's policies on the Jesuit and Polish questions.[53]

On March 30, while the tariff committee was still in the early stages of its work, Ernst Lieber succumbed to a lung infection. Though he had been away from the Reichstag for over a year, he had expected to return to parliamentary activity in the early future. His prolonged illness had finally brought him the respect and affection of the Catholic people that he had long desired. Lieber had been loudly greeted when he appeared at the Catholic Congress of 1901. But he undoubtedly felt a deep sense of frustration over his failure to bring about the revocation of the anti-Jesuit law which might have justified in their eyes the support he and his party had given to the government on the major naval bills of 1898 and 1900. His bitter reference at the Congress to the ruling authorities who "trample on our backs" because Catholics were committed to the monarchical system reflected his state of mind clearly enough.[54]

Lieber's death, unlike Windthorst's just ten years earlier, was not a major political event. Nevertheless most of his colleagues and the leading party newspapers expressed their respect for the deceased parliamentarian. Eugen Richter paid him the highest praise in saying that Lieber had the rare ability of being able to master all types of legislative proposals and problems and had forced the government to take him into consideration at all times.[55] Even *Vorwärts,* the official organ of the Social Democratic party, was cautiously respectful of him and underscored its belief that he did not belong to the reactionary wing of the Center.[56] Franz Mehring, the prominent left-wing Socialist editor, was caustically critical of the deceased Centrist leader, however, since he claimed that Lieber had converted his party into an instrument of government use.[57] That Lieber had not achieved a final peace with Julius Bachem and Hermann Cardauns before his death was evident in the statement of the *Kölnische Volkszeitung* that it was probably more accurate to say that he had been the "fraction's speaker" rather than its leader.[58]

Lieber's death was a serious blow to his party, though its full cost was not immediately evident in 1902. Nevertheless, he had found it difficult to adjust to some of the Center's newer needs. His reluctance to approve of the interconfessional trade union movement revealed that he, like Windthorst before him, feared above all else that some of the bishops might withdraw their support from the party. He had tried persistently though unsuccessfully to win the approval of the influential Free Conservatives for the Center's motion on works councils,[59] but he had been unwilling to make social legislation one of his major objectives. Lieber had come to maturity at a time when questions of national union, church and state relations, constitutional rights, and a free economy had been the crucial topics of national political debate.[60] It was not strange that he found himself closer to the National Liberals than he did to some members of his own party except where matters touching on the freedom and privileges of the Catholic Church were concerned. Unlike Julius Bachem and some other regional Centrist leaders, he had not been seriously concerned with the question of parity in state appointments. His major objectives seem to have been the liberation of the Catholic Church and the elevation of the Center to a position of permanent partnership with the monarchy in the domestic governance of Germany. He had a special attachment to the two organizations that made it possible for the Catholic minority to direct the activities of the Reichstag, the Center itself, and the Peoples' Association which sought to ensure the continuing loyalty of the Catholic lower classes to that party.[61]

In the course of the summer of 1902 the tariff committee, after ninety sessions, finally completed its work

[50] In December, 1903, Porsch threatened to resign all his positions in the Landtag Center except for his seat on its executive committee because of the open conflict between the *Kölnische Volkszeitung* and the Silesian Center over the Polish question in Silesia: Porsch to Alois Fritzen, December 14, 1903, Porsch Papers, V17b.

[51] Bachem, *Zentrumspartei* 7: pp. 476–477.

[52] Schulthess, *Geschichtskalender* 43 (1902): p. 95.

[53] Rotenhan to Bülow, January 13, 1902, GFMA University of Michigan, Microcopy, Roll 110.

[54] See above p. 88.

[55] *Freisinnige Zeitung,* April 2, 1902.

[56] *Vorwärts,* April 2, 1902.

[57] Mehring, *Gesammelte Schriften* 14: pp. 453–456.

[58] *Kölnische Volkszeitung,* April 1, 1902.

[59] *Der Tag,* May 13, 1906.

[60] Spahn, *Lieber,* pp. 63–64.

[61] At the Osnabrück Catholic Congress of 1901, he called on his auditors to be loyal to the Center and the Peoples' Association, the two institutions with which he had been intimately associated. See fn. 28 above.

on the nine hundred provisions of the government bill. While the committee, led by the Center, rejected the extreme demands of agrarian groups, it reported out rates on the basic grains that were from a half-mark to a mark higher than those requested by the government. Bülow seriously contemplated the possibility that the Reichstag would reject his proposals.[62] During the second reading of the bill he was to reveal the effects of the strain he had undergone.[63]

The Center could not afford, however, to risk a serious conflict with the government or the loss of a comprehensive tariff bill. But it is more likely that its leaders looked upon Bülow's plight as an opportunity to secure worth-while concessions from him for their party. Their eagerness to do so was evident in their agreement on November 27 to accept the rates on wheat and rye in the government measure; in return Bülow accepted a somewhat higher tariff level for barley. The Christian peasants' associations, except for those in the lower Rhineland, approved the compromise.[64] The *Westdeutscher Arbeiterzeitung,* in stark contrast to the Social Democratic party journals, had long advocated moderate protection for the producers of foodstuffs, though it had also called for the reduction of tariffs on coffee, fats, rice, and gasoline. It welcomed the settlement between the government and the Center even though those tariffs, highly unpopular among workers, remained in force.[65]

Bülow had experienced difficulty in finding an adequate basis for effective negotiations with the Center. Arenberg tried to secure his acceptance of parliamentary allowances but the chancellor chose to take the advice of Friedrich von Holstein who was still opposed to them.[66] He agreed, however, to pledge the government's support of pensions for widows and orphans. The chancellor undoubtedly did so over the advice of the Imperial Treasury even though the pensions would not be paid before 1911.[67]

But it was unlikely that the Centrist leadership would have gone so far to meet the chancellor on the tariff bill unless he had committed himself to a larger concession. Bülow had told Spahn in the late summer that the expulsion article of the anti-Jesuit law would be rescinded during the next parliamentary session.[68] While there is no explicit evidence to that effect, he apparently made a specific pledge to the Center's leaders during their final negotiations in late November. It would be difficult to explain otherwise why most of the agarian groups in the Confederation of Peasants' Associations approved of the Center's substantial acceptance of the government's tariff proposals. The bill became law before the chancellor learned that he could not overcome the resistance of some states to any change whatsoever in the anti-Jesuit law. That setback was to be painful to him, the Center, and prominent Catholic churchmen like Kopp.

The Center's commitment to the chancellor involved considerably more than the promise of its votes. The Social Democrats and Radicals had carried on a vigorous press campaign against the tariff bill for over a year; they had demonstrated during the debates on the censorship bill that it was possible to frustrate the will of a majority by skillful obstruction. The Social Democratic leaders were confident that they could delay a final vote on the bill until the eve of the elections of June, 1903, or after them by long speeches on each article of the tariff measure and by an insistence on quorums for each debate. In the past the Center had always been sensitive about the rights of the Reichstag and of minorities. It was also the tradition of the house that its members deliberated on each part of a budget or tariff measure. But the Centrist leadership was now more concerned to demonstrate to the government that it could bring about the passage of major legislation in the face of a determined oppositional minority.

Bülow and Spahn agreed on two proposals to counter the obstructionist tactics of the Social Democrats and those Radicals willing to support them. Aichbichler, an agrarian Centrist from Bavaria, introduced a motion to the Reichstag at an early point in the second reading which permitted deputies to vote by card rather than by voice. Bülow had talked with Ballestrem in advance and the president had assured him that he would not rule against the motion.[69] Despite strong objections from the Social Democrats and the Radicals the motion carried on November 14. A more radical measure was a Spahn proposal which called for a single vote *en bloc* of the nine hundred-odd tariff articles. Because of his reputation as a prominent agrarian the Center and the government prevailed upon Wilhelm von Kardorff of the Free Conservative party to give the motion his name.[70] On November 27 Kardorff presented the proposal to revise the Reichstag's traditional procedure to the parliament.

The debates at the third reading of the tariff proposals were probably the angriest in the history of the Reichstag before World War I; on one occasion there

[62] Bachem, *Zentrumspartei* **6**: pp. 150–151; Bülow to Holstein, *Holstein Papers* **4**: p. 266.

[63] Radziwill, *Lettres* **3**: p. 32.

[64] Müller, *Im Spiegel der Geschichte*, p. 852.

[65] *Westdeutscher Arbeiterzeitung,* November 30, 1902; December 14, 1902.

[66] *Holstein Papers* **4**: p. 272.

[67] Bachem, *Zentrumspartei* **6**: pp. 149–150, 162. According to the Imperial secretary of the treasury the deficit for 1902 was almost fifteen million marks: *Frankfurter Zeitung,* November 24, 1902. Seven years later the government announced there was no money in the Treasury to pay the pensions: *Deutsche Zeitung,* February 16, 1909.

[68] Karl Bachem, notes dated September 16, 1902. Bachem Papers, File 170.

[69] Bülow's memoirs contain a garbled account of his conversation with the Reichstag president. He does not indicate whether Ballestrem also committed himself in the same manner on the more important Kardorff motion which I treat below: Bülow *Memoirs* **1**: p. 583.

[70] Bachem, *Zentrumspartei* **6**: p. 157.

was near violence. But the anger was essentially an expression of the frustration, disappoinment, and anticipation of defeat felt by the Social Democrats after Ballestrem permitted Kardorff to submit his motion. Ballestrem claimed that he had not been aware of that proposal before its presentation to the Reichstag and acknowledged that it was not in accordance with Article 19 of the parliament's code; nevertheless, he insisted that he could not reject a motion which enjoyed the support of a majority of the deputies. The Reichstag president was eager, however, to save what he could of his reputation for impartiality and he also ruled that the house should debate the measure adequately before it voted on it.[71] During the last night of the third reading of the tariff bill itself, Ballestrem ignored Spahn who had a prior claim to the floor and recognized a Social Democratic speaker who filibustered for eight hours.[72] But since most of the Radicals refused to join in the obstructionist campaign, the majority finally prevailed and the tariff bill was carried during the early morning hours of December 14, 1902.

The tactics of the Center's leaders in the final reading of the tariff bill revealed the high importance they attached to its passage before the new year. The government had feared that the Social Democrats might be able through their own obstructionist methods to force the postponement of the final voting on the measure till the last months before the elections of June, 1903. The Center had put Bülow in its debt by its acceptance of the government's rates on wheat and rye and by its relentless tactics in bringing about an early decision on the whole bill. But the Centrist leaders undoubtedly believed that they had to provide some satisfaction for their own agrarians and the Conservatives whose assistance could be helpful on cultural and social legislation. That they felt they were playing for high stakes was evident in their willingness to risk the loyalty of their working-class electors by associating their party prominently with a tariff measure which would make German food prices the highest in the western world.[73]

The outcome of the Reichstag elections of June, 1903, undoubtedly strengthened Bülow and Posadowsky in their belief that the government had to put special reliance upon the Center's good will. The Social Democrats won one million new votes and twenty-five additional seats, an achievement which shook Imperial officials and conservatives throughout Germany. The Center had been one of the targets of the Social Demo-

cratic campaign against the promoters of the "hunger tariff." While it lost five mandates, it retained its traditional strength in industrial regions and increased its popular vote by four hundred thousand ballots. Ironically enough the Social Democrats had made most of their gains at the expense of the Radicals who had almost uniformly disapproved of the tariff proposals.[74] It was now more apparent than ever before that the Free Conservatives, National Liberals, and Radicals were only secure in Prussian state elections which were still based on class suffrage.

During the months following Lieber's death there was no competition for the succession to his position. In the final debates on the tariff bill Peter Spahn functioned as the leading negotiator and first speaker for his party. Spahn possessed important political and personal qualifications for the office of party leader. A native of Nassau like Lieber, he had been a close friend of his predecessor. He had held Rhenish mandates in the Reichstag and Landtag for many years, however, and enjoyed the backing of the influential Rhineland contingent in the Reichstag fraction. A jurist of distinction, Spahn had also sat part-time for many years as a judge in Prussian courts. In the contest over the tariff bill he had shown that he was a shrewd tactician, firm in resolve, and apparently cool under pressure. But he also had obvious limitations as a leader. Spahn was reserved and somewhat colorless in personality. That he lacked Windthorst's and Lieber's passion for political power and influence and their judgment as well was evident from his decision to retain his Prussian judicial position after his accession to the party leadership.[75] He was certainly a respectable candidate for that office but it was a revealing commentary on conditions in his party that he did not have to compete seriously with some of his colleagues for it.

The political calm in Berlin after the passage of the tariff bill and the good relations between the Center and the government actually concealed a serious thinness in the party's leadership ranks. The Center had experienced serious difficulties in recruiting promising young men to its ranks after the conclusion of the Kulturkampf negotiations in the late 1880's.[76] One of Lieber's friends wrote him in May, 1898, on the eve of the parliamentary elections, that the list of Centrist candidates for the Reichstag was unimpressive."[77] It was unfortunate therefore that Julius Bachem and Felix Porsch, the most talented of Windthorst's younger

---

[71] *Frankfurter Zeitung,* November 28, 1902; December 3, 1907.

[72] During the debates on the Kardorff motion and the tariff bill itself and afterward Centrist deputies complained over Ballestrem's rulings. The rumors that he would resign his chair did not die down till the early months of 1903. Radziwill, *Lettres* 3: pp. 45, 50; Bachem, *Zentrumspartei* 6: pp. 163–164.

[73] Barkin, *Debate over German Industrialization,* p. 253 ff.; Johannes Ziekursch, *Politische Geschichte des neuen Deutschen Reiches* (3 v., Frankfurt/M, 1925–1930) 3: p. 178.

[74] Bachem, *Zentrumspartei* 6: pp. 189–190. Arenberg undoubtedly reflected the government's point of view when he said that the outcome of the elections could not have been worse: Radziwill, *Lettres* 3: p. 67.

[75] The *Berliner Tageblatt* of April 7, 1902, thought that his retention of the judgeship might limit his independence. The more serious aspect of his decision was that his south German colleagues came to look upon him as a Prussian official.

[76] See above chapter 2, p. 20.

[77] Heinrich Brauns to Lieber, May 30, 1898. Lieber Papers, Speyer, Envelope *Personliche Angelegenheiten, I.*

lieutenants, could not sit in the Reichstag Center and that Georg von Hertling only attended the parliamentary sessions irregularly.[78] For a party which had to lead a coalition, negotiate regularly with the government, and maintain contacts with its own electorate, the Center lacked depth in its leadership.

In January, 1904, Alois Fritzen, the prominent Rhineland Centrist and chairman of the Prussian Center, did not return to the Landtag. The parliamentary fraction then elected Felix Porsch to be its chairman. According to Karl Bachem, Fritzen gave up his mandate because of weak health.[79] But two political considerations of some moment may have contributed also to his resignation of the chairmanship of the Prussian Center which was also the position of leadership in that party. The rivalry between provincial groups in the Center was keen and Fritzen's position may have become untenable after the succession of another Rhineland Centrist to the leadership of the Reichstag Center after Lieber's death. Nevertheless, the decisive factor leading to Porsch's election was probably the revival of the school question in Prussian politics. In March, 1903, the Prussian government and the Cartel parties had entered into an agreement that they would introduce and approve a new school support bill. Porsch had been one of the major speakers for the Center in the debates on the Zedlitz proposal of 1892. More important was the fact that he, Ballestrem, and Kopp had close ties with the Prussian Conservatives who were to represent the Center's point of view on some aspects of the new bill.

The interest of the government and the Cartel parties reflected the financial embarrassment of towns and cities confronted with rising costs of elementary and secondary education but especially the rural communities in eastern Prussia where the Conservatives were politically dominant. But all municipalities felt the strain in considerable measure and even the Radicals were convinced that there had to be a school law which would provide substantial state support for the schools. Since the Center favored such a measure for financial and other reasons, the new bill was assured of broad support and eventual approval.

In contrast to its practice in 1892, the Prussian Center did not figure prominently in the inter-party negotiations, committee deliberations, and parliamentary debates on the school proposal, though Porsch was undoubtedly active in the inter-party negotiations on that measure. There were two apparent reasons for the modest role that the Centrist leaders elected to assume in the public or semi-public discussions of the school

bill. The Cartel parties had agreed that it should establish the legal equality of the existing interconfessional schools with the more numerous confessional schools.[80] But the Center could not have been surprised by that agreement since the interconfessional school had been a fixture for many years in some Prussian provinces. The more probable explanation of the Center's reserve was the desire of its leaders to do nothing that would arouse liberal public opinion against a school bill which was actually highly satisfactory to the Catholic Church.[81] The measure stipulated that all confessional schools should retain their character, a provision that covered approximately ninety-five per cent of all the Prussian schools. It also put them on a sounder financial basis. The bill contained no provision for the Churches' control over the teachers of religion and their instructional materials, but the conclusion is probably warranted that the ministers of public worship and education had gone out of their way to avoid conflicts with Catholic bishops on those issues since the Zedlitz debacle.[82]

The changes that took place in the Vatican's diplomacy after Leo XIII's death in June, 1903, contributed significantly, of course, to the improvement of the atmosphere in which the Center worked with the Imperial government. Rampolla, aware that his pro-French policy was in ruins, had extended himself to make William II's visit to the Vatican in May of that year a success.[83] Nevertheless Kopp participated significantly in the successful effort of the anti-Rampolla bloc in the conclave to prevent the election of the secretary of state as pope.[84] The successful candidate, Pius X, and Cardinal Merry del Val, Rampolla's successor, were ultra-conservative in orientation and inclined to seek cordial relations with Austria-Hungary and Germany.

---

[78] Hertling hoped to secure a Bavarian cabinet position at some time but in the early Bülow years he wanted to become the first Imperial minister to the Vatican. Cardinal Kopp convinced the chancellor that he should not establish such a position. Franciscus Hanus, *Die Preussische Vatikangesandschaft 1747–1920* (2 v., Munich, 1953) 2: p. 391.

[79] Bachem, *Zentrumspartei* 6: pp. 185–209.

[80] Hess, *Kampf um die Schule*, p. 143. The Catholic Congress of 1904 passed a formal resolution which condemned by implication the interconfessional school: *VGVkD zu Bochum* (Bochum, 1902), pp. 114–115.

[81] Bachem, *Zentrumspartei* 6: p. 279.

[82] *Ibid.*, pp. 281–286. Hess, *Kampf um die Schule*, pp. 134–141. *Kölnische Volkszeitung*, October 24, 1906.

[83] Josef Schmidlin, *Papstgeschichte der Neuesten Zeit* (4 v., Munich, 1933–1939) 2: pp. 431–433; 3: pp. 95–96. Bülow, *Memoirs* 1: pp. 599–605.

[84] Cardinal Puzyna of Cracow, then a city in the Austrian state, caused Rampolla's defeat by asserting the ancient right of the Hapsburg emperors to veto the election of any candidate of whom they disapproved. Kopp encouraged the nervous Puzyna to carry out the assignment given him by Emperor Francis-Joseph of Austria-Hungary: *Ibid.*, pp. 610–611. Hutten-Czapski, *Sechig Jahre* 2: pp. 435–437. Radziwill, *Lettres* 3: p. 87. Kopp wrote to Peter Spahn that he had not been told by either William II or Bülow to vote against Rampolla and that the cardinal secretary of state would have been highly acceptable to the chancellor: Morsey, *Wichmann-Jahrbuch für Kirchengeschichte in Bistum Berlin*, 1967–1969: p. 63, fn. 83. The actual point is that Kopp knew how Emperors William II and Francis Joseph felt about Rampolla, so he did not need instructions from anyone. For Bülow's feeling of relief about the outcome of the election: Radizwill, *Lettres* 3: p. 87.

There can be no doubt that Bülow and the Centrist leaders felt highly satisfied with each other by 1904. Because of the Center's contribution to the success of the tariff bill, the chancellor, unlike his predecessors, did not have to contend with an antagonistic Conservative party. The Prussian government's introduction of the new school bill to the Landtag in January, 1904, was pleasing to the Center, but an action taken by the Federal Council in April of the same year had a wider symbolic importance. In the course of that month the Council voted in favor of the deletion of the expulsion article of the anti-Jesuit law. It is improbable that any German state had recently expelled a Jesuit or a member of any other banned religious order. Nevertheless, the article had been of political importance since it was an act of legal exception against certain groups of Catholics.[85] The removal of the expulsion paragraph was, in the thinking of the leading Centrists, the first step to the abolition of the whole law.

Not all the prominent Centrists in or outside Berlin shared the enthusiasm of the Spahn and Porsch circles for Bülow. The chancellor, relatively youthful and confident, represented the *Weltpolitik* which the Rhineland Center had always disliked. His desire to satisfy Bülow was probably the reason why Porsch refused to enter an electoral pact with moderate Polish leaders in Silesia before the Prussian elections of 1903.[86] But the Rhineland Centrists had their own links with the Imperial government. The achievements of the Social Democrats in the national elections of 1903 had strengthened Julius Bachem's conviction that the Center and the government could not afford to deal fitfully with the social and labor questions. He and his colleagues in the Rhineland Center counted heavily upon Arthur von Posadowsky-Wehner, the vice-chancellor and secretary of the interior, to initiate new legislation for the working classes and full rights of organization for unions, in particular those in the Christian trade union movement.

The chief spokesman for Julius Bachem in the Reichstag Center was not his young cousin, Karl Bachem, but Karl Trimborn who had first entered the national parliament in 1896. Karl Bachem was a member of the Center's leadership group and more sympathetic to Bülow than his cousin liked. Trimborn, the chairman of the Rhineland Center and the deputy-chairman of the People's Association, had gradually supplanted his close friend, Franz Hitze, as the Center's expert on social legislation. Through his experiences in his native Cologne, work in the Peoples' Association and his friendship with Hitze,[87] Trimborn had acquired an impressive knowledge of social problems. He was one of the Center's best speakers and probably the most attractive member of the whole Reichstag fraction because of his warm personality and ready humor. He had established a close relationship with Posadowsky after that official became secretary of the interior in 1897 and with some of the Conservatives who shared the Center's interest in the urban social problem.

The Center party had been in a position after the defeat of Posadowsky's prison house bill in November, 1899, to make life difficult for the secretary of the interior and vice chancellor. *Vorwärts* had revealed that Posadowsky solicited money from the Central League of Industrialists for the purpose of publishing propaganda in favor of the bill before its defeat. That revelation was intensely embarrassing to the secretary of the interior, and the Center was insistent that some official had to pay a penalty for the acceptance of the fund. The Centrist leaders were satisfied with the government's willingness to sacrifice Posadowsky's chief assistant since they already knew that the secretary of the interior was not disinclined to a course of moderate social reform.[88] Indeed Posadowsky was all the readier to do so after the Center demonstrated conclusively to him in its abrupt rejection of the prison house bill that it expected the Imperial government to concentrate on positive social legislation.

The collaboration between Posadowsky and the Center extending from 1900 to 1906 fell into two even periods. Between 1900 and 1903, the year of the impressive success of the Social Democrats in the Reichstag elections, the vice-chancellor with the Center's support concentrated largely on the reform or further development of earlier worker insurance or protection programs. From 1903 to 1906 Posadowsky showed increased interest and energy in legislation beneficial to trade unions.

In the late spring of 1899, following the first setback of the prison house bill, Posadowsky had introduced a bill to improve the administration of old-age insurance. It required the richer provincial insurance societies to aid the weaker associations with their payments. In 1901 the Reichstag passed legislation making industrial courts mandatory for all communities with populations of twenty thousand or more and the government itself alloted two million marks for work-

---

[85] Bachem, *Zentrumspartei* 6: p. 210. The Baden government agreed to abstain from voting on a Prussian proposal to delete the expulsion paragraph of the law in return for certain pledges from the Center regarding the shaping of the financial reform bill of 1904. Male religious orders were barred from Baden prior to the revolution of 1918, so the attitude of its government was probably one of the major obstacles to the revocation of the whole anti-Jesuit law.

[86] See above pp. 90–91. They eventually reached an agreement on that issue before the Prussian elections of 1908. On the agreement: Porsch to Naperalski, May 19, 1908. Porsch Papers, File 17b.

[87] Cardauns, *Karl Trimborn,* pp. 111–112. The more unsympathetic sketch of Trimborn in Klaus Epstein's study on Matthias Erzberger reflects the differences between Erzberger and Trimborn after World War I: Klaus Epstein, *Matthias Erzberger,* p. 43.

[88] Karl Bachem, notes dated October 29, 1900. Bachem Papers File 154. Born, *Staat und Sozialpolitik,* pp. 180–182.

ers' housing, an amount it increased in succeeding years. In 1903 Posadowsky won the Reichstag's approval for a measure to increase sickness benefits from thirteen to twenty-six weeks. Before the Center approved the measure it insisted successfully that a provision be deleted that would have barred all persons from the local administration of the funds who could not qualify for jury duty.[89]

Prior to the elections of 1903 the Rhineland Centrists made no progress, however, in trying to convince the Imperial government that it should take a positive attitude toward trade unions. Between 1893 and 1902 it had presented nine interpellations in the Reichstag to the government regarding the question of granting full corporate rights to them. In November, 1902, Julius Bachem informed an assembly of the Catholic press association that the survival of the Center depended upon its response to that issue.[90] During the course of that year the Congress of Christian trade unions voted to establish a general secretariat at Cologne and in January, 1903, the first holder of that office, Adam Stegerwald, a south German labor leader, took up his activity there.[91]

In January, 1904, Karl Trimborn presented the fourteenth Reichstag interpellation to the government regarding its views on the trade union question. On that occasion he found the vice-chancellor was ready to consider the possibility of introducing legislation to the Reichstag that would provide private and public legal rights to the unions. Trimborn and Posadowsky had undoubtedly agreed in advance that the interpellation should be made and that the vice-chancellor should respond positively to it.[92]

Two events of some magnitude led Posadowsky to revise his thinking on the trade union question. The achievements of the Social Democrats in the elections of June, 1903, was obviously one. The government could not revert to the old policy of repression if it wished to retain the Center's support and that of some of the National Liberals as well. Its new policy of modest social reform had failed to halt the growth of the Social Democratic movement. The second event which impressed Posadowsky was the apparent success of the "German Workers' Congress" staged by Stegerwald and other non-Socialist trade unionist leaders at Frankfurt am Main in the summer of 1903. Approximately six hundred thousand laborites from Christian trade unions, other unions, and the Catholic and Evangelical workers' associations attended the congress. It passed a series of resolutions calling upon the government to provide for the extension of coalition rights, the provision of a uniform and liberal law of association and assembly throughout the empire, the granting of adequate legal competence to unions, and the establishment of workers' chambers.[93]

The continued growth of the Social Democratic movement and the apparent potential of the Christian trade unions combined with the urging of the Rhineland Centrists convinced Posadowsky that the government should adopt a new attitude on the issue of unions' rights. Like the Center, he was now certain the Christian trade union movement could become a successful competitor of the Social Democrats and win labor's support for the monarchy. In the discussions which he initiated on that question in the Federal Council during 1904 he pointed out that agricultural, industrial, commercial, and banking associations were permitted a high degree of organization denied to unions and extensive legal rights. For reasons that remained obscure, he refused to consider the introduction of legislation establishing works councils or workers' chambers. He invariably fell back on the old argument that they would be dominated by Social Democrats and be dangerous to industry. He was only willing to consider the creation of boards representing both industry and labor and sitting under the chairmanship of a government official with a limited right to discuss matters of interest to both economic groups. In all likelihood Posadowsky believed that he could not convince the Cartel parties and industrial leaders that the government should sponsor legislation in favor of both the unions and workers' chambers.[94]

The Center's leaders were encouraged, nevertheless, by Posadowsky's constructive conduct in a major strike which broke out in the private coal mines of the Ruhr in January, 1905. In contrast to the conduct of the Clemenceau government in France when it was confronted with a big strike in the mines of the Pas de Calais later that year, Posadowsky refused to send troops into the area or to permit owners to use strike breakers. He was impressed by the contrast between the orderliness and discipline of the recent strike with its predecessor of 1889 when the miners had been unorganized. Although one hundred ninety-five thousand of the two hundred twenty-four thousand miners in the Ruhr participated in the January strike, there was no violence or destruction of property. The three major trade union groups, the Free Trade unions, the Liberal unions, and the Christian Miners' Association, had all participated in the mass undertaking.[95]

During the period of the economic conflict, Posadowsky announced he would introduce a new Prussian mine bill to the Landtag in the immediate future. In collaboration with a committee chaired by Peter Spahn he worked out a bill that was probably a model for its time. It went far to resolve the specific grievances of the miners but also provided for the establishment of

[89] *Ibid.*, pp. 177–184.

[90] *Augustinus-Blatt,* Nr. 11, Krefeld, November, 1902.

[91] Josef Deutz, *Adam Stegerwald* (Cologne, 1952), pp. 40–41; Bachem, *Zentrumspartei* **9**: p. 133.

[92] Born, *Staat und Sozialpolitik,* pp. 188–189.

[93] *Ibid.*, pp. 180–191. Schaedler: *VGVkD zu Regensburg* (Regensburg, 1904), p. 157.

[94] Born, pp. 191–192.

[95] *Ibid.*, pp. 184–186.

a works council in all mines to be elected by secret vote of the workers.[96] The general bill on trade unions that the vice-chancellor intended to submit to the Reichstag in November, 1905, was a document which set limits to the legal powers unions would have under a new law and to the types of workers who could belong to them. Local authorities had to approve their statutes before they could be registered in the official books of the state. They could be held responsible if their members damaged property during a strike and the members themselves could be fined if the union exceeded its area of legitimate activity. The union could lose its rights if it engaged in a political strike. No provision was made for the right of agricultural laborers to form unions although the Center and the *Westdeutscher Arbeiterzeitung* had insisted they should have the right to do so since the debates on the prison house bill.[97]

The new Posadowsky bill on legal rights for trade unions did not reach the Reichstag in 1905–1906, however. The German government was then deeply concerned about the outcome of its diplomatic conflict with France and Great Britain over the independence of Morocco and was uncertain whether the question could be settled peacefully. The Prussian minister of war, Karl von Einem, insisted in the Prussian Ministerial Council in December that the government should consider whether new repressive legislation should be introduced against the Social Democrats because of their alleged influence on new recruits in the army. Only a few weeks earlier August Bebel had stated in the Reichstag that the government should not rely upon the loyalty of the German working class if it did not attend to its needs and legitimate desires. Although the Social Democrats gave no cause in public assemblies or in the Reichstag in the parliamentary year 1905–1906 for new legislation or police action against their party, the government withheld the submission of the Posadowsky measure to the Reichstag till the following autumn.[98]

The Center did not feel the same confidence in Tirpitz that they did in either Bülow or Posadowsky in the period between 1900 and 1906. Its leaders were to become increasingly uneasy about his ambitions to make Germany one of the great naval powers. But they were immediately concerned with the task of making the secretary of the navy accept the control of the Reichstag and themselves over the program of naval construction so that he would not create further financial problems for the empire and serious political difficulties for themselves. That proved to be a difficult undertaking since Tirpitz, encouraged by his successes with the bills of 1898 and 1900 and prodded by William II, was eager to continue a policy of further naval building.

The first disagreements between the Center and Tirpitz came in the early months of 1902. During the debates of the budget committee on the second naval bill of 1900 Tirpitz had agreed to the withdrawal of his request for six large cruisers, supposedly intended for foreign service. He knew that the naval yards could not begin work on them until 1906 because of their other building tasks. Unlike William II, the secretary of the navy was not interested in using money, ships, and manpower for anything but a strong navy which could be a match in home waters for Great Britain in a future war. His apparent building goal was a home fleet of sixty battleships so it is likely that he hoped to be able to present the Reichstag with a new naval bill for a third double squadron in the next few years.[99] In January, 1902, *Vörwärts,* the Social Democratic journal, published a Tirpitz memorandum which revealed that the naval secretary intended to ask the Reichstag to approve a proposal calling for five battleships and a single cruiser at an early date instead of the six cruisers deleted from the second naval bill.[100]

The Centrist leaders did not appear to be upset over the *Vorwärts* exposure of Tirpitz's secret planning. They were busy then with the tolerance and tariff bills. Because of the Reich's serious financial problems they were not willing to consider any changes in the naval program before 1905–1906. Therefore, they let the tight-fisted Müller-Fulda, no admirer of Tirpitz in any case, deal with the secretary of the navy.[101] The Center's financial expert warned Tirpitz that the Reichstag had not committed itself to the approval of the six cruisers dropped from the naval bill of 1900 and that it would be time enough to consider them in 1905–1906. He deliberately spoke of cruisers and not

[96] *Ibid.,* pp. 187–188; Karl Bachem, notes dated April 13, Bachem Papers, File 223.

[97] Born, *Staat und Sozialpolitik,* p. 193 ff. *Ibid.,* p. 160. *Westdeutscher Arbeiterzeitung,* January 4, 11, 18 and February 1, 1902.

[98] Born does not provide a detailed explanation of why some Prussian ministers became worried about the trade unions in 1905. After the Ruhr strike they may have had second thoughts about the wisdom of granting legal rights to the Christian unions. The *Kölnische Volkszeitung* of July 5, 1906, stated that the Prussian government may have become concerned over the reorganization of the Confederation of the Christian Miners in 1905. It went on to say that the Christian unions had to be energetic in their defense of their members but that they were carrying on the old struggle against the Social Democratic unions.

[99] Most historians who have written on Tirpitz's plans think that a battleship fleet of this size was his primary objective: see Volker Berghahn, *Der Tirpitz Plan: Genesis und Verfall einer innenpolitischen Krisenstrategie unter Wilhem II* (Düsseldorf, 1971), pp. 112 ff.; also P. M. Kennedy, "Tirpitz, England and the Second Naval Law of 1900: A Strategical Critique," *Militär-geschichtsliche Mitteilungen,* 1970, no. 2: pp. 33–57.

[100] Schulthess, *Geschichtskalender* **43** (1902): pp. 28, 34.

[101] According to Lieber, Müller-Fulda had become soured over the failure of either the emperor or Tirpitz to acknowledge his labors on behalf of the second naval bill of 1900: Lieber to Tirpitz, December 8, 1900, Bundes-archiv-Militärarchiv, Freiburg. Nachlass Tirpitz (N253), **4**: pp. 182–183. Copy in possession of Patrick J. Kelly.

of battleships.[102] In the next few years he and Schaedler were to make difficulties for the secretary of the navy on minor budgetary matters.[103]

Nevertheless, Spahn and Gröber finally realized that they would have to speak out unequivocally to the secretary of navy on the question of naval expansion. Like Lieber in the mid and later 1890's, they were keenly sensitive to any efforts on the part of the government or non-governmental organizations to bring the Reichstag under the pressure of an artificially stimulated public opinion for their military plans.

In the early months of 1904 the feelings between the Center and Tirpitz suffered new strains because of his relations with the Naval League. At that time General August Keim, the general director of the League, emerged as the leading advocate of naval expansion in the empire. Keim, an aggressive militarist, initiated a campaign for the early introduction of a third naval bill which would add a third double squadron of battleships to the navy by 1912, although the law of 1900 was not to achieve completion until 1917. In April, 1904, the general executive committee of the Naval League formally approved Keim's proposal and plan for a national campaign of propaganda in its favor.[104] Keim disputed the estimates made by Müller-Fulda in March, 1904, of the costs of a third double squadron, approximately eight hundred million marks, but they were probably accurate enough. The *Kölnische Volkszeitung* tried to engage Keim in a responsible debate about the manner in which a third major naval program could be financed, only to be told that the Naval League could not take a position on that complex question of financial policy.[105]

Although Müller-Fulda depicted Keim as "a new [General] Boulanger" in the Budget Committee in March, 1904, the Center did not worry so much over the general as it did over Tirpitz's secret relations with him. The secretary of the navy disapproved of the efforts of the Navy League to take the lead in determining what the next steps in the navy's building program should be and he found General Keim to be a nuisance in his insistence that heavier artillery was more important to a battleship than navigability.[106] But Tirpitz undoubtedly thought that Keim and the Navy League could be useful in putting pressure on the Reichstag and the Center for a further rapid expansion of the navy.[107]

The Centrist leaders were still eager to preserve the reputation their party had won of being reliable on national issues and of having brought about the passage of the first two naval laws. They were prepared to advocate the approval of a supplementary bill for the construction of six cruisers in the session of 1905–1906 when the proposals for a major finance reform would be ready. But they were also determined to show Tirpitz and the emperor that they would not be forced by the artificial agitation of the Navy League into a new expansionist program. They were right that official encouragement of the Keim program would be counter-productive and might endanger the supplementary bill of 1905–1906.

In the parliamentary session of 1904–1905 the Center made it clear to the secretary of the navy and to its parliamentary allies what its priorities were in national defense. During the first months of the Navy League's agitation Spahn had said with marked emphasis that it was the army and not the navy which would have to fight the battles that would be decisive for Germany's future.[108] In the course of the session of 1904–1905 the Center enabled the Prussian minister of war, General von Einem, to bring a moderate army bill through the Reichstag without a reduction.[109] In the debates in early February, 1905, Gröber, a spokesman often selected by his colleagues when they wanted to be unpleasant, told the Reichstag that the Navy League had used the argument that further expansion of the navy would be justified because of the "colossal amount of national property" protected by them. He intended to address the Free Conservatives, and the National Liberals, both parliamentary patrons of the Navy League, when he added that the taxes for such an expansion should be borne by "large-scale commerce and big industry" which profited most from that service and not by the lower classes.[110]

But Tirpitz was a realist and the Center was more important to the success of his policies than the Navy League. During the winter of 1904–1905 he fought off William II himself when the emperor insisted he submit a supplementary bill to the Reichstag for more big ships.[111] In late February, 1905, he told the Budget Committee that the Navy League had no influence on the government and expressed regret it had sought to promote the cause of its own building program. Keim correctly concluded that Tirpitz had sacrificed his connections with the League in favor of a better understanding with the Center. Later that spring Tirpitz told the Reichstag that he would ask the parliament to approve six cruisers in the next session.[112]

It was apparent that Tirpitz and Spahn reached an agreement in the late spring or summer of 1905 about

[102] *Reichstag Verhandlungen*, February 2, 1902: p. 3994.

[103] Schulthess, *Geschichtskalender* **44** (1903): p. 169; **45** (1904): pp. 28, 64.

[104] Generalleutnant August Keim, *Erlebtes und Erstrebtes. Lebenserinnerungen* (Hanover, 1925), p. 99.

[105] Gröber: *Reichstag Verhandlungen*, February 5, 1905: p. 4797.

[106] Keim, *Erlebtes*, p. 105.

[107] *Ibid.*, p. 111. Berghahn, *Der Tirpitz Plan*, p. 480.

[108] *Reichstag Verhandlungen*, April 14, 1904: p. 2033.

[109] Bachem, *Zentrumspartei* **6**: pp. 254–257.

[110] *Reichstag Verhandlungen*, February 5, 1905: p. 4798.

[111] Patrick J. Kelly, "The Naval Policy of Imperial Germany" (Ph.D. diss. Georgetown University. 1970), pp. 269–274. William II had apparently hoped for some years to secure Tirpitz's acceptance of a new type of ship, a fast heavy cruiser: Berghahn, *Tirpitz Plan*, p. 206.

[112] *Ibid.*, p. 486.

the supplementary naval bill of 1905–1906. The naval secretary had been forced to deny that the government approved of the work of the Navy League. In the future the naval secretary would apparently negotiate only with the Center about his further plans for the building program. In the session of 1905–1906 both were to ignore the demand of the Navy League that the lifetime of battleships and other heavily armed ships be shortened. The Center was eager to establish a dual relationship with Tirpitz at the expense of the Navy League and it was ready to give him approximately what he desired. The six cruisers were to be heavy enough to take their places in the battle line and would not go off on foreign service. In the regular naval budget Tirpitz planned to ask for funds to convert the battleships still to be built into dreadnoughts in imitation of the recent British example.[113] Tirpitz had reason to be satisfied with the outcome of his differences with the Center over the agitation of the Navy League.

8. THE END OF THE GOVERNMENT-CENTER COALITION

You say that we are no longer "the healthy party of opposition" of 1893 whose politics had been a joy to the voters. You are correct there in some degree that a change has taken place in our relationship to the government and that it is more difficult today to make our policy more plausible to the voters than it was earlier.
Karl Bachem to Müller-Fulda, January, 1905.[1]

Up to now Bülow's strength has lain in the fact that people believed he could get along with the Center better than anyone else. In this he was considered a specialist.
Friedrich von Holstein, February, 1907.[2]

The Center's leaders became increasingly aware in the years of their close collaboration with Bülow of the growing insistence from nationalist, liberal, and some Protestant quarters that the government should attempt to form a new coalition without their party. They were also sensitive to the heightening of confessional temperatures due in substantial measure to the Center's favored position in the existing coalition, the chancellor's ties with its leaders, and the modification of the anti-Jesuit law. Spahn and his colleagues were reasonably confident, however, about the future of their partnership with the government at the end of the legislative year, 1904–1905.[3] Their relations with the

chancellor were easy and there appeared to the government to be no practicable alternative to the Center as an ally of the Cartel parties. The Radicals were split into three independent and small fractions whose total Reichstag membership after 1903 was substantially less than half of the Center's and the government still regarded the Social Democrats as dangerous enemies of the monarchical system.

Nevertheless, the links between the Center and the government were subject to severe strains in the session of 1905–1906 and were broken in December, 1906. In the early months and fall of 1906 Spahn and his intimate associates were not in control of the party and the chancellor had suffered an erosion of the influence he had enjoyed earlier with the emperor. It was ironic that the break did not come over the staggering budgetary demands the government made on the Reichstag but over colonial issues which had always been amenable to compromises between the chancellors and the Center in the past.

Neither the government nor the Reichstag had paid adequate attention to the needs of the German colonial program prior to the winter of 1905–1906. Bismarck had hesitatingly acquired the four African colonies, Southwest Africa, East Africa, the Cameroons, and Togo, with the expectation that chartered companies, in imitation of some British models, would take over both their administration and economic exploitation. But even in those colonies where such companies existed the government had to step in and assume the burdens of administration at an early date. Bismarck and his successors did not attempt, however, to set up a separate colonial civil service and most of its officials were recruited from the Foreign Office, of which the Colonial Department was a part until 1907, or from other sections of the Imperial government. And despite all of the official emphasis upon *Weltpolitik* after 1894, Hohenlohe and Bülow did not take substantially greater interest in the colonies than Caprivi whose unenthusiasm for them had been notorious.

The members of the Windthorst circle, like their Radical allies of the 1880's, had been unhappy over Bismarck's acquisition of a modest German empire overseas. They assumed that they would continue to be dependent on the home country for financial support for a long time or possibly in an individual case like that of Southwest Africa permanently so. Windthorst also feared that the possession of the colonies would permit later German governments to argue that a large navy was necessary for their defense.[4] Political ex-

---

[113] I develop the accommodation between the Center and the naval secretary at greater length in the next chapter, pp. 105–109.

[1] Letter dated January 22, 1905. Bachem Papers, File 223.

[2] *Holstein Papers* 4: p. 454.

[3] Two of the most respected political publicists of the period, Hans Delbrück, the editor of the *Preussische Jahrbücher*, and Friedrich Naumann, were systematic critics of the Center party. Georg von Hertling had expressed alarm to Hermann Cardauns in 1903 over the amount of anti-Catholic feeling he found in Berlin: letter of February 24. 1903, Hertling-Cardauns Correspondence. In a letter to Müller-Fulda, dated January 22,

1905, Karl Bachem justified the leaders' coalition policy with the claim that the adoption by the Center of an oppositional course could lead to a "Bloc des Gauche" like the ruling anticlerical and leftist coalition in France or "an anti-Center coalition." Fn. 1 above.

[4] *Verhandlungen des Reichstages*, January 10, 1890: p. 941; February 4, 1890: p. 1302; February 6, 1890: p. 1348. He and his party were pleased over the Anglo-German treaty of June, 1890, in which Germany received Heligoland in return for its

pediency dictated, however, that the Center adopt a positive position on the colonial question. While Windthorst always tended to be somewhat reserved in his statements, Lieber and his colleagues were emphatic that Germany had to pursue a colonial policy because she was a great nation which had to assume responsibilities for the cultural, moral, and material well-being for a less fortunate part of the world.[5]

However, the Center never gave more than qualified approval to the colonial program.[6] Nor did it want to be drawn into a detailed consideration of the conditions in the colonies and the government's policies there. Windthorst had protested against Bismarck's decision in 1886 to exclude the Reichstag from the exercise of any legislative power over them, but Lieber and his successors did not challenge the monarchy's monopoly of that power. While they may have thought it would be politically unwise to do so, it is also likely that they were happy to be excluded from any serious responsibility for colonial affairs beyond a concern for the work of the Catholic missionaries and for economy in the expenditures of the Colonial Department.

The qualified character of the Center's support of the colonial program, its concern with economy, and its sensitivity to the views of Catholic missionary societies were related factors in the formulation of its policy.[7] There were no Catholic groups who were eager to promote German imperialism for economic or nationalist reasons and no Catholic explorer and imperialist like Carl Peters who had sought to defy Bismarck himself in his efforts to expand Germany's possessions in East Africa. The fact that Franz von Arenberg served from the mid-1890's to his death in 1907 as the chairman of the Berlin branch of the German Colonial Society had little or no impact on his co-religionists.[8] They, like most Catholics in western and central Europe, were affected by neo-imperialism

only to the extent of its association with missionary activity. They were able to identify themselves with the religious and cultural efforts of the missionaries in a way which they could not with the administration or German business enterprises in the colonies.

As churchmen, the Centrists were undoubtedly sincere in their personal interest in the work of the missionaries. But they were also aware there was considerable apathy in the south and southwest and even in the west toward the whole colonial program. In June, 1894, the editors of the *Kölnische Volkszeitung* agreed with Chancellor Caprivi that the less Germany owned of Africa the better off she would be.[9] The Rhineland Center had to change its tune after the Hohenlohe administration emphasized the importance of the colonies to Germany, but the *Historisch-politische Blätter* was undoubtedly expressing Bavarian Centrist attitudes in its essentially negative stand on the whole program from its initiation to the great debates on the colonial scandals in 1905–1906.[10]

The difficulties that the Centrist leaders encountered in trying to overcome Catholic apathy or hostility to the colonial program was compounded by the campaign that the Radical Peoples' and the South German Peoples' parties had carried on against it without interruption since its beginning. No German parliamentarian had as impressive a knowledge of budgets, financial and economic affairs as Eugen Richter, the head of the Radical Peoples' party and the leading bourgeois critic of the monarchy. Richter also had a gift for sharpening his criticism through ridicule. In 1896 he pointed out that less than one thousand Germans lived in all the colonies and most of them did so at the expense of the Imperial treasury. He claimed that the total amount of exports to the colonies in the previous year had been about ten million marks, chiefly in the form of "beer, wine, champagne, powder, guns, and salt for the civil servants and the military."[11]

In the Hohenlohe and Bülow periods the Center had to perform a delicate tightrope act on the colonial question. It was eager to demonstrate its loyalty to Germany's overseas program but also to convince its electorate that by doing so it was aiding the missions. During most of the 1890's Lieber and his colleagues carefully examined the reports of abuses committed by some German officials against natives including their alleged misconduct with native women. They referred sometimes to their concern about such cases in the open Reichstag to inform Catholic voters of their attention to complaints about the colonial administrators. But they made it plain that they considered such abusive or criminal acts to be isolated incidents or products

renunciation of claims to Zanzibar and wider territories in east Africa: Windthorst in the Reichstag: *ibid.,* Lieber's journal, June 18, 1890. They were also relieved by the treaty because they feared an Anglo-German rivalry which could lead to a costly naval competition between the two governments.

[5] Lieber: *Verhandlungen des Reichstages,* February 17, 1894: pp. 13–15. Fritzen: *ibid.,* December 9, 1895: p. 23.

[6] Franz von Arenberg was to state in 1905 that he could have become the director of the Colonial Department without any effort if it had not been for the reserved attitude of his party toward the colonial program: Bachem, *Zentrumspartei* **6**: p. 339.

[7] Erzberger: *Verhandlungen des Reichstages,* December 14, 1905: p. 331.

[8] I have been unable to determine conclusively why Arenberg was so active in the Colonial Society. While he may have made some investments in the colonies, my own assumption is that he, a former diplomat, acted for the government in trying to win Center support for the colonial program and for his church in representing mission interests with the government. He had been highly pleased when he received an invitation to address the Catholic Congress of 1894 on the subject of the missions: Ernst Lieber to Gröber, June 9, 1894, Lieber Papers, Speyer, *Briefe* 1892–1897.

[9] *Kölnische Volkszeitung,* June 9, 1894.

[10] In 1905 it was to describe the colonies as "highly worthless" and as being heavily dependent on subsidies: **106**: p. 133.

[11] *Reichstag Verhandlungen,* March 16, 1896: p. 1498.

of carelessness and not typical examples of official conduct.[12]

In the late 1890's Centrist speakers ceased referring to the misdeeds of colonial civil servants. It was hardly due to the fact that the government had raised the qualitative level of administrators or that the officials themselves avoided conflicts with missionaries of strict moral views. The probable explanation is that Arenberg, the Reichstag reporter for the colonial budget and Bülow's old friend, dealt with specific cases of differences between missionaries and officials behind the closed doors of the Colonial Department with its director. Some critics of the Center, inclusive of some of Arenberg's non-Catholic friends, believed that he kept a black list which contained the names of officials not cooperating with the missionaries.[13]

Bülow's willingness to support that practice was probably part of his general effort to eliminate all potential elements of friction between the government and its most important ally in the Reichstag. But it may have been due in some measure to the greater demands that the government had begun to make on the Reichstag in the form of subsidies for private companies to undertake the building of railroads in the African colonies in the same years that Tirpitz introduced his first major naval bills to the Reichstag. The leaders of the Center, inclusive of the mercurial Müller-Fulda till 1904, acknowledged that the new policy was realistic on the grounds that these colonies would never attract significant investments and become self-sufficient without adequate communications.[14]

The combination of the government's increasing emphasis upon its new railroad policy and the outbreak of extensive rebellions in Southwest Africa in the early winter of 1903–1904 did lead, however, to an increased attention on the part of the Center's leaders to colonial budgets and problems, particularly in the Reichstag session of 1904–1905. It was calculated that the war in that colony, the poorest of Germany's major African possessions, would cost the empire at least one hundred million marks a year before its conclusion. Although the Center approved most of the colonial budget, it was discriminating in its voting on the proposed subsidies for railroad companies and for compensation to settlers and businessmen who had lost property in the Southwest African uprisings.[15]

During that session Matthias Erzberger, a Centrist deputy from the small Württemberg group, sat for the first time as a member of the large Center contingent in the prestigious and powerful Budget Committee. He had become the youngest member of the Reichstag when he entered in 1903. Erzberger early revealed the ambition, driving energy, political courage and power of speech that were to make him one of the most effective deputies in the Reichstag by 1914. Like Windthorst he had no interests other than politics except those connected with his religion. He had nearly all the qualifications necessary for a career as a parliamentary statesman except an inner balance which probably reflected his lack of an advanced education and the inability to examine himself with critical detachment.[16]

As a young editor in the late 1890's Erzberger had been active in the promotion of the interconfessional trade union movement in southwestern Germany. In the normal course of events he would have devoted himself as a new deputy to central economic and social questions more than to colonial issues if he had not become aware of a conflict involving missionaries and local German officials in the colony of Togo.[17] The awakening of his interest in colonial affairs through his acquaintance with that happening was to be fateful for two heads of the Colonial Department and pro-

---

[12] Hans Spellmeyer, *Die deutsche Kolonialpolitik im Reichstag* (Stuttgart. 1931), p. 69. Hans Pehl, *Die deutsche Kolonialpolitik und das Zentrum 1884–1914* (Limburg, 1934), p. 55. As Pehl points out, Lieber and Arenberg were outspokenly critical of Karl Peters for the offenses he had committed in East Africa. It should be added that one of these was in effect legal murder, the hanging of his former concubine on the grounds of treason, and that at the time he came under Centrist fire, March, 1896, he was one of the leaders of the agitation for a big navy.

[13] The ex-Jesuit and bitter enemy of the Center, Count Paul Hoensbroech, said in his newspaper, *Deutschland,* in April, 1904, that he had been informed that a Centrist deputy close to the chancellor, obviously Arenberg, had decisive power in the personnel matters of the Colonial Department; quoted in the *Deutsche Zeitung,* April 7, 1904. Some of Arenberg's associates in the Colonial Society made the same kind of statements after his death in February, 1907. See Spitzenberg, *Tagebuch,* p. 471. Their claims were probably excessive but the resentments that German bureaucrats later felt against Erzberger and Hermann Roeren for their interference in the internal affairs of the colonial administration had their origins in Arenberg's earlier exercise of influence.

[14] Richard Müller and Hubert Sittart, *Der Deutsche Reichstag von 1898 bis 1903* (Cologne, 1903), pp. 13–14. Pehl, *Kolonialpolitik und das Zentrum,* p. 61. Spellmeyer, *Kolonialpolitik im Reichstag,* p. 87.

[15] *Ibid.,* pp. 102–103.

[16] Georg von Hertling recognized his talents, but complained in 1906 about his lack of education and power of self-criticism: letter to Julius Bachem, April 10, 1906, Hertling Papers, Bundesarchiv, IV, File 35. The *Frankfurter Zeitung,* which was essentially sympathetic to him in its appraisal of his career, commented on August 22, 1921, after his assassination, that there was something "uneven" in his personality.

[17] Bachem, *Zentrumspartei* 6: pp. 349–350. In his study of Erzberger, *Matthias Erzberger and the Dilemma of German Democracy* (Princeton, 1959), Klaus Epstein devoted only a few pages to his subject's campaign against the colonial administration in 1905–1906 and chose to treat it at length in his article: "Erzberger and the German Colonial Scandals, 1905–1911." *English Historical Review* **84** (1959): pp. 637–664. The article is a most useful account of the campaign and of Erzberger's views on colonial reform. Epstein did not attempt, however, to grapple seriously with the question of why Erzberger became involved in the debates over the colonial program or why he was so hostile to the Colonial Department. He implied that it was essentially due to Erzberger's indignation over the scandalous conditions which existed in the German colonial system, while acknowledging that Erzberger was looking for a field of legislative activity in which he would be the leading authority in his party.

gressively embarrassing for the senior Centrists and the chancellor himself.

In early 1903 there had been differences between some Catholic missionaries and a district officer over the punishment of natives. Later that year they came into conflict again because of the relationships between some officials, the district officer among them, and young native girls. The dispute took a bizarre turn in that a higher German official arrested several priests and confined them without trial; some weeks later the acting governor of Togo intervened and ordered their release. The missionaries, outraged over the affair, insisted that the officials immediately involved in the dispute and in the arrests should be recalled or transferred. Franz von Arenberg and the officials of the Colonial Department tried to work out a compromise which called for the transfer of the leading participants on both sides.[18] The superior of the missionaries was not willing to accept that political settlement which he thought was unjust to the priests and asked Hermann Roeren to bring the case and its background to the attention of the colonial director. The missionary superior, armed with documents from the files of the colony administration given him by a young official, Wistuba, apparently a Catholic, met with Oswald von Stuebel, the colonial director in November, 1904. As a result of their meeting, one official was dismissed from the civil service and some others were transferred to other colonies, while the missionaries involved in the earlier controversy remained in Togo.[19]

It was unusual that Roeren, not Arenberg, the long-time contact between the Center and the Foreign Office, represented the missionary society in its negotiations with the head of the Colonial Department. The Togo affair had aspects to it that may have been disconcerting to Arenberg and the other senior leaders of the Center. It involved the dismissal or disciplining and transfer of several civil servants. The access of missionaries to government files through Wistuba was a still more serious matter. It was a grave breach of discipline on Wistuba's part and in the course of the next year authorities instituted proceedings against him. Hermann Roeren soon became his protector. Roeren was a sincere man but he had the reputation of representing Catholic causes and points of view in legislative and political matters with a narrow zeal. Some years later he was to become the leading figure in a conservative Catholic movement to oppose the efforts of Julius Bachem and the Centrist leaders to promote interconfessionalism in the Catholic labor movement and, though to a lesser extent, in the Center.[20]

In the last months of the coalition between the Center and the government Roeren was to appear as a divisive figure, antagonizing Bülow and other officials. Nevertheless, he did not play an active part in the campaign of exposure which Erzberger and the Social Democrats waged against the Colonial Department in 1905–1906. He appeared to be preoccupied with the task of persuading the government to drop the charges against Wistuba and with non-colonial issues.[21] While he may have secretly encouraged Erzberger in his onslaughts on the Colonial Department, it is likely that the younger man did not need any encouragement from Roeren.

Not enough attention has been paid in the past to the fact that Erzberger was a south German, though not a particularist in the Bavarian sense of that term. He came from a region where there was a strong tradition of anti-Prussianism and opposition to *Weltpolitik*.[22] His mentor and patron, Adolf Gröber, had long been a member of the Center leadership group and supported its traditional policies of collaboration with the government, but he occasionally expressed his dislike for the Prussian bureaucracy in his speeches.[23] Despite his relative youthfulness Erzberger himself appeared to lack the respect that his Prussian Centrist colleagues appeared to feel for the higher officials of the Prussian-German state.

In the budget committee debates of 1904–1905 on the colonies, Erzberger's contacts with some colonial officials had been abrasive. He was sharply critical of the plan presented by Karl Helfferich, the young economics expert of the Colonial Department, to set up a special bank and currency in German East Africa and claimed that it would benefit big business but not agriculture.[24] He was emphatic in insisting that his party would not approve funds to aid settlers and merchants who had lost property because of the Southwest African rebellions and he was curious about the propriety of the monopoly contract the Colonial Department had awarded to Tippelskirch, a military supply

Roeren since Karl Bachem complained about Roeren's lack of tact in handling the measure in the parliament: Karl Bachem, notes dated March 9, 1900. Bachem papers, File 111. On Roeren's later differences with Julius Bachem over the interconfessional labor movement see his *Zentrum und Kölner Richtung* (Trier, 1913). The Centrist leaders had forced him out of the Reichstag before the appearance of his brochure.

[21] *The German Elections of 1907*, p. 43, fn. 60.

[22] He was to say after the break between the government and his party in December, 1906, that Catholics were loyal monarchists but they disliked *Weltpolitik*: Radziwill, *Lettres* 3: p. 284.

[23] The slender and cautious biographical sketch by Hermann Cardauns, *Adolf Gröber* (M. Gladbach, 1921) does not reveal this side of him. He liked to say of himself, in a play upon his name, that he could be "gröber" (more gross). Klaus Epstein writes of him that "his prepared orations in the Reichstag . . . made ministers tremble." *Erzberger*, p. 41.

[24] See the objective treatment of their dispute in John Williamson, *Karl Helfferich, 1872–1924* (Princeton, 1970), pp. 70–74. Williamson concludes that Helfferich's schemes, the work of a young academic theorist, were impractical.

[18] Karl Müller, *Geschichte der katholischen Kirche in Togo* (Kaldenkirchen 1958), pp. 173–174.

[19] On the Togo affair: *ibid.*, pp. 165–176: George D. Crothers, *The German Elections of 1907* (N.Y., 1941), pp. 41–42.

[20] Roeren had taken the leading part in trying to promote the passage of the Center's censorship bill of 1900. There was probably some tension then between the Bachem cousins and

firm, in connection with the campaigns in the same colony.[25]　He had apparently established his reputation as a critic of the colonial administration because material on it flowed to him that spring and summer from a variety of sources, inclusive of disaffected officials, businessmen who had failed to secure contracts, and missionaries.

But Erzberger did not depend alone on the complaints and materials of persons who had grievances, legitimate or otherwise, against the Colonial Department.　The Reichstag had closed down earlier than usual because of the Moroccan crisis between Germany and France, and Erzberger, who spent most of his summer in Berlin, also worked through parliamentary reports and proceedings and governmental documents on the colonies.　He discovered that the Colonial Department sometimes had been seriously inaccurate in its reporting to the Reichstag.　In addition, Director Stuebel and Karl Helfferich had not revealed some important facts about the transfer of the Cameroon railroad concession which had involved, among other things, kickbacks from the new to the old directors and a failure on Helfferich's part to provide the Reichstag with a full estimate of the total costs of the railroad's construction.　Moreover, there was a growing realization in Germany in 1905 that the uprisings in Southwest Africa had been due in substantial degree to serious grievances on the part of the natives.　The administration of Director von Stuebel, a victim of a long tradition of government neglect of the colonies and his own lack of experience in colonial affairs, was finally discredited by the outbreak of native disorders in East Africa in midsummer.　His position had already been undermined when Erzberger attacked his administration in a series of articles in the *Kölnische Volkszeitung* in which he claimed that there had been improprieties in the transfer of the Cameroon railroad concession and that the government had granted monopolistic contracts for supplies to the troops in Southwest Africa.[26]　After an appropriate waiting period of about two months the government announced that Stuebel had been appointed minister to Norway.[27]

At some point before the publication of his articles Erzberger had become acquainted with O. Poeplau, a junior civil servant in the Colonial Department and a friend of Wistuba.　Poeplau had long been disaffected with his superiors because they had not given him the promotion he desired.　In 1902 he had delated them to Stuebel and to the chancellor himself without success and the superiors had tried to bring about his early retirement.　Two years later he gave material which could incriminate them to other officials to a Radical deputy who asked the chancellor to investigate Poeplau's charges.　Instead Bülow ordered proceedings instituted against the young official.　Poeplau later brought the same or similar documents to Erzberger who was to use some of the material in his exposures of the colonial administration in the Reichstag session of 1905–1906.　In September, 1905, and shortly after the Colonial Department began Poeplau's trial, Erzberger sought to intervene on his behalf with Friedrich Loebell, the chief of the Imperial Chancellory, Bülow's assistant.　He apparently stated or implied that Poeplau would publish his material and that it would be difficult for his party to approve colonial programs if the chancellor did not drop the charges or make them part of a wider investigation of the Colonial Department.　Loebell refused to make either concession and the chancellor himself was to adhere rigidly to the regulations in insisting that both Poeplau and Wistuba had to be tried in an administrative court for revealing the contents of confidential government documents to unauthorized persons.[28]

Erzberger made his unsuccessful intervention on Poeplau's behalf about two months before the opening of the Reichstag in which he began his sustained attacks on the Colonial Department.　It is logical, therefore, to pose the question whether there was a causal connection between that failure and his later hostile parliamentary campaign against the Colonial Department.　Klaus Epstein, in his sympathetic study of Erzberger, insists that the Centrist politician did not try to bring about the dismissal of charges against Poeplau since he knew that Poeplau's trial was under way.　He claims that Erzberger hoped at best that the chancellor would order an investigation of Poeplau's charges in the belief that it would put the official's illegal conduct in a better light and that Erzberger made no threats in the course of his efforts.[29]

Nevertheless, it is difficult to avoid the conclusion that Erzberger mounted the broad assault on the Colonial Department, in which he made critical remarks about Bülow as well, in part for the reason that he wanted to put pressure on the chancellor and the new colonial director, Prince Ernst von Hohenlohe-Langenburg, to drop the charges against his informant.　Erzberger was a more robust politician in 1905–1906 than his biographer described him and throughout his career he never worried about legal niceties, though he certainly had both ideal and purely political motives for his campaign.　It is also likely that he made veiled

[25] Spellmeyer, *Kolonialpolitik im Reichstag,* p. 100.　Pehl, *Kolonialpolitik und das Zentrum,* p. 66.

[26] Williamson treats in some detail the manner in which Helfferich had handled the transfer of the concession for the Cameroon railroad and concludes, rightly I believe, that Helfferich made an effective defense of his conduct in that affair. He does stress the fact, however, that Helfferich had kept back the information about the amount of money the new company would have to pay its predecessor for earlier construction.

[27] There had been rumors in Berlin before the appearance of Erzberger's articles that Stuebel would be given such a post: *Allgemeine Zeitung,* September 2, 1905.

[28] *Verhandlungen des Reichstages,* December 14, 1905 : p. 332. Epstein, *Erzberger,* pp. 405–407.　And see Crothers, *The German Elections of 1907,* pp. 41–42.

[29] Epstein, *Erzberger,* pp. 405–407.

threats to Bülow's subordinates in the Chancellery that his party would oppose colonial programs in the future if the government continued with its plan to try Poeplau.[30]

But Erzberger's campaign also owed some of its incentive to the resentment all Centrists felt over the appointment of Prince Hohenlohe-Langenburg to the directorship of the Colonial Department shortly before the Reichstag opened in late November, 1905. In fairness to Bülow, it should be recalled that he was deeply involved in the diplomatic negotiations for the international conference on the Moroccan dispute and that Hohenlohe's appointment reflected the difficulty of finding someone in the actual colonial administration who was both competent and satisfactory to the Center. Hohenlohe's qualifications seemed to be that he was married to a cousin of the emperor, was unemployed after serving as the regent of a small German state, and had some interest in colonial affairs, and they were to be ranked in that order. But even if his qualifications had been better the chancellor had made a serious political mistake in agreeing to his appointment at William II's request. The attacks of the Evangelical League on the Center were at their peak in 1905 and Hohenlohe was the son of one of the founders of the League and a prominent member himself.[31] To make matters worse he insisted that the government ask the Federal Council and the Reichstag to heighten the prestige of his new position by converting the Colonial Department into a Secretariat of Colonial Affairs independent of the Foreign Office. His appointment and Erzberger's campaign against his administration were to contribute significantly to the bitter press disputes between the Free Conservatives and the National Liberals, who were his protectors, and the Center, his critics, in 1906.

Some political observers compared Erzberger during the session of 1905–1906 with Eugen Richter who was then inactive because of a terminal illness.[32] They noted, however, that he avoided the great Radical's purely negative approach and associated himself in principle with the colonial program. Erzberger, as a member of the Center party, could not have advocated the abandonment of the German colonial empire. His short-range aim was to secure the rights of the Reichstag to share in the legislative process for the colonies and to enable it through that participation to produce a basic policy stressing consideration of the rights of the natives as the prime objective of German colonial policy. His recommendations were actually quite conservative since he did not demand self-government for the natives much less the right to ultimate independence.[33]

Nevertheless, Erzberger's assaults on the colonial administration were far more massive than the earlier attacks of either Richter or the Social Democrats. He warned that the whole African empire was on the point of collapse because of the widespread native unrest which threatened to paralyze German government in Southwest Africa, East Africa, and the Cameroons.[34] As Richter had so often done, he stressed the small size of the German population in the colonies—under six thousand in 1905—and the incidental amount of trade between the homeland and the colonies, approximately three hundred eighteen million marks worth, between 1884 and 1905.[35] But he probably scored heaviest on three issues: the number of officials who were under charges for the commission of serious abuses or the failure of the Colonial Department to punish lesser officials who had committed them, the continued exploitation of natives by land and commercial companies which included the illegal use of forced labor, and the number of monopolistic contracts involving excessive profits which the government had awarded to privileged German firms.[36]

In his campaign Erzberger steered clear of all references to the question of the personal moral habits of officials. When he referred to the missionaries he did so for the purpose of demonstrating their concern about the future of German rule and the missions in the colonies where official German representatives and businessmen were disliked or hated. He quoted a Protestant missionary, apparently from Southwest Africa, as saying that the rebels would respect the lives of missionaries, Englishmen, Boers, and bastards but not those of German soldiers or officials.[37] Later he told the Reichstag that Catholic missionaries in East Africa had said they would have to close their missions if the natives were driven off the land and became nothing more than shepherds and day laborers.[38]

Erzberger's campaign against the colonial administration added to the tension which already existed between the middle parties, the Free Conservatives and National Liberals, and the Center. The further strengthening of the Center's parliamentary position

---

[30] Like Epstein, Crothers is more sympathetic to Erzberger and Roeren than he is to the government in the Poeplau and Wistuba affairs. But Crothers suggests that Erzberger may have used a threat to create embarrassment for the government through the publication of Poeplau's materials; *The German Elections of 1907*, p. 43.

[31] Julius Bachem was so concerned about the appointment that he asked Arenberg whether the goverment did so to offend the Center. Arenberg replied in the negative and said that he could have secured the directorship if his party had not been reserved in its attitude toward the colonies: Bachem, *Zentrumspartei* **6**: p. 339. William II may have insisted upon Hohenlohe's appointment to placate the Evangelical League because Bülow had selected several Catholics for important administrative or judicial positions in the previous half-year. See below p. 107.

[32] Schulthess, *Geschichtskalender* **47** (1906): p. 445.

[33] Epstein, *EHR* **84** (1959): pp. 662–664.

[34] *Verhandlungen des Reichstages*, December 14, 1905: p. 320.

[35] *Ibid.*, pp. 320–321.

[36] *Ibid.*, pp. 321–324.

[37] *Ibid.*, December 2, 1905: p. 87.

[38] *Ibid*, March 23, 1906, p. 2234.

after the elections of 1903 and its intimate relationship with the Conservatives had reduced the influence of the two other Cartel parties in the government coalitions in the Reichstag and the Prussian Landtag. They were also sensitive to the heightened attacks of the Evangelical League on the Center. But they had been the traditional advocates of a German *Weltpolitik* and colonial policy which could add to German prestige and the economic interests of German big business.[39]

In retrospect, it should be recognized that Erzberger's charges, despite some inaccuracies, were substantially correct. Some prominent colonial officials were under charges or already on trial as Erzberger claimed, and even the National Liberals, leading apologists for the colonial bureaucracy, admitted in the spring of 1906 that certain officials would have to be removed.[40] Bernard Dernburg, Hohenlohe's successor, was to decide after a review of the contracts with business firms transporting or supplying the colonial troops that some would have to be canceled. But Erzberger's presentation of conditions in the colonial service was almost unrelievedly black and stained the reputation of the government itself when it was involved in the most serious international crisis of its brief history.[41] The severe defects of the colonial administration were primarily due to the fact that William II, his chancellors after 1894, and the middle parties had preferred to concentrate their thinking and energies on the splendors of naval power and a foreign policy of prestige rather than on the responsibilities Germany had incurred through her acquisition of colonies. In December, 1905, Bülow, while not going into any detail on matters concerning the colonies, frankly admitted that "great mistakes" had been made in their administration.[42] But the Center had been derelict, too, though not to the same degree, since it had not wanted to become seriously involved in the affairs and problems of the colonial administration and was only ready to approve the creation of structures in the colonies if they were economically viable. It was undoubtedly the greatest achievement of Erzberger and the Social Democratic critics of the colonial service that both the government and its Reichstag allies decided after the spring of 1906 to adopt a more responsible policy.

Nevertheless, neither the chancellor nor the leaders of the Center recognized the potential political proportions of the German colonial question in December, 1905. They were overwhelmed with what they judged to be far more important matters: the chancellor with the forthcoming Algeciras Conference on Morocco and both he and the Center with other legislative problems that would come up in the next session of the Reichstag. The government was ready to make more serious demands upon the Center and the Reichstag than it had had to do since the introduction of the tariff bill in the late fall of 1901. First of all, Tirpitz wanted them to approve the supplement to the naval bill of 1900 which called for the building of the six cruisers for foreign service deleted from the earlier law. In fact, the naval minister went beyond the original proposal since the new ships were to be heavy cruisers which could be used in the battle line with the new dreadnoughts which the navy planned to build. Tirpitz also expected the Reichstag to approve funds for the replacement of the battleships still to be built under the law of 1900 by dreadnoughts and for the widening of the North Sea-Baltic Sea Canal.[43]

The senior Centrists were not really worried that they would have trouble in finding sufficient support in their party for the naval program. They were thoroughly skeptical of the belief of naval enthusiasts that Germany could catch up with Great Britain in her naval construction, but they did not say so openly.[44] As they had done in 1898 and 1900, they were only concerned that the new building be financed by taxes which would not offend the Center's working-class supporters. In all probability they sensed that the continuation of the Moroccan crisis and Great Britain's involvement in it on the side of France would provide a sufficient argument against opponents in the parliamentary groups hostile to the government's request.

Above all, the leading Centrists were concerned in the session of 1905–1906 with tax and finance questions. After the opening of the Reichstag the *Historisch-politische Blätter* had made the magisterial statement that "it is very clear that the financial question moves more and more into the foreground and will be decisive for all political questions."[45] The expenses for the navy and army, the Chinese intervention of 1900, and the suppression of the rebellions in Africa had caused an increase in the national debt by nearly forty-one million marks since 1900. The total amount of the debt would be approximately three and a half billion marks by March, 1906. In addition, the government was supposed under the provisions of the tariff law of 1902 to make sufficient savings each year to

[39] Robert Witt, *Die Finanzpolitik des Deutschen Reiches 1903 bis 1913* (Lübeck and Hamburg, 1970), pp. 78–81. For a more detailed treatment of the tensions between the Cartel parties and the Center see the older work by Theodor Eschenburg, *Das Kaiserreich am Scheideweg. Bassermann, Bülow und der Block* (Berlin, 1929), passim.

[40] *HpB* **127** (1906): p. 77.

[41] Oddly enough two higher officials who served with some success in the colonies were Catholics: Count Zech, who was the governor of Togo in 1905–1906 and Albrecht von Rechenberg who became governor of East Africa in 1906. Rechenberg, a trained diplomat, was apparently a man of high competence: John Iliffe, *Tanganyika and German Rule* (Cambridge, 1969), ch. 4.

[42] *HpB* **126** (1905): p. 77.

[43] Hansgeorg Fernis, *Die Flottennovelle im Reichstag 1906–1912* (Stuttgart, 1934), pp. 105–107.

[44] Karl Bachem to Spahn, November 12, 1905; notes of same on a leadership meeting, dated November 29, 1905, Bachem Papers, File 239.

[45] **136** (1905): p. 203.

finance the operations of the orphans' and widows' fund which was to come into operation in 1911.[46]

Spahn and his intimates were aware before 1905 that they would finally have to impose the policy of a direct tax upon the government and their own conservative and Bavarian members. Lieber and Gröber had sometimes tried to frighten government officials and the Cartel parties with their threats that the Center would insist on direct taxes to finance military programs but they were not serious in their warnings. But after its approval of the tariffs on foodstuffs in 1903, and the success of the Social Democrats in the elections of the next year, the senior Centrists had to become serious about the necessity of such a levy and opted for an inheritance tax. Article six of the naval law of 1900, which they had drafted, stipulated that future naval construction could not be financed by levies on articles of mass consumption and it set close limits to their freedom of action in the tax committee.[47]

During the crucial months between mid-January and early May the leading Centrists, Spahn at their head, were to be tied down in the nearly fifty sessions of the tax committee. They were not equipped to debate with Erzberger on colonial issues except when they were related to budgetary matters or broad administrative policies. They were not actually prepared to cope with all the demands made on them in the session of 1905–1906. Windthorst and Lieber had sacrificed all other satisfactions, including those of regular family life, to their political careers. But Peter Spahn had retained his Prussian judgeship after his succession to the party leadership in 1903. In November, 1906, Bülow secured his elevation to the presidency of the superior court of Schleswig-Holstein, a charge which kept him away from Berlin three days in every week. Gröber, Hertling, and Schaedler were absent from Berlin for extended periods of time because of legislative duties or other responsibilities in their own states. Karl Bachem, the only member of the inner leadership group who seemed to be regularly in Berlin, was neurotic about his health and was undoubtedly overworked.[48]

Bülow had become alarmed in September, 1905, over the amount and extent of criticism of his administration from Centrist sources. He turned therefore to Cardinal Kopp for assistance. He learned from Kopp that there was no Center leader with substantial authority in the party. Kopp implied to the chancellor that he was unable himself to carry on any meaningful

negotiations with the party for that reason.[49] It is probable that Bülow was not so much concerned about Erzberger, a youthful member of the tiny Württemburg delegation in the Center, as he was about the dissident leaders of the major regional parties. In his first years as chancellor, Bülow had collided with Franz Schaedler, the leader of the Bavarian Reichstag group. Schaedler and Franz Pichler, an agrarian expert, were priests who wished in particular to promote the Center's efforts to recover full freedom for the Catholic Church and its religious orders. But the lay agrarians were by far the most powerful influence in the Bavarian state party and in the Reichstag delegation. Their interests did not extend beyond Bavaria itself and they were completely negative on national issues. In February, 1905, their leader, Georg Heim, had caused serious obstruction in a parliamentary committee of the new commercial treaty with Austria because he disliked some of its features.[50] In April of that year Georg von Hertling, possibly at Bülow's request, had formally chided in print the Bavarian agrarians in the party for not putting the higher needs of the Center ahead of its immediate interests. The hostile reaction from the Bavarian Center and its press against Hertling's person was so severe he thought seriously of moving to another part of Germany.[51]

It was the Rhineland delegation which held the pivotal position in the Center, however, and the chancellor was deeply perturbed in 1905 over the coldness of the *Kölnischer Volkszeitung* toward his person and the regularity of its editorial criticism of the government's actions.[52] He was well aware that its editors had ruined Miquel's promising career through their unrelenting attacks on his person and policies. Bülow was clearly alarmed over the fact that the Cologne paper had published Erzberger's articles against the Colonial Department in September, 1905.[53]

There is no doubt that Julius Bachem wanted to intimidate the government by threatening it with the

---

[46] See above chapter 7, p. 83.

[47] Witt, *Finanzpolitik*, pp. 95–96. At a leadership meeting in November, 1905, Spahn and his colleagues stressed their party's commitment to their working-class supporters in proposing a tax reform in the forthcoming legislative session: Karl Bachem, notes dated November 12, 1905. Bachem Papers, File 239.

[48] The poor health of its leading members, especially after Lieber's initial collapse, was a frequent subject of discussion in Center circles. The *Kölnische Volkszeitung* dealt with it twice in 1905, on April 18 and June 10.

[49] Cardinal Kopp told a German official that the Center had no leader and that it was hard to negotiate with the party for that reason: Rotenhan to Bülow, September 12, 1905. GFMA, University of Michigan Microcopy, Roll 110.

[50] Bachem, *Zentrumspartei* 6: p. 248.

[51] Karl von Hertling, unpublished manuscript on his father, Hertling Papers, Bundesarchiv, File 56.

[52] On March 7, 1905, it pointed out that the government had not issued a denial regarding a statement made by an official of the Evangelical League who claimed that Prince Henry had said he and his brother, the emperor, approved of the Evangelical League and its work. During the early summer it made complaints about the lack of governmental regard for Catholics in its judicial appointments. In the late summer, the *Kölnische Volkszeitung* claimed that the Reichstag's rights were in danger because the government had sent troops to Southwest Africa without parliamentary approval: *Allgemeine Zeitung*, September 23, 1905.

[53] He accompanied William II to the Rhineland for the army maneuvres in mid-September and conferred at length with Schorlemer, the new superior-president: *ibid.*, September 15, 1905.

danger of stern opposition from the Center. He had apparently failed to influence his cousin Karl, a member of the governing group of the Reichstag Center, in that direction. But it was evident that Julius Bachem and Müller-Fulda, a somewhat unwilling supporter of the tariff bill of 1902, helped to create the crisis in the committee on the Austrian trade treaty because Müller-Fulda sided with the Bavarian agrarians in their obstruction to the agreement.[54] After Georg von Hertling came into conflict with his agrarian colleagues in Bavaria, his old friends at the *Kölnische Volkszeitung* published the article which he wrote in defense of his views. But to Hertling's considerable chagrin they did not come to his defense for tactical reasons.[55] The Erzberger articles which they published in early September were a further part of their own careful campaign against the government.

Bachem and Cardauns were undoubtedly alarmed over the staggering increase in the national debt caused in substantial measure by the *Weltpolitik*, navalism, and colonialism they disliked. In the early Bülow years they were struggling to help the Christian trade union movement get under way and they believed the government would be wise to concentrate more on the domestic struggle with the Social Democrats. They would have undoubtedly preferred Posadowsky to Bülow as chancellor of the empire.[56] Nevertheless, the two Rhineland leaders were realists and they knew that the emperor, not a chancellor, would decide the course of Germany's external policies.[57] Their opposition was merely tactical in intent.

They were obviously convinced that the Center's loyal support of the government over a period of almost a decade had produced paltry results. The repeal of the expulsion article of the anti-Jesuit law had been more important for its symbolic effect than it had been for the collective freedom of the members of the Jesuit, Dominican, and other banned orders.[58] If the leaders of the Reichstag Center thought immediately in terms of the return of the religious orders and confessional school laws, Julius Bachem and Cardauns were more concerned with the immediate needs of regional parties like their own. Prior to the late summer of 1905 the Prussian government had occasionally promoted Catholics to important judicial positions but none to a high administrative post in its provinces in over forty years. Bülow had also failed to take any initiative on the old proposal of the Rhineland Center that the Imperial government should provide for parliamentary allowances, a reform which Julius Bachem thought would cure the prevalent absenteeism among south German Centrists.[59]

Bülow was unusually sensitive to press criticism and he realized in the spring of 1905 that the Prussian government would have to make some concrete gestures to the Rhineland Center. He was undoubtedly aware that the *Kölnische Volkszeitung* had complained in March because the Prussian Ministry of Justice had appointed a Protestant to the presiding judgeship of the Rhineland superior court, a position which had been previously held three times by Catholics. Two months later the government announced the appointment of Rudolf von Seckendorf, the undersecretary of state in the Prussian Ministry of Justice and a Catholic to the chief judgeship of the Imperial Court at Leipzig. Seckendorf's appointment had not halted the criticism of the government in the *Kölnische Volkszeitung*, so in August, Bülow brought about the promotion of Clemens von Schorlemer, the son of the old Centrist dignitary, to the superior-presidency of the Prussian Rhineland.[60] But like Seckendorf, the younger Schorlemer, had always remained at a distance from the Center party. To the chancellor's disappointment and concern the Erzberger articles against the Colonial Department followed some weeks after the announcement of Schorlemer's appointment. It is quite probable that the nearly simultaneous designation in mid-November of Hohenlohe-Langenburg, a prominent Protestant dignitary, to the colonial directorship and of Spahn's promotion to the presiding judgeship of provincial superior court in Protestant Schleswig-Holstein reflected the concern of Bülow to satisfy both Protestants and Catholics.[61]

In the parliamentary session of 1905–1906, however, the Rhineland Centrists, except for the small conventicle of integralists from Trier, drew progessively away from Erzberger. That they were doing so was not immediately obvious because they were upset over Hohenlohe-Langenburg's appointment and the government's proposal to make his position into a Secretariat for Colonial Affairs. They were aware that a general assault on the whole colonial system extending from the Colonial Department to the local administration would justify Hohenlohe-Langenburg's claim that he should have more power than he possessed as colonial director. On December 6 Fritzen told the Reichstag that his party was not pleased about the plan to reorganize the central administration of the colonial service. He added that there were many "dark corners" in the colonial administration but that the reform should begin at the lower levels.[62] And much as they disliked the Hohenlohe-Langenburg appointment, Rhine-

---

[54] See the first quotation at the head of this chapter, p. 99. On Müller-Fulda's obstructionism in the committee deliberations on the Austrian treaty: Bachem, *Zentrumspartei* **6**: p. 248.

[55] Karl von Hertling, see above fn. 51.

[56] Cardauns, *Trimborn*, pp. 112, 113.

[57] Karl Bachem to Spahn, November 12, 1905. Bachem Papers, File 239.

[58] Karl Bachem to Müller-Fulda, January 22, 1905, *ibid.*, File 223. Müller-Fulda had made a statement to that effect in a letter to Karl Bachem.

[59] *Kölnische Volkszeitung*, June 10, 1905.

[60] Bachem, *Zentrumspartei* **6**: pp. 218–219.

[61] For the Spahn appointment: *ibid.*, pp. 219–220.

[62] *Verhandlungen der Reichstages*, December 6, 1905: p. 135.

land Centrists had to recognize that the government had made a handsome symbolic gesture to the Center in its promotion of Spahn. Around the end of January, 1906, the Reichstag passed a Center bill for parliamentary allowances. Though it is not clear at what date the chancellor did so, Bülow must have told the Center's leaders before mid-March that the Federal Council would approve this old request of the Rhineland Center.[63]

During the course of the debates over the colonial questions Julius Bachem and his intimates apparently became increasingly worried that the Erzberger campaign could lead to the breakup of the Center-Conservative partnership and to the isolation of the party in the next parliamentary election. Far more was at stake for the leaders of the Rhineland Center than there was for Erzberger and his South German friends since a political quarrel between the government and the Center over a national issue would necessarily affect the relationship between the Center and the Conservatives in Prussia. Most of the leaders of the Reichstag Center were Prussians and they undoubtedly anticipated or shared Bachem's concern. His alarm was evident in his article written for the *Historisch-politische Blätter* in March, 1906, "Wir mussen den Turm heraus," in which he called upon Centrist leaders, probably in regional parties, to bring about the election in certain districts of Protestants who shared the cultural, constitutional, and social aims of the Center party.[64] The once proud boast of the Centrist leaders that they had a small but respectable Protestant membership was no longer a reality since there were no Protestants left in the Prussian Center and apparently only two in the Reichstag fraction.[65] He had correctly foreseen that in a new election the middle parties and possibly the Radicals would stress the Catholic confessional character of the Center and make it difficult for the Protestant Conservatives to continue their partnership.

By the latter part of February or early March the senior Prussian leaders of the Center, inside and outside the Reichstag, decided they would have to take stern measures to control Erzberger. They agreed with him about the need for reform, in particular that colonial policy had to be based on cultural considerations, that the Reichstag should participate in legislation for the colonies, and that the Colonial Department had to be more reliable in its reports to the parliament.[66] Most of them were old pupils of Windthorst's school of po-

litical diplomacy and they had sought to influence Erzberger by working on him behind the scenes and going along with his campaign to a limited degree. But their reliance upon tactful persuasion failed and so Spahn decided to rebuke him publicly in the Reichstag.

The senior leaders obviously felt that because of its sheer breadth Erzberger's campaign could be harmful to their relations with the government, but they were especially concerned about those aspects of it that reflected on the honor and competence of the bureaucracy and its administrative independence. In late February, Erzberger had attacked the personnel director of the Colonial Department on the grounds that he had been supposedly unjust to a young informant of Erzberger by the name of Koch. On March 14 Spahn made a rare appearance in the chamber of the Reichstag. He praised the work of the better colonial officials and noted that all colonial powers experienced problems in securing reliable civil servants. But then he turned directly to the theme of parliamentary intervention in the internal affairs of the civil service and charged that it could not function properly if the Reichstag mixed directly in its personnel matters.[67] Two days later Wilhelm Schwarze, the colonial expert of the party, defended government officials in East Africa against an earlier Erzberger charge that they were responsible for the uprisings because they had imposed the hut tax on the natives and had countenanced the forced labor practices of certain companies. Schwarze insisted that natives had to be made to work and that officials could not be held responsible for the exploitative practices of independent corporations, a statement that expressed the economic philosophy of the Colonial Department itself.[68] Shortly after the Spahn speech the *Kölnische Volkszeitung* and *Tremonia*, the leading Centrist journal in Westphalia, stated tactfully but firmly that Spahn was the leader of the party and inferred that Erzberger should be seen and heard less.[69]

The Spahn-Schwarze assault on Erzberger was a complete fiasco as far as the efforts to discipline him were concerned. Erzberger calmly stated in the Reichstag a few days later that both he and the leader were entitled to their different views. Most of the fraction supported him against the leader[70] who had undoubtedly further weakened his authority by recently accepting a high judicial position in the Prussian state. Shortly after the debate Georg Heim vigorously defended Erzberger before a Center assembly in Munich and the Bavarian Center press soon took up the same position. But it was undoubtedly most indicative of what the state of opinion was throughout the south on the whole colonial controversy that the press of the Baden Center after some delay followed the same

[63] *HpB* **137** (1906): pp. 139–140, 302. The Federal Council was apparently still considering the proposal on March 21: Karl Bachem, notes on that date, Bachem Papers, File 239.
[64] *HpB* **137**: pp. 376–386.
[65] Karl Bachem to Joseph Dahlmann, S.J., June 1, 1906, *ibid.*, p. 239. Bachem expressed the concern that his cousin felt over the disappearance of Protestant members from the Center and the efforts of the Evangelical League to depict the Center as a purely Catholic confessional party.
[66] Spahn, *Verhandlungen der Reichstages*, March 15, 1906: p. 2028; Crothers, *The German Elections of 1907*, p. 35.
[67] *Ibid.*, p. 2029.
[68] Spellmeyer, *Kolonialpolitik im Reichstag*, p. 112.
[69] Bachem, *Zentrumspartei* **6**: pp. 345–346.
[70] Karl Bachem, notes dated March 21, 1906, Bachem Papers, File 239.

course.[71] Theodor Wacker, the state Centrist leader, had earlier tried to avoid the negativism of the Bavarian particularists on national issues. More significant still was the fact that Erzberger was able to make a veiled attack on Bülow himself later that month in the *Schlesische Volkszeitung,* the organ of Cardinal Kopp and the Silesian Center.[72]

Spahn and his intimates were undoubtedly severely handicapped in trying to defend the bureaucracy and in the timing of that defense. Most Centrists probably sympathized with Poeplau, Wistuba, and Koch, the official and informant whom Erzberger had defended in a speech in late February, and thought the unpopular Colonial Department wanted to prosecute them as part of a "cover-up." Hohenlohe-Langenburg and his senior aides did not demonstrate an interest in reform. In their defense it should be recognized that they had to be primarily concerned with the suppression of the native rebellions in Southwest Africa and East Africa. But they continued to stress the importance of the railroad building program and took no steps to cancel the more offensive monopoly contracts with military suppliers. They were hampered in some degree by their dependence on political support from the parties of big business and nationalism, the Free Conservatives and National Liberals. The session was in its last weeks before Basserman, the National Liberal leader, acknowledged that some "unworthy officials" would have to be removed.[73]

Bülow, helpless to act otherwise, had also frustrated the Center on two issues of traditional importance to its back-benchers. He had refused in mid-January to take any action toward the restoration of a reserve officer's commission after the officer had been dismissed from the army for rejecting the duel as a method of defending his military honor. Despite the monarchy's earlier efforts to restrict dueling, William II and Bülow, out of deference to the Prussian military traditions of the officers' corps still refused to adhere to the course that the monarchy had earlier appeared ready to follow.[74] And throughout the session Bülow, rather than upset the states where the concept of the state church was rigidly upheld, refused to identify the government with the Center's modified bill of toleration which called for individual religious freedom throughout the empire. The prospect of parliamentary allowances had not taken the edge off the resentments felt by many Centrist back-benchers when Spahn criticized Erzberger, the major symbol of opposition to the Prussian-German government.

As the Reichstag moved into its final weeks of work in May, 1906, the senior Centrist leaders were probably uncertain how the Erzberger campaign would affect their longtime ties with the government. They finished the debates on the naval supplementary bill and on the financial reform in a state of near euphoria. But the outcome of the Reichstag voting on the question of a supplementary budget proposal for further railroad construction in Southwest Africa and on the establishment of a Secretariat for Colonial Affairs on May 26 had a deflationary effect on their spirits.

The naval bill and the additional requests for the navy in the general budget had posed no problems at their second reading in late April. The leading Centrists had not really anticipated serious difficulties but, as Karl Bachem noted, the requests floated through the Reichstag because of the general hostility felt toward the British government over its anti-German conduct in the recent Algeciras Conference.[75] They had taken a special pride, however, in their achievement in bringing about the major reform of the tax system and finances in mid-May. It was in fact an impressive demonstration of the virtuosity of its leaders in masking the impact of new taxes on individual Catholic social groups. They adamantly overrode the opposition of the Conservatives and their own agrarians insisting on an inheritance tax whose passage they secured with the support of the Social Democrats, Radicals, and ethnic parties. But they had been careful to exclude immediate heirs from its provisions and to extend themselves to work out its terms with the Conservatives so as to restrict its application to landed properties as much as possible. They also approved taxes on cigarettes and breweries which producers would pass on to consumers and on railroad fares, except for those of the fourth class.[76]

The uncertain state of mind of Spahn and his colleagues about their party's relations with the monarchy had little to do with Bülow's practical evaluation of their achievements and efforts and more with William II's emotional responses to their performance on specific measures for the colonies. It was undoubtedly due to Bülow's initiative that the emperor wrote the chancellor an open letter on May 21 praising "the patriotic collaboration of the representatives of the German people" in reforming the national financial system.[77] Bülow still demonstrated a positive attitude toward Spahn and the other senior leaders at the end of the Reichstag session. But the chancellor had suffered a physical collapse in the Reichstag on April 5 and was not in condition to wrestle with William II on matters involving the Center and colonial issues in the last weeks of the parliamentary session.

The Center's leaders knew that they could not afford to associate their fraction with the proposal that would make Hohenlohe-Langenburg a secretary of state for colonial affairs. Spahn had sought to justify the Cen-

[71] *Tagliche Rundschau,* March 30, 1906.
[72] See fn. 70 above.
[73] See fn. 39 above.
[74] Spitzemburg, *Tagebuch,* p. 455.

[75] Notes dated April 13, 1905, Bachem Papers, File 239. Fernis, *Die Flottennovellen,* pp. 38–40, 70.
[76] Karl Bachem, notes on the fraction caucus, February 21, 1906. *Ibid.,* File 241. Witt, *Finanzpolitik,* pp. 123–131.
[77] Bachem, *Zentrumspartei* **6:** p. 303.

ter's opposition to that measure in terms of national interest that appeared relevant because of the recent Moroccan controversy. He said during the second reading on March 27 that it would be unwise to separate control of colonial affairs from foreign policy because colonial questions did impinge from time to time on foreign policy.[78] But there were a large number of absentees during the voting on the bill in the second reading and the proposal to create a Secretariat for Colonial Affairs was passed. It is probable that the Center's caucus before the third reading on May 26 left its members free to vote as they saw fit. Of the eighty-two who were in the Reichstag chamber on that day, all but seventeen voted against the measure.[79]

The rejection of the proposal for an independent colonial secretariat was proper, though it was probably an example of a case where many Centrists voted the right way for the wrong reasons. But the leaders of the party were keenly aware of William II's involvement in the attempt to elevate the rank of his relative. The anger that the emperor expressed toward Spahn over the Center's failure to approve the extension of the Southwest African railroad a few hours earlier was due in part to the embarrassment over his own failure on Hohenlohe's behalf among his relatives.[80]

In light of the knowledge that he had of the emperor's personal interest in Hohenlohe's promotion and the hostility of most of his colleagues to it, Spahn made a tactical mistake in not insisting that the Center vote for the Southwest African railroad. He was aware that the Colonial Department, determined to promote the economic development of the colony, had not given the correct reason for its construction in claiming that it would be used to move troops for the suppression of the rebellions which were, in fact, nearly over. Spahn wanted to use approval of the railroad as a bargaining counter to commit the government to an early reduction of the number of troops in the colony, a tactic he was to repeat briefly in the fall. It is likely that he was following the old Center tactical policy of coupling the approval of highly expensive measures with a modest degree of economy.[81] Since the Colonial Department and the government did not respond favorably to his tactic, the Center voted against the railroad extension.

The debates and controversies within the Center over colonial issues had already created extensive strain among the members of the leadership group. Spahn was embittered over Erzberger's conduct and resented the earlier exposure which the *Kölnische Volkszeitung* had provided for him in September, 1905.[82] Caught in

the middle between his old ally Spahn and his friend Erzberger and between Prussian Catholic interests and South German emotions, Gröber had become ill-tempered and disinclined to follow a consistent course of supporting the government. Hertling had been critical of the party leadership and undoubtedly assumed that he could have done better if he had been in Spahn's place.[83]

Spahn's pessimism deepened in the course of the summer recess. After his annual visit to the chancellor's summer home on the North Sea he concluded that Bülow intended to break off his old connection with the Center since the chancellor had avoided serious political conversation with him. His fears in that respect were undoubtedly reinforced some weeks later by a government release announcing that Bülow had entertained first Spahn and then a prominent member of the Radical Peoples' party at his summer residence. Then in early September the chancellor announced the appointment of Bernhard Dernburg, a former member of the Radical Alliance, as the successor of Hohenlohe-Langenburg to the directorship of the Colonial Department.[84]

Bülow had become increasingly doubtful over the course of the summer about the ability of the government and the Center to work together. In June he had defended the conduct of its leaders against the criticism of a senior foreign official who enjoyed the confidence of William II, saying that they had to demonstrate to their electors that they were independent of governmental control.[85] But by mid-summer he became more aware of William II's continued hostility toward the Center which reflected, Bülow thought, the influence of Protestant groups who were upset over the partial revocation of the anti-Jesuit law and the ruler's resentment over the Erzberger attacks on the Colonial Department.[86] Then his old friend, Franz von Arenberg, warned the chancellor that he would have more difficulty with the Center in the next parliamentary session.[87]

There was evidence, however, that the senior leaders of the Center had regrouped their forces in the course of the long recess. Spahn and Gröber were a team again. They visited Bülow and Dernburg a few weeks before the opening of the Reichstag and apparently came away satisfied that they had demonstrated their good will to the chancellor and the new colonial director. Their leading south German colleague, the Bavarian Schaedler, was to be respectful in his remarks to Dernburg in the Reichstag at the end of the month. Gröber had apparently persuaded Erzberger to abandon his press attacks on the Colonial Department in the course

[78] Schulthess, *Geschichtskalender* **47** (1906): p. 82.
[79] Crothers, *The German Elections of 1907*, pp. 39–40.
[80] William II and the railroad: *ibid.*, p. 37.
[81] Martin Spahn: "Das Jahr 1906" in *Das Deutsche Volk*, July 15, 1928.
[82] His resentment was evident in the manner in which he responded in a Center caucus to the preferences of its editors for new taxes. *Kölnische Volkszeitung*, May 20, 1906.

[83] Hertling to Julius Bachem, April 10, 1906. Hertling Papers, IV, 35.
[84] Crothers, *The German Elections of 1907*, p. 44.
[85] Bülow, *Memoirs* **2**: p. 283.
[86] *Ibid.*
[87] *Ibid.*

of the summer and much to Bülow's satisfaction Erzberger had yielded up to a law officer the government documents he had acquired from Poeplau.[88] Though he was to bring out still more disturbing evidence of mismanagement in the Colonial Department, Erzberger was to be generous in his demeanor toward Dernburg in his first speech of the Reichstag session. In Cologne, Julius Bachem was apparently eager to see the Center and the government let by-gones be by-gones, for Posadowsky was to introduce his long-delayed bill on the granting of corporate rights to trade unions soon after the opening of the parliament.[89]

Yet it was clear that Arenberg had been correct in his assessment of attitudes toward the government in certain Centrist circles. Accommodating though Bülow had been to the Center in its earlier attempts to intervene in the personnel of the Colonial Department in the past, he had not dared to terminate the administrative proceedings against Wistuba and Poeplau or to make them part of a wider investigation of the colonial service. Angry over the chancellor's refusal to aid Wistuba in any way, Hermann Roeren had retained possession of the documents from the files of the Colonial Department which the young ex-civil servant had given him. That Roeren would try to make trouble for the government in the Reichstag was evident from a speech he gave in Trier in late October. He had a penchant for strong, sometimes vituperative language. In his remarks he claimed that the German colonial system was "rotten" and needed to be reformed. Roeren went on to say that his party should not approve any part of the colonial budgets until the government provided the Reichstag with rights to participate in the control of the colonies.[90] Some two weeks later when Bülow and Dernburg met with Spahn and Gröber the two officials informed the Centrist leaders that they wanted freedom to treat Roeren as they saw fit if he attacked the Colonial Department.[91]

Roeren did not speak for himself alone. Conservative Catholics—integralists and aristocrats, backed by some influential bishops—had apparently formed an alliance for the purpose of arousing Catholic opinion against the colonial administration in Berlin. In the spring of 1906 Georg von Hertling, a Centrist long close to Bülow, had been critical of Erzberger's campaign and his party's role in the defeat of the plan for a separate Colonial Office. But in early October he told a Westphalian Catholic audience that the Colonial Department had not been careful enough in its selection of officials. Hertling also expressed doubt whether

the new director, Dernburg, would be able to clean house in the Department.[92]

Hertling and Roeren were not natural allies. The Bavarian aristocrat disagreed fundamentally with the negative attitude of the integralists toward the universities. He believed that Catholic leaders, lay and clerical, should make a systematic effort to improve the attendance of young Catholics at universities and to encourage their interest in science.[93] It is conceivable that Hertling, then at a low point in his political career, recognized an opportunity to achieve popularity by identifying himself with the Catholic campaign against the Colonial Department. He was to be more active in Center affairs after 1906 and eventually became its leader in the fall of 1908.[94] But Hertling had always preferred to pin his hopes for high office on the patronage of the chancellor, Bavarian courtiers, or cardinals rather than on the vagaries of popular favor. Most likely his shift of position on the colonial issue reflected both his susceptibility to hints from persons in high places, and a strong desire to be in step with popular Catholic attitudes toward the government.

Shortly before Spahn and Gröber met with the chancellor and Dernburg, *Germania* published two editorials on November 6 and 11 which also called for the reformation of the colonial administration. The editorials claimed that the colonial program was too expensive and did not promote the Christianization of the natives. They implied, however, that the government could restore the faith of the Center in the Colonial Department if it dispersed the dominant group of officials in that office.[95] Since Erzberger was then supporting the efforts of Spahn and Schaedler to restore working relations with Bülow one can only conclude that the editorials reflected the influence of Ballestrem and Cardinal Kopp over the editors. Kopp had long been on close terms with Hertling and Bishop Korum of Trier, the district represented by Roeren.[96]

The message contained in the Roeren and Hertling speeches and in the *Germania* editorials was clear enough: the government should carry out a vigorous shake-up of the Colonial Department. In his first speech of the new Reichstag session on December 3 Roeren was to bring out new sensational accounts of criminal acts committed by local German officials against natives, some of them heinous in character. He was obviously sincere in his remarks and a majority of the Reichstag approved them. But Roeren also dilated at some length on the refusal of the governmental authorities to halt the disciplinary proceedings

---

[88] Crothers, *Elections of 1907*, p. 77.

[89] *Ibid.*, p. 82, fn. 42. The Reichstag debated the bill in its first reading from November 25 to 27. Giesberts stated that his party would not approve the measure unless the government extended it to agricultural laborers. Trimborn had spoken more positively about the measure in an earlier speech. Born, *Staat und Sozialpolitik*, p. 202.

[90] Crothers, *Elections of 1907*, p. 71.

[91] Spahn, "Das Jahr 1906," (*Das Deutsche Volk*).

[92] Crothers, pp. 71–72.

[93] Hertling, *Erinnerungen* 2: p. 167 ff.

[94] Bachem, *Zentrumspartei* 7: p. 9.

[95] Crothers, *The German Elections of 1907*, p. 73.

[96] For Ballestrem's financial investment in *Germania* see above chapter 3, fn. 4 Kopp and Korum were the leading Catholic opponents of the interconfessional Christian trade union movement.

against Wistuba, the young civil servant who had given official documents to missionaries involved in the Togo dispute.[97] It was evident in the speeches made by Hertling and Roeren that they had doubts about the government's willingness or ability to reform the colonial administration and that it was more eager to punish young officials who had violated administrative regulations regarding secrecy in the handling of official documents than it was to ferret out other civil servants who had committed serious abuses against natives.[98]

But it is probable that leading conservative Catholics, laymen and high clergymen, wanted to send signals of disapproval to the chancellor over his recent appointments to the colonial directorship: first a prominent, though essentially inoffensive, member of the Evangelical League, then a former banker and stock exchange speculator who had belonged to one of the Radical parties. They would have preferred a colonial director who came out of a more traditional bureaucratic and orthodox Protestant background. Their allies among the Prussian Conservatives had firm convictions on that score, for the *Kreuzzeitung,* the leading Conservative journal, hinted that Dernburg might be Jewish.[99] Friedrich von Holstein revealed the real cause of the Conservatives' dislike of the Dernburg appointment when he expressed the fear that Bülow, having broken the rule that ministers had to be from Conservative backgrounds, might bring other Radicals into governmental ministries. As one might have expected, Holstein also resented the attacks made by Reichstag deputies on the bureaucracy of the colonial department.[100]

In his first appearance before the Reichstag on November 28 Dernburg made a favorable impression on those members who were not principled opponents of German colonialism. Bülow, while he had acknowledged in his own earlier speech that the colonial administration was going through a crisis, was mainly interested in absolving himself and the government from any responsibility for it and in defending the bureaucracy in the colonial service which he extolled for its loyalty, energy, conscientousness and integrity. He implied that certain deputies and the press were more responsible for the crisis than any officials.[101] Dernburg was obviously aware, however, that he had to overcome considerable opposition or apathy toward the German colonial administration and its programs if he

were to be a success in his new office. He sought first of all to rebut the traditional Radical and Bavarian Centrist argument that the colonies had no economic future and would continue to be a drag on the home economy and German taxpayers. He also announced his intention of dissolving business relations with firms which had made excessive profits from their monopolistic contracts with the Colonial Department and of punishing officials who had committed abuses against the natives.[102]

In their speeches Schaedler and Erzberger, the first two Centrist spokesmen, tried to avoid any friction with the government. They claimed that the earlier parliamentary criticisms of the colonial administration were justified on the grounds that the facts of the conditions in the colonies were responsible for the crisis in the system, not the publicity given to them by deputies or editors. Erzberger also disputed statements that Bülow had made about the Poeplau case. But their posture toward the chancellor was defensive rather than aggressive. And while Erzberger and Schaedler disagreed with Dernburg on some points of his speech, they took positive stands toward him. *Germania* and the *Kölnische Volkszeitung* also expressed satisfaction with the introductory appearance of the new colonial director.[103]

Bülow and Dernburg were proven right, however, in their earlier assumption that they would run into difficulties with Hermann Roeren. His speech of December 3, offensive though it was to Dernburg, was probably aimed at Bülow in the first instance. The chancellor had not changed his mind about the disposition of the Wistuba case. In his own remarks to the Reichstag he had ignored messy facts so that he could make a broad defense of the reputation of the colonial bureaucracy. In his own speech Roeren contrasted the idealism of Wistuba and the Togo missionaries, whom the ex-civil servant had tried to assist, with the materialism and brutality of some other German officials. He implied that the administrative standards of the German colonial system were lower than those of some other nations by saying that natives in nearby French and British territories referred to the German possessions as the "whip colonies" because of the extensive use made by German officials of that instrument for penal purposes.[104] Roeren's speech revealed how flimsy Bülow's defense of the colonial administration had been. Therefore, Dernburg and Bülow decided that the colonial director should concentrate on other issues in their counterattack against Roeren.

The colonial director, as his later policies demonstrated, took a highly serious view of his new responsibilities. But like Bülow he was not in a strong

[97] *Verhandlungen des Reichstages,* December 3, 1906: pp. 4085–4093.

[98] Dernburg was to force their superiors to transfer the priests involved in the Togo controversy to other posts in early 1907. He may have made that decision only after the break between the government and the Center in mid-December 1906. On the transfer: Müller, *Geschichte der katholischen Kirche in Togo,* pp. 177–178. The priests were bitter about it.

[99] Bachem, *Zentrumspartei* **6**: p. 354.

[100] *Holstein Papers* **4**: pp. 525–526.

[101] *Verhandlungen des Reichstages,* November 28, 1906: pp. 3959–3961.

[102] Pehl, *Kolonialpolitik und das Zentrum,* p. 73.

[103] *Ibid.* Spellmeyer, *Kolonialpolitik im Reichstag,* p. 120; and *HpB* **138**: p. 949.

[104] *Verhandlungen des Reichstages,* December 3, 1906: pp. 4088, 4092.

enough political position to speak frankly about the administrative failures of the Colonial Department, admissions that would have made his position untenable with the higher officials in his department and in the wider Prussian bureaucracy. A newcomer to parliamentary debate, he was heavy-handed and tactless in his efforts to rebut Roeren and other critics of the colonial administration. He skipped over the Togo controversy but remarked obliquely that there were some missionaries who did not act as they should and who were "black sheep," an apparent reference to the priests who had accepted government documents from Wistuba. In his discussion of that case he questioned Roeren's competence as a Prussian judge. Dernburg read letters which Roeren had written to the chancellor on Wistuba's behalf during the previous session; one contained the veiled threat that the Center might vote against the new colonial budget if Wistuba were punished for his violation of administrative regulations.[105] Bülow and Dernburg were obviously trying to demonstrate to the Reichstag that Roeren's attacks on the Colonial Department were motivated by a desire for revenge against the government because it had refused to submit to his pressure in the Wistuba case.

It is probable that any other prominent Centrist would have responded to Dernburg with restraint. But Roeren's ultra-conservative convictions had undoubtedly prejudiced him against the new colonial director. Dernburg, a liberal of Jewish descent and a former banker and speculator on the stock exchange, was a symbol to him of the modern aggressive businessman whom Catholic integralists and corporatists distrusted and disliked. In his own attempt at a rebuttal he recalled Dernburg's "stockjobbing" past and said that his previous business activity would not bear examination. Roeren would have put himself in a better light if he had avoided personalities and put heavier stress on the fact that Stuebel, the former colonial director, had asked him to try to calm Wistuba and that Bülow had not taken offense over his efforts to secure a favorable settlement of Wistuba's case.[106]

In the heat of the debate Dernburg revealed the government's aggressive attitude toward the Center itself and how much its officials had resented that party's influence over personnel policy in the Colonial Department. He claimed that the Center had tried to exercise a "backstairs" influence on that department and that the time had come for the government "to lance that abscess."[107]

Nevertheless, the Center's leaders were appalled over Roeren's severe attack on the Colonial Department and his intemperate remarks about Dernburg's reputation and mannerisms. While Erzberger was permitted to make a moderate defense of Roeren's speech on De-

cember 4, Ballestrem, the Center president of the Reichstag, reprimanded Roeren for his unparliamentary language before the session began. Roeren stated later in its course that he had acted by himself when he had attempted to aid Wistuba by writing on his behalf to the chancellor in the previous winter.[108] Leading Centrist journals stressed the claim that the party had not been involved in his efforts on Wistuba's behalf or in his confrontation with Dernburg.[109]

Yet it must have been evident to the leading Centrists that the rank-and-file members of their party would be even less willing to approve the supplementary budget of the Colonial Department than they had been in the first days of the debates of the period November 28 through December 4. Dernburg had undoubtedly offended many Centrists by his oblique but offensive reference to the missionaries in the Togo controversy as "black sheep"; the priests had been imprudent in their dealings with Wistuba but they had been drawn into the affair by their concern for natives' welfare. And all members of the party must have been offended to some degree by Dernburg's claim that their party had attempted to exercise an unconstitutional "backstairs" influence since all other bourgeois parties had engaged in the same practice in the past.[110] In fact, that charge revealed Dernburg's inexperience in high politics. Because of the new resentments in the party against the chancellor and the colonial director, Spahn and the other leaders had more reason than ever to be sensitive on matters of budgetary economy.

Either the leadership group or a Center caucus had decided that Spahn should demand a sharp reduction in the number of troops in Southwest Africa within the immediate future and reject a further extension of the new railway in that colony. The leaders believed that the rebellion there was flickering out and that the colonial authorities could complete the suppression by an ample use of police units. Therefore, Spahn insisted that the government should present a plan to the Reichstag before April 1, 1907, which would provide for the reduction of the regular military forces to two thousand five hundred men Since most of the Radicals

[105] *Ibid.*, pp. 4104–4105.

[106] *Ibid.*, p. 414.

[107] Pehl, *Kolonialpolitik und Zentrum*, p. 79. Spellmeyer, *Kolonialpolitik im Reichstag*, pp. 119–120.

[108] *Ibid.*, p. 120.

[109] Crothers, *German Elections of 1907*, p. 82. Pehl, *Kolonialpolitik und Zentrum*, pp. 78–79. *HpB* **138**: p. 949.

[110] Pehl and Spellmeyer agree that Dernburg's rough handling of Roeren and his aspersions on the Center itself influenced to a greater or lesser degree the manner in which many of its members responded to the government's supplementary budget for the colonies. Pehl adds that the struggle between the party and the government had become an "inner necessity" for both: *Kolonialpolitik und das Zentrum*, p. 85. I assume that many members of the party were influenced by their sympathy for the Togo missionaries and Wistuba. Walther Rathenau, the prominent business executive, threw light on the political importance of the Togo controversy when he made the half-serious remark that he could not become colonial director because he could not handle "negro women and other tasks": Walther Rathenau, *Tagebuch 1907–1922*. H. Pogge von Strandmann, ed. (Düsseldorf, 1967), p. 56.

had favored such a cut, the Centrist leader apparently thought that Bülow would have to seek a compromise with his party. Spahn and his colleagues in the Budget Committee took an accommodating stand however on the railroad issue on December 12–13, though they insisted that the government should promote its building by a loan rather than by a grant from its own funds.[111]

In all probability the Centrist leaders would have sought a compromise with Bülow's troop issue, too, if they had fully realized that the chancellor could not accept their proposal. Bülow and other Imperial officials warned Spahn or some of his colleagues that the government could not promise before April 1 that it would reduce the troops in Southwest Africa below the level of eight thousand men. The chancellor suggested to Spahn that his party should offer a compromise based on the proposal of Bruno Ablass, a Radical deputy, which simply stipulated that the government should consider a lowering of its military forces in the colony when local authorities thought it safe to do so. But Spahn believed that his party could take the risk of adhering to its own motion at the second reading in the expectation that it could secure a compromise with Bülow at the third reading if the government was adamant in its insistence on its own proposal. The Reichstag voted down both the Ablass and government measures on December 14, however, and before the Center could present its own proposal the chancellor read the order of dissolution. A long period of collaboration between the monarchy and the Center on important legislation had come to an end.

The Center was unfortunate in its decision to challenge the government on an issue involving a constitutional principle. William II was the supreme commander of the military forces in Southwest Africa and was responsible for their security and that of the civilian colonists. But the Reichstag had the right and responsibility of examining and passing on the colonial budget. Most likely Spahn and his colleagues knew that the military authorities were in disagreement among themselves over the number of troops needed for the final suppression of the rebellion in Southwest Africa.[112]

The breach between the monarchy and the Center in December, 1906, was due, however, to personal and political factors, not to a disagreement over constitutional powers or any substantial issue. As the senior Centrists suspected afterward, William II was responsible for the government's decision to dissolve the ties with their party and for its refusal to renew the coalition in February, 1907, after the parliamentary elections. A few days after the dissolution of the Reichstag he said in a loud voice at a diplomatic dinner that "it was time to deliver a stiff blow to all those persons of the Center who were insolent enough in their au-

dacity to think they could govern me."[113] The emperor was basically resentful of a party that did not respond positively to his own person and the Center had never been warm toward him. An alliance in which his personality was an important factor could not survive the combination of the Center's restraints upon his personal rule, the complaints of Protestant courtiers and the Evangelical League about the monarchy's reliance upon a Catholic party, and the resentments of William II and the bureaucracy against the Erzberger-Roeren assaults on the Colonial Department.

Nevertheless, it was the Erzberger campaign against the colonial administration and the widespread support it received in the Center and wider Catholic press which led to the breakdown of the party's relationship to the government. The surprising popularity of Erzberger's assaults on the colonial service had three related causes. First of all it appealed to the substantial numbers of Catholics, especially those in the south and southwest, who had always disliked the new *Weltpolitik* and navalism if only for financial reasons. Secondly, many Catholics relished revelations which were embarrassing to the Prussian-Germany bureaucracy from which they were largely excluded. And finally the Erzberger exposures appeared to demonstrate that the colonial administration obstructed the moral and humanitarian efforts of the missionaries, the only German overseas undertakings in which the great majority of Catholics were interested. Despite their commitment to monarchism, most Catholics did not find themselves in harmony with some major policies of their ruler and the bureaucracy through which he ruled Germany.

EPILOGUE

The break between the Imperial monarchy and the Center in December, 1906, was an interruption of their relationship, not its end. Nevertheless, the most significant phase of their legislative collaboration and of the Center's hopes about the benefits to be derived from it lay behind them.

Despite their mutual need for a political alliance the Centrist leadership and Imperial officials had needed approximately a decade to forge that relationship. The Imperial government and the Center were both complex institutions and neither was under the control of a single person until near the turn of the century. William II wanted to be his own first minister but he lacked the political passion, application, and understanding necessary for that position. He failed to understand that the system of constitutional monarchy could only work properly if the government respected its parliamentary partners and understood their problems. To do so William II would have had to meet with the leaders of the Center and other parties from time to time in serious political talks. But he had the mentality of a courtier and was not interested in bourgeois

111 Bachem, *Zentrumspartei* 6: p. 363 f. Crothers, *German Elections of 1907*, p. 79 f.
112 Witt, *Finanzpolitik des Deutschen Reiches*, p. 154, fn. 16.
113 Radziwill, *Lettres* 3: p. 267.

politicians who were rarely seen at court functions. In Julius Bachem's words there was "no connecting link between the monarchy and the people."[1]

The tension between the monarch and the Center undoubtedly owed much to the influence that the powerful Prussian Conservatives exercised on Imperial affairs through the person of William II and to the impotence of the Center in the political life of Prussia. The ruler's contempt for the Center and the Reichstag reflected the impressive strength of his position in that state where his authority rested on the concept of divine right, the most powerful part of the German armed forces, and the support of the Conservatives. But in the course of the heated Reichstag debates over the commercial treaties of 1893–1894 William II learned that the Conservatives did not offer fealty to his person out of conviction alone. The emperor was hostile to European republicans and to persons who sanctioned their governments, as Cardinal Rampolla had learned, but his eagerness to undertake a new repressive campaign against the Social Democrats after the early summer was increasingly due to his desire to placate the angry Junkers and their party. After the army-bill conflict of 1893, it proved to be the one major governmental enterprise that the Center could not support.

It is undoubtedly significant that the struggles between the monarch and the Reichstag over the two important programs in which William II was deeply interested, repressive legislation against the Social Democrats and naval expansion, began and ended in the same parliamentary sessions. In March, 1895, Lieber prevailed upon his reluctant associates to approve four new cruisers because he was aware that the monarch was angry over the Center's delaying tactics in the committee deliberating on the anti-revolution bill. Exactly two years later a rebellious Center chose to make substantial cuts in the naval budget even though it knew that its Prussian sister party would reject the bill on associations in the early future. With the exception of his rival, Cardinal Kopp, Lieber was more sensitively aware than any other Catholic dignitary of the extreme tensions between the monarch and the Center in 1897 when Tirpitz drafted his first naval bill.

It is logical to ask whether Lieber made the decision in that year to seek his party's approval of the first naval bill because he had growing doubts about the Center's ability or willingness to be identified with the monarch's anti-Socialist campaign. In the recent past Catholic editors and pastors had shown fear that their newspapers and associations might also come under the prescriptions of laws aimed primarily at Social Democrats. Regional Centrist leaders in the Rhineland and the Ruhr were becoming increasingly sensitive about the image their party had among workers who were the objects of growing Social Democratic agitation. His party's inability to support the monarchy's anti-Socialist

campaign sharpened the edge of Lieber's anxiety about the unsatisfactory nature of the Center's relation with William II but it was not the cause of that concern. He undoubtedly came to the separate conclusion that the Center would have to identify itself with the Tirpitz naval plans because William II was determined that they become law. The Conservatives, Free Conservatives, and National Liberals liked to boast that they deserved the name "national parties" because they had always subordinated their own views on army and navy proposals to those of the monarchy. Lieber wanted his party to be more than just another member of the government coalition; he sought the leading position for the Center in that alliance and was willing that it should make the financial and psychological sacrifices involved in adopting the monarch's naval policy in place of its own.

There was a definite connection, nevertheless, between the Center's capitulation on the naval question and the marked change in the monarchy's social policy. Julius Bachem and the Rhineland Centrists were profoundly disturbed in the late fall of 1899 over the introduction of a second large naval proposal only two years after the presentation of the first measure. Because of the Rhineland Centrists' resistance, Lieber had to abandon his efforts to demonstrate that the Center was a reliable member of the governmental coalition by its support of the prison house bill. His party treated that measure with contempt in November, 1899, because it knew that the monarch needed its votes for the second Tirpitz proposal.

While Julius Bachem felt depressed over the continuing acceleration of German naval expansion, he undoubtedly found some compensation in the compromises reached between his party and the government during and after the naval debates of 1900. The government and the Cartel parties agreed that any new taxes for the construction of ships would not be levied on articles of mass use as they had earlier done in 1898. On the face of things a party which wanted to demonstrate that it was committed to the security of labor rights and organization could feel that it had come out of the parliamentary year 1899–1900 in good political condition. It had put an end to the monarchy's long campaign to secure legislation against the Social Democratic movement and its unions and it had won assurances that the lower classes would not suffer financially from the implementation of the new naval bills. And at an early date its leaders knew that the vice-chancellor, Posadowsky, would initiate a more extensive if moderate program of social legislation than he had earlier anticipated.

Lieber and his colleagues were unaware, of course, that they had participated in the making of a naval policy which would have tragic consequences for Germany.[2] They had known before Tirpitz's appointment

---

[1] *Kölnische Volkszeitung*, January 20, 1909.

[2] See the first quotation in chap. 5, p. 63.

to the Naval Secretariat that the advocates of a big navy hoped to make Germany the equal of Great Britain as a naval power. They were legitimately skeptical of their government's ability to catch up with its great naval rival and rightly so since they had no intention of trying to squeeze enough money out of German taxpayers, their own first of all, for such an ambitious undertaking. Lieber had told Tirpitz in their first talks that his party would not approve any naval objective that involved the creation of a fleet strong enough to attack enemy shores and harbors.[3] The Center apparently believed that it could not approve the assumption of aggressive strategies by either the army or navy. But it was evident enough that Lieber and his party friends saw the question of naval expansion in a financial context and did not consider its possible impact on Germany's relations with foreign powers.

The implicit compromise between the monarchy and the Center over the difficult issues of naval expansion and repression of the Social Democrats contributed substantially to the realization of the intimacy that characterized the relations between the Centrist leaders and Bülow after 1902. But it cannot be stressed too much that Bülow was able to cultivate close ties with the Center because he, unlike Caprivi and Hohenlohe, did not have to face a hostile Conservative party in the Landtag. The Center leaders had reassured the Conservatives and their own Bavarian associates during the debates on the second naval bill that they would support an agrarian tariff in 1902. Indeed Bülow's main worry during the long debates on that complex bill was that the Center would insist on higher rates on grains than the government could accept.

Lieber's collapse in January, 1900, made it easier for his leading colleagues to move their party into a closer relationship with the Conservatives. If anything, Lieber's old distaste for the Junker Conservatives had deepened in the mid- and late 1890's—his bitter resentment against Miquel over that minister's connivance with them during the Prussian canal-bill debates was proof enough of that fact. He had responded enthusiastically to evidence provided by Lujo Brentano in 1897 that more Germans were now engaged in industry and commerce than in agriculture.[4] Though he did not say so, Lieber probably assumed that the growing industrialization of Germany would undermine the hegemonial political position of the Conservatives in the foreseeable future. His reserve toward the censorship bill in the spring of 1900 and his enthusiasm for the toleration measure of that fall, which was intended to appeal to the liberal idealism of the middle parties, revealed how much he hoped that the Center could work together with the National Liberals and Free Conservatives from time to time.

Yet it is difficult to see how even a healthy Lieber could have persuaded his party to refrain from a policy of close collaboration with the Conservatives. The angry response of many Catholic editors and other Catholics to the anti-revolution bill of 1895, a measure they partly associated with the National Liberals and Free Conservatives, the prime advocates of the Kulturkampf, showed how much animosity there was in Catholic circles toward the middle parties. Lieber had succeeded afterward in bringing his party together with the middle parties, but especially the National Liberals, because of the Conservatives' extremism on constitutional and economic issues. (At that time the Christian peasant association movement whose leaders decidedly favored a Center-Conservative Coalition lacked a substantial Bavarian base; by the end of the decade that was no longer the case. By the first years of the new century the agrarians, thanks no doubt to their dominant role in Bavarian Centrist politics, were the most influential economic group in the national Center.[5] They were to hold that position until 1920 when the Bavarian Centrists left the German Center.)

Despite the clear and convincing evidence of the importance of the agrarians to the Center, it was patent that the confidence and support of the clergy were more vital to its existence as a strong party. With their aid, the leadership could impose some restraints on economic interest groups like the agrarians who tended to be egotistical. The Center's inability to make any real headway on the repeal of the whole anti-Jesuit law undoubtedly made its leaders even more eager to satisfy the needs and desires of the secular clergy, especially in Prussia, its main base of power. But the Center could achieve those objectives only with the aid of the Conservatives. After 1897 the two parties brought to passage a number of bills improving the financial status of the Protestant and Catholic clergies, but as Windthorst had recognized at an early date the vital question to the clergy was the future of the Prussian confessional school. Neither he nor his immediate successors were able to secure the kind of school law that the Catholic Church desired. Therefore, the Conservatives won new recognition among the Catholic clergy by acting as a friendly surrogate in the debates on the school bill of 1904–1906.

Though the Junkers were not seriously interested in social legislation for industrial workers, enough Conservatives were so that their party was more helpful to the Center in the passage of its social legislation or Posadowsky's than the middle parties. It would have been fateful for the Center if it had appeared merely as an enemy of the Social Democrats rather than as a respectable rival of that party in the competition for labor's favor. The Rhineland Centrists were especially appreciative of the assistance their national party

[3] Chap. 5, p. 68.

[4] Lieber to Brentano, November 8, 1897. Lieber-Brentano Correspondence.

[5] Richard Müller-Fulda to Karl Bachem, November 19, 1928. Bachem Papers, File 96.

received from the Christian Conservatives in Adolf Stöcker's circle. When Julius Bachem called in 1906 on other regional leaders of the Center to run or support some Protestant candidates he meant that they should look above all others to Stöcker's friends in the Conservative party.

It is impossible to tell whether the leaders of the Center or of the Conservatives were more embarrassed by Erzberger's campaign against the Colonial Department in 1905–1906. Most likely some, perhaps many of Erzberger's supporters would have been less willing to follow him if the government had appointed another bureaucrat with Conservative connections to the directorship of the department instead of a Prince Hohenlohe-Langenburg or a Dernburg. The Conservatives were unhappy over Bülow's decision to expel the Center from the official coalition and they were to break with him in July, 1909, so that they could bring about the restoration of the old alliance with the Catholic party. It should be stressed that they had good reason to do so since they stood to profit more from that relationship than the Center would.

In theory all Germans, inclusive of Catholics, Jews, and workers, were equal before the law in the empire and the states; in practice those three groups suffered from varying degrees of discrimination under the monarchy. At the end of sixteen years of leadership in the Reichstag the Center's leaders could not claim that they had substantially improved the position of educated Catholics in the administrative services of Prussia and the wider empire. The Prussian Ministry of the Interior had a mixed record in its appointments of Catholics to prestigious positions at the county level. It tended to select Catholic county councilors in those areas of the Rhineland and Westphalia with heavy Catholic populations because the county councilors had to work closely with county assemblies which were predominantly Catholic in membership. But in 1910 there were to be only twelve county councilors in the remaining ten Prussian provinces, inclusive of three which had Catholic majorities but in which Catholics did not control the county assemblies. The imparity in administrative appointments was most evident in the Prussian and Imperial ministries in Berlin where the ministers or secretaries of state, the ministerial directors, the heads of departments, and the ranking councilors were rarely Catholic.[6] Though they denied it

publicly, high Prussian and Imperial officials acknowledged to each other that the monarchy wanted to keep Catholic appointments to a minimum.[7]

It is unlikely to say the least that the Center's leaders could have prevailed upon the government to make significant changes in the policies of the Imperial and Prussian departments on the question of Catholic appointments and to put pressure upon other state governments to imitate its example. The higher bureaucrats, Protestant clergy, the Conservatives, and the Evangelical League were determined to keep Catholic participation in state service to a minimum. Nevertheless the Prussian-German government would have been forced to improve its performance on the parity question if the Center had given a high priority to that issue. But it was revealing that the most prominent spokesmen for the Center in the struggle for equality in the civil service were chiefly Rhineland Centrists who followed in the footsteps of their first leaders, the Reichenspergers, who had initially complained about imparity in Prussian state appointments in the 1850's. The leaders of the Reichstag Center may have hoped that the Prussian state would change its policies vis-à-vis Catholic civil servants in the future, but they were never willing to run the risk of straining relations with the government and the Conservatives by a vigorous insistence that government authorities open up more high offices to Catholics.[8]

The fact of the matter was that the leaders of the Center were unable to exert their tactical skills and the favorable parliamentary position to maximum advantage in an effort to achieve all the constitutional rights to which lay Catholics and the members of religious orders were theoretically entitled. Ernst Lieber had acknowledged shortly before his death that his party's principled commitment to the monarchical system im-

---

[6] Bachem, *Zentrumspartei* 9: pp. 64–68; J. C. G. Röhl, "Higher Civil Servants in Germany, 1890–1900," *Journal of Contemporary History* 2 (July 1967): pp. 101–121; and Lysbeth W. Muncy, "The Prussian *Landräte* in the Last Years of the Monarchy: A Case Study of Pomerania and the Rhineland in 1890–1918," *Central European History* 6 (December, 1973): pp. 299–338. Muncy claims that Centrists, especially in areas where they were politically strong, were really dissatisfied with the Prussian government's reluctance to appoint members of their own Center party to high offices, but for constitutional and political reasons they had instead to complain about discrimination against all Catholics. That is an accurate but

only partial explanation of the views and tactics of the Rhineland Centrists and other regional Center parties. It should be remembered that the great majority of the higher Prussian officials were closely associated with the Conservative party and that some of the Conservative county councilors actually agitated against the Prussian canal bill of 1899 even though it had been approved by the ruler and the Prussian ministerial council.

In any event the numbers of Catholics holding positions of some dignity in the Prussian service was relatively small. Muncy points out that the Prussian government was embarrassed in World War I when it wanted to appoint more Catholic county councilors but learned that the number of younger Catholic officials who could qualify for promotion to that office was very low. *Ibid.*, p. 334, fn. 101.

[7] Otto von Mühlberg, the under secretary of state for foreign affairs, wrote Bülow on July 16, 1909, that the Catholic minority could easily create "a serious disturbance" if it made "strong demands" upon the state "beyond the strictly ecclesiastical sphere." GFMA, University of Michigan microcopy, Roll 110.

[8] The above letter from Mühlberg to Bülow seems to indicate that the Centrist leaders may have been pressing the issue of parity for Catholics in the Prussian civil service in 1909. At that time, however, their party was in opposition and they were eager to drive Bülow from office.

posed limits on its political freedom of action.[9] While the Centrist leaders and the Catholic upper classes were monarchists for other reasons as well, the interests of the Catholic Church were of paramount importance in the Center's preference for the monarchical governmental form.

There was considerable truth in Felix von Löe's assertion that the Center was "an association of pastors." The party maintained an impressive stability from 1874 to 1918[10] because it gave highest priority to causes which meant most to the clergy: the preservation of the confessional character of the primary and secondary schools in Catholic districts, parity of treatment for the Catholic clergy with the Protestant ministry in the states' programs of financial support, censorship of literature, the stage, and exhibitions, and the return of the religious orders. The Prussian Catholic clergy believed that the position of the church in public life could be maintained only with the firm assistance of the monarchy and the Center-Conservative coalition, though it was evident that the Conservatives opposed the repeal of the anti-Jesuit law. Therefore the Center's leadership exercised caution in its advocacy of equality for educated Catholics in government service and actually opposed the introduction of working-class suffrage in Prussia.

The approach of the Centrist leaders to politics was basically defensive; they thought that their church would be more secure in its rights and privileges under the existing state and Reich constitutions in which the ruler appointed his ministers and shaped policies than it would be in a democratic order in which an anticlerical majority of Radicals and Social Democrats might exercise those powers.[11] They combined with the Conservatives to uphold class suffrage in Prussia so as to keep the Social Democrats from entering the Landtag in substantial numbers, though they did not admit to it publicly.[12] Windthorst, Lieber, and the

later party leaders insisted, of course, on the maintenance of the Reichstag's democratic suffrage since they knew that the Prussian-German bureaucracy could be arbitrary when it was not checked by a strong majority in the national parliament.

Despite the discrimination against Catholics most of the senior Centrists were more at home in the Second Empire than they were to be in the Weimar Republic. The description that Otto Braun, the Social Democratic minister-president of Weimar Prussia, gave of Hugo am Zehnhoff, his Centrist cabinet colleague and respected member of the Reichstag Center before 1914, would fit most of them: "He was a social-minded and personally a very sympathetic man, but he had a rigid Catholic conservative political and philosophical orientation and was decidedly hostile to socialist ideas."[13] Since their religion kept them from achieving ministerial positions, except in Bavaria, they found substitute gratifications. They felt that they and their party performed vital if secondary roles in the governance of Germany. Lieber, Spahn, Arenberg, Hertling, Trimborn, and Müller-Fulda met regularly with either the chancellor, the secretary for foreign affairs, the secretary of the interior, or with other high Imperial or Prussian officials. Lieber's pronounced self-consciousness and Spahn's gravity of manner in their appearances before the Reichstag or the annual Catholic congresses were expressive of the importance they attached to their positions in public life.

It is more important to know, however, whether the Catholic educated and working classes found other sufficient compensation for the discrimination they experienced in many parts of the empire before World War I.[14] Like their Socialist rivals, Catholic leaders, clerical and lay, had created numerous professional, vocational, and cultural organizations in addition to the Center parties themselves and they provided some opportunities for employment and leadership to Catholics with higher education and instruction for workers. And since members of their church were not significantly

---

[9] See above chap. 7, p. 88.

[10] The Center held seventy-three of the one hundred and four mandates that were in the continuous possession of one party from 1874 to 1918. H. Goldschmidt, "Parteiwesen," *Jahresberichten für deutsche Geschichte,* 1928: p. 340.

It is also important to remember that the Center depended heavily on the clergy to exercise influence on the response of Catholic peasant and worker associations to sensitive economic legislation like the commercial treaties and tariff bills.

[11] For the authoritative Centrist doctrine on the best form of government, constitutional monarchy, consult: Georg Wellstein, "Konstitutionalismus," *Staatslexikon* (3rd rev. ed.) **3**: pp. 427–451. Wellstein was a prominent member of the party. His reasoning was that constitutional monarchy provided the best security for minorities.

[12] Karl Bachem stated in 1913 that the establishment of universal suffrage in Prussia was "a life and death question" for the Center since it would be beneficial to the Social Democrats. Letter to Lambert Lensing, August 23, 1913. Bachem Papers, File 78. In his history of the Center, Bachem tries to put the Center's views on Prussian working-class suffrage in a more

ideal light: *Zentrumspartei* **6**: p. 216. Near the end of the war the Centrist leaders, under pressure from their own laborites to advocate the introduction of democratic suffrage in Prussia, made a careful study of its possible effects and decided that it would not hurt their party. And from 1921 to 1933 the Prussian Center worked comfortably in coalition with the Social Democrats.

[13] Otto Braun, *Von Weimar bis Hitler,* (New York, 1940), p. 98.

[14] I should point out that the Centrist leadership was engaged from about 1906 or 1907 in a bitter struggle with integralist Catholics, who were supported by Cardinal Kopp and Bishop Korum, over the question whether Catholic workers could belong to the interconfessional Christian trade union movement. For Catholic labor that issue was more important in the years before the war than the question of equal suffrage in Prussia. See: Ernst Deuerlein, "Der Gewerkschaftstreit," *Theologische Quartalschrift,* **139** (1959): pp. 40–81.

represented in the economy, the universities, and the arts, one can assume that they took some satisfaction in the part played by the Center in the governing of the national state. But in the long run pride in the Center's leadership of the Reichstag and its ties with the Imperial government could not provide adequate compensation for the lack of complete civic rights to those Catholics who were even more keenly aware of the economic, social, and cultural disadvantages of their situation. It was not surprising therefore that many of them were to watch the collapse of their monarchical government in 1918 without concern or regret.

SELECT BIBLIOGRAPHY

UNPUBLISHED MATERIALS

For the period 1890–1900 this study depended heavily on the extensive papers of Ernst Lieber. His widow, left in financial distress with a large family, attempted to sell them to the Peoples' Association but the negotiations broke down. It was fortunate that they did so because the Gestapo was to confiscate the contents of the Peoples' Association archive in 1933. Several years before the outbreak of World War I Frau Lieber sold a sizable collection of her husband's papers to Cardinal Kopp who then deposited them in his diocesan archive. That part, removed to safer quarters during World War II, is in the same depository, now the Archiwum Archidiecezjalne of the archdiocese of Wrocław. In the late 1920's Dr. Wilhelm Winckler, then a member of its staff, prevailed upon the Pfalzische Staatsbibliothek at Speyer to purchase another large segment of the remaining body of Lieber papers. It is probably not as valuable as the Wrocław collection, but I found it to be most useful for my research. A third part of the papers, essentially a residue, is still in the possession of Dr. Ernst Lieber in Camberg, Germany, the sole surviving grandson of the one-time Center leader and the owner of the ancestral home. It includes a journal kept by Ernst Lieber in the form of letters to his wife which is invaluable for the years 1890–1892, though Lieber neglected it pretty much after the latter date. In addition to the originals or copies of other correspondence between Lieber and party friends, the Camberg collection contains copies of the occasional letters written by Lieber in the 1890's to Lujo Brentano, the close friend of his youth.

The Archiwum Archidiecezjalne at Wrocław also possesses the papers of Cardinal Kopp and Felix Porsch. The Kopp papers are rich in correspondence on the army bill conflict of 1893 and contain letters to and from Lieber, Porsch, Ballestrem, Huene, Caprivi, and high churchmen both in Rome and in Germany. There are also notes or memoranda on papal audiences and additional correspondence with high government officials and churchmen. It is my assumption that much of the more sensitive Kopp correspondence and other papers is not accessible to scholars, since the materials available for research in 1965, extensive though they were, could have been only a relatively small part of the papers of a leading churchman who had sat in both the upper chambers of the Prussian and Austrian parliaments, acted as the chief negotiator for the Prussian bishops with the state, and was in frequent communication with the Prussian, Austrian, and Papal authorities. The Felix Porsch papers contain a letter from Franz X. Seppelt, the diocesan archivist to Cardinal Bertram, Kopp's successor in Breslau, dated July, 1931, in which the writer recommended that all Kopp's letters to Porsch be added to the Kopp papers because they contained so many criticisms of Center politicians. The Porsch collection does possess a sizable number of letters from Kopp to Porsch but they treat chiefly of the affairs of the Silesian Center. Felix Porsch apparently destroyed a considerable part of his own papers, but his *Nachlass* at the Archiwum Archidiecezjalne was useful for this study because there are letters from Lieber in it as well as some Lieber materials that Porsch took over from the Lieber papers.

The other source of materials for this study and the prime source for the years after Lieber's first serious illness in 1900 was the papers of Karl Bachem at the Stadt Köln Historisches Archiv, Cologne. Bachem began conscientiously to collect documents on his party soon after his election to the Reichstag in 1889 and they include letters to and from himself, interviews with senior colleagues on important events and decisions in the Center's history, personal notes, memoranda, records of fraction meetings, and extensive newspaper clippings. His papers also contain materials from the files of the *Kölnische*

Volkszeitung. It is evident from the documents which Bachem carefully collected for his party's history, which he later wrote, that he expected later professional historians to be more frank about his party than he was himself.

I was also able to consult the remains of the correspondence of Georg von Hertling at the Bundesarchiv in Koblenz, and copies of the letters exchanged between Hertling and Hermann Cardauns for over a half-century, thanks to the generosity of the late Professor Ernst Deuerlein of Munich. Professor Josef Becker of Augsburg was generous enough to send copies of some letters written by Rudolf von Buol to Albrecht von Stötzingen, a Baden Catholic dignitary, and of some entries from the journals of Robert Bosse, the Prussian minister of cults and education between 1893 and 1901. Professor David King was kind enough to send me his personal copies of some entries regarding the Center in the diaries of Adolf Marshall von Bieberstein, now in the Politisches Archiv of the Foreign Ministry at Bonn.

The various collections of microfilm copies of documents from the German Foreign Ministry in the United States were sometimes of high worth for my research, especially for the years from the late Windthorst period through the summer of 1893. I used the following collections: National Archives, Microcopy T 149, Rolls 12, 24, 28, 304 and 305; University of California T139, Roll 36 and University of Michigan, T139, Rolls 110, 113, and 127.

PRINTED SOURCES

The *Stenographische Berichte der Verhandlungen des deutschen Reichstages* for the period 1890–1907 were of course indispensable for this study; I also made some use of the *Stenographische Berichte der Verhandlungen des Preussichen Abgeordnetenhauses.* It would be difficult to overestimate the value of the *Verhandlungen der Generalversammlungen der Katholiken Deutschlands* for the years covered in this study, since they often revealed the thinking of the Center's leaders on important political and socio-economic issues of the times.

NEWSPAPERS, REVIEWS, AND RELATED PUBLICATIONS

The Center newspapers of greatest use for my research were *Germania,* the *Kölnische Volkszeitung,* and the *Deutsche Reichszeitung,* the leading Catholic integralist journal. I also found it worth while to consult the *Frankfurter Zeitung,* the *Kölnische Zeitung,* and *Vörwarts.* Both the Lieber and Bachem papers contain extensive newspaper clippings from a wide arrangement of newspapers associated with the Center or some other party.

The *Historische-politische Blätter* was most useful for a better understanding of Bavarian Catholic reactions to governmental policies and to developments within the Center. It also provided several anonymous articles by Julius Bachem. *Le Correspondant,* the French Catholic review, often carried reports or articles on Center and German Catholic affairs between 1890 and the last years before World War I. Karl Muth's distinguished review, *Hochland,* founded in 1903, contains occasional articles and reviews on the Center in the period before 1914.

CENTER PARTY HISTORIES, MEMOIRS, BIOGRAPHIES AND RELATED WORKS

Needless to say, this study profited from the existence of Karl Bachem's monumental *Vorgeschichte, Geschichte und Politik der deutschen Zentrumspartei* (9 v., Cologne, 1929–1932). Bachem's formal training in law, his experience in journalism, his parliamentary service, and his devotion to the

Center equipped him to produce a monumental history of his party. It is in many respects a great work, though it is sometimes apologetic, evasive, or silent on important matters and in a few instances misleading. But it should be realized that he often preserved documents that could be used by later historians to correct his own history.

Martin Spahn's little brochure, *Das Deutsche Zentrum* (Mainz and Munich, 1906) provides interpretive material. Wilhelm Hankemer, an Essen Centrist editor, also wrote a popular short history of the Center: *Das Zentrum, die politische Vertretung des katholischen Volksteils* (Essen, 1927). It has some useful information. Rudolf Morsey's major study of the Center after 1917 has some incidental material on the party for the period before 1914; *Die Deutsche Zentrumspartei, 1917–1923* (Beiträge zur Geschichte des Parlamentarismus und der politischen Parteien, Band 32) (Dusseldorf, 1966).

For background purposes I also found it worth while to use the *Staatslexikon*, ed. by Julius Bachem, (5 v., 3rd rev. and 4th ed., Freiburg im Breisgau, 1908). The *Staatslexikon* was one of the major publications of the Görres Society and its articles on constitutional, social, and economic issues reflected the thinking of Catholic leaders like Julius Bachem and Georg von Hertling, the longtime president of the society, in short, views of the dominating leadership group in the Center and Catholic society itself.

Members of the Center left relatively little autobiographical or memoir materials of a substantial nature. Of all the party members active at any time in the period covered by this study Georg von Hertling alone left any personal account of his political career. His *Erinnerungen aus meinen Leben* (2 v., Munich and Kempten, 1919–1920) are gracefully and entertainingly written, but Hertling died before he got beyond 1899. His son, Karl, added a chapter for the period 1899–1902. Karl von Hertling also left an incomplete and unpublished manuscript which was of some use to me for the years 1903–1907. It is now in the Hertling papers at the Bundesarchiv in Koblenz, File 56. Neither father nor son revealed many secrets. Karl von Hertling later contributed a chapter entitled "Bülow, Hertling, Zentrum," to the collective work: *Front Wider Bülow*, edited by Friedrich Thimme (Munich, 1931). It is of some use.

There are only a few biographies of other Center personalities. The best is undoubtedly Klaus Epstein's study of Erzberger: *Matthias Erzberger and the Dilemma of German Democracy* (Princeton, 1959). Martin Spahn's *Ernst Lieber als Parlamentarier* (Gotha, 1906) was more a short political work than a critical historical study, but it is occasionally quite revealing about Lieber's limitations. Hermann Cardauns wrote two short biographies of prominent Centrist leaders: *Adolf Gröber* (M. Gladbach, 1920) and *Karl Trimborn* (M. Gladbach, 1922). Neither represented a major undertaking on the author's part and they are only of limited value, although numerous quotations from Trimborn's letters makes his sketch the more useful of the two. Paul Siebertz's *Karl Fürst zu Löwenstein* (Munich, 1924) is uncritical and usually irrelevant to the Center's history after 1890 but it provides material on the conflict between the party and its agrarian elements in the early and mid-1890's.

OTHER MEMOIRS, JOURNALS, AND BIOGRAPHIES

One of the most valuable sources on the Center's relations with the government and the emperor is Prince Chlodwig zu Hohenlohe-Schillingfurst's *Denkwürdigkeiten der Reichskanzlerzeit*, ed. by Karl A. von Müller (Stuttgart and Berlin, 1931). It is a selection of journal entries, memoranda, and letters. His successor, Bernhard von Bülow, left disappointing recollections of his relations with the Center: *Memoirs* (4 v., London, 1932). His remarks are often either superficial or vacuous. General, later Field Marschal, von Waldersee had only incidental contacts with Center personalities but his journal notes are useful for the light they throw on William II's views

of the Center: *Denkwürdigkeiten des General-Feldmarschalls Alfred Grafen von Waldersee*, ed. by Heinrich Otto Meisner (4 v., Berlin, 1925). I also found helpful random references to the Center in the reminiscences of Eugen von Jagemann, *25 Jahre des Erlebens und Erfahrens* (Heidelberg, 1925). Jagemann was the Baden envoy to Berlin in the 1890's.

There are biographies of some prominent government officials or other party leaders which I found most helpful. Easily the most important is Hans Herzfeld's *Johannes von Miquel* (2 v., Detmold, 1938). Sigismund von Kardorff's life of his father, *Wilhelm von Kardorff, Ein Nationaler Parlamentarier im Zeitalter Bismarcks und Wilhelm II, 1828–1909* (Berlin, 1936), was also helpful in part. The biography of Rudolf von Bennigsen by Hermann Oncken has only occasional references to the Center party after 1890: *Rudolf von Bennigsen, Ein deutscher liberaler politiker* (2 v., Stuttgart, 1910).

PUBLISHED COLLECTIONS OF DOCUMENTS, AND RELATED WORKS OF REFERENCE WITH MATERIALS ON THE CENTER

Molt, Peter, *Der Reichstag vor der improvisierten Revolution* (Opladen, 1963). The author has collected some useful materials on the social and vocational backgrounds of Center party members.

Mommsen, Wilhelm, *Deutsche Parteiprogramme* (Munich, 1950).

Schwarz, Max, ed., *MdR Biographisches Handbuch der deutschen Reichstages* (Hannover, 1965).

Rassow, Peter, and Karl E. Born, eds., *Akten zur Staatlichen Sozialpolitik in Deutschland, 1890–1914* (Historischen Forschungen, No. 3) (Wiesbaden, 1959). Most useful, especially the reports of the Bavarian envoy to Berlin, Count Lerchenfeld on political conditions there.

Reichstag-Handbuch, 1890, 1893, 1898, 1903, 1907, edited by and published by the Bureau of the Reichstag, Berlin, in the same years.

WORKS ON INSTITUTIONS CLOSELY RELATED TO THE CENTER

There is a handy commentary on the speeches and resolutions made at the annual Catholic Congresses on social questions by P. Dr. E. Filthaut, O.P., *Deutsche Katholikentage, 1848–1958 und Soziale Frage* (Essen, 1960). There is also an older and official general work on the congresses down to 1903: J. May, *Geschichte der Generalversammlungen der Katholiken Deutschlands* (Cologne, 1904). Both books are uncritical. Hans Buchheim's *Ultramontanismus und Demokratie, Der Weg der deutschen Katholiken im 19, Jahrhundert* (Munich, 1963) deals in substantial measure with the Catholic Congresses and with Karl zu Löwenstein, although his central theme has to do with the efforts of prominent German Catholic laymen like Löwenstein to secure a larger role in German Catholic and international Catholic affairs for laymen like himself. I fail to see, however, any connection between Löwenstein, a gentle reactionary, and democracy.

Two useful studies are those by Wilhelm Kisky on the Augustine League: *Der Augustinus-Verein zur Pflege der katholischen Presse von 1898 bis 1928* (Düsseldorf, 1928) and Emil Ritter on the Peoples' Association: *Die katholisch-soziale Bewegung Deutschlands im neunzehnten Jahrhundert und der Volksverein* (Cologne, 1954). Kisky offers some useful information on the differences between Lieber and the Bachem press bloc but even more on the struggle between the Rhineland Center and its dissident agrarian wing.

Ritter's detailed monograph is partly based on a manuscript left by August Pieper, the secretary-general of the Peoples' Association. His study conveys some of the dynamism and impressive activity of that organization: in its holding of courses, production of materials on the social question, and promotion of the Center's interests among Catholic voters.

MONOGRAPHS OR OTHER STUDIES WITH MATERIAL ON THE CENTER

Barkin, Kenneth D., *The Controversy over German Industrialization 1890–1902* (Chicago, 1970). This a most useful monograph on its subject, but it is thin and sometimes unreliable in its treatment of the Center.

Berghan, Volker, *Der Tirpitz-Plan: Genesis und Verfall einer innen-politischen Krisenstrategie unter Wilhelm II* (Düsseldorf, 1971). A valuable study but it does not contain much material on the Center and its response to the naval bills of 1898 and 1900.

Born, Karl, *Staat und Sozialpolitik seit Bismarcks Sturz.* (Historische Forschungen im Auftrag der Historischen Kommission der Akademie der Wissenschaften und der Literatur.) Band I (Wiesbaden, 1957). This is an indispensable monograph on the German state, the political parties, and the social question.

Crothers, George, *The German Elections of 1907* (New York, 1940). Despite its age, this is still a worth while study of the relations between the German government and the parties in the decade before World War I.

Fernis, Hansgeorg, *Die Flottennovellen im Reichstag 1906–1913* (Stuttgart, 1934). Helpful on the Center and the naval budget debates of 1906 and its background.

Goebel, Hans, *Die Militarvorlage, 1892–1893*. Münster Universität Ph.D. dissertation (Munster, 1935). Provides useful material on the reaction of the Center press to the Caprivi army bill.

Kehr, Eckart, *Schlachtflottenbau und Parteipolitik, 1894–1901* (Historische Studien, Heft 197) (Berlin, 1930). Kehr's study of the political and economic background of the naval programs of the years 1898 and 1900 is still impressive. It is unfortunate that he had to rely upon the Center press and did not have access to party documentation during his research for the parts on the Center. He rightly assumed that Lieber and his colleagues sought power for their party but he was unable to expose their state of mind because of his research problems.

Kelly, Patrick J., "The Naval Policy of Imperial Germany," Georgetown University Ph.D. dissertation (Washington, D.C., 1970). This study, based on side use of microfilm copies of official German naval documents, was a useful guide to some aspects of Tirpitz's naval policy and his relations with William II.

King, David B., *Marschall von Bieberstein and the New Course, 1890–1897* (University Microfilms Inc., Ann Arbor, Michigan, 1965). Based on his diary, this is an excellent study of Marschall. It also offers worth-while insights into the functioning of the German government between 1890 and 1897.

Morsey, Rudolf, "Georg Kardinal Kopp, Fürst-bischof von Breslau, 1887–1914," *Wichmann Jahrbuch für Kirchen Geschichte im Bistum Berlin* **21–24** (1967–1969): pp. 42–65. This is the best article on Kopp.

Müller, Klaus, "Zentrumspartei und Agrarische Bewegung im Rheinland 1882–1903," in: *Im Spiegel der Geschichte—Festgabe fur Max Braubach,* Konrad Repgen and Hans Skalweit, eds. (Münster, 1965), pp. 828–857.

Nipperdey, Thomas, *Die Organisation der deutschen Parteien vor 1918* (Düsseldorf, 1961). This is a very useful book on the structure and organization of the bourgeois parties. Nipperdey points out that the Center was led, like other bourgeois parties, by an elitist group of Catholic dignitaries who coopted their successors. He also notes that the leaders did not need to build up a more democratic electoral organization because they were able to rely upon the services of the Peoples' League.

Pehl, Hans, *Die deutsche Kolonialpolitik und das Zentrum 1884–1914*. Frankfurt Universität Ph.D. dissertation (Frankfurt a.M., 1934). Reliable monograph based on Reichstag debates and press comments on colonial affairs.

Puhle, Hans-Jurgen, *Agrarische Interessenpolitik und Preussische Konservatismus im Wilhelmische Reich (1893–1914)*. Schriftenreihe des Forschungsinstitut der Friedrich Ebert Stiftung (Hannover, 1966). Helpful to this study because the author shows how difficult it was for the Agrarian League to penetrate the Christian peasants' associations.

Röhl, J. C. G., *Germany without Bismarck* (Berkeley and Los Angeles, 1967). This is a substantial study of the unsuccessful efforts of higher Prussian and German officials led by Holstein to bring William II under control. However, some major governmental bills or legislation, the Caprivi army bill, the Miquel financial reform, and the anti-revolution measure of 1894–1895 get only superficial consideration or no treatment at all.

Witt, Peter-Christian, *Die Finanzpolitik des deutschen Reiches 1903 bis 1913: Ein Studie zur Innenpolitik des Wilhelminischen Deutschland* (Lübeck and Hamburg, 1970). This is an excellent study of Germany's financial problems in the period 1903–1913 and of the manner in which the government and the Reichstag tried to deal with them.

SUPPLEMENT

I came on the three following works after I had submitted my own manuscript to the publisher:

Becker, Josef, *Liberaler Staat und Kirche in der Ära von Reichsgründung und Kulturkampf. Geschichte und Strukturen ihres Verhältnisse in Baden 1860–1976*. Veröffentlichungen der Kommission für Zeitgeschichte (Mainz, 1973). Becker treats the major conflict between the liberals and the Catholics in Baden which began several years before the Kulturkampf in Prussia. He comes to the interesting conclusion that Baden Catholics became satisfied with the interconfessional school system because adequate provision was made in it for confessional instruction and clerical participation in the supervision of the schools.

Lill, Rudolf, *Die Wende im Kulturkampf. Leo XIII, Bismarck und die Zentrumspartei 1878–1880*. Sonderausgabe "Quellen und Forschungen aus italienischen Archiven und Bibliotheken," Band 50, Band 52. (Tübingen, 1973). The author stresses Windthorst's belief that separation of church and state would come in the future and that the Catholic Church would have to depend "upon forces which would defend it without legal privileges and in competition with other forces."

Weber, Christoph, *Quellen und Studien zur Kurie und zur vatikanischen Politik unter Leo XIII: Mit Berücksichtigung des Beziehungen des Hl. Stuhles zu den Dreibundmächten* (Bibliothek des Deutschen Historischen Instituts in Rom, number 45. Tubingen, 1973). The author has an impressive knowledge of the details and intricacies of Vatican diplomacy during Leo XIII's pontificate. While I agree with him that Leo XIII did not make a serious effort to change the Center's stand on the Caprivi army bill of 1892–1893 it is important to remember after all that the pope did attempt to influence its final decision. Weber implies, wrongly in my judgment, that William II changed his position on the Zedlitz school bill of 1892 under pressure from Free Conservative industrialists who had been financially generous to him.